Public Documents from Sinnār

African Historical Sources
Number 1

Public Documents from Sinnār

Jay Spaulding and Muhammad Ibrāhīm Abū Salīm
Editors

Michigan State University Press
East Lansing, Michigan
1989

Michigan State University Press
East Lansing, Michigan 48823-5202

Printed in the United States of America

All Michigan State University Press books are produced on paper which meets the requirements of American National Standard for Information Sciences—Permanence of paper for printed materials. ANSI 239.48-1984 ♾

Published on the recommendation of the International Council for Philosophy and Humanistic Studies and with the financial assistance of the National Endowment for the Humanities.

UNION ACADÉMIQUE
FONTES HISTORIAE AFRICANAE,
SERIES ARABICA XI

Library of Congress Cataloging-in-Publication Data

Public documents from Sinnār.
(African historical sources; no. 1)
Includes bibliographical references.
1. Sudan — Charters, grants, privileges. 2. Law — Sudan — Sources. I. Spaulding, J. L. (Jay L.) II. Abū Salīm, Muhammad Ibrāhim. III. Series.
LAW 348.624′025 89-12896
346.240825
ISBN 0-87013-280-6

This book is respectfully dedicated to the memory
of the founders of Sudanese historical
writing in Arabic,
among them:

Muḥammad al-Sayyid b. Dōlīb
Aḥmad, *sīd al-qūm* to Sultan Ismā`īl b. Bādī
Aḥmad b. `Īsā al-Anṣāriyābī
Muḥammad al-Nūr b. Ḍayf Allāh
Aḥmad b. al-Ḥājj Abū `Alī

CONTENTS

THE CENTRAL GOVERNMENT

THE NORTHERN PROVINCIAL GOVERNMENT

OTHER

ACKNOWLEDGEMENT

About fifteen years ago the authors of this volume undertook to prepare a collection of public documents from Sinnār, the texts available at that time having been gathered and set by M. I. Abū Salīm and an English translation and notes prepared by Jay Spaulding. Due to a series of unfortunate circumstances beyond the authors' control, however, this collection never appeared. With the passage of time many new documents became available and scholarly understanding of eighteenth and early nineteenth-century Sinnār advanced, so that a thorough revision of the original project became essential. This was begun by Jay Spaulding in 1985, and the present volume is the result. The authors are keenly aware that discoveries during the next decade may require further and comparable reinterpretation of the material offered here; however, we nevertheless feel that this uncommonly precise and detailed set of sources for Sinnār deserves prompt dissemination and attention.

We acknowledge the following institutions for permission to publish the texts of documents from their collections: the National Records Office, Khartoum (Sudan), the Sudan Archive, University of Durham and the Library of the School of Oriental and African Studies, University of London (United Kingdom). We are grateful to John Hunwick, `Alī `Osmān Muḥammad Ṣāliḥ and Robin Thelwall for permission to adapt materials initially published in *Fontes Historiae Africanae Arabicae: Bulletin d'Information* and *Sudan Texts Bulletin*, and we acknowledge our debt to the prior scholarly contributions of A. J. Arkell, P.M. Holt, Ṣādiq al-Nūr, al-Ṭayyib Muḥammad al-Ṭayyib, `Izz al-Dīn al-Amīn and Neil McHugh. Our editors John Hunwick (Northwestern University), and Harold Marcus and David Robinson (Michigan State University) have sustained this project with good will and sound advice, and our colleague Lidwien Kapteijns (Wellesley College) has read several drafts of the manuscript and shared numerous insights drawn from her extensive experience with the Arabic literature of the precolonial Sudan. Dr. Hazem Sayed facilitated our adaptation of computer software to the present project.

Finally, we gratefully acknowledge the institutional support of the National Records Office, the African Studies Centers of Michigan State University and Boston University, the Department of History and the Africana Studies Program at Kean College of New Jersey, and UNESCO, which through the Conseil International de la Philosophie et Sciences Humaines authorized the issue of this volume as a contribution to its *Fontes Historiae Africanae* series. The United States National Endowment for the Humanities, Division of Research Programs, Texts, Translations, helped support this publication through a grant to the Association for the Publication of African Historical Sources.

Wellesley,
January 1989

A NOTE ON CONVENTIONS

Eighteenth-century Sudanese Arabic is an idiom of beauty, power, and precision. Its conventions differ in some minor respects from those of Classical Arabic, but rarely to a degree that raises questions about meaning; only in the latter case does the present study call attention to its idiosyncracies. The Arabic texts given below follow the sources from which they are derived, and the English translations are based on the texts. Words left untranslated have been transliterated according to the Middle East Times system, and a glossary of brief working definitions is appended. A few familiar place names (for example, Khartoum) are spelled according to modern English conventions in the translations; less familiar ones are transliterated and capitalized.

There are several differences between eighteenth-century Sudanese Arabic and twentieth-century American English usages in regard to personal names and titles. Arabic names often indicate an individual's parentage through use of the word *ibn*; the present study expresses this in English through the abbreviation "b.", for example, Aḥmad b. `Īsā, "Aḥmad, the son of `Īsā." The feminine equivalent to *ibn* is usually *bint;* where this word appears in the Arabic text it is transliterated and written in full in the English translation. Eighteenth-century Sudanese Arabic often substitutes its own words *walad* or *wad* for the Classical Arabic *ibn*; where these words appear they are also transliterated and written in full. Many group names are compounded with *awlād*, the plural of *walad* or *wad*.

In the eighteenth-century Sudan it was not uncommon for an individual to be generally known not by his given name, but as the son of his father (or sometimes, his mother); thus Muḥammad the son of Rajab the son of Muḥammad Abū Likaylik usually appears in the records of the day as Wad

Rajab. Moreover, in such a case a child in the next generation might well be known as the son of an individual whose name began with *walad*; for example, one witness to Document 6 below bears the name Muḥammad walad Walad Ḍūyū. The appearance of the word *walad* twice in succession in an eighteenth-century Sudanese Arabic document is not an error, as P. M. Holt has incorrectly maintained, but an accurate reflection of contemporary naming practices. Omission of the second *walad* in the name of the individual mentioned above would wrongly excise one whole generation from the family history his name was designed to preserve.

Classical Arabic names inflect according to their grammatical role in discourse, and in a few cases visible vestiges of this survive in eighteenth-century Sudanese texts. The present study translates a fixed nominative form regardless of what appears in the Arabic text; thus Abū Bakr is always Abū Bakr, and Dhu'l-Ḥijja is always Dhu'l-Ḥijja. Many Arabic names and titles are constructed with the definite article *al-*. Where the definite article appears at the beginning of or within an individual's name and titles the present study either omits it, translates it, or transliterates it by the fixed forms al- or 'l- according to context. Where the documents give lists of names connected by the particle *wa* ("and"), the conjunction has been dropped in translation.

According to standard conventions Arabic titles should be transliterated and italicized, while Arabic names should be capitalized but not italicized. Rigorous adherence to these rules, however, would violate the spirit of eighteenth-century Sudanese usage, for an individual's titles of personal status or office constituted an integral and important part of his name. In the translations below, whenever a title is considered to form an integral part of a proper name it is capitalized but not italicized; when a title stands alone it is italicized but not capitalized. The familiar titles "sultan" and "shaykh" are considered to be English; thus, for example, "shaykh" is only italicized when it forms part of a longer title whose complete meaning would not generally be understood, and only capitalized when it is part of a person's name. An exception will be made for the Funj titles *mankarūkan* or *mankrōknā* and *sawākira*, which are not Arabic; these are always italicized in deference to their special status. In a few exceptional cases a title conveys a coherent meaning that benefits from translation; thus the *wakīl ḥōsh khāl al-malik* is "the agent of the compound of the maternal uncle of the king." Often, however, the significance of a title is uncertain even when its literal meaning is known; for example, little would be gained by making the *muqaddam al-sajjāda* the "foreman of the carpet." The translators have used their best judgment; in all cases of doubt, recourse may be had to the Arabic texts.

INTRODUCTION

The Historical Setting.--The northern Nile Valley Sudan is home to one of the world's oldest cultural traditions, characterized for more than three millennia by the presence of state forms of government and by literacy. The leaders of successive regimes chose to write in diverse languages; sometimes these were indigenous (Meroitic, Nubian), but at other times preference was given to a language of current cultural eminence in the wider eastern Mediterranean world (Ancient Egyptian, Greek, Arabic). The present volume offers a collection of government documents from one segment of this long written history, records produced in the period A.D. 1702-1821 and couched in the Arabic language. If these documents testify eloquently to continuity in the Sudanese tradition of literate statecraft, they also afford invaluable insight into the particular circumstances of their age of origin. Further consideration of these themes must be placed within a more specific historical context.[1]

The fourteenth and fifteenth centuries witnessed an important transition in the northern Sudan. The large kingdoms of medieval Nubia disintegrated into their lesser constituent parts as innovations in agriculture stimulated a reorganization in political economy, while invading Egyptian armies, nomadic Arab immigrants, and pioneering Muslim merchants and missionaries introduced a new set of Mediterranean cultural influences. Political unity was restored in about 1500 under Islamic auspices; the Sudanese monarch of the new Funj dynasty was recognized in neighboring lands as "the king of the Nubian Muslims."[2] During the next century and a half the leaders of the Funj government were quite familiar with the practice of writing. For example, in the 1520s the traveler David Reubeni found that King `Amāra might pay handsomely in gold for an Arabic book imported from Makka; or again, the Ethiopian visitor of 1629-1632 Zaga Christ could communicate with Rubāṭ and his family by means of written letters.[3] Yet there is little indication that these earlier Funj kings themselves chose to make use of written documents in the conduct of their administration. Indeed, a pre-Arabic system of numerical calculation survived even as late as the early nineteenth century, when tax payments were still routinely recorded by means of the strings of beads that constituted the Nubian abacus.[4] Significantly, Zaga Christ noted the absence in his day of a genre of government documents later to become common in the Sudan, the written *laissez-passer*. That Zaga Christ understood the significance of such documents may be inferred from his own use of one in Egypt; at Girga a pasha gave him "lettres de passeport pour toute l'Egypte enchargea à tous les Bachas, Bays, & Sangiacs, de le recevoir selon que sa qualité portoit. Ces patentes eurent l'effect pretendu."[5] In the Sudan, however, Rubāṭ responded to his request for safe passage out of the country not with the familiar written certificate of later years, but by assigning a *sokārī*, an escort of men "pour guides & sauf-conduite."[6] In short, the earlier Funj kings understood and responded appropriately to the writings of others, but did not elect to make use of the practice themselves.

Toward the middle of the seventeenth century Rubāṭ's son and successor Bādī II (1054/1644-1645 to 1092/1681) abandoned the custom of maintaining a mobile court and brought his roving capital to rest; henceforth the Funj kingdom was often known by the name of his new fixed seat of government, Sinnār.[7] Bādī b. Rubāṭ continued to respond to written communications from abroad. For example, when the Armenian bishop Hovannes wished to travel from Ethiopia to Egypt via Sinnār in 1678-1680, "The king [Yohannes I of Ethiopia] then wrote a letter of recommendation to the king of Sennar, called Badin . . . . We delivered the letter of the king of Ethiopia to the king of [sic] Badin. He stood up with all his soldiers, kissed the letter and put it on his [fore]head."[8] In contrast to his predecessors, however, Bādī is also said to have produced written documents of his own. The earliest presently known text attributed to the government of Sinnār is a letter of about 1654 from the "Arabs of Funj, otherwise known as Sinnār" to the Ethiopian emperor, in which it was claimed that Sinnār had eliminated an Ottoman governor of Sawākin irksome to the Ethiopians and Sudanese alike: "Behold, we have killed the pasha. Should we now experience the threat of war from the Turks, send one of your generals to our aid."[9] While the authenticity of this example of state correspondence is questionable, it illustrates accurately enough a second important genre of Funj government documents which, like the *laissez-passer*, were to become common in the years to follow.

From the beginning the Funj kings had given tangible expression to their Islamic convictions through patronage and grants of land and privilege to holy men, known in Sudanese Arabic as *fuqarā'* (singular *faqīh*).[10] Yet in regard to religious usages also the reign of Bādī b. Rubāṭ witnessed several new developments. It was Bādī who built the first mosque in Sinnār (his father had laid the foundations); he undertook to enhance the status of the Funj kingdom in the wider Islamic world through the dispatch of royal gifts to worthy religious causes abroad, and one need not doubt that his charity toward the holy men of his own land was commensurate.[11] These local beneficiaries of Bādī's generosity were no longer immigrant missionaries from afar or rare Sudanese individuals with a foreign education, for by the middle of the seventeenth century most holy men of Sinnār were born and trained within the Funj kingdom.[12] A final important feature of Bādī's grants to holy men was that at least some of them were said to have been recorded in writing.[13] In later years similar charters were to constitute the third major genre of official Funj government documents; none from Bādī's reign, however, are known to be extant.

By the dawn of the eighteenth century the kingdom of Sinnār had reached its apogee of wealth and power, and approached its greatest geographical extent. Over the course of its remaining century and a quarter of independent but troubled existence, it began to accumulate a considerably more extensive and instructive literature of primary historical sources. The documents of the present collection are among the most important of these, but they are subtle, so that often the full significance of the information they convey can only be appreciated by placing them within their wider historical and historiographical context. While no attempt will be made to replicate here the full scope of an extended study of this theme undertaken elsewhere, even a brief introductory survey may provide some useful perspectives.[14]

During the prosperous reign of Bādī III (1103/1691-1692 to 1128/1715-1716) a number of European visitors to Sinnār wrote descriptions of the Funj kingdom.[15] The writings of these early eighteenth century travelers are of great importance because they unequivocably describe a powerful and centralized kingdom run by secular noblemen according to traditional constitutional principles. They inspire one to take seriously indeed the power and authority of the individuals whose names and titles appear in even the earliest documents of the present collection. Later European travelers, though they encountered Sinnār in far less fortunate circumstances, usually shared their predecessors' interest in the conduct of government; in addition to valuable comments on the conditions of their own day, their accounts contribute many meaningful details that illuminate the older constitutional structure and clarify its function. For example, they explain the duties of many of the titled officials named in the documents, and they reveal that the older society of Sinnār had comprised several legally distinct classes of people--subject commoners, *fuqarā'*, foreigners, slaves, and noblemen--whose status before the law differed one from another.[16] This clarification of the sociological and legal context lends a new depth of significance, for example, to the series of actions described in Doc. 47, where the appeal of a group of *fuqarā'* to the sultan is referred back to a provincial governor with instructions to have their case adjudicated by the local

Islamic judge, the *qāḍī*, according to Islamic law, the *sharī`a*. What was one's personal legal status? To which court was one subject? To which system of law? These were perennial issues of public life in eighteenth century Sinnār. Conspicuous also is the fact that the present collection of documents is concerned primarily with relations between noblemen and *fuqarā'*, and only secondarily with relations among noblemen, or between noblemen and foreigners. Commoners appear but rarely, for example, as the objects of a royal grant to a *faqīh* (Doc. 24). This highly selective class emphasis is a strong and inherent bias of the present study.

The political history of eighteenth century Sinnār was eventful and dramatic, and from the middle of the century on, it became increasingly clear to contemporaries that the world around them was changing forever. One response was the birth of formal Sudanese history-writing in Arabic, an effort to which several individuals who figure prominently in the documents below made pioneering contributions. For Aḥmad b. `Īsā, and after him Aḥmad b. al-Ḥājj Abū `Alī, the most relevant story was that of the deeds of the kings and the chronicle of their ill fortune, while Muḥammad al-Sayyid walad Dōlīb reflected upon the origins and ethnic composition of Sinnār, and Muḥammad al-Nūr b. Ḍayf Allāh constructed a masterful collective biography of the men and women who had advanced the cause of Islam in the Sudan.[17] These writers, and others whose names remain less well known, have contributed in broad outline a history of events for eighteenth century Sinnār. The names of even the earliest sultans were retrieved from the depths of memory, together with a few anecdotal fragments of information about them.[18] On the surer ground of the eighteenth century, one is told of the fall of the old matrilineal Funj dynasty in 1719, followed by the brief tenure of the good king Nōl and the long and eventful reign of his son Bādī IV (16 Shawwāl 1136/8 July 1724 to 2 Ramaḍān 1175/27 March 1762). The chroniclers then speak of the rise of the Hamaj, and the subordination of the sultans after 1762 to Muḥammad Abū Likaylik and his heirs, their mighty *wazīrs*. They conclude with the spread of discord among the Hamaj lords, and the collapse of government into interminable civil war. The travel account of James Bruce captures some of the high drama of the days of Abū Likaylik himself, while that of John Lewis Burckhardt probes the depths of political and social decadence at the local level on the eve of colonial conquest.[19] What the present set of documents adds to this story, notably through the witness rosters to the charters issued by noblemen, is exquisite specificity about the composition of the group in power, both in the national capital and in the northern provincial capital, at a series of numerous points in time between 1729 and 1820. Some of the potential of this information for improving the narrative history of the period has been exploited in another study.[20]

The beneficiaries of the dissipation of government authority in Sinnār were those whose primary allegiance was to middle class values and institutions as sanctioned by Islamic law; their characteristic contribution to society was the city, and as the kingdom fell apart over the course of the eighteenth century, its towns increased in number from one to twenty. The experience of the Majādhīb of al-Dāmir, who built a small rural religious enclave into a prosperous emporium through commercial acumen and royal largesse (Docs. 63, 64, 65) provides an archtypical example. Town leaders such as the shaykhs of Arbajī or al-Ḥalfāya won positions at the courts of failing noblemen, and Islamic holy men served them as judges.[21]

One early eighteenth century traveler included a translation of the *laissez-passer* given to him by Bādī III on his departure in 1702 (Doc.1). With that sole exception, all the documents of the present collection originate from the troubled "Heroic Age" that followed the overthrow of the old Funj dynasty; they should be interpreted in terms of the gradual decline and increasingly questionable legitimacy of the central government, and the corresponding rise of a self-assertive urban-based Islamic middle class. In legal terms, one may perceive the fragmentation of traditional royal authority in that while in the beginning only the sultan is said to have created official state documents, by the reign of Bādī IV such documents were also being issued by other court officials (Docs. 4, 6) and by at least one provincial governor (Doc. 45); thereafter, as the fortunes of the central government declined, the number of issuing authorities expanded to include not only the Hamaj *wazīr*s but also many lesser dignitaries.

A second legal theme apparent in the documents below is an extended conflict between royal customary justice (*'urf* or *'āda*) and middle-class Islamic *sharī'a*. For example, the very adoption of written Arabic documents to record grants to *fuqarā'* may probably be seen as a departure from time-honored tradition, and the shift in the conditions of such a grant from limited delegated rights (as found for example in Docs. 23 or 24) to the full alienation of property recorded elsewhere may be interpreted in similar terms. Further indications may be found in the conspicuous irregularities that surround the issue of documents by the Islamic judges traditionally if ambiguously associated with the courts of noblemen. At Sinnār, for example, an early *qāḍī* (Doc. 4) apparently had no choice but to rely for witnesses upon the ordinary panel of sultanic courtiers who would also have witnessed a royal document, while a later *qāḍī* (Doc. 33) was able to assert his Islamically more correct prerogative of assembling as witnesses a group of local holy men. Or again, at the northern provincial capital of Qarrī an early *qāḍī* (Doc. 46) may be observed giving justice to individuals of middle-class Islamic legal status when told to do so by a king (Doc. 47), while later *qāḍī*s (Docs. 55, 61) regularly sit beside their secular lord at his court to assure the middle-class constituency that his rulings (Docs. 54, 60) are acceptable according to the *sharī'a*. The present collection of government documents by definition excludes the terminal stage in the process of disintegration of governmental control over the administration of justice, whereby members of the Islamic middle class wrote their own private legal documents according to the principles found in handbooks of the *sharī'a* and themselves nominated *qāḍī*s to pass judgment on the basis of what appeared in them.

Physical and Formal Characteristics of the Documents.--The present volume contains 67 documents originally written in Arabic by officials of the Funj kingdom of Sinnār between 1702 and 1820. Documents 1 through 43 were created by agents of the central government in the capital, 44 through 61 by officials of the northern provincial government, and the remainder by scribes of lesser leaders. Within each geographically defined corpus the documents are arranged chronologically. Each document is accompanied by a brief introduction, an English translation, and notes; a glossary has been provided for terms left untranslated. The majority of texts have been set by the editors on the basis of originals in the possession of private individuals in the Sudan, photocopies of which have been deposited in the National Records Office in Khartoum. In some cases the texts have been derived from an original in the NRO, a nineteenth or twentieth-century copyist's version of an original document, or a photocopy published by other scholars; in a few instances imperfect English translations of apparently authentic but otherwise unavailable documents have been included. The source for each text and, where relevant, a record of previous publication, will be given in the introductions to the individual documents.

The documents were written with a reed pen on one side of large sheets of a variety of high-quality imported trade papers, the study of which will not be undertaken here. The ink, manufactured locally, has faded to a russet color where exposed to sunlight.[22] Documents were often folded for careful preservation by their keepers; holes are comparatively rare, but damage along the folds or around the periphery of a document is common, and in a few cases an entire folded fragment is missing. The language of the documents is formal and solemn; only occasionally does the use of direct discourse introduce brief expressions of the colloquial idiom. The script is clear and workmanlike and exhibits few peculiarities; where it does, we follow the original. The writer of a document often began by placing a short prayer near the top of a sheet of paper, leaving a wide margin to the right, little if any to the left, and a space for one or more impressions of the seal below. The seal was apparently added after the main portion of the document was written (Doc. 35), though additional comments were sometimes inserted thereafter. By convention, we center one copy of the seal text in the appropriate position. The written text resumed below the seal, (or began at that point on the page if no seal was used), and when the text reached the bottom of the page, the sheet was turned upside down to allow further writing in the wide margin. We have indicated the end of a line of original text with a slash (/), and the transition to writing in the margin with a double slash (//).

The documents of the present collection, to a greater or lesser degree, exhibit formal characteristics that repay diplomatic analysis.[23] All are public documents, created by government officials in the discharge of their civic duties, as opposed to private writings of a personal character by such officials or documents made by individuals outside the structure of government. The public documents of Sinnār may be divided into those which possess legal content and those which do not; in the present collection the latter category is represented by Doc. 11 (a colophon) and Doc. 13 (a drum inscription), while all others ask to be understood in a legal context. The documents with legal content may be divided into those in which the authority of witnesses other than the issuing official is invoked and those in which it is not. Documents in the latter category are couched in the form of a letter from an official to one or more subordinates; normally each contains a command that must be obeyed, together with explanatory material (Docs. 17, 29, 31, 34, 43, 44, 57). A distinctive sub-genre is the *laissez-passer* (Docs. 1, 19, 20, 21). The majority of documents in the present collection invoke the authority of witnesses other than the issuing official; such a document is a *ḥujja* or charter (*notitia*, *Beweisurkunde*). The structural features of a Sinnār *ḥujja* are comparatively complex, and deserve extended formal analysis.

The Structure of Sinnār Charters

Allowing for many imperfections in the existing record due to lacunae in the original documents, copyists' interpolations, and flawed translations, the charters of Sinnār exhibit a fairly high degree of standardization in their formal structure. Noteworthy is the apparent absence of evolutionary development in this regard over the period 1729-1820; in form, the earliest extant charters greatly resemble the latest, and if the genre had an indigenous Sudanese prehistory, that remains obscure. It would seem that the creator of a document enjoyed considerable liberty to transpose the order of structural elements within a document, particularly within the body or central portion, and occasionally even to omit some, without compromising the validity of the document. Similarly, while some clauses are phrased almost identically in virtually all documents, others display considerable variation. It would seem fair to conclude that while written texts may well have been available at many courts to serve as examples to the creator of a new document, the latter was free but not obliged to copy them; rather, the formal coherence of Sinnār charters as a genre should probably be attributed to a tradition of chancery usages preserved orally within the ruling institution.[24] These circumstances render it unlikely that the formal characteristics of eighteenth-century Sinnār charters could have been derived directly from any single foreign source, nor do the corresponding charter literatures from historically plausible donor cultures seem to offer convincing models.[25] However, the possible existence of a more limited exchange of stylistic influences between Sinnār and other lands need not be excluded, and would repay further investigation.

The Sinnār charters conform to an apparently almost universal characteristic of the genre in their division into three parts, a body (*ṣadr*) enclosed by introductory and concluding protocols. The following discussion introduces the charter's component clauses in the order in which they most commonly occur.

More tentatively, it also addresses the difficult question of the relationship between the various portions of the charter and the social and legal realities of the historical experience of Sinnār.

The Introductory Protocols

(1) INVOCATIO.-- The written text of all intact Sinnār charters begins with an invocation of the name of God and mention of His prophet. In some cases this meditation is extended into a longer introductory prayer, often poetic in form but thoroughly conventional in content (for example, see Doc. 18). The *invocatio* serves to establish the fundamental religious and cultural context within which all aspects of the charter's creation and subsequent interpretation are to be evaluated.

(2) SEAL.--All intact sultanic charters and many documents issued by subordinate officials bear one or more impressions of the seal of the authority in whose name the document was created.[26] Through the application of his seal, the issuing authority formally recognized the authenticity of the document itself and the validity and force of its contents.[27] Not all issuing authorities seem to have possessed seals, however--in one instance a set of alphanumeric characters were written by hand in the place of the seal (Doc. 48)--and the absence of a seal did not in itself invalidate a document. In one case (Doc. 46) a seal was used to authenticate the *subscriptio* of a witness, the latter having been appended at some considerable interval after the creation of the rest of the document, and quite possibly at a different place. One item in the present collection (Doc. 37) consists solely of a seal impression, otherwise unknown. The written text of a seal normally contains the name of its owner, a statement of his trust in God, and the date of the creation of the seal; in some cases, the date is absent or difficult to read.

(3) LEGAL CHARACTERIZATION OF THE CHARTER.--Most charters from Sinnār explicitly identify themselves as such through the use of the term *ḥujja*, "charter" (Doc. 62); by way of exception, a few do not (Docs. 45, 59, 65). In most cases the designation *ḥujja* is followed by a term specifying the system of law from which the charter derived its authority and according to which it was to be interpreted; in Sinnār this meant either Islamic law (*sharī`a*) administered by a qualified Islamic judge (*qāḍī*) or Funj customary law (*`urf* or *`āda*) administered by the sultan or in his name by a subordinate nobleman. Thus a litigant who received a favorable ruling from both a *qāḍī* and a nobleman was said to have won vindication by both *sharī`a* and *`āda* (Doc. 52).

Five documents in the present collection were issued by *qāḍī*s and identify themselves, through the designation *ḥujja shar`īya*, as charters to be interpreted according to Islamic law (Docs. 4, 33, 46, 55, 61); additional characterizations include the terms *qāṭi`a* or *qaṭ`īya*, "definitive," *sunnīya*, "according to the *sunna*," "legitimate," and *Mālikīya*, "to be interpreted according to the Mālikī *madhhab*." It is possible to further specify the content of the *sharī`a* as understood in the courts of Sinnār by observing that a *qāḍī* relied not only upon his own expertise, but also upon the authority of several standard handbooks of Mālikī Islamic law.[28]

All intact charters issued by the sultans and some by subordinate officials designate themselves documents at customary law through the terms *ḥujja sulṭānīya wa-wathīqa mulūkīya*, "a sultanic charter and royal document" (Docs. 2, 5, 7, 8, 9, 10, 12, 14, 15, 18, 22, 24, 25, 26, 28, 32, 35, 40, 42, 63, 64, 66, 67).[29] Variations which carry a similar intent include *ḥujja sulṭānīya*, "a sultanic charter" (Docs. 38, 39), *ḥujja wa-wathīqa mulūkīya*, "a charter and royal document" (Docs. 6, 27) and *ḥujja qaṭ`īya wa-wathīqa mulūkīya*, "a definitive charter and royal document" (Doc. 58). The royal quality of customary justice was not dependent upon its administration by the king himself. As the contemporary traveler James Bruce observed, "It is the custom . . . to have an arm chair left empty in the middle of the hall where justice is administered [at subordinate courts], which represents the sovereign, and to which obeissance is made."[30] When a subordinate nobleman gave judgment, "The form was--'The *muk* [king] says.'"[31] A number of such noblemen acknowledged the derivative character of their jurisdiction by designating their charters *ḥujja far`īya*, "a subsidiary charter" (Docs. 49, 52, 53, 56, 66). Others omitted reference to the king but did link themselves to customary law through expressions such as *ḥujja qaṭ`īya wa-wathīqa `urfīya* or *`ādīya*, "a definitive charter and customary document" (Docs. 30, 48, 50, 51) or *ḥujja `ādīya wa-wathīqa*, "a customary charter and document" (Doc. 54). The contrast between the standard formula employed by the sultans and the variety of designations to be found among their subordinates probably reflects the uncertain legitimacy of the latter's charter-issuing authority.

(4) PLACE OF ISSUE.--Most charters indicate the place in which they were written (*muḥarrara*) by the scribe and approved (*marḍīya*) by the issuing authority. The broadest geographical designations are *bi-diyār al-Funjīya*, "in the Funj territories" or *bi-mamlakat Sinnār*, "in the kingdom of Sinnār." Documents from the northern province often use the expression *bi-nawāḥī Qarrī*, "in the regions of Qarrī [the traditional provincial capital]," and those from the district of Shandī *bi-diyār* "in the territories of" *Shandī*. Specific locational designations include *bi-Sinnār* or *bi-madinat Sinnār*, "in (the city of) Sinnār" and *bi-bandar* ("in the *bandar* of") al-Tumayd, Qarrī, al-Ḥalfāya and Shandī. The term *bandar* meant a center for the conduct of trade, and its proliferation among towns outside the national capital reflects the rise of private

commerce during the eighteenth century at the expense of the older royally administered trade.[32] When a town is mentioned, the name is usually followed by the epithets *al-maḥrūsa al-maḥmīya*, "the divinely guarded and protected" (familiar from the usages of the Islamic heartlands) and a brief prayer for its well-being.[33]

(5) INTITULATIO.--The numerous titles employed by issuing authorities of Sinnār charters (and letters) vary greatly, both between noblemen and among the documents issued by a single lord. They draw freely upon the nomenclature common to rulers of the Islamic heartlands,[34] and reflect the timeless duties of a Muslim prince or judge to command the good and prohibit evil. Noteworthy, in contrast to the documents of Dār Fūr and the other sultanates of the western Sudan, is the absence of a claim to the Caliphal title of *amīr al-mu'minīn*.[35] This study will confine itself to examination of only a few features of the titles of Sinnār lords which seem to have relevance to contemporary circumstances in the Sudan.

Since it was highly desirable that a lord should have achieved his position through sound hereditary succession, whenever possible he would be introduced as the descendant of his predecessors. When a place of issue for a document is given the issuing authority is usually introduced as *mutawallīhā*, "her warden," and the son of her warden. An effective governor must master equally "her far places and near, her nomads and sedentaries." He should be a source of equitable justice and compassion to whom any subject could appeal.[36] When a Funj lord spoke formally from the throne, directly and not via the *manamalecna* or court "linguist," his words had the force of law; this feature of customary procedure is reflected in the expression *idhā qāla ṣadaq, wa-idhā takallam bi'l-ḥaqq naṭaq,* "when he speaks he speaks the truth, and when he speaks the truth he has ordained."[37] Since the people of Sinnār observed the astronomical position of the Pleiades in order to ascertain the time of the onset of the rainy season, one may perhaps read an oblique reference to the presumed powers of the king over the forces of nature in the assertion that his influence "ascends to the Pleiades and gathers in clouds."[38]

The high king claimed the title "sultan, the son of the sultan." Subordinate territorial lords usually used the title "shaykh" and identified themselves in terms of family relationship that defined them as members of the hereditary nobility. By way of exception, during the last years of Sinnār a few territorial lords designated themselves the shaykh or *malik* of certain groups of subjects (Docs. 48, 52, 56) or claimed an ancestry outside the traditional nobility (Docs. 64, 67). Subordinate servants of the central or provincial governments identified themselves by their court titles such as *amīn* (Doc. 6), *qāḍī* (Docs. 4, 33 [Sinnār]; 46, 55, 61 [Qarrī]), or *wazīr* (Docs. 17, 29, 31, 39, 42).[39] Several Hamaj *wazīr*s styled themselves "*amīn* of the army" of the sultan (Docs. 29, 30, 31, 39, 42).

(6) INSCRIPTIO.--Many charters issued by noblemen (not by *qāḍī*s) contain an *inscriptio*, usually in the form *ilā [ḥaḍrat] kulli man taqif ʿalayhī hādhihī al-wathīqa wa'l-nāẓir li-mā fīhā min al-ḥaqīqa*, "To [the presence of] all who read this document and see the truth therein." Variations may be found in Docs. 2, 59, 60, 64, and 67.

The Body of the Charter

(7) TRANSITIONAL EXPRESSION.--The transition from the introductory protocols to the *ṣadr*, the body of the charter, is signified by the *baʿdīya*, consisting of the terms *ammā baʿd*. In the present study the form "Thereafter:" is used to translate the *baʿdīya*.

(8) DISPOSITIO.--The *dispositio* begins by naming again the issuing authority introduced in the *intitulatio*, and states the legal action he has performed giving rise to the creation of the charter. This action may be expressed in the first person or the third (compare Docs. 2, 3) through a limited number of verbs, and the differences between these terms divide the charters into several categories. The first, signified by the term *taṣaddaqa*, "bestow as alms," may be called originating charters; these are in no way dependent upon prior actions or conditions. A second, most frequently indicated by the verbs *tammama* or *amḍā* ("confirm," "ratify"), may be called confirming charters, for they serve to validate anew actions taken in the past. A third category employs the verb *abṭala*, "nullify;" the purpose of such a charter is to render null and void actions taken in the past. Finally, the charter of a *qāḍī* records his act of giving judgment, usually through the verb *ḥakama*.[40] The *dispositio* then names the parties who are affected by the action; an originating or confirming charter has one or more beneficiaries, while the charter of a *qāḍī* or a nullifying charter names both a victorious party and a defeated one. A confirming charter names the person or persons whose previous actions are to be confirmed. The *dispositio* then states what is conveyed by the action of the issuing authority. In the broadest sense, this object of the action of the charter consists of a set of legal rights and privileges, which may be called generically a *jāh* or "grant."[41] Sometimes the grant is described in terms of the religious motivations of the issuing authority, for example, as *ṣadaqa*, "a gift of alms" (Docs. 18, 25, 32).[42]

In a predominantly agricultural social setting most meaningful grants of rights could not fail to impinge upon the system of land tenure, if only indirectly; for purposes of formal analysis, however, it is useful to distinguish between those charter grants in which rights over land constituted the direct and primary object of the issuing authority's action and those in which they did not. Among the latter, exemplified by Doc. 3, the donor not only granted a special personal status to the beneficiary but also extended these immunities and privileges to his relatives and followers; moreover, members of the privileged group thus constituted were at liberty to move freely throughout the kingdom, bearing their status with them. A grant might transfer groups of subjects from their previous lord to the beneficiary (Docs. 24, 59), or bestow upon him the right to own slaves (Doc. 24). In other cases a grant conveyed administrative privileges, or the right to sponsor a market (Doc. 23).[43]

In most cases the object of a charter grant in Sinnār was a a set of rights over land, often described in general terms as a *dār* or "estate."[44] In one instance (Doc. 10) the grant is said to consist of a *zarība*, literally a protective enclosure of thorn branches, but probably to be understood here as the homestead such a fence was constructed to defend; in all other cases the land granted was apparently intended for non-residential use. Two grants (Docs. 35, 42) were said to consist of *rufā'īya* lands, pastoral lands as opposed *ḥaḍarīya* or sedentary lands, to *ṭīn* or cultivable land, and particularly to cultivable rainlands, *ṭīn . . . arḍ maṭar mawāt,* "cultivable land . . . virgin rainland" (Doc. 39) or *arḍ mawāt wa-būr laisa fīhā 'ammār*, "barren wasteland with no cultivation on it" (Docs. 48, 49). A final and very important category consisted of riverine lands; these included the *jarf* or sloping riverbank innundated annually by the Nile flood (Doc. 40) and the immediately adjoining flat lands beyond the crest of the *jarf* that could be irrigated mechanically by ox-driven waterwheel or *sāqīya* (Docs. 8, 45). Within the high and comparatively permanent banks of the Nile, the floods deposited low, shifting banks or islands of very fertile soil; these too became the object of grants (Docs. 14, 64). The large grant recorded in Doc. 24 conveyed lands both pastoral and sedentary, riverine and rainlands.

For legal purposes each unit of non-residential land conveyed by a charter grant must be defined in terms of the prevailing system of land survey. With the exceptions to be noted below, this usually meant designating the boundaries according to *al-arkān al-arba`a*, "the four corners" (Doc. 25); to the north (*al-sāfil*, literally "downstream"), south (*al-ṣa`īd*, literally "upstream"), west (*al-gharb*) and east (*al-ṣubḥ*, *al-qibla*). It was said that "all land has a name," that of the tenant according to customary tenure,[45] and particularly in the wide regions that were not irrigated, a grant could sometimes be sufficiently defined by naming its adjoining neighbors (Docs. 2, 39). Sometimes other relatively fixed features of the landscape such as roads, reservoirs, rivers, springs, perennial rain pools, trees, rocky peaks, cemeteries, riverbank watering places, or seasonal watercourses also helped serve this purpose (Docs. 28, 39, 42). Less frequently, man-made boundary marks such as blazes on trees or stone markers were used (Doc. 59); conspicuously, a number of boundary segments in Doc. 24 were defined in terms of *turūs* (singular, *turus*), low earthen banks constructed around the lower sides of a cultivated rainland field to hold runoff. In many cases, however, a more precise survey system was necessary.

A basic unit of linear measure in Sinnār was the cubit or *dhirā`*, "a measure consisting of the length of the forearm from the elbow to the extremity of the middle finger with the addition of six fingers crosswise."[46] A certain number of cubits constituted the standard *`ūd* or rod for purposes of land measurement, but since this number varied from one community to another, so did the length of the rod, and it was necessary for any document using the term *`ūd* to specify the number of cubits that comprised it, for example (Doc. 63), a rod "of three cubits," *wa-dhirā`hā abū thalātha*. In the measurement of rainland (Doc. 33) the rod was used to define a measure of area called the *jad`a*, a square of 60 rods (in some districts, 64 rods) on each side.[47]

> "Only linear measure was employed in the survey of irrigated riverine lands. Each landholding began at the *mirin*, an imaginary line that followed the center of the riverbed (or the middle of the channel if there were islands), and extended inland east or west (but not both) to the

> limits of possible cultivation . . . . The up- and downstream boundaries of a landholding, called *fāṣils*, were drawn at right angles to the midriver *mirin* and parallel to one another, and the size of a landholding [Docs. 55, 63, 65] was measured by the linear distance between the *fāṣil*s along the *ḥaram al-sār*, a second imaginary line running parallel to the midriver *mirin* along the east and west banks at the crest of the *jarf*. (In some villages where the *jarf* was unusually wide additional boundaries, also called *mirins*, were drawn across it at intervals, parallel to the *ḥaram al-sār* [Docs. 50, 58]). The distance between *fāṣils* tended to be drawn at the limits of the irrigating capacity of a waterwheel, and each landholding unit--which like the waterwheel itself was termed a *sāqīya* [Docs. 8, 45]--included both irrigated land and its appertaining *jarf*.[48]

Certain further details of the survey system of riverine lands will be considered below in the introductions to individual documents.

(9) NARRATIO.--All charters issued by *qāḍīs* and some issued by noblemen contain a summary of the relevant circumstances that led up to the legal action that occasioned the issue of the document. In the document of a *qāḍī* the primary preoccupation is the conduct of litigation before the ruling judge, with assurances that the correct procedure has been followed and the judge's ruling well grounded in the *sharī'a*. In documents issued by noblemen the *narratio* constitutes a broad, brief, and undoubtedly selective history of the object of the charter grant; emphasis is given to previous actions by the courts and to establishing the jurisdiction of the current issuing authority. In some cases extended quotations from previous documents are included.

(10) ARENGA.--The *arenga* of a Sinnār charter is found only in the documents issued by noblemen, and usually consists of variations on the comparatively fixed formula, "A gift of alms for the sake of God and the messenger, asking for reward in the life to come, for a day in which neither wealth nor sons suffice, unless one comes to God with a secure heart."

(11) CORROBORATIO.--This portion of a charter defines the status of the object of a charter grant following the completion of the legal action by the issuing authority recorded in the *dispositio*. This status often includes a negative component consisting of immunity from obligations and encumbrances that would otherwise obtain; from these the object of the charter is said to be *sālima musallama*, "completely free." The immunities granted may be divided into a majority which may be assumed to originate from the traditional usages of Sinnār and a smaller subset which reflect the intrusion of the money economy and commercial capitalist usages during the eighteenth century.[49] The meanings of many of the former remain conjectural; taken as a whole, they probably delineate much of the structure of obligation of a Sinnār subject to his lord.[50] The context suggests that three terms--*shurūr*, *maḍārr*, and *subul*, sometimes (Doc. 12) said to be *`ādīya* or "customary"--are more general and comprehensive than the ensuing list of specific immunities introduced by the expression *lā `alayhā*, "it is not subject to . . . ."

When the object of a charter grant consists primarily or exclusively of personal privileges (Docs. 3, 59) or administrative authority (Docs. 23, 24, 28), it is defined largely in terms of immunities; the object is said to have become a grant of *jāh* if within the code of customary law (Doc. 24) or a gift (*`aṭā'*) if an alienation from it (Doc. 28). In the frequent case that a grant consists primarily of land, however, the issuing authority usually adds a statement that defines the land as being henceforth the property (*milk*) of the beneficiary, and sometimes (Doc. 38) specifies that he also enjoys the rights of possession (*ḥawz*) and usufruct (*taṣarruf*). In such cases the property donated is alienated from the land tenure system of Sinnār. The definitive quality of this alienation is emphasized by the introduction of a temporal dimension to the grant and the specification of its future owners until the end of time; for example (Doc. 18), a grant is said to have become the property of the beneficiaries, "for them and their descendants, and their descendants' descendants. They shall bequeath it from heir to heir until God inherits the earth and those upon it, and He is the Best of Heirs."

(12) SANCTIO.--The body of a nobleman's charter normally concludes with an admonition not to trouble (*ta`āraḍa*) or challenge (*tanāza`a*) the beneficiary of the grant; sometimes other prohibitions, notably against trespass, are also expressed (Doc. 59). Often special warning is given to the generality of government officials, and occasionally (Doc. 10) specific individuals are mentioned as likely potential offenders. In a few cases a penalty is named for violation of the terms of the charter; for example (Doc. 56), "He who troubles them after that is subject to the reckoning; whoever challenges concerning it, be they one, two, or more, I will fine him a camel." In most cases the threat of royal displeasure, sometimes (Doc. 3) emphasized grammatically through use of the energetic mood, is deemed sufficient deterrent: "Beware, then beware of disobedience, and let the disobedient blame none but himself."

The Concluding Protocols

(13) SUBSCRIPTIO.--According to Islamic legal principles, "with God, two witnesses suffice."[51] Both noblemen and *qāḍīs* in Sinnār, however, obtained the endorsement of a larger number of suitable and influential witnesses. The witness clauses of a nobleman's charter typically begin "there were present and witnessed to it," followed by a roster of the names and titles of incumbent court members in the handwriting of the document's scribe. Taken as a whole, these court rosters constitute an important source for the study of the government of Sinnār after 1729, and repay further examination.[52] For example, they indicate that while the court of a district lord (Doc. 66) consisted largely of groups of his kinsmen, the court of a provincial governor (Doc. 50) also contained some titled officials, and that of a sultan, many; this study will focus upon the titled officials of the rosters of sultanic charters. The composition of the sultan's court changed during the course of the eighteenth century. The rosters of charters issued during the minority of Bādī IV before 1745 may serve here as a standard against which subsequent changes may be evaluated; the latter will be discussed below in the introductions to the individual documents.

Given the protocol of hierarchy that obtained at the sultan's court, one may infer that the witnesses of a charter roster appear in an order that approximates their rank at court.[53] The first two positions, sometimes designated those of the *amīn* and the *jundī,* were held on an hereditary basis by members of a single family said to be kinsmen of the king himself.[54] The third position belonged to the *sīd al-qūm*, the maternal uncle of the king.[55] During one stage in the minority of Bādī IV his maternal uncle Ismā`īl occupied this position in person, but normally the maternal uncle was represented by an agent, the *wakīl ḥōsh khāl al-malik.* The second group of court officials were the provincial governors of Sinnār, the shaykhs of Qarrī, Alays, al-Baḥr, al-Tāka, Bayla, Atbara, al-Qarbīn, and Kordofāl (Kordofan). In early charters the *amīn,* the *jundī*, and the provincial governors are identified only by a single personal name; this sufficed to identify hereditary Funj noblemen who were incorporated into the sultan's own matriclan through dynastic marriage in each generation.[56] In later years, as patrilineal principles of descent began to gain currency, these noblemen began to use names in which they designated themselves the sons of their fathers.[57] A third group of court officials were titled bureaucrats and military officers, some of whom seem to have been slaves; the functions of several offices in this category are not known, for example, those of the *malik bursāj* and the *muqaddam al-sajjāda*. The *muqaddam al-sawākira* was responsible for the *sawākira* or princely hostages, "locked up tighter than the cloistered nuns of Christendom."[58] The *muqaddam al-quwwārīya* was in charge of the treasury. The *muqaddam al-qawāwīd*, a military officer, also supervised the corps of pages assembled by the sultan from among the sons of his nobles. The *muqaddam al-khayl* commanded the sultan's cavalry, while the *muqaddam bayt al-`udda* supervised the arsenal where war materiel was gathered or manufactured. In later years, as the sultan's control over the military affairs of his kingdom dissipated, most of these military titles disappeared from the rosters of sultanic charters. A final important category of sultanic courtiers were Islamic dignitaries, the *qāḍī*, the *khaṭīb* and the muezzin of the Sinnār mosque, and the scribe who wrote the document. From the beginning, these individuals used names revealing a preference for patrilineal descent. In broad terms, these were the "twenty old men" of the Sinnār court who surrounded a Funj king of the early eighteenth century.[59]

Two major subsequent modifications in the court structure of Sinnār left their imprint upon the witness rosters of the later sultanic charters. When Bādī IV assumed personal power between 1744 and 1752, he greatly expanded the size of his court; the older set of courtiers were balanced against new parties of Islamic holy men, of urban leaders such as the Shaykh of Arbajī, and of minor noblemen entitled *arbāb*. With the Hamaj coup of 1762, places were found in the charter rosters for the regent (*wazīr*) himself and for various lesser Hamaj officials.[60]

The two charters in the present collection issued by *qāḍī*s of Sinnār differ sharply in regard to witnesses. The 1733 charter of the *qāḍī* `Abd al-`Azīz (Doc. 4) is witnessed by the incumbent members of the royal court and does not differ significantly in that regard from a sultanic document of the same period (Docs. 2, 5). In the 1799 charter of the *qāḍī* `Umar (Doc. 33), however, the witnesses consist exclusively of Islamic holy men and no courtiers are present. Further, the judge has not only placed his seal upon the document, but has written an endorsement in his own handwriting in the margin. The three charters issued by *qāḍī*s of Qarrī (Docs. 46, 55, 61) follow the conventions of Doc. 33 in regard to witnesses. In the case of Doc. 46, it is known from other sources (Doc. 47) that the written endorsements by various Islamic holy men in their own handwriting and the seal of the *qāḍī* of Sinnār `Abd al-`Azīz were added some time after the completion of the original document in response to a challenge by the defeated party. While the witness rosters of Docs. 55 and 61 consist exclusively of Islamic holy men, secular courtiers witnessed the corresponding princely documents issued on the same two occasions by the Shaykh of Qarrī (Docs. 54, 60).

(14) **DATES.**--In contrast to the colorful irregularities that characterize private documents from Sinnār,[61] the charters, when intact, express the date in simple and conventional Islamic terms. In some cases only the month of the year of issue is given, but usually the precise date, and sometimes the day of the week and time of day.

NOTES

[1]For the early Sudan, its kingdoms and languages, see William Y. Adams, *Nubia: Corridor to Africa* (Princeton: 1977), Abdelgadir Mahmoud Abdulla, ed., *Studies in Ancient Languages of the Sudan* (Khartoum: 1974), and Peter L. Shinnie, "The Ancient Languages of the Northern Sudan," in Robin Thelwall, ed., *Aspects of Language in the Sudan* (Londonderry: 1978), pp. 82-96. A survey of the period A.D. 1500-1820 may be found in R.S. O'Fahey and J.L. Spaulding, *Kingdoms of the Sudan* (London: 1974), and a detailed study of the eighteenth century in Jay Spaulding, *The Heroic Age in Sinnār* (East Lansing: 1985).

[2]Spaulding, *Heroic Age*, p. xvii and note 9. For the transitional period, see Yūsuf Faḍl Ḥasan, *The Arabs and the Sudan from the seventh to the early sixteenth century* (Edinburgh: 1967), Jay Spaulding, "The End of Nubian Kingship in the Sudan," in M.W. Daly, ed., *Modernization in the Sudan* (New York: 1985), pp. 17-28, Lidwien Kapteijns and Jay Spaulding, "History, Ethnicity and Agriculture in the Sudan," in Jill Craig, ed., *The Agriculture of the Sudan* (Oxford: forthcoming), and J.L. Spaulding and Jay Spaulding, "The Democratic Philosophers of the Medieval Sudan: Pigs," forthcoming in *Sprache und Geschichte in Afrika.*

[3]Eduard Biberfeld, *Der Reisebericht des David Reubeni* (Berlin: 1898), pp. 7-8; Jean de Sainte Marie, *Les estranges evenemens du voyage de son altesse, le serenissime prince Zaga-Christ d'Ethiopie* (Paris: 1635), pp. 27-28.

[4]Jay Spaulding, "Numerical Notation and Token Counters in Nubia," *Findings* (1985): 9-12. If these well-attested medieval Sudanese usages survived into the nineteenth century, an age when writing on paper in the Arabic language had gained general ascendancy in the region, it is reasonable to assume that they would have enjoyed at least equal importance during the intervening centuries of less extensive Arabic influence. For a contrary view, which holds with "profound misgivings" that this line of argumentation is "a prescription for the arbitrary selection of data," see P.M. Holt, "A New History of [sic] Funj," *Journal of African History* 27, 3 (1986):563. The reader may judge.

[5]Sainte Marie, *Zaga-Christ*, pp. 49-50.

[6]Ibid., p. 28.

[7]As early as 1635 Zaga Christ used both the terms "Royaume de Fungi" and "Royaume de Senar" in reference to the kingdom through which he passed on the way from Ethiopia to Egypt (Sainte Marie, *Zaga-Christ*, pp. 7, 12). A second seventeenth-century example of the parallel use of the terms "Funj" and "Sinnār" for the kingdom of the Sudanese Nile Valley is the written testimony of the Ethiopian monk Gregory in Rome in 1654; he referred to "the Arabs of Funj ["*Fundio*"], otherwise known as Sinnār ["*Synnâr*"]:" Anonymous [Hiob Ludolf?], *Sonderbarer Lebens-Lauf Herrn Peter Heylings aus Lübec* (Halle: 1714), pp. 192-193 (Ethiopic text) and pp. 193-195 (German translation). During the sixteenth century Ottoman governmental records from Sawākīn referred to the Nile Valley kingdom as *vilâyet-i Func*, but by the dawn of the eighteenth century they had followed the prevailing historical trend and adopted the expression *vilâyet-i Sinnar*. See Cengiz Orhonlu, *Habeş Eyaleti* (Istanbul: 1974), Documents 2 and 3, pp. 185, 182, (both of these documents are sixteenth century, but only Document 3 is dated [9 Şevval 971/21 May 1564]) and Document 77, p. 247 (Zilhicce 1112/May-June 1701). For a defense of the viewpoint that these and others err in referring to Sinnār by that name, see Holt, "A New History of [sic] Funj."

[8]E. van Donzel, *Foreign Relations of Ethiopia, 1642-1700* (Istanbul: 1979), p. 182.

[9]Anonymous, *Peter Heylings*, pp. 193-195.

[10]For an introduction see Neil McHugh, "Holymen of the Blue Nile: Religious Leadership and the Genesis of an Arab Islamic Society in the Nilotic Sudan, 1500-1850," Ph.D Diss., Northwestern University, 1986. A primary source of fundamental importance is Yūsuf Faḍl Ḥasan, ed., *Kitāb al-ṭabaqāt . . . ta'līf Muḥammad al-Nūr b. Ḍayf Allāh* (Khartoum: 1971), hereafter cited as *Ṭabaqāt.*

[11]al-Shāṭir Buṣaylī `Abd al-Jalīl, ed., *Makhṭūṭat Kātib al-Shūna fī ta'rīkh al-sulṭāna al-Sinnārīya wa'l-idāra al-Miṣrīya* (Cairo: 1961), p. 10; hereafter cited as *Makhṭūṭa.*

[12]Spaulding, *Heroic Age*, p. 152; McHugh, "Holymen," pp. 109-164.

[13]See below, Docs. 3, 27, 30; *Ṭabaqāt*, pp. 347-348.

[14]An extended treatment may be found in Spaulding, *Heroic Age.*

[15]See O'Fahey and Spaulding, *Kingdoms*, pp. 68-78, and the sources cited therein. Of particular importance are Theodoro Krump, *Hoher und Fruchtbarer Palm-Baum des Heiligen*

Evangelij (Augsburg: 1710) and the account of Charles-Jacques Poncet in William Foster, ed., *The Red Sea at the Close of the Seventeenth Century* (London: 1949), pp. 93-165.

[16]Spaulding, *Heroic Age*, pp. 76, 113, 154-155.

[17]Jay Spaulding, "The Chronicle of Aḥmad b. `Īsā," *Sudan Texts Bulletin* 6 (1984): 37-43, and *Heroic Age*, p. 195.

[18]Jay Spaulding and `Abd al-Ghaffār Muḥammad Aḥmad, "The Sinnār King-List of the *sīd al-qūm* Aḥmad," *Fontes Historiae Africanae Arabicae: Bulletin d'Information* 7-8 (1982-1983): 38-42.

[19]James Bruce, *Travels to Discover the Source of the Nile*, 2nd ed. (Edinburgh: 1805); John Lewis Burckhardt, *Travels in Nubia*, 2nd ed. (London: 1822).

[20]Spaulding, *Heroic Age*, pp. 299-451.

[21]Ibid., pp. 139-237.

[22]See Terence Walz, "The Paper Trade of Egypt and the Sudan in the Eighteenth and Nineteenth Centuries," in Daly, *Modernization*, pp. 29-48. Near-contemporary information was given by Giovanni Battista Brocchi: "The paper in these lands comes from Cairo. Ink is made of soot which adheres to the terra cotta disk on which they cook the wafers [of *kisra*] that take the place of bread. The pen is from the cane of a native durra, "white durra," which is cultivated on lands irrigated by *sāqīya* [waterwheel]; pens are also made of the stalk of *nāl* grass, or of another called *tammām*, and these are excellent." (*Giornale delle osservazioni fatte ne'viaggi in Egitto, nella Siria e nella Nubia* [Bassano: 1843], Vol. 5, pp. 301-302.)

[23]The present discussion draws upon Adolf Grohmann, *Allgemeine Einführung in die Arabischen Papyri nebst Grundzügen der Arabischen Diplomatik* (Wien: 1924).

[24]As R.S. O'Fahey and M.I. Abū Salīm (*Land in Dār Fūr* [Cambridge: 1983], p. 23) observe in regard to the early twentieth-century court of `Alī Dīnār in Dār Fūr, there probably existed "an intermediate stage in the evolution of bureaucratic practice whereby the mechanisms for the issuing of documents with a more or less standard format existed, but not for consistently registering and preserving copies . . . . It would seem, therefore, that while incoming letters, tax records and the like were kept at court, outgoing correspondence was not copied and stored." A similar situation seems to have prevailed in Sinnār.

[25]For an introduction to the formal conventions of the Islamic heartlands, see W.

Björkman, G.S. Colin, H. Busse, J. Reychman, and A. Zajaczkowski, "Diplomatic," *The Encyclopaedia of Islam*, 2nd ed. (Leiden: 1965), Vol. 2, pp. 301-316, and Claude Cahen, "Notes de Diplomatique Arabo-Musulmane," *Journal Asiatiques* 251 (1963): 311-325. Some geographically and chronologically relevant points of comparison would include S.M. Stern, "Two Ayyūbid Decrees from Sinai," in his *Documents from Islamic Chanceries* (Oxford: 1965), pp. 9-38 and Hans Ernst, *Die mamlukischen Sultansurkunde des Sinai-Klosters* (Wiesbaden: 1960). For medieval Nubia, see `Alī `Osmān Muḥammad Ṣāliḥ, "The Economy and Trade of Medieval Nubia," Ph.D Diss., Christ's College, Cambridge University, 1978, pp. 221-238. For Ethiopia, see Madeleine Schneider, "Deux actes de Donation en Arabe," *Annales d'Ethiopie* 8 (1970): 79-88 and G.W.B. Huntingford, *The Land Charters of Northern Ethiopia* (Addis Ababa: 1965). For Dār Fūr, see Muḥammad Ibrāhīm Abū Salīm, *al-Fūr wa'l-arḍ: wathā'iq tamlīk* (Khartoum: 1975), O'Fahey and Abū Salīm, *Land in Dār Fūr*, R.S. O'Fahey, *State and Society in Dār Fūr* (London: 1980), and Lidwien Kapteijns and Jay Spaulding, *After the Millennium* (East Lansing: 1988).

[26]For a discussion of Sudanese seals and sealing practices, see Muḥammad Ibrāhīm Abū Salīm, *al-Khatm al-Dīwānī fi'l-Sūdān* (Khartoum: 1983).

[27]Grohmann, *Einführung*, p. 83.

[28]The fundamental work most commonly cited is the *Mukhtaṣar* of Khalīl b. Isḥāq, also referred to as *al-Muṣannif*, "The Author," for whom see M. ben Chenes, "Khalīl b. Isḥāq," *The Encyclopaedia of Islam*, 2nd ed. (Leiden: 1978), Vol. 4, p. 964. According to ben Chenes, the *Mukhtaṣar* is "so obscure because of its conciseness that it can only be understood by means of a commentary," and understandably therefore several commentators are cited also. Notable are Ṣaḥnūn b. `Abd al-Salām b. Sa`īd b. `Abd al-Salām al-Tanūkhī, Abū `Abd Allāh Muḥammad al-Khorāshī, `Abd al-Bāqī b. Yūsuf al-Zurqānī, and Muḥammad b. Ibrāhīm al-Tatā'ī. For an introduction to their writings, see Carl Brockelmann, *Geschichte der Arabischen Litteratur* (Weimar: 1898-1902), Vol. 1, pp. 176-178 and Vol. 2, pp. 183, 316-318, and David Santillana, *Istituzioni di Diritto Musulmano Malichita* (Rome: 1925), Vol. 2, pp. 647, 655, 658.

[29]P.M. Holt renders *mulūkīya* very freely as "customary," but the more literal translation "royal" is to be preferred; see his "Four Funj Land-Charters," in his *Studies in the History of the Near East* (London: 1973), pp. 111-112.

[30]Bruce, *Travels*, Vol. 6, p. 283.

[31]Lord Prudhoe, "Extracts from private Memoranda kept by Lord Prudhoe on a journey from Cairo to Sennar, in 1829, describing the Peninsula of Sennar," *Journal of the Royal Geographical Society* 5 (1835): 49.

[32]Lidwien Kapteijns, "The Organization of Exchange in Precolonial Western Sudan," in Leif O. Manger, ed., *Trade and Traders in the Sudan* (Bergen: 1984), pp. 49-80; Jay Spaulding, "The Management of Exchange in Sinnār, c.1700," in Manger, *Trade and Traders,* pp. 25-48, and Lidwien Kapteijns and Jay Spaulding, "Precolonial Trade Between States in the Eastern Sudan, c.1700 - c.1900," *African Economic History* 11 (1982): 29-62.

[33]For example, see J. Wansbrough, "A Mamlūk Commercial Treaty concluded with the Republic of Florence 894/1489," in Stern, *Islamic Chanceries*, pp. 39-80.

[34]For example, see the sources cited above, note 25.

[35]Kapteijns and Spaulding, *Millennium*, p. 10; O'Fahey and Abū Salīm, *Land in Dār Fūr*, p. 151.

[36]For the precolonial Sudanese use of *miskīn* to mean "subject," see Kapteijns and Spaulding, *Millennium*, p. 8, and Lidwien Kapteijns, *Mahdist Faith and Sudanic Tradition* (London: 1985), pp. 40, 248.

[37]See Spaulding, *Heroic Age*, pp. 9-14, and the sources cited therein. For another viewpoint, see Holt, "A New History of [sic] Funj," p. 563. Holt, who is not familiar with the accounts of eyewitnesses to the practice of Funj royal justice, advances on textual grounds the objection that "The two clauses are identical in meaning, and convey no more than the formal eulogy, 'When he speaks, he speaks the truth.'" In support of this view he proposes that "The passage and its context are in rhymed prose (*saj`*), and here we have two parallel clauses with inversion in the second for the sake of the rhyme;" in other words, according to Holt, the second clause should read *wa-idhā takallam naṭaq bi'l-ḥaqq*. Holt is certainly correct in identifying the mode of expression as *saj`*, and his argument must fall precisely because the demand of the *saj`* genre for an end-rhyme, in this case on the letter *qāf*, was already satisfied by the original text as written; Holt's arbitrary inversion of *bi'l-ḥaqq* and *naṭaq* in the second clause would affect the conformity of the passage to the prosodic conventions of *saj`* in no way whatsoever. What Holt's strained and artificial attempt to

distort the text as written does do, however, is to remove the force of the verb *naṭaq*, a term which conveys the literal sense of "pronounce," and in the present context, "pronounce judgment"--or, as we have rendered the idiom, "ordain."

[38]Brocchi, *Giornale*, Vol. 5, p. 656.

[39]Since `Adlān b. Muḥammad Abū Likaylik was not yet *wazīr* at the time he issued Doc. 30, he identified himself as a "son of the *wazīr*;" see Jay Spaulding, "Two documents from the days of Nāṣir b. Muḥammad Abū Likaylik, Hamaj Regent of Sinnār," *Fontes Historiae Africanae Arabicae: Bulletin d'Information* 7-8 (1982-1983): 33-37. His son Muḥammad b. `Adlān also identified himself as a "son of the *wazīr*" (Docs. 35, 38, 43); although he dominated political life in Sinnār during its last years, he did not attempt to usurp the title of the last titular Hamaj *wazīr* Ḥusayn b. Muḥammad Abū Likaylik.

[40]The originating charters in the present collection are Docs. 6, 8, 9, 35, 38, 42, 45, 48, 50, 59, 63, 64, and 65. Doc. 16 is a nullifying charter and Docs. 4, 33, 46, 55, and 61 were issued by *qāḍīs*; the remaining charters confirm previous actions.

[41]On the basis of the Dār Fūr charter literature, O'Fahey and Abū Salīm (*Land in Dār Fūr*, pp. 17-18) correctly conclude that the term *jāh* appears most frequently in cases where the bestowal of immunities and rights over people upon the beneficiary are more important than rights over land. As Doc. 24 in the present collection indicates, however, in Sinnār a grant of *jāh* may also include rights over land; the comprehensive translation "grant" seems preferable.

[42]For a discussion of why some donors may have chosen to define their grants in these terms, see Spaulding, *Heroic Age*, p. 160 and note 37.

[43]For a discussion of the wider historical significance of these grants, see Spaulding, *Heroic Age*, pp. 155-157.

[44]The very large and exceptional grant recorded in Doc. 28, in effect the cession of a whole province, probably deserves to be considered in a category by itself; however, its unusual qualities are not revealed by its thoroughly conventional formal characteristics.

[45]Spaulding, *Heroic Age*, pp. 269-270.

[46]Brocchi, *Giornale*, Vol. 5, p. 256.

[47]Ibid., p. 429.

[48]Spaulding, *Heroic Age*, pp. 85-86.

[49]Ibid., pp. 157-158.

[50]Some possible meanings are suggested in the glossary. Discussion may be found in Muḥammad Ibrāhīm Abū Salīm, *al-Fūnj wa'l-arḍ: wathā'iq tamlīk* (Khartoum: 1967), pp. 31-33 and Jay Spaulding, "Taxation in Sinnār," *Northeast African Studies* 6, 1-2 (1984): 127-146.

[51]Claude Cahen, "A Propos des Shuhūd," *Studia Islamica* 31 (1970): 71-79.

[52]Spaulding, *Heroic Age*, pp. 15-19; 51-56.

[53]Ibid., pp. 14-15.

[54]Brocchi, *Giornale*, Vol. 5, pp. 344-345; 540-543.

[55]Spaulding, *Heroic Age*, pp. 33-36.

[56]Ibid., pp. 21-38.

[57]Ibid., pp. 215-218.

[58]Krump, *Palm-Baum*, p. 283. For an introduction to the court offices mentioned below, see Spaulding, *Heroic Age*, pp. 15-19; 23; 26-27; 66-67; 72-73.

[59]Poncet in Foster, *Red Sea*, p. 103.

[60]Spaulding, *Heroic Age*, pp. 214-218; 313-316; 320-321.

[61]Ibid., pp. 196-197.

DOCUMENT 1

Document 1 is a *laissez-passer* issued by Sultan Bādī III to the Franciscan missionaries Theodoro Krump and Antonio della Terza on their departure from Sinnār on 1 May 1702. The translation given here is derived from Krump's travel account, where he calls it a "Copy of the letter of recommendation given to me and Father Antonio della Terza in Arabic by the king, which I have translated into German with my own hand."[1] (The explanatory comments in parentheses were added by Krump himself.) The probable authenticity of the king's letter and the general accuracy of Krump's translation are supported by the similarity between this document and the other *laissez-passers* from Sinnār (Docs. 19, 20, 21) and the sultanates of the western Sudan.[2] Krump described the circumstances of the document's issue as follows:

> On the first of May [1702] Father Pasquale and I were granted a royal audience. I opened by saying that since the king's first personal physician, Father Pasquale, had returned, I was inclined to go back to Egypt with the caravan to seek my fortune. Although the king would rather have had me here, he did not want to hinder me, and at once ordered Shaykh Ismā`īl to deliver to me one of his best dromedaries from his court stable. He then ordered his secretary to prepare a royal letter for me and Father Antonio della Terza . . . . It should say that wherever we went on the journey people should supply us, as royal servants, with everything necessary for ourselves and our camels and servants. I heartily thanked him for this great favor. After a few hours had passed the letter of recommendation and a very beautiful and excellent dromedary were brought to me at our dwelling by a *mursāl*

> [messenger]. [He] also reported that before my departure I should come once more to an audience, for the king wanted to give me several ounces of gold on account of my faithful service to himself and his subjects. I . . . thanked him very politely.[3]

Several individual features of the letter deserve comment. In Krump's usage the term "Turk" means "Muslim" and bears no specific ethnic connotation. "One calls Christians *mu`allim* in Turkey," Krump noted. "It simply means 'Mister,' and is commonly applied to merchants and craftsmen. Yūnus was my name, Sulaymān was Father Antonio della Terza, and Yūsuf, Father Pasquale [da Montella]. We had to use names that were known to both Christians and Turks."[4] Shaykh Ismā`īl was Krump's chosen court representative and protector at the time of his departure.[5] The letter is addressed to the Shaykh of Qarrī, Muḥammad, in whose service Krump, as court physician, had recently experienced some misadventure; the northern governor was also at odds with his king.[6] When the royal caravan accompanied by the departing missionaries passed Qarrī, Krump scrupulously avoided entering Shaykh Muḥammad's capital, and the governor probably never saw the sultan's letter.

Copy of the letter of recommendation given to me and Father Antonio della Terza in Arabic by the king, which I have translated into German with my own hand.

From the great glory of the king of the Turks, the high king, the lord of countless generations, who at all times is busy in ordering the affairs of the world and of religion, with confirmation and strengthening of the many and important affairs of the Turks, may God the Almighty raise him over the whole world and increase his vassals and slaves, for he is worthy of it, possessing the highest wisdom and most subtle understanding, he whose name is renowned throughout the whole world, partly because of his keen justice, partly also because of his great mercy; he displays his deep and clever insights at all times, and courage both toward his vassals and toward foreign strangers, our mighty king, a son of the king, Bādī [the son of] King Unsa. May God increase the days of his life and renew his great felicity through the influence of the great and precious Qur'ān and the holy prophet Muḥammad. Amen.

The king greets you, O Shaykh Muḥammad (this is the viceroy who has under him the whole kingdom of Nubia and Qarrī and as far as the Red Sea; the other viceroys and governors are also called "shaykh"), and says to you: If *Mu`allim* Yūnus and *Mu`allim* Sulaymān, who wish to go to Egypt, come to you and show you this letter, order all your subjects, vassals and slaves that no one, whoever he may be, shall do them the least harm, offense or injustice. They shall let them pass wherever they will, freely and without hindrance, for *Mu`allim* Yūnus, who has been my physician, has done much good for me and my kingdom, and in his place he has left me *Mu`allim* Yūsuf (that was Father Pasquale). I further order you, O Shaykh, to provide everything necessary for them, their servants and camels throughout your realm. Do it for my sake, for they are worthy. If they wish to stay in your lands, as it may seem good to them, or to turn aside to the right hand or the left, you shall not in any way oppose them, but give them the greatest help in obtaining whatever they desire.

This is my mighty will and incontrovertible command, which should be sufficient so that they need no other writings of recommendation. Through your good offices and commands the king in Dongola will give to them everything that they need.

Farewell, and the blessings of our great prophet be upon you and all our kingdoms. Sinnār, 1 May 1702.

[1]Krump, *Palm-Baum*, pp. 354-356.

[2]Kapteijns and Spaulding, *Millennium*, Docs. 15, 26, 27, 28, 86.

[3]Krump, *Palm-Baum*, pp. 354-355.

[4]Ibid., p. 356. For the Franciscan missionaries, see G. Giamberardini, *I viaggiatori francescani attraverso la Nubia dal 1698 al 1710* (Cairo: 1963) and G.M. Montano, *L'Etiopia Francescana nei Documenti dei secoli XVII e XVIII* (Quaracchi: 1948). Records of their Jesuit companions and rivals may be found in C. Beccari, *Rerum Aethiopicarum Scriptores Occidentales Inediti a saeculo XVI ad XIX* (Rome: 1905-1917).

[5]Spaulding, *Heroic Age*, pp. 113-114.

[6]For his impending revolt against Bādī III, see O'Fahey and Spaulding, *Kingdoms*, pp. 74-77.

DOCUMENT 2

Document 2 is a confirming charter issued by Sultan Bādī IV during Rajab 1141 (31 January to 1 March 1729) to Faqīh Muḥammad walad al-Shaykh [Abū . . .] concerning the estate of al-Daqāqāt and to Faqīh Ḥammad concerning a purchased property. The text is based upon the photocopy published by Sadik Nur.[1] This is the earliest extant dated charter from Sinnār. One of its functions is to give royal sanction to the sale of land between private individuals, a precaution characteristic of the early days of private property in Sinnār.[2] Noteworthy is the presence at court of the young sultan's maternal uncle Ismā`īl, and the frequent use of singular personal names among the court officials of the witness roster.

باسمك يا كريم بسم الله الرحمن الرحيم الحمد لله الذى بلغ الرسول و نحن امنا بما يقول

الواثق بالله و الرسول
ابن السلطان نول
السلطان بادى ١١٢٧

حجة سلطانية و وثيقة ملوكية من حضرت من ايده الله بالنصر و التمكين / و الرفع و التحصين و جعله ظلا ظليلا ياوى اليه كل مسكين الذى هو فى الدنيا سعيد / و فى الاخرة ان شاء الله شهيد من انطوى باطنه على الصفا و ظاهره على الصدق و الوفا / الصادق فى قوله الامين فى فعله الذى اذا قال صدق و اذا تكلم بالحق نطق مولانا / السلطان بن السلطان السلطان بادى بن السلطان نول نصره الله الرحمن الرحيم /

بجاه القرءان العظيم و النبى الكريم ءامين ءامين يا رب العالمين الى كل من تقف عليه / هذه الوثيقة و الناظر لما فيها من الحقيقة من المقاديم و الشيوخ و الجراى الذى من / تحتهم فى حد ملكى خصوصا الشيخ بادى ولد سرير و الذى ياتى من بعده و بعد فان / السلطان المبرور المويد المنصور تمم ملكية دار الفقيه محمد ولد الشيخ (. . . .)[3]/ دار الدقاقات و جميع زراعتهم التى فى ملكهم و ايضا تمم ملكية الدار الذى اشتراها / الفقيه حمد من احمد ولد حمد المعلومة الحدود من جهة الصبح ولد حبيب و من جهة / الغرب الزين و من جهة السافل حامد و من جهة الصعيد حليو فصارت هذه الدار / ملك الفقيه حمد و ذريته و ذرية ذريته الى ان يرث الله الارض و من عليها و هو / خير الوارثين فهى جاه الله و رسوله سالمة مسلمة من جميع الشرور و السبل و المضار / لا احد يقربها و لا يدنيها الحذر ثم الحذر من الخلاف و المخالف لا يلوم الا نفسه

حضر ذلك و شهد به /
الشيخ يونس ولد الجندى محمد
و الشيخ ارداب
و الشيخ اسماعيل
و الشيخ دياب شيخ (قرى)
و الشيخ / شاطر شيخ اليس
و الشيخ بادى ولد هاكيت
و الشيخ عوض شيخ التاكة
و الشيخ محمد قيلى شيخ بيله
و الشيخ عثمان شيخ القريين
و الشيخ عبد الله شيخ السواكره
و خميس سلطان فور /
و الارباب ايدوا جد الملك
و الشيخ رجب مقدم الخيل
و الشيخ نايل مقدم العدة
و الشيخ / بادى شيخ البحر
و الشيخ محمود شيخ القواريه
و الشيخ شلنكى شيخ السجادة

و الملك محمد ملك برساج /
و القاضى عبد الحميد
و الخطيب عبد الحفيظ ولد نونو
و الارباب محمد بكومة
و الارباب دفع الله ولد / الشامى
و الفقيه عمار بن الفقيه ابو النقا
و الفقيه يعقوب حميرا

و مسطر الحروف محمد بن / عبد الغانى و كفا بالله شهيدا تحرير ذلك فى شهر رجب المبارك سنة ١١٤١

In Thy name, O Generous One. In the name of God, the Merciful, the Compassionate. Praise be to God, Who sent the messenger. We believe in what he says.

He who trusts in God and the messenger
The son of Sultan Nōl
Sultan Bādī 1137/1724-1725

A sultanic charter and royal document from the presence of him whom God has supported, aided, invested, elevated, strengthened, and made a protecting shelter with whom every subject may seek refuge. He is happy in this world and, if God wills, in the next will be a martyr. His interior is purity, his exterior truth and fidelity. Truthful in word and trustworthy in deed, when he speaks he speaks the truth, and when he speaks the truth he has ordained, our lord the sultan, the son of the sultan, Sultan Bādī, the son of Sultan Nōl. May God, the Merciful, the Compassionate, grant him victory through the influence of the sublime Qur'ān and the eminent prophet. Amen, amen, O Lord of the Universe.

To all who read this document from among the *muqaddams* and shaykhs and the *jarāī* who are under them throughout my kingdom, especially Shaykh Bādī walad Sarīr and whoever may come after him.

Thereafter: The pious, divinely assisted and victorious sultan has confirmed the ownership of the estate of Faqīh Muḥammad walad al-Shaykh [Abū ? . . .], the estate of al-Daqāqāt and all the cultivation that they [the beneficiaries] own. Furthermore, he has confirmed the ownership of the estate that Faqīh Ḥammad purchased from Aḥmad walad Ḥammad. The boundaries are known: on the eastern side, Walad Ḥabīb; on the western side, al-Zayn; on the northern side, Ḥāmid; on the southern side, Ḥilyū. The estate has become the property of Faqīh Ḥammad, his descendants, and his descendants' descendants, until God inherits the earth and those upon it, and He is the Best of Heirs. It is a grant for [the sake of] God and His messenger. It is completely free from all *shurūr*, *subul*, and *maḍārr*. Let no one draw near or approach it. Beware, then beware of disobedience, and let the disobedient blame none but himself.

There were present and witnessed to it:

Shaykh Yūnus, son of the *jundī* Muḥammad
Shaykh Irdāb
Shaykh Ismā`īl
Shaykh Diyāb, Shaykh of Qarrī
Shaykh Shāṭir, Shaykh of Alays
Shaykh Bādī walad Hākīt
Shaykh `Awaḍ, Shaykh of al-Tāka
Shaykh Muḥammad Qaylī, Shaykh of Bayla
Shaykh `Uthmān, Shaykh of al-Qarbīn
Shaykh `Abd Allāh, *shaykh al-sawākira*
Khamīs, Sultan of the Fūr
Arbāb Īdū, grandfather of the king

Shaykh Rajab, *muqaddam al-khayl*
Shaykh Nāyil, *muqaddam al-`udda*
Shaykh Bādī, Shaykh of al-Baḥr
Shaykh Maḥmūd, *shaykh al-quwwārīya*
Shaykh Shalnakī, *shaykh al-sajjāda*
Malik Maḥmūd, *malik bursāj*
the *qāḍī*, `Abd al-Ḥamīd
the *khaṭīb*, `Abd al-Ḥafīẓ walad Nūnū
Arbāb Muḥammad Bakōma
Arbāb Daf` Allāh walad al-Shāmī
Faqīh `Ammār b. al-Faqīh Abu'l-Naqā
Faqīh Ya`qūb Ḥamīran

The writer of the letters is Muḥammad b. `Abd al-Ghanī. With God, two witnesses suffice. That was written in the blessed month of Rajab in the year 1141.

[1]Sadik Nur, "Land Tenure during the Time of the Fung," *Kush* 4 (1956): Plate IV. See also Abū Salīm, *al-Fūnj wa'l-arḍ*, pp. 137-138.

[2]Spaulding, *Heroic Age*, pp. 157-158.

[3]Lacuna.

DOCUMENT 3

Document 3 is a confirming charter issued by Sultan Bādī IV to Faqīh Bishāra b. al-Faqīh `Alī b. Bursī in 1145/1732-1733. The text has been derived from a partial copy preserved in Aḥmad b. Ismā`īl al-Azharī's manuscript entitled *Khulāṣat al-iqtibās fī ittiṣāl nasabinā bi'l-Sayyid al-`Abbās.*[1] The author of this genealogical work wrote that he was copying the charter letter by letter from an original document in his possession at that time, but he did not claim to have reproduced the entire document; indeed, he specifically mentioned the existence of seals and introductory materials which were not copied. Comparison with other charters of the period tends to inspire confidence in the authenticity of the portion preserved.

هذا الجاه كتبته[2] للفقيه بشارة ابن على بن برسى بان لا يتعرض عليه / و اخوانه و اولاده و اصهاره و اهله و جميع من ينسب اليه او يلتجى به بان / لا يتعرض عليه احد من العمال الذين فى البلاد و انا[3] السلطان بادى ابن / السلطان نول تممت[4] ما فعله السلطان بادى ابن السلطان ارباط من تجويه الفقيه بشارة ابن الفقيه على ابن برسى هو و من معه جاها لله و للرسول / حرمه للدين و جاهه الذى فى يده من بعده لا يطلب عليه لا حسب و لا عادة / و لا عانة و لا قوار و لا جباية و لا علوق و لا متورت و لا شى قل او جل / من جميع مضار السلطنة لا فى الحضر و لا فى السفر ان شرقوا او غربوا /[5] فكل من تعرض له او دناه لا يلومن الا نفسه و الحذر الحذر من الخلاف و المخالف / لا يلومن الا نفسه انتهى

This is the grant which I have written[6] for Faqīh Bishāra b. al-Faqīh `Alī b. Bursī, so that no one shall trouble him, his brothers, his sons, his relatives by marriage, his family, and all who are his kinsmen or who attach themselves to him. Let none of the *`ummāl* who are in the land trouble him. I, Sultan Bādī b. al-Sultan Nōl, have confirmed what Sultan Bādī b. al-Sultan Irbāṭ[7] did in his grant for Faqīh Bishāra b. al-Faqīh `Alī b. Bursī, for him and whomever is with him. It is a grant for [the sake of] God and the messenger out of respect for religion, and his grant shall [also] be for him who comes after him. Let no one demand *ḥasab*, *`āda*, *`āna*, *quwwār*, *jabāya*, *`ulūq*, *matūra*, nor any of the *maḍārr* of the sultanate, great or small, whether [they are] settled or traveling, whether they are in the east or the west. Let anyone who troubles him or approaches him blame none but himself. Beware, then beware of disobedience, and let the disobedient blame none but himself.

[1]Sudan Archive, University of Durham, G//S 555(4), uncatalogued, from the papers of Douglas Newbold. The editors are grateful to Dr. R.S. O'Fahey for calling this work to their attention. For an earlier published version see Jay Spaulding, "A Charter of Sultan Bādī b. Nōl of Sinnār, 1145/1732-3," *Fontes Historiae Africanae Arabicae: Bulletin d'Information* 9-10 (1984-1985): 8-11. A second copy of the document may be found in National Records Office, Khartoum, Intelligence 5/1/3, "Nisba of Ahmed al-Azhari." An English translation of this work has been published by P.M. Holt as "The genealogy of a Sudanese holy family," *Bulletin of the School of Oriental and African Studies* 44 (1981): 262-272. The first source is to be preferred to the second; notably, it contains the verb bearing the act of confirmation for which purpose the charter was issued.

[2]Intelligence 5/1/3 reads كتبه .

[3]Intelligence 5/1/3 reads وا ن .

[4]Missing from Intelligence 5/1/3.

[5]Intelligence 5/1/3 reads ان اشرقوا او اغربوا ,

[6]Holt's reading ("Holy Family," p. 268) is "[The sultan] has written this."

[7]Bādī II b. Rubāṭ.

DOCUMENT 4

Document 4 is a charter containing a ruling of the *qāḍī* of Sinnār `Abd al-`Azīz, issued in Sha`bān 1145 (17 January to 14 February 1733). The text is based upon a copy prepared by El Fatih El Houssein El Hasan.[1] The ruling illustrates a common theme of the Heroic Age in Sinnār, the gradual extinction of the landholding rights of women under traditional terms of tenure in favor of aggrandizing middle-class landowners through purchase, with the support of the *qāḍī* and the *sharī`a*.[2] (The unusual dependence of this early eighteenth-century *qāḍī* upon the witness of royal courtiers has been noted.) Significantly, the defeated litigant identified herself in matrilineal terms as Kanīna the daughter of Ḥalītī the daughter of Rawḍa; her rejected claim, insofar as it may be reconstructed from the hostile court record, seems to have rested upon the expectation of inheritance from her maternal uncle. The victorious purchasers were members of the `Arakīyīn, a prominent family of *fuqarā'* with numerous landholdings along the middle course of the Blue Nile; the disputed estate has not been otherwise located. Noteworthy is the reference to the "estate of the king's son," one example of the cluster of demesne holdings established by each family of the territorial nobility around its capital, in this case the royal family, in the environs of Sinnār.

فهذا لنا فيه شهاده ان لا الاه الا الله و ان محمد رسول الله صلى الله عليه و سلم و فيه حجه شرعيه محرره مرضيه قاطعه مالكيه بالديار الفنجيه بمدينه سنار المحروسه المحميه اجلها الله تعالى لدا متوليها و الحاكم يومئذ بما فيها اقضى قضاه الاثام محرر القضايا و الاحكام ما من النقض العلاقه الخير من سارت بذكره الركبات و تعطرت بند حديثه الطيب ساير البلدات سببيه زمانه و سحبان وقته و اوانه الفايق على اقرانه خاب من

رام غايته و خسر من طلب نهايته الذى سيضع خطه و مهره الكويعين اعلاه لطف الله به و تولاه و زاد فى علاه مولاه الواثق بالملك العبدى القاضى المالكى الشريف عبد العزيز بن السيد محمد المهدى ادام الله ايامه الزاهره و اسعده فى الدنيا و الاخره امين و بعد فان كنينه بنت حليتى بنت روضه حضرت عند الحاكم الشرعى اعزه الله و حضروا اولاد الفقيه الامين و هم احمد و الفقيه حمد النيل و الفقيه ابو عاقله فلما حضروا جميعا اقرت كنينه بان خالها الفقيه حمد ولد خليل باع على الفقيه محمد الامين الدار المعروفه بحدبت روضينه بثمن مقداره و مبلغ وقيتين ذهب و مثقال و قبض الثمن جميعه فى حال صحه بدنه و سلامه عقله و خلوه من كل مانع شرعى فهذا ما اقرت به كنينه من البيع و الشرى و خلاص الثمن و قطعت نزاعها و دعواها و التزمت دعوى اختها مك البلوح و ضاعت حجتها و صارت الدار المذكوره بحدودها المعلومه فحدها من جهه الصبح الخور خور الفعج و من جهه السافل الطريق طريق الكبر و من جهه الغرب الكوع و من جهه الصعيد درب الحديبه و صارت هذه الديار ملكا و حوزا لاولاد الفقيه الامين بالشرى الصحيح الشرى المتقدم من ابيهم الفقيه محمد الامين فلا دعوى لكنينه و لا لاختها دعوى و لا طلب و لا فضه و لا ذهب و لا يمينا بالله اذا وجب خصوصا شيوخ دار ولد الملك و الحذر ثم الحذر من الخلاف و المخالف لكلامى لا يلومن الا نفسه

حضر ذلك و شهد به
الشيخ رحمه بن الشيخ يونس
و الجندى يونس
و الشيخ اسماعيل خال الملك
و الارباب ايدو جد الملك
و عبد الله بن الشيخ عجيب
و الشيخ محمد بن على
و الشيخ ابو شوه شيخ الحواكره
و الشيخ شاع الدين شيخ البحر
و الشيخ محمد مقدم السجاده
و الشيخ حمد شيخ القربين
و القاضى ابراهيم
و الارباب محمد ولد بكومه
و الفقيه عمار بن الفقيه ابو النقا
و احمد بن الفقيه باتكورا

و مسطرها فقير الله تعالى محمد بن عبد الغنى و كفى بالله شهيدا فى شعبان سنه
١١٤٥ من الهجره النبويه على صاحبها افضل الصلاة و السلام

A charter according to Islamic law, definitive and Mālikī, written and approved in the Funj territories, in the city of Sinnār, the divinely guarded and protected, may God Most High exalt her, in the presence of her warden, the governor at the present time of what is in her, the chief judge of crimes and writer of rulings and judgments not to be declared void, the best of those at whose mention knees bend, whose discourse of legal paragraphs emits perfume, the best among other nations of his day and age in his [interpretation of] causalities and applications, whose readings are superlative; whoever desires to match his standards will fail, and he who seeks to equal his record will lose. He will place both his signature and his seal upon [this document]. May God befriend and care for him, and may his Master increase his eminence, he who trusts in the King, His servant the Mālikī *qāḍī*, Sharīf `Abd al-`Azīz b. al-Sayyid Muḥammad al-Mahdī. May God prolong his radiant days and make him happy in this world and the hereafter. Amen.

Thereafter: Kanīna bint Ḥalītī bint Rawḍa appeared before the Islamic judge, may God strengthen him, and there appeared also the Awlād al-Faqīh al-Amīn, they being Aḥmad, Faqīh Ḥammad al-Nīl, and Faqīh Abū `Āqila. When they all were present Kanīna affirmed that her maternal uncle, Faqīh Ḥammad walad Khalīl, had sold to Faqīh Muḥammad al-Amīn the estate known as Ḥadabat Rōḍina for a price whose magnitude and amount was two *waqīya*s and a *mithqāl* of gold. He had taken the whole price in a state of good bodily health and sound mind, being free from all canonical impediments. It was this which Kanīna affirmed concerning the sale and purchase, and the payment of the price. Her challenge and her plea have been cut off. The plea of her sister, Makk al-Balūḥ, remained, but her document was lost. The boundaries of the said estate are known. Its boundary on the eastern side is the *khōr*, Khōr al-Fa`j; on the north the road, the road of al-Kubur; on the west al-Kū`a; on the south the road of al-Ḥudayba. The estate has become the property and possession of the Awlād al-Faqīh al-Amīn through a valid act of purchase previously effected by their father, Faqīh Muḥammad al-Amīn. Neither Kanīna nor her sister has a plea, nor a claim, neither to silver nor to gold, nor to an oath by God if it should be required by [anyone], especially the shaykhs of the estate of the king's son. Beware, then beware of disobedience, and let him who disobeys my word blame none but himself.

There were present and witnessed to it:
Shaykh Raḥma b. al-Shaykh Yūnus
the *jundī*, Yūnus
Shaykh Ismā`īl, maternal uncle of the king
Arbāb Īdū, grandfather of the king
`Abd Allāh b. al-Shaykh `Ajīb
Shaykh Muḥammad b. `Alī
Shaykh Abū Shōwa, *shaykh al-sawākira*[4]
Shaykh Shā` al-Dīn, Shaykh of al-Baḥr
Shaykh Muḥammad, *muqaddam al-sajjāda*
Shaykh Ḥammad, Shaykh of al-Qarbīn
the *qāḍī*, Ibrāhīm
Arbāb Muḥammad walad Bakōma
Faqīh `Ammār b. al-Faqīh Abu'l-Naqā
Aḥmad b. al-Faqīh Bātkūran

Its writer is the *faqīr* of God Most High, Muḥammad b. `Abd al-Ghanī. With God, two witnesses suffice. In Sha`bān of the year 1145 from the *hijra* of of the prophet, upon whose master the best of prayers and peace.

[1]El Fatih El Houssein El Hasan, "The Fung and Mehadyia At Abu Haraze Site," B.A. Honours Diss., Dept. of Archaeology, University of Khartoum, 1977-1978 (no pagination).

[2]Jay Spaulding, "The Misfortunes of Some--The Advantages of Others: Land-Sales by Women in Sinnār," in Margaret Jean Hay and Marcia Wright, eds., *African Women and the Law: Historical Perspectives* (Boston: 1982), pp. 3-18.

[3]Spaulding, *Heroic Age*, pp. 39-41.

[4]The copyist has read "*ḥawākira*."

DOCUMENT 5

Document 5 is a confirming charter issued by Sultan Bādī IV to Faqīh Muḥammad b. al-Faqīh Aḥmad b. al-Shaykh `Abd al-Raḥmān b. al-Shaykh `Abd al-Raḥīm "The Seller of Rain" in Sha`bān 1145 (17 January to 14 February 1733). The text is derived from a photocopy published by Sadik Nur.[1] Shaykh `Abd al-Raḥīm was a younger contemporary of Bādī II b. Rubāṭ; he was a disciple in Sufism to Shaykh Muḥammad b. Īsā "Suwwār al-Dhahab" in the Gezira, where his landholding was probably located.[2]

الحمد لله و الصلاة و السلام على نبيه

الواثق بالله و الرسول
ابن السلطان نول
السلطان بادى ١١٣٧

حجة سلطانية و وثيقة ملوكية من حضرت سلطان المسلمين و ناصر / شريعة سيد المرسلين و ناشر لواء العدل و الفضل على كافة العالمين حافظ البلاد / و ناصر العباد و قامع اهل الظلم و الفساد و رحمة الله سبحانه و تعالى للحاضر و الباد / مولانا السلطان بن السلطان الملك المظفر المعان السلطان بادى بن المرحوم / السلطان نول زيدت ايام عدله و جددت ليالى سعده بجاه محمد و ءاله ءامين / الى كل من تقف عليه هذه الوثيقة و الناظر لما فيها من الحقيقة و بعد فان السلطان المنصور المويد المبرور تمم للفقيه محمد بن الفقيه احمد / ابن الشيخ عبد الرحمن (...)[3] الشيخ عبد الرحيم بياع المطر دار جده الشيخ / عبد الرحيم المذكور التى فى يدهم من جدهم للوقت و هى الدار معلومة الحدود حدها / من جهة السافل بلاد عثمان بن دل و تطلع الى ام عشيره و العزازه النازلين فيها / العتاقه دارهم القديمه و حفير كرى و من جهة الصبح حفير ولد المرقوب و من جهة / الغرب (...)[3] حصحوص و من جهة الصعيد (...)[3]

حدود الدار المذكورة دار الشيخ عبد الرحيم بياع المطر من الجهات الاربعة تممها لهم ابتغاء / لوجه الله تعالى و طلبا للثواب فى يوم الماب لا ينازعه فيها منازع و لا يتعرض له فيها معارض / سالمة مسلمة من جميع الشرور و المضار و السبل لا احد يتعرض ذرية الشيخ عبد الرحيم / بياع المطر فيها لهم و لذريتهم و ذرية ذريتهم الى ان يرث الله الارض و من عليها و هو خير / الوارثين فمن تعرض لهم فيها فقد تعرض للهلاك خصوصا شيوخ دار ولد الملك / و الحذر ثم الحذر من المخالفه و المخالف لكلامى لا يلومن الا نفسه

حضر ذلك و شهد به

الشيخ رحمه / بن الشيخ يونس
و الجندى يونس
و الشبخ اسماعيل خال الملك
و الارباب ايدوا جد الملك /
و الشيخ عبد الله بن الشيخ عجيب
و الشيخ محمد بن على
و الشيخ ابو شوه شيخ السواكره
و الشيخ شاع الدين شيخ البحر
و الشيخ محمد مقدم السجاده
و الشيخ حمد شيخ القربين
و القاضى ابراهيم /
و الارباب محمد ولد بكومه
و الفقيه عمار بن الفقيه ابو النقا
و احمد بن الفقيه باتكورا

و مسطرها / فقير الله تعالى محمد بن عبد الغنى و كفا بالله شهيدا فى شعبان سنة ١١٤٥ من الهجرة / النبوية على صاحبها افضل الصلاة و السلام

Praise be to God, and prayers and peace upon His messenger.

He who trusts in God and the messenger
The son of Sultan Nōl
Sultan Bādī 1137/1724-1725

A sultanic charter and royal document from the presence of the sultan of the Muslims, upholder of the law of the lord of the messengers, who spreads the banner of justice and excellence throughout the universe, the guardian of the lands and helper to the worshipers, who removes the people of tyranny and corruption, the mercy of God (praise be to God Most High) upon the quick and the dead, our lord the sultan, the son of the sultan, Sultan Bādī, son of the late Sultan Nōl. May the days of his justice be increased and the nights of his good fortune be renewed, through the influence of Muḥammad and his family. Amen.

To all who read this document and see the truth therein.

Thereafter: The pious, divinely assisted and victorious sultan has confirmed to Faqīh Muḥammad b. al-Faqīh Aḥmad b. al-Shaykh `Abd al-Raḥmān [b.] al-Shaykh `Abd al-Raḥīm "The Seller of Rain" the estate of his forefather the said `Abd al-Raḥīm, which has been in their possession from [the days of] their forefather to the present. The boundaries of the estate are known. Its northern boundary is the land of `Uthmān b. Dalla, and it runs up to Umm `Ushayra and al-`Azāza, where it adjoins their old estate held previously and the reservoir of Kurrī. On the eastern side [its boundary is] the reservoir of Walad al-Marqūb; on the western side [. . .] Ḥaṣḥūṣ; on the southern side [. . .]. He has confirmed for them the boundaries on the four sides of the said estate, the estate of Shaykh `Abd al-Raḥīm "The Seller of Rain," for the sake of God Most High, asking for reward in the life to come. Let no challenger challenge him concerning it. Let no troublemaker trouble him in it. It is completely free from all *shurūr*, *maḍārr*, and *subul*. Let no one trouble the descendants of Shaykh `Abd al-Raḥīm "The Seller of Rain" concerning it. It is for them, their descendants, and their descendants' descendants until God inherits the earth and those upon it, and He is the Best of Heirs. He who troubles them concerning it has exposed himself to destruction, especially the shaykhs of the estate of the son of the king. Beware, then beware of disobedience, and let him who disobeys my words blame none but himself.

There were present and witnessed to it:

Shaykh Raḥma b. al-Shaykh Yūnus
the *jundī*, Yūnus
Shaykh Ismā`īl, maternal uncle of the king
Arbāb Īdū, grandfather of the king
Shaykh `Abd Allāh b. al-Shaykh `Ajīb
Shaykh Muḥammad b. `Alī
Shaykh Abū Shōwa, *shaykh al-sawākira*
Shaykh Shā` al-Dīn, Shaykh of al-Baḥr
Shaykh Muḥammad, *muqaddam al-sajjāda*
Shaykh Ḥammad, Shaykh of al-Qarbīn
the *qāḍī*, Ibrāhīm
Arbāb Muḥammad walad Bakōma
Faqīh `Ammār b. al-Faqīh Abu'l-Naqā
Aḥmad b. al-Faqīh Bātkūran

Its writer is the *faqīr* of God Most High, Muḥammad b. `Abd al-Ghanī. With God, two witnesses suffice. In Sha`bān of the year 1145 from the *hijra* of the prophet, upon whose master the best of prayers and peace.

[1]Sadik Nur, "Land Tenure," Plate V.

[2]*Ṭabaqāt*, p. 347

[3]Lacuna.

DOCUMENT 6

Document 6 is an originating charter issued by the *amīn al-sulṭān* Raḥma b. Yūnus for Shaykh Ya`qūb b. al-Shaykh Muḥammad Zayn on 23 Dhu'l-Ḥijja 1146/27 May 1734; Sultan Bādī IV subsequently confirmed this grant (Doc. 7). The text is based upon a copy preserved in the papers of A.J. Arkell.[1] The beneficiary was a member of the community of *fuqarā'* of the Ya`qūbāb living near "Huggag" (al-Ḥujjāj), about five miles west of the Blue Nile near Wad el Haddad Station.[2] This document gives a glimpse of the procedure through which a grant was implemented; an emissary of the donor demarcated the boundaries in the presence of the steward of the land. The witnesses are not titled courtiers but the personal entourage of the *amīn*, consisting largely of his kinsmen and slave soldiers.

فهذه حجة / و وثيقة ملوكيه بسنار المحروسة المحميه اجلها الله تعالى لدا متوليها و الحاكم / يوميذ بما فيها ريس الفرسان و اشجع الشجعان صندوق الامان المعروف بالخير / و الاحسان الواثق بالملك المنان الشيخ رحمه ابن المرحوم الشيخ يونس امين / السلطان كان الله حيث كان و حرسه بالسور و ايات القران امين اما / بعد فالشيخ رحمه ابن المرحوم الشيخ يونس تصدق على الشيخ يعقوب بدار فى ارض ام / مراحيك صدقه لابتغاء وجه الله تعالى و طلبا لثواب الدار الاخرة ليوم لا ينفع / فيه مال و لا بنون الا من اتا الله بقلب سليم و معلومة الحدود من الجهات / الاربعة من جهه الصبح الطنضبه و نقر هنتوله و من جهة الصعيد عزاز جرووره / و حفير ولد بلال و من جهة الغرب ام مراحيك يمشى الحد مسفل بنظرة مسفل / الى عن درب امطلحه يمشى مصبح بناظر الطنضبه و يركز فوق طين الشيخ / يعقوب المشترى و مرسال الشيخ رحمه ابن الشيخ يونس (قال)[3] لا احد يقربه و لا يدنيه / و لا يقف على بابه و حمد ولد خيار راعى الدار حضر على قطع الدار

حضر و شهد بذلك

الشيخ بشر اخيه
و كتفا اخيه
و وارت اخيه
و هارون اخيه
و نصر اخيه
(و منصور)[4] /
و الارباب مسعود
و على ولد نوير
و الارباب محمد ولد ولد ضويو
و على ولده /
و مضوى مقدم القواويد
و الطاهر الغدوى
و عمر الغدوى
و حسن قواد الشيخ
و زايد / الحراس
و مصطفى السودان
و سعيد المراجنة
و اسماعيل اخو الشيخ رحمه
و انقله / اخيه
و شوال اخيه
و رمضان
و على ولده
و صابون
و كوراب
و عبد العاطى /
و الارباب ابراهيم ولد بدوى

و مصطر الاحرف محمد ابن الفقيه احمد / كاتب و شاهد ضحا الخميس ثلاثه و عشرين في ذى الحجة / سنة ماية و سته و اربعين من بعد الالف من الهجرة النبويه / على ساكنها افضل الصلاة و ازكى التسليم

This is a charter and royal document [issued] in Sinnār, the divinely guarded and protected, may God Most High exalt her, in the presence of her warden, the governor at the present time of what is in her, the chief of knights, bravest of the brave, the repository of trust, known for kindness and good deeds, he who trusts in the King, the Benefactor, Shaykh Raḥma, son of the late Shaykh Yūnus, *amīn al-sulṭān*. May God be with him wherever he is, and protect him with chapters and verses of the Qur'ān. Amen.

Thereafter: Shaykh Raḥma, son of the late Shaykh Yūnus, has bestowed as alms upon Shaykh Ya`qūb an estate in the land of Umm Marāḥīk, alms for the sake of God Most High, asking for reward in the life to come, for a day in which neither wealth nor sons suffice, unless one comes to God with a secure heart. The boundaries are known on the four sides: on the eastern side al-Ṭunḍaba and Naqr Hantūla; on the southern side `Azzāz Jarūra and the reservoir of Walad Bilāl; on the western side Umm Marāḥīk; the boundary runs in a northward direction as far as the path of Umm Ṭalḥa, and runs eastward in the direction of al-Ṭunḍaba above the cultivable land Shaykh Ya`qūb purchased. The messenger of Shaykh Raḥma b. al-Shaykh Yūnus [said], "Let no one draw near to him or approach him, or stop at his gate." Ḥammad walad Khayyār, guardian of the estate, was present for the delimitation of the estate.

There were present and witnessed to that:

Shaykh Bashar, his [Raḥma's] brother
Kitfā, his brother
Wārit, his brother
Hārūn, his brother
Naṣr, his brother
(Manṣūr)[4]
Arbāb Mas`ūd
`Alī walad Nuwayyir
Arbāb Muḥammad walad Walad Ḍūyū

`Alī, his son

Maḍuwī, *muqaddam al-qawāwīd*

al-Ṭāhir al-Ghadawī

`Umar al-Ghadawī

Ḥasan, *qawwād al-shaykh*

Zāyid al-Ḥurrās

Muṣṭafā al-Sūdān

Sa`īd al-Murājina

Ismā`īl, brother of Shaykh Raḥma

Anqala, his brother

Shawwāl, his brother

Ramaḍān

`Alī, his son

Ṣābūn

Kōrāb

`Abd al-`Aṭā

Arbāb Ibrāhīm walad Baduwī

The writer of the letters is Muḥammad b. al-Faqīh Aḥmad, scribe and witness, on the morning of Tuesday, 23 Dhu'l-Ḥijja in the year 1146 from the *hijra* of the prophet, upon whom the best of prayers and purest peace.

[1]School of Oriental and African Studies, University of London, Arkell Papers, Box 1, File 5, Piece 82. A photocopy and translation have been published in Holt, "Land-Charters," Plate I and p. 105.

[2]Holt, "Land-Charters," p. 104. For an introduction to the Ya`qūbāb see H.C. Jackson, *Notes on the Yacubabi Tribes of Sennar* (Khartoum: 1912), and McHugh, "Holymen."

[3]Inserted by the editors.

[4]Crossed out by the copyist.

DOCUMENT 7

Document 7 is a confirming charter issued by Sultan Bādī IV to Shaykh Ya`qūb b. Muḥammad Zayn on 1 Muḥarram 1147/3 June 1734; it confirms the grant of the *amīn* Raḥma (Doc. 6). The text is based upon a copy preserved in the papers of A.J. Arkell.[1] The appearance of the *khaṭīb* `Abd al-Laṭīf among the courtiers of this early roster tends to identify him with the party of the young king's maternal uncle. After Bādī assumed personal power, he killed `Abd al-Laṭīf in 1170/1756-1757, and to Bādī's opponents, this execution provided a degree of justification for his ensuing overthrow.[2]

حجة سلطانية و وثيقة ملوكية من حضرت سلطان الاسلام و جامع كلمة / الايمان و مدمر
اهل البغا و الطغيان[3] مالك ملوك البر و اليم ناظر مصالح جماهير الامم ماسس /
بقاع الكرم و الالطاف هادم اساس (دور)[3] الاعتاف الذي اذا توجه استقبله / الفتح
و الظفر من ادرع المسلمين سحايب فضله الذى اختاره الله على العباد امينا و كان /
الله حافظا و امينا مولانى السلطان ابن السلطان الملك المظفر المعان السلطان / بادى ابن
المرحوم السلطان نول زيدت ايام عدله و جددت ليالى سعده بجاه محمد و اله / امين
الى كل من تقف عليه هذه الوثيقة و الناظر لما فيها من الحقيقة و بعد / فان السلطان
المبرور المويد المنصور تمم و امضا ما فعله الشيخ رحمة ابن الشيخ يونس / من الصدقة
على الشيخ يعقوب ابن الشيخ محمد زين بدار فى ارض ام مراحيك صدقة ابتغاء لوجه
تعالى و طلبا للثواب فى يوم المناب و هى معلومة الحدود فى وثيقة / الشيخ رحمة
المذكور من الجهات الاربعة من الصبح الطنضبة و نقر هنتوله و من الصعيد / عزاز
جروره و حفير ولد بلال و من القرب ام مراحيك يمشى الحد بنظره مسفل / الى عند
درب ام طلحة يمشى مصبح يناظر الطنضبة و يركز فوق طين الشيخ يعقوب / المشترى
لا حد يقربه و لا يدنيه و لا يقف له على طريق و حبله المرمى لا يشيله زول / و ماءه
الازرق لا يشربه فى ذالك سالمة من جميع الشرور و المضار و الحذر ثم الحذر من
المخالفة و المخالف لا يلوم الا نفسه

حضر ذالك و شهد به

الشيخ رحمة ابن / الشيخ يونس
و الجندى يونس
و الشيخ اسماعيل خال الملك
و الارباب ايدوا جد الملك /
و الشيخ شاع الدين درويش شيخ البحر
و الشيخ حمد شيخ القربين
و الشيخ محمد / مقدم السجادة
و القاضى ابراهيم
و الخطيب عبد اللطيف
و عمار ابو النقا

و مسطر / الوثيقه محمد عبد الغنى و كفا بالله شهيدا اول يوم من محرم لسبعة / و اربعين وماية بعد الالف من الهجرة النبوية على صاحبها افضل الصلاة / و السلام

A sultanic charter and royal document from the presence of the sultan of Islam, who consolidates the authority of the faith and destroys the people of wrongdoing and oppression, ruler of the kings of land and sea, who orders the affairs of the peoples of the nations, the founder of places of kindness and benevolence, who demolishes the foundations of loathsome practices, who encounters conquest and victory whenever he sets forth, who shelters the Muslims with the clouds of his excellence, he whom God has chosen as guardian over the worshipers (may God be his Protector and Guardian), our lord the sultan, the son of the sultan, the victorious and divinely aided king, Sultan Bādī, son of the late Sultan Nōl. May the days of his justice be increased and the nights of his good fortune renewed, through the influence of Muḥammad and his family. Amen.

To all who read this document and see the truth therein.

Thereafter: The pious, divinely assisted and victorious sultan has confirmed and ratified what Shaykh Raḥma b. al-Shaykh Yūnus did in regard to the gift of alms to Shaykh Ya`qūb b. al-Shaykh Muḥammad Zayn of an estate in the land of Umm Marāḥīk. [It is] a gift of alms for the sake of God Most High, asking for reward in the life to come. Its boundaries on the four sides are known from the document of the said Shaykh Raḥma: on the east al-Ṭunḍaba and Naqr Hantūla; on the south `Azzāz Jarūra and the reservoir of Walad Bilāl; on the west Umm Marāḥīk. The boundary runs northward to the Umm Ṭalḥa road, then eastward toward al-Ṭunḍaba, terminating beyond the land Shaykh Ya`qūb purchased. Let no one draw near or approach him, nor pause near him along the way. Let no one carry off [even] the rope he has thrown away, nor drink of his blue water.[4] It is free from all *shurūr* and *maḍārr*. Beware, then beware of disobedience, and let the disobedient blame none but himself.

There were present and witnessed to it:

Shaykh Raḥma b. al-Shaykh Yūnus
the *jundī*, Yūnus
Shaykh Ismā`īl, maternal uncle of the king
Arbāb Īdū, grandfather of the king
Shaykh Shā` al-Dīn Darwīsh, Shaykh of al-Baḥr
Shaykh Ḥammad, Shaykh of al-Qarbīn
Shaykh Muḥammad, *muqaddam al-sajjāda*
the *qāḍī*, Ibrāhīm
the *khaṭīb*, `Abd al-Laṭīf
`Ammār Abu'l-Naqā

The writer of the document is Muḥammad ʿAbd al-Ghanī. With God, two witnesses suffice. The first day of Muḥarram in [the year] one thousand one hundred forty-seven from the *hijra* of the prophet, upon whose master the best of prayers and peace.

[1]School of Oriental and African Studies, University of London, Arkell Papers, Box 1, File 5, Piece 81. A photocopy and translation have been published in Holt, "Land-Charters," Plate II and pp. 105-106.

[2]*Makhṭūṭa*, p. 23.

[3]Inserted by the editors.

[4]This expression implies that the beneficiary is not to be disturbed in any way, even the smallest.

DOCUMENT 8

Document 8 is an originating charter issued by Sultan Bādī IV to Faqīh al-Sayyid [b.] `Abd al-Hādī b. al-Shaykh Muḥammad walad Dōlīb. The text was taken from the original by the editors.[1] The top of the document, probably bearing the *invocatio*, is truncated; so is the bottom line or lines containing the name of the scribe and the date. A fragment of the lower right-hand corner is also missing. The beneficiary was a member of the prominent *fuqarā'* family, the Awlād Dōlīb.[2] The grant included the bestowal of a *sāqīya* landholding, probably in or near the village of al-Kadarō, on the east bank of the Nile north of al-Ḥalfāya. A probable relative chronology may be established on the basis of the witness roster. It is likely that the document was issued after the fall of the king's maternal uncle Ismā`īl, which took place during 1156/1743-1744.[3] Since in Doc. 8 `Abd al-Laṭīf had not yet been replaced as *khaṭīb* through the restoration of the older holder of that office `Abd al-Ḥafīẓ walad Nūnū, it is possible that Doc. 8 would have been issued in 1156/1743-1744, after the fall of Ismā`īl but before the issue of Doc. 9 later that year. It is reasonably certain that Doc. 8 preceded the issue of Doc. 12 in Rajab 1166/May 1753, by which time several major officeholders had been replaced.

الواثق بالله و الرسول

ابن السلطان نول

السلطان بادى ١١٢٧

حجة سلطانية و وثيقة ملوكية بمدينة سنار المحروسة المحمية اجلها الله تعالى / لدا متوليها الذي ايده الله بالنصر و التمكين و الرفعة و التحصين و جعله ظلا ظليلا ياوي / اليه كل مسكين الذي هو في الدنيا سعيد و في الاخرة ان شا الله شهيد من انطوي باطنه / علي الصفا و ظاهره علي الصدق و الوفا الصادق في قوله الامين في فعله الذي اذا قال صدق / و اذا تكلم بالحق نطق مولانا السلطان بن السلطان السلطان بادي بن السلطان / نول نصره الله الرحمن الرحيم بجاه القرءان العظيم و النبي الكريم امين امين يا رب العالمين / الي حضرت كل من تقف عليه هذه الوثيقة و الناظر لما فيها من الحقيقة و بعد فان السلطان / المبرور الموبد المنصور تصدق علي الفقيه السيد عبد الهادى بن الشيخ محمد ولد دوليب بساقية / الشقايق المعلومة الحدود و المكان فحدها من جهة السافل حسن ولد عرفات / و من جهة الصعيد عجيب ولد كريو الي عند خور المنقلبه و من عند الخور حديدها / من جهة الصعيد علي ولد الحاج و من جهة السافل الكشوناب و من جهة الصباح (...)[4] / دار ولدعجيب و من جهة الغرب اصل البحر المعلوم الله الله لا احدا يتعرض لهذه الصدقة / و صار الدار المذكورة بحدودها المعلومة ملكا للفقيه السيد و ذريته لاتباع و لا / و لا[5] فيها منازع صدقة خالصة لوجه الله و طلبا للثواب فى دار الماب و ليوم لا ينفع / فيه مال و لا بنون الا من اتي الله بقلب سليم سالمة مسلمة من جميع الشرور و السبل / و المضار لا عليها دم و لا حسب و لا علوق و لا نزول و لا كليقة و لا سنسنه و لا مخلا / و لا سبلة من السبل و حكم داره في يده من جهة الحربة و الحجر و نوكد عليكم يا جميع الشيوخ و المقاديم و الجراي الذين من تحتهم الى حد ملكي كله خصوصا / اونسه ولد سرير و من بعده الي قيام الساعة لا احدا يتعرض لهذه الصدقة / و من تعرض لها فقد عرض نفسه للهلاك و الحذر ثم الحذر من المخالفة و المخالف / لا يلوم الا نفسه

حضر ذلك و شهد به

الشيخ بشر
و الجندي محمد
و الشيخ عزوزه وكيل / حوش ناصر خال الملك
و الشيخ عبد الله شيخ قري
و الشيخ سليمان شيخ اليس
و الشيخ على / ولد شاور شيخ التاكة
و الشيخ على ولد حسن شيخ اتبره

و الشيخ محمد قيلي شيخ بيله /
و الشيخ قاسم شيخ القربين
و الشيخ فاطر شيخ البحر
و الشيخ محمود مقدم القوارية /
و الشيخ ادريس مقدم السواكره
و السلطان خميس سلطان فور المسبعات
و الشيخ / (على ولد تومه مقدم)[6] الخيل
و الشيخ نايل مقدم العدة
و الشيخ جابر مقدم / (القواويد)[6]
(و الشيخ)[4] اونسه ولد جمعه
و الشيخ ادم ولد كورى
و الملك نوار ملك برساج /
(و الشيخ محمد مقدم)[7] السجاده
و القاضى عبد الحميد
و الخطيب عبد اللطيف
و الارباب دفع الله /
(... ولد اونسه)[8]
(و الفقيه مونه)[8]
و الفقيه عثمان
و تكل الله (....)[4]

He who trusts in God and the messenger
The son of Sultan Nōl
Sultan Bādī 1137/1724-1725

A sultanic charter and royal document [issued] in the divinely guarded and protected city of Sinnār, may God Most High exalt her, in the presence of her warden, whom God has supported, aided, invested, elevated, and strengthened, and made a protecting shelter with whom every subject may seek refuge. He is happy in this world and, if God wills, in the next will be a martyr. His interior is purity, his exterior truth and fidelity. Truthful in word and trustworthy in deed, when he speaks he speaks the truth, and when he speaks the truth he has ordained, our lord the sultan, the son of the sultan, Sultan Bādī, the son of Sultan Nōl. May God, the Merciful, the Compassionate, grant him victory through the influence of the sublime Qur'ān and the eminent prophet. Amen, amen, O Lord of the Universe.

To the presence of all who read this document and see the truth therein.

Thereafter: The pious, divinely assisted and victorious sultan has bestowed as alms upon Faqīh al-Sayyid [b.] `Abd al-Hādī b. al-Shaykh Muḥammad walad Dōlīb the *sāqīya* [called] "al-Shaqāyiq." The boundaries and location are known. Its boundary on the northern side is Ḥasan walad `Arafāt; on the southern side `Ajīb walad Kiryū as far as Khōr al-Munqalba. From the *khōr*, its boundary on the southern side is `Alī walad al-Ḥājj, and on the northern side al-Kashūnāb. On the eastern side [it is] the land of Walad 'Ajīb; on the western side the known riverbed. God, God, let no one trouble this gift of alms. The said estate, its boundaries known, has become the property of Faqīh al-Sayyid and his descendants to follow. There is no challenger concerning it. It is a gift of alms purely for the sake of God, asking for reward in the life to come, for a day in which neither wealth nor sons suffice, unless one comes to God with a secure heart. It is completely free from all *shurūr*, *subul* and *maḍārr*. It is not subject to *damm*, *ḥasab*, *`ulūq*, *nuzūl*, *kalīqa*, *sinsina*, *mukhlā*, nor any *subul*. The government of his estate, in regard to troops and rocks,[9] is in his possession. We command you peremptorily, all you shaykhs and *muqaddams*, and the *jarāī* who are under them throughout my kingdom, all, especially Ūnsa walad Sarīr and whoever may [come] after him until the hour of resurrection, let no one trouble this gift of alms. He who troubles it has exposed himself to destruction. Beware, then beware of disobedience, and let the disobedient blame none but himself.

There were present and witnessed to it:

Shaykh Bashar
the *jundī*, Muḥammad
Shaykh `Azūza, agent of the compound of Nāṣir, maternal uncle of the king
Shaykh `Abd Allāh, Shaykh of Qarrī
Shaykh Sulaymān, Shaykh of Alays
Shaykh `Alī walad Shāwir, Shaykh of al-Tāka
Shaykh `Alī walad Ḥasan, Shaykh of Atbara
Shaykh Muḥammad Qaylī, Shaykh of Bayla
Shaykh Qāsim, Shaykh of al-Qarbīn
Shaykh Fāṭir, Shaykh of al-Baḥr
Shaykh Maḥmūd, *muqaddam al-quwwārīya*
Shaykh Idrīs, *muqaddam al-sawākira*
Sultan Khamīs, Sultan Fūr al-Musabba`āt
Shaykh [`Alī walad Tūma, *muqaddam*] *al-khayl*
Shaykh Nāyil, *muqaddam al-`udda*
Shaykh Jābir, *muqaddam* [*al-qawāwīd*]
[Shaykh Ūnsa] walad Jum`a
Shaykh Ādam walad Kūrī
Malik Nuwwār, *malik bursāj*
[Shaykh Muḥammad, *muqaddam*] *al-sajjāda*
the *qāḍī*, `Abd al-Ḥamīd
the *khaṭīb*, `Abd al-Laṭīf
Arbāb Daf` Allāh
[. . .] walad Ūnsa
Faqīh Mūna
Faqīh `Uthmān
Takalla Allāh, [Sultan of Borqu][10]
[. . .]

[1]For a published version see Abū Salīm, *al-Fūnj wa'l-arḍ*, pp. 65-66.

[2]*Ṭabaqāt*, pp. 348-349 (Muḥammad walad Dōlīb) and pp. 373-374 (ʿAbd al-Hādī b. Muḥammad walad Dōlīb).

[3]Spaulding, "Nubian Kingship," p. 18.

[4]Lacuna.

[5]Dittography in original.

[6]Lacuna. A conjectural reading of the missing text has been restored on the basis of Doc. 9.

[7]Lacuna. A conjectural reading of the missing text has been restored on the basis of Doc. 7.

[8]Conjectural reading; see Abū Salīm, *al-Fūnj wa'l-arḍ*, p. 66.

[9]This expression implies that the beneficiary is to enjoy full control over the property granted.

[10]Lacuna. For the title of Takalla Allāh, see Doc. 14.

DOCUMENT 9

Document 9 is an originating charter issued by Sultan Bādī IV to Faqīh Muḥammad al-Sayyid b. al-Shaykh `Abd al-Hādī b. Muḥammad Dōlīb and to Faqīh Dōlīb b. Muḥammad in 1156/1743-1744. The text was taken by the editors from the original.[1] The top of the document, bearing part of the *invocatio*, is damaged, and a fragment at the lower right-hand corner is missing. The grant includes the village of the Awlād Dōlīb at al-Kadarō.

(باسمك يا كريم)[2] بسم الله (الرحمن الرحيم)[2] الحمد لله الذى بلغ الرسول و نحن (امنا بما يقول)[2]

الواثق بالله و الرسول
ابن السلطان نول
السلطان بادى ١١٢٧

حجة سلطانية و وثيقة ملوكية بمدينة سنار المحروسة المحمية اجلها الله تعالى / لدا متوليها الذى ايده الله بالنصر و التمكين و الرفعة و التحصين و جعله ظلا (ظليلا)[2] / ياوى اليه كل مسكين الذى هو فى الدنيا سعيد و في الاخرة ان شاء الله شهيد من انطوى / باطنه على الصفا و ظاهره على الصدق و الوفا الصادق فى قوله الامين فى فعله / الذى اذا قال صدق و اذا تكلم بالحق نطق مولانا السلطان بن السلطان السلطان بادى بن السلطان نول نصره الله الرحمن الرحيم بجاه القرءان العظيم و النبى الكريم / امين امين يا رب العالمين الى كل من تقف عليه هذه (الوثيقة)[2] و الناظر لما فيها من الحقيقة و بعد فان السلطان المبرور المويد المنصور تصدق / على الفقيه محمد السيد بن الشيخ عبد الهادى بن الشيخ محمد ولد دوليب و الفقيه / دوليب بن الفقيه محمد بدار الكدرو المعلومة الحدود و البقعه فحدها / من جهة الصعيد المشايخة و من جهة السافل الجعليين و من جهة الغرب / مرن الجعليين المعلوم و من جهة الصبح درب الجمل

المعلوم صدقة / لوجه الله تعالى و طلبا للثواب فى دار الماب و ليوم لا ينفع فيه مال و لا بنون / الا من اتى الله بقلب سليم و صارت الدار المذكورة بحدودها المعلومة ملكا / لهؤلاء المذكورون و لذريتهم و ذرية ذريتهم الى ان يرث الله الارض و من عليها / و هو خير الوارثين سالمة مسلمة من جميع الشرور و السبل و المضار لا عليها دم و / و[3] لا حسب و لا علوق و لا نزول و لا تورات و لا كليقة و لا مخلا و لا سنسنة و لا عاده و لا عانه و لا سبلة حجر دارهم عندهم فى ايدهم و حكم دارهم / فى ايدهم و حربتها فى ايدهم الله الله لا احدا يقربها و لا يدنيها و لا يقف / عليهم و نوكد عليكم يا جميع الشيوخ و المقاديم و الجراى الذين من تحتهم / الى حد ملكى كله خصوصا الشيخ اونسه ولد سرير و من بعده الى قيام الساعة / لا احدا منكم يتعرض لهذه الصدقه و من تعرض لها بعد كلامى هذا فقد عرض نفسه / للهلاك و الحذر ثم الحذر من المخالفة و المخالف لا يلوم الا نفسه

حضر ذلك و شهد / (به)

(الشيخ)[4] بشر
و الجندى محمد
و الشيخ عزوزه وكيل حوش ناصر خال الملك
و الشيخ عبد الله / (شيخ)[4] قرى
و الشيخ سليمان شيخ اليس
و الشيخ على ولد شاور شيخ التاكة /
(و الشيخ على)[4] ولد حسن شيخ اتبره
و الشيخ محمد قيلى شيخ بيله
و الشيخ قاسم شيخ القربين
(و الشيخ فاطر شيخ)[4] البحر
و الشيخ محمود شيخ القوارية
و الشيخ ادريس مقدم السواكره /
(و السلطان)[4] خميس سلطان فور المسبعات
و الشيخ على ولد تومه مقدم الخيل
(...) / (...)
شيخ جابر مقدم القواويد

و الشيخ ادم ولد (كورى)[4] // (...)
(و الخطيب)[2] عبد الحفيظ (ولد نونو)[2] /
و الفقيه عثمان / (...)
السلطان البرقاوى
و الفقيه / محمد بن عبد الغنى

و كاتب الوثيقه / يعقوب حميرا و كفا بالله شهيدا / سنة ١١٥٦ من الهجرة / النبوية
على صاحبها افضل الصلاة و ازكى السلام

[In Thy name, O Generous One.] In the name of God, [the Merciful, the Compassionate]. Praise be to God, Who sent the messenger. We [believe in what he says].

He who trusts in God and the messenger
The son of Sultan Nōl
Sultan Bādī 1137/1724-1725

A sultanic charter and royal document [issued] in the divinely guarded and protected city of Sinnār, may God Most High exalt her, in the presence of her warden, whom God has supported, aided, invested, elevated, and strengthened, and made a protecting shelter with whom every subject may seek refuge. He is happy in this world and, if God wills, in the next will be a martyr. His interior is purity, his exterior truth and fidelity. Truthful in word and trustworthy in deed, when he speaks he speaks the truth, and when he speaks the truth he has ordained, our lord the sultan, the son of the sultan, Sultan Bādī, the son of Sultan Nōl. May God, the Merciful, the Compassionate, grant him victory through the influence of the sublime Qur'ān and the eminent prophet. Amen, amen, O Lord of the Universe.

To all who read this [document] and see the truth therein.

Thereafter: The pious, divinely assisted and victorious sultan has bestowed as alms upon Faqīh Muḥammad al-Sayyid b. al-Shaykh ʿAbd al-Hādī b. al-Shaykh Muḥammad walad Dōlīb and Faqīh Dōlīb b. al-Faqīh Muḥammad the estate of al-Kadarō. The boundaries and the location are known. Its boundary on the southern side is al-Mashāyikha, on the northern side the Jaʿaliyīn, on the western side the known *mirin* of the Jaʿaliyīn, and on the eastern side the known camel path. [It is] a gift of alms for the sake of God Most High, asking for reward in the life to come, for a day in which neither wealth nor sons suffice, unless one comes to God with a secure heart. The said estate, its boundaries known, has become the property of these the aforementioned, their descendants, and their descendants' descendants, until God inherits the earth and those upon it, and He is the Best of Heirs. It is completely free from all *shurūr*, *subul*, and *maḍārr*. It is not subject to *damm*, *ḥasab*, *ʿulūq*, *nuzūl*, *tūrāt*, *kalīqa*, *mukhlā*, *sinsina*, *ʿāda*, *ʿāna*, nor a single *subul*. The rocks of their estate belong to them and are in their possession. The governance of their estate is in their possession, and its troops are in their possession.[5] God, God, let no one draw near to it, nor approach it, nor pause near them. We command you peremptorily, all you shaykhs and *muqaddam*s, and the *jarāī* who are under them throughout my kingdom, especially Shaykh Ūnsa walad Sarīr and whoever may come after him until the hour of resurrection, let no one of you trouble this gift of alms. He who troubles it after these my words has exposed himself to destruction. Beware, then beware of disobedience, and let the disobedient blame none but himself.

There were present and witnessed [to it]:

[Shaykh] Bashar
the *jundī*, Muḥammad
Shaykh ʿAzūza, agent of the compound of Nāṣir, maternal uncle of the king
Shaykh ʿAbd Allāh, [Shaykh] of Qarrī

Shaykh Sulaymān, Shaykh of Alays
Shaykh `Alī walad Shāwir, Shaykh of al-Tāka
[Shaykh `Alī] walad Ḥasan, Shaykh of Atbara
Shaykh Muḥammad Qaylī, Shaykh of Bayla
Shaykh Qāsim, Shaykh of al-Qarbīn
[Shaykh Fāṭir, Shaykh] of al-Baḥr
Shaykh Maḥmūd, *shaykh al-quwwārīya*
Shaykh Idrīs, *muqaddam al-sawākira*
[Sultan] Khamīs, Sultan Fūr al-Musabba`āt
Shaykh `Alī walad Tūma, *muqaddam al-khayl*
[. . .]
Shaykh Jābir, *muqaddam al-qawāwīd*
Shaykh Ādam walad [Kūrī]
[. . .]
[the *khaṭīb*,] `Abd al-Ḥafīẓ [walad Nūnū]
Faqīh `Uthmān
(Takalla Allāh?), Sultan al-Borqāwī
Faqīh Muḥammad `Abd al-Ghanī

The writer of the document is Ya`qūb Ḥamīran. With God, two witnesses suffice. The year 1156/1743-1744 from the *hijra* of the prophet, upon whose master the best of prayers and purest peace.

[1]For a published version see Abū Salīm, *al-Fūnj wa'l-arḍ*, pp. 59-61.

[2]Lacuna. A conjectural reading of the missing text has been restored from Doc. 2.

[3]Dittography in original.

[4]Lacuna. A conjectural reading of the missing text has been restored from Doc. 8.

[5]This expression implies that the beneficiaries are to enjoy full control over the property granted.

DOCUMENT 10

Document 10 is a confirming charter issued by Sultan Bādī IV to Faqīh `Abd al-Hādī walad Muḥammad walad `Abd al-Hādī walad Dōlīb in Rajab 1157/10 August - 8 September 1744, renewing his rights to the homestead (*zarība*) of his forefather Muḥammad walad Dōlīb. The text has been taken by the editors from the original.[1] The document is worn around the periphery with some loss of text on all sides; one large fragment at the lower right-hand corner is missing, as is a second containing the first half of eight lines near the beginning. Noteworthy is the inclusion of "selling" and "buying" among the demands of external society against which this charter was drafted to grant immunity; for a comparison, and possible motive for the inclusion of this clause, see Doc. 33. The *sanctio* contains specific warnings to an unusually large number of possible transgressors, including not only `Abd Allāh walad `Ajīb the governor of the northern province and his rival Musnad walad Ibrāhīm, leader of the Jamū`īya,[2] but also the governors of a number of small subdistricts in Dongola. It is probable that the ancestral *zarība* of Muḥammad walad Dōlīb should be understood to include his tomb, which is located at al-Dabba near the border between Dongola and the Shāīqīya country.[3] (For a second grant drawn up to include the tomb of the beneficiary's forefather, see Doc. 12).

الواثق بالله و الرسول
ابن السلطان نول
السلطان بادى ١١٢٧

حجة سلطانيه و وثيقه ملوكيه بمدينة سنار المحروسة المحمية (اجلها / الله تعالى لدا متوليها الذى ايده)[4] الله بالنصر و التمكين و الرفعه و التحصين و جعله (ظلا / ظليلا ياوي اليه كل مسكين)[4] الذى هو فى الدنيا سعيد و في الاخرة ان شاء (الله شهيد / من انطوى باطنه على)[4] الصفا و ظاهره على الصدق و الوفا الصادق فى قوله / (الامين فى فعله الذى)[4] اذا قال صدق و اذا تكلم بالحق نطق مولانا السلطان / (بن السلطان السلطان)[4] بادى بن السلطان نول نصره الله الرحمن (الرحيم / بجاه القرءان العظيم)[4] و النبى الكريم امين امين يا رب العالمين الى (حضرت / كل من تقف عليه هذه)[4] الوثيقة و الناظر لما فيها من الحقيقه و بعد فان (السلطان / المبرور المويد المنصور)[4] تمم للفقيه عبد الهادى ولد محمد ولد عبد الهادى / ولد دوليب زريبة جده محمد ولد دوليب التى هى سابق بيده لا من جيرانه [5] / و لا من جيرانه و لا من نسابته الذى فى زريبته لا احدا يقربهم و لا (يدنيهم)[4] / و لا يتعرض لهم فى جاههم لا فى قليل و لا فى كثير و لا فى بيع و لا شرا و لا فى (تورات)[4] / و لا فى دم و لا فى مخلا و لا فى كسره و انهم سالمين مسلمين من جميع الشرور (و السبل)[6] / و المضار و الحذر لا احدا يقربهم و لا يدنيهم و لا يقف لهم على طريق حبلهم (المرمى)[7] / لا يشيله زول و نوكد عليكم يا جميع الشيوخ و المقاديم و الجراى الذين من تحتهم / الى حد ملكى كله خصوصا الشيخ عبد الله ولد عجيب و شيوخه و مقاديمه و ملوك ضنقله و جرايهم خصوصا الشيخ مسند ولد ابراهيم و جرايه و خدامه و الشيخ سوه / ولد محمد ولد الوناوى و جرايه و خدامه و الارباب محمد ولد الملك على و جرايه / و خدامه و الملك عون الله ملك الخندق و جرايه و خدامه و الملك الزبير / و جرايه و خدامه و الملك موسى ولد امامه ولد الدفار و خدامه و جرايه / و الملك صلاح و خدامه و جرايه و ملوك الجابرية و خدامهم و جرايهم / و جميع من هو تحت ملكى لا احدا منكم يتعرض لهذا الجاه و من تعرض (لها بعد)[6] كلامى هذا فقد عرض نفسه للهلاك و الحذر ثم الحذر من المخالفة (و المخالف / لا يلوم)[6] الا نفسه

حضر ذلك و شهد به

الشيخ بشر
و الجندى محمد
و الشيخ عبد الله شيخ قرى /

(و الشيخ سليمان شيخ اليس)[4]
(و الشيخ على ولد شاور)[4] شيخ التاكة
و الشيخ على شيخ اتبرة
و الشيخ محمد قيلى شيخ (بيله)[4]
(و الشيخ فاطر)[8] شيخ البحر
و الشيخ محمود مقدم القواريه/
(و السلطان)[8] خميس سلطان فور المسبعات
و الشيخ جابر (مقدم / القواويد)[4]
(و الشيخ على ولد تومه)[4] مقدم الخيل
و الشيخ عزوزه مقدم حوش ناصر خال (الملك)

(. . .) // بالله (شهيدا) تمم فى شهر الله رجب سنة ١١٥٧ (الف و مايه و سبعه) و خمسين من الهجرة على صاحبها (افضل الصلاة و ازكى السلام)

He who trusts in God and the messenger

The son of Sultan Nōl

Sultan Bādī 1137/1724-1725

A sultanic charter and royal document [issued] in the divinely guarded and protected city of Sinnār, [may God Most High exalt her, in the presence of her warden, whom God has supported], aided, invested, elevated, and strengthened, and made [a protecting shelter with whom every subject may seek refuge]. He is happy in this world and, if God wills, in the next will be [a martyr. His interior is] purity, his exterior truth and fidelity. Truthful in word [and trustworthy in deed], when he speaks he speaks the truth, and when he speaks the truth he has ordained, our lord the sultan, [the son of the sultan, Sultan] Bādī the son of Sultan Nōl. May God, the Merciful, [the Compassionate], grant him victory [through the influence of the sublime] Qur'ān and the eminent prophet. Amen, amen, O Lord of the Universe.

To [the presence of all who read this] document and see the truth therein.

Thereafter: [The pious, divinely assisted and victorious sultan] has confirmed to Faqīh `Abd al-Hādī walad Muḥammad walad `Abd al-Hādī walad Dōlīb the *zarība* of his grandfather Muḥammad walad Dōlīb, formerly in his possession and not that of his neighbors, nor of his kinsmen by marriage who are in his *zarība*. Let no one draw near or [approach them], nor trouble them in their grant, not in little and not in much, neither in selling nor in buying, not in [*tūrāt*], *damm*, *mukhlā*, or *kisra*, for they are completely free from all *shurūr*, [*subul*], *maḍārr*, and *khidam*. Let no one draw near or approach them, nor pause near them along the way. Let no one carry off [even] the rope they have [thrown away]. We command you peremptorily, all you shaykhs and *muqaddams*, and the *jarāī* who are under them throughout my kingdom, all, and especially Shaykh `Abd Allāh walad `Ajīb, his shaykhs and *muqaddams*, the kings of Dongola and their *jarāī*, especially Shaykh Musnad walad Ibrāhīm, his *jarāī* and servants, Shaykh Sowwah walad Muḥammad walad al-Wanāwī, his *jarāī* and servants, Arbāb Muḥammad walad al-Malik `Alī, his *jarāī* and servants, Malik `Awn Allāh the king of al-Khandaq, his *jarāī* and servants, Malik al-Zubayr, his *jarāī* and servants, Malik Mūsā walad Imāma walad al-Duffār, his servants and *jarāī*, Malik Ṣalāḥ, his servants and *jarāī*, the kings of al-Jābirīya, their servants and *jarāī*, and all who are under my authority; let no one of you trouble this grant. He who troubles [it after] these my words has exposed himself to destruction. Beware, then beware of disobedience, and let [the disobedient blame] none but himself.

There were present and witnessed to it:

Shaykh Bashar
the *jundī*, Muḥammad
Shaykh `Abd Allāh, Shaykh of Qarrī
[Shaykh Sulaymān, Shaykh of Alays]
[Shaykh `Alī walad Shāwir], Shaykh of al-Tāka

Shaykh `Alī, Shaykh of Atbara
Shaykh Muḥammad Qaylī, Shaykh of [Bayla]
[Shaykh Fāṭir], Shaykh of al-Baḥr
Shaykh Maḥmūd, *muqaddam al-quwwārīya*
[Sultan] Khamīs, Sultan Fūr al-Musabba`āt
Shaykh Jābir, [*muqaddam al-qawāwīd*]
[Shaykh `Alī walad Tūma], *muqaddam al-khayl*
Shaykh `Azūza, *muqaddam* of the compound of Nāṣir, maternal uncle of the king
[. . .]

With God, [two witnesses suffice]. It was completed in God's month of Rajab in the year 1157, [one thousand one hundred] fifty-[seven] from the *hijra*, upon whose master [the best of prayers and purest peace].

[1]For a previously published version see Abū Salīm, *al-Fūnj wa'l-arḍ*, pp. 62-64.

[2]Father of the recipient of Docs. 19 and 20.

[3]*Ṭabaqāt*, p. 349.

[4]Lacuna. A conjectural reading of the missing text has been taken from Doc. 9.

[5]Dittography in original.

[6]Lacuna. A conjectural reading of the missing text has been taken from Doc. 12.

[7]Lacuna. A conjectural reading of the missing text has been taken from Doc. 7.

[8]Lacuna. A conjectural reading of the missing text has been taken from Doc. 8.

DOCUMENT 11

Document 11 is a colophon concluding a Qur'ān manuscript and dated 9 Sha`bān 1159/27 August 1746; it was prepared in Sinnār for donation by Sultan Bādī IV to Faqīh Muḥammad al-Ḥājj Sa`d, leader of the *fuqarā'* community of the `Abābsa of Nādī in the Rubāṭāb country. The text has been taken by the editors from the original.[1] This royal donation is one expression of Sultan Bādī's vigorous policies in support of *fuqarā'* following his personal assumption of power in 1156/1743-1744.[2]

The `Abābsa Qur'ān consists of a set of unbound pages, some of them illuminated, housed in a hand-tooled case of brown oiled leather. The book is a cherished heirloom of the family, and the final page containing the colophon shows signs of having been handled much more frequently than the rest of the book. In the course of usage, substantial portions of the margins have been lost. The surviving written text of the final page may be divided into three portions on the basis of the size of the script and the orientation on the page; the handwriting appears to be that of one man.

A. The first portion, written in a small script consistent in scale with that of the rest of the book, consists of eighteen lines of text arranged down the center of the page in two inverted pyramids:

و قد تم على يد كاتبه / أفقر الورى و أحوجهم / الى رحمة ربه المولى / ذاك عبد الله
بن / محمد لقب / بدريش / الحداد / غفر / الله / له / و لوالديه و لمشايخه و
لاخوانه و لاخواته و لجميع المسلمين و للا / جداد و كان الفراغ منه نصف نهار
الاثنين من شهر / الله المبارك الاصم شعبان لتسعة ايام / خلت منه من شهور سنة الف
و ماية / و تسعة و خمسين من الهجره / النبوية على ساكنها / افضل الصلاة و
اتم السلام

It has been completed by the hand of its writer, the poorest of mortals and the one among them most in need of the mercy of his Lord the Master. That is `Abd Allāh b. Muḥammad, with the *laqab* D.R.Y.Sh. al-Ḥ.D.Ā.D.[3] May God forgive him, his two parents, his shaykhs, his brothers, his sisters, all the Muslims, and the forefathers. The completion of it was at noon on Monday in God's blessed month of Sha'bān *al-aṣamm*,[4] when nine days of it had passed, in the months of the year one thousand one hundred fifty-nine from the *hijra* of the prophet, upon whom the best of prayers and most complete peace.

B. The second portion, couched in the largest script, would require the reader of **A** to rotate the page ninety degrees clockwise. The text begins at the lower right corner of the page, after rotation, and follows the base of the page to its approximate midpoint. The surviving fragment reads: "this *maṣḥaf*. . . ."

. . . هذا المصحف . . .

C. The third portion, written in a script of intermediate size, would require the reader of **B** to rotate the page one hundred eighty degrees. The text begins at the upper right corner, after rotation, and consists of at least four lines in the upper margin and at least three in the lower; the initial line or lines of text in the upper margin are missing, as are substantial parts of the Qur'ānic text in the lower margin. According to the `Abābsa, this portion of the colophon contained the sultanic dedication of the volume to their family, and many members of the community committed it to memory. The missing opening of the text as taught to Aḥmad al-Mu`taṣim reads: "From Sultan Bādī b. Muḥammad to Faqīh Muḥammad."

من السلطان بادى بن محمد الى الفقيه محمد

This reading from the orally-preserved traditions of the community does not inspire complete confidence. In all other documents from Sinnār in which his name appears, Sultan Bādī is designated the son of Nōl and not Muḥammad; the use of *ilā* seems incorrect because the preposition *`alā* is employed in a parallel construction in the passage to follow and finally, this reading would assume that the written grant was couched in a verbless form. While verbless charter grants were indeed issued by the *makk*s of Taqalī during the period of Dār Fūr hegemony over the region,[5] these southern documents display many unusual features and it is doubtful that they should be employed as models here; further, the use of *`alā* in the surviving text strongly suggests that a verb existed at the beginning of the passage.[6] An alternative and entirely conjectural reading, prepared with the preceding discussion in mind, might read: "Sultan Bādī b. Nōl has bestowed this Qur'ān as alms upon the Faqīh Muḥammad."

ان السلطان بادى بن نول قد تصدق بهذا المصحف على الفقيه محمد

The surviving portion of text in the upper margin continues: "al-Ḥājj Sa`d and his descendants after him. It is not to be sold, or made over [to someone else] until Thou shalt inherit the earth and those upon it, and Thou art the Best of Heirs."

الحاج سعد و على ذريته من بعده لا يباع / و لا يورث حتى ترث الارض و من / عليه
و أنت خير الوارثين /

The lower margin consists of a scriptural passage (Qur'ān 2:181), written without the customary vocalizations:

فمن بدله بعد ما سمعه فانما اثمه / (على) الذين يبدلونه ان (الله سميع عليم (

"Whoever alters it [the bequest] after having heard it, [should be aware that] the sin of doing so devolves only upon those who alter it. Surely God is Hearing, Knowing."[7]

[1]For a previously published version see Aḥmad al-Mu`taṣim al-`Abbās, `Alī `Osmān Muḥammad Ṣāliḥ, and Jay Spaulding, "A Colophon from Eighteenth-Century Sinnār," *Fontes Historiae Africanae Arabicae: Bulletin d'Information* 6 (1981): 13-18. The editors extend special appreciation to Mr. Aḥmad al-Mu`taṣim and his family for permission to consult and to publish this work, and to Professor J.O. Hunwick for advice.

[2]Spaulding, *Heroic Age*, pp. 212-215.

[3]Islamic holy men in Sinnār were often known by a nickname, which was sometimes said to possess a mystical import; the significance of this individual's *laqab,* however, is not known. Informants agreed that the correct reading of the first part of his name was Darīsh, but rejected the otherwise-plausible reading of the second part as al-Ḥaddād on the grounds that no respectable person would willingly be identified with a smith, even in a figurative or arcane sense; they proposed the alternative al-Ḥidād ("the mourning"), but this would seem to require a difficult reinterpretation of "Darīsh" to complete the construct.

[4]This epithet, "the deaf," is more frequently given to the month of Rajab.

[5]Historisk Institutt, Universitetet i Bergen, SK 1.1/1, SK 2.1/2, SK 3.1/3, SK 4.1/4, SK 5.1/5, SK 6.1/6. These documents were collected by Janet Ewald, who offers a discussion of them in "Leadership and Social Change on an Islamic Frontier: The Kingdom of Taqali, 1780-1900," Ph.D Diss., University of Wisconsin-Madison, 1982, Vol. 2, pp. 322-331.

[6]The editors are grateful to J.O. Hunwick for this insight.

[7]The translation given here was supplied by J.O. Hunwick.

DOCUMENT 12

Document 12 is a confirming charter issued by Sultan Bādī IV to Faqīh `Abd al-Raḥmān b. al-Faqīh Khōjalī in Rajab 1166/4-31 May 1753, bestowing upon him a grant that included the land in which Shaykh Khōjalī was buried. The text has been taken by the editors from the original.[1] A fragment at the center of the bottom of the document is missing. The site of the grant lay on the east bank of the Nile immediately below the confluence within modern Khartoum North, where the tomb is to be found today. The eminent early eighteenth-century holy man Shaykh Khōjalī b. `Abd al-Raḥmān died on 18 Jumāda II 1155/20 August 1742. He was succeeded as the leader of the Khōjalāb community by his son Aḥmad Bishāra, whose tenure as *khalīfa* was six years.[2] The present grant of the ancestral tomb to a second son, `Abd al-Raḥmān,[3] suggests that the latter may have succeeded to the leadership of the Khōjalāb after the passing of Aḥmad Bishāra in about 1161/1748. The immunity clauses of this charter seem to allude to freedom from demands for tobacco. The question of the legitimacy of the use of tobacco by Muslims was a point of controversy among Sudanese holy men, and a demand for tobacco from those who abhored it would certainly have been very offensive. Alternatively, such immunity might also have appealed to smokers, for reasons made clear by the traveler John Lewis Burckhardt:

> The insolence of the slaves [in Berber] . . . is in nothing more displayed than their behavior in regard to smoking; if they see a stranger with a pipe in his mouth, they often take it from him without saying a word, and are unwilling to return it before they have smoked it out. To a smoker . . . nothing can be more disagreeable.[4]

The witness roster to this document is the earliest extant testimony to Sultan Bādī's expansion of his court to include numerous *fuqarā'*, as well as other new elements, following his personal assumption of power.[5]

باسمك يا كريم بسم الله الرحمن الرحيم الحمد لله الذى ايد الشريعة المحمدية بالادلة / و القواطع الحكمية المنزلة على خير البرية / الحمد لله الذى بلغ بالرسول و نحن امنا بما يقول

الواثق بالله و الرسول
ابن السلطان نول
السلطان بادى ١١٢٧

حجة سلطانية و وثيقة ملوكية بمدينة سنار المحروسة المحمية / اجلها الله تعالى لدا متوليها الذى ايده الله بالنصر و التمكين و الرفعة / و التحصين و جعله ظلا ظليلا ياوى اليه كل مسكين الذى هو فى الدنيا سعيد و فى الاخرة ان شاء الله شهيد من انطوى باطنه على الصفا و ظاهره / على الصدق و الوفا الصادق فى قوله الامين فى فعله الذى اذا قال صدق و اذا تكلم بالحق نطق مولانا السلطان بن السلطان السلطان بادى بن / السلطان نول نصره الله الرحمن الرحيم بجاه القرءان العظيم و النبى الكريم ءامين ءامين يا رب العالمين الى حضرت كل من تقف عليه هذه الوثيقة و الناظر لما فيها / من الحقيقة و بعد فان السلطان المبرور المويد المنصور (. . .) / (. . .) الشيخ عبد الله ولد عجيب و ولده الشيخ مسمار و ولده الشيخ / محمد الامين من تمامت صدقت الدار على الفقيه عبد الرحمن ابن الفقيه خوجلى / بالدار التى فيها قبر الفقيه خوجلى و هى معلومة الحدود و البقعة / فحدها من جهة السافل الزرقاب و من جهة الصعيد الضنيقيله و من جهة / الصبح درب الجمل و من جهة الغرب انتها البحر و حدها فى المشارع من جهة الصعيد مشرع الحاج عالم و من جهة السافل مشرع فافوا و هذا كله ابتغاء / لوجه الله تعالى و طلبا للثواب فى دار الماب و ليوم لا ينفع فيه مال و لا بنون / الا من اتى الله بقلب سليم و صارت هذه الدار المذكورة بحدودها المعلومة / صدقة و ملكا للشيخ عبد الرحمن ابن الشيخ خوجلى و لذريته و ذرية ذريته / لا ينازعهم فيها منازع و لا يتعرض لهم متعرض سالمة مسلمة من جميع الشرور و السبل / و المضار لا عليها جساره و لا خساره و لا نزول و لا ضيافه من ناس قرى او من ناس سنار / و لا يغشاهم احدا فى حلتهم و لا ماءهم الازرق يشربه انسان و لا فيكم الجميع من يعرب /

دواية التنباك عندهم و لا عادة و لا عانة و لا شيء من السبل العادية و نوكد عليكم / يا جميع الشيوخ و المقاديم و الجراى الذين من تحتهم الى حد ملكى خصوصا انتم / يا ناس قرى الشيخ محمد الامين ولد مسمار و جرايه و من ياتى بعدهم الى قيام الساعة / لا احدا منكم يتعرض لهذه الصدقه و من تعرض لها بعد كلامى هذا فقد عرض نفسه / للهلاك و الحذر ثم الحذر من المخالفة و المخالف لا يلوم الا نفسه

حضر ذالك و شهد به

الشيخ / انقله ولد يونس
و الجندى محمد ولد دريش
و الشيخ عزوزه شيخ حوش ناصر خال الملك /
و الشيخ محمد الامين ولد مسمار ولد عجيب شيخ قرى
و الشيخ سليمان ولد بادى شيخ اليس /
و الشيخ عبد الله ولد عوض شيخ التاكة
و الشيخ سبت ولد حيدر شيخ اتبره
و الشيخ عبد العاطى / ولد الشيخ محمد قيلى شيخ بيله
و الشيخ قاسم شيخ القربين
و الشيخ الضو ولد ارباب شيخ البحر /
و الشيخ على كرار ولد عمر شيخ كردفال
و الشيخ محمد ولد محمود شيخ القوارية
و الشيخ / شنبول ولد (نوه شيخ اربجى)[6]
(و الشيخ)[6] ادريس ولد نايل مقدم السواكرة
(و السلطان بدر)[6] / ولد السلطان (خميس سلطان فور المسبعات)[6]
و السلطان حماد ولد مادبه
و السلطان / (محمد القمراوى)[6] سلطان قمر
و الشيخ (. . .)
و الشيخ على ولد حمد الله (شيخ) الداخل
و الملك (. . .) / عبد الحى (. . .) //
سليمان ولد (. . .) /
و عبد الكريم اخيه
و الارباب عبد / (الكريم)[6] ولد الحكيم عبد السلام المغربى

و الارباب / احمد الشوبرى ولد الفقيه بلول حمد /
و الارباب على ولد رضوان
و الارباب / مرسال ولد اكد
و الشريف سالم ولد الشيخ / جعفر العلوى
و الشريف عبد الله ولد / السيد الشوبرى
و الشريف ضياب ولده /
و الشريف احمد ولد المكحل
و الفقيه عثمان /
و الحاج محمد الصليحاوى
و الفقيه عبد الرحمن / ولد جابر
و الفقيه محمد الامين الحرادابى /
و الفقيه الزاكى ولد العجب
و الحاج عمران ولد / الحاج سعيد
و الفقيه محمد ولد مدنى / ولد عبيدى
و الفقيه محمد ولد الفقيه (حسن)[6] / الطاحونى
و الفقيه محمد ولد ابو الحسن / المشهور بتور المتون
و الفقيه بلول ولد / ركابى (. . .) نسيب الملك
و الفقيه انوار ولد / عبد الحليم المغربى رجل الحلفا (. . .)
الجنيد ولد طه
و الفقيه تاج الدين / عبد الرازق (معتوق)[6] الملك
و الفقيه (عبد الحفيظ)[7] / ولد نونو
و ابراهيم (. . .) / ولد ولد النجدى
و الفقيه عبد الهادى / ولد دوليب
و الفقيه (. . .)
و الفقيه سالم ولد نعيم
و الفقيه مدنى ولد محمد ولد مدنى /
و الفقيه احمد ولد (. . .)
و الفقيه رحمة الله الصليحاوى
و الفقيه / يوسف ولد ولد ونيسه
و الفقيه ابو بكر / ولد ام سيكه
و الفقيه يعقوب حميرا /

و مسطر الحروف ابنه ابراهيم شاهد بذالك / و كفا بالله شهيدا تحرير ذلك في شهر
الله الحرام / الفرد رجب من شهور سنة ٦٦ سنة / الف و ماية ٦٦ من الهجرة
النبوية / على صاحبها افضل الصلاة و السلام

In Thy name, O Generous One. In the name of God, the Merciful, the Compassionate. Praise be to God, Who has confirmed the Muḥammadan law with proofs and definitive judgments, that descended on the best of creation. Praise be to God, Who sent the messenger. We believe in what he says.

He who trusts in God and the messenger
The son of Sultan Nōl
Sultan Bādī 1137/1724-1725

A sultanic charter and royal document [issued] in the divinely guarded and protected city of Sinnār, may God Most High exalt her, in the presence of her warden, whom God has supported, aided, invested, elevated, and strengthened, and made a protecting shelter with whom every subject may seek refuge. He is happy in this world and, if God wills, in the next will be a martyr. His interior is purity, his exterior truth and fidelity. Truthful in word and trustworthy in deed, when he speaks he speaks the truth, and when he speaks the truth he has ordained, our lord the sultan, the son of the sultan, Sultan Bādī, the son of Sultan Nōl. May God, the Merciful, the Compassionate, grant him victory through the influence of the sublime Qur'ān and the eminent prophet. Amen, amen, O Lord of the Universe.

To the presence of all who read this document and see the truth therein.

Thereafter: The pious, divinely assisted and victorious sultan [has confirmed and ratified that which][8] Shaykh `Abd Allāh walad `Ajīb, his son Shaykh Mismār, and his son Shaykh Muḥammad al-Amīn [have done][8] in regard to the confirmation of the gift of alms of an estate to Faqīh `Abd al-Raḥmān, son of Faqīh Khōjalī, the estate in which is located the tomb of Faqīh Khōjalī. Its boundaries and location are known: its boundary on the northern side is al-Zuruqāb; on the upstream side al-Danīqīla; on the east, the camel path; on the west it ends at the river. It is bounded by watering places: on the southern side the watering place of al-Ḥājj `Ālim; on the northern side the watering place of Fāfū. All this is for the sake of God Most High, asking for reward in the life to come, for a day in which neither wealth nor sons suffice, unless one comes to God with a secure heart. The said estate, its boundaries known, has become a gift of alms and property of Shaykh `Abd al-Raḥmān b. al-Shaykh Khōjalī, his descendants, and his descendants' descendants. Let no challenger challenge them concerning it. Let no troublemaker trouble them in it. It is completely free from all *shurūr*, *subul*, and *maḍārr*; it is not subject to *jusāra*, *khusāra*, *nuzūl*, nor *ḍiyāfa* on the part of the people of Qarrī or of the people of Sinnār. Let no one visit them in their village, nor any person drink of their blue water. No one among all of you may demand the drug tobacco from them. It is not subject to *`āda*, *`āna*, nor any of the customary *subul*. We command you peremptorily, all you shaykhs and *muqaddam*s, and the *jarāī* who are under them throughout my kingdom, especially you, O people of Qarrī, Shaykh Muḥammad al-Amīn walad Mismār and his *jarāī*, and whoever may come after them until the hour of resurrection, let none of you trouble this gift of alms. He who troubles it after these my words has exposed himself to destruction. Beware, then beware of disobedience, and let the disobedient blame none but himself.

There were present and witnessed to it:

Shaykh Anqala walad Yūnus
the *jundī*, Muḥammad walad Darīsh
Shaykh `Azūza, shaykh of the compound of Nāṣir, maternal uncle of the king

Shaykh Muḥammad al-Amīn walad Mismār walad `Ajīb, Shaykh of Qarrī
Shaykh Sulaymān walad Bādī, Shaykh of Alays
Shaykh `Abd Allāh walad `Awaḍ, Shaykh of al-Tāka
Shaykh Sabat walad Ḥaydar, Shaykh of Atbara
Shaykh `Abd al-`Aṭā walad al-Shaykh Muḥammad Qaylī, Shaykh of Bayla
Shaykh Qāsim, Shaykh of al-Qarbīn
Shaykh al-Ḍaw walad Arbāb, Shaykh of al-Baḥr
Shaykh `Alī Karrār walad `Umar, Shaykh of Kordofāl
Shaykh Muḥammad walad Maḥmūd, *shaykh al-quwwārīya*
Shaykh Shanbūl walad [Nūh, Shaykh of Arbajī]
[Shaykh] Idrīs walad Nāyil, *muqaddam al-sawākira*
[Sultan Badr] walad al-Sultan [Khamīs, Sultan Fūr al-Musabba`āt]
Sultan Ḥammād walad Mādiba
Sultan [Muḥammad al-Qimrāwī], Sultan of Qimr
Shaykh [. . .]
Shaykh `Alī walad Ḥammad Allāh, [Shaykh] of al-Dākhil
Malik [. . .] `Abd al-Ḥayy [. . .]
Sulaymān walad [. . .]
`Abd al-Karīm, his brother
Arbāb `Abd [al-Karīm], son of the physician `Abd al-Salām al-Maghribī
Arbāb Aḥmad al-Shōbarī walad al-Faqīh Balūl Ḥammad
Arbāb `Alī walad Raḍwān
Arbāb Mursāl walad Akad
Sharīf Sālim walad al-Shaykh Ja`far al-`Alawī
Sharīf `Abd Allāh walad al-Sayyid al-Shōbarī
Sharīf Ḍiyāb, his son
Sharīf Aḥmad walad al-Mikḥal
Faqīh `Uthmān
Ḥājj Muḥammad al-Ṣulayḥāwī
Faqīh `Abd al-Raḥmān walad Jābir

Faqīh Muḥammad al-Amīn al-Ḥarādābī
Faqīh al-Zākī walad al-`Ajab
Ḥājj `Imrān walad al-Ḥājj Sa`īd
Faqīh Muḥammad walad Madanī walad `Abīdī
Faqīh Muḥammad walad al-Faqīh [Ḥasan] al-Ṭāḥūnī
Faqīh Muḥammad walad Abu'l-Ḥasan, known as "Tōr al-Matn"
Faqīh Balūla walad Rikābī [. . .], a kinsman by marriage of the king
Faqīh Anwār walad `Abd al-Ḥalīm al-Maghribī, "The Man of al-Ḥalfā"
[. . .]
Junayd walad Ṭaha
Faqīh Tāj al-Dīn `Abd al-Rāziq, [a freedman] of the king
Faqīh [`Abd al-Ḥafīẓ] walad Nūnū
Ibrāhīm [. . .] walad Walad al-Najdī
Faqīh `Abd al-Hādī walad Dōlīb
Faqīh [. . .]
Faqīh Sālim walad Na`īm
Faqīh Madanī walad Muḥammad walad Madanī
Faqīh Aḥmad walad [. . .]
Faqīh Raḥmat Allāh al-Ṣulayḥāwī
Faqīh Yūsuf walad Walad Wanīsa
Faqīh Abū Bakr walad Umm Sīka
Faqīh Ya`qūb Ḥamīran

The writer of the letters and witness to that is his son Ibrāhīm. With God, two witnesses suffice. That was written in God's holy month *al-fard* Rajab from the months of the year 66, the year one thousand one hundred 66 from the *hijra* of the prophet, upon whose master the best of prayers and peace.

[1]For a previously published version see Abū Salīm, *al-Fūnj wa'l-arḍ*, pp. 101-103.

[2]*Ṭabaqāt*, pp. 190-201.

[3]Ibid., pp. 309-310.

[4]Burckhardt, *Travels in Nubia*, pp. 206-207.

[5]Spaulding, *Heroic Age*, pp. 214-215.

[6]Lacuna. A conjectural reading of the missing text has been taken from Doc. 14

[7]Lacuna. A conjectural reading of the missing text has been taken from Doc. 2.

[8]Conjectural reconstruction.

DOCUMENT 13

Document 13 is an inscription on a copper kettledrum preserved in the family of the Funj sultans. According to A.E. Robinson, "Mek [Sultan] Nasr, the lineal descendent of Mek Badi [VI] the Fung Sultan who surrendered [to the Turks in 1821] possesses a nehas [*naḥās*] or copper drum . . . . Tradition states that this drum is the original Fung drum and [that] the gold was removed in times of stress by the persons into whose hands it passed."[1] The text reads:

نقارة الدار نقارة السلطان
عمارة بن السلطان عدلان
جدهم الكبير الجاء
من لول عمرها السلطان
بادى بن السلطان نول
نصره الله
امين

The drum of the land
The drum of Sultan `Amāra the son of Sultan `Adlān
Whose ancient forefather came from Lūl
Sultan Bādī the son of Sultan Nōl caused it to be made
May God grant him victory
Amen

[1] A.E.R.[obinson], "The Fung Drum or Nehas," *Sudan Notes and Records* 4 (1921): 211-212.

DOCUMENT 14

Document 14 is a confirming charter issued by Sultan Nāṣir b. Bādī to the Awlād al-Shaykh Khōjalī on 15 Dhu'l-Qa`da 1175/7 June 1762. The text has been taken by the editors from the original, which is intact and easily legible.[1] The witness roster illustrates the changes in court personnel that immediately followed the Hamaj coup of 27 March 1762; conspicuous is the prominent position accorded the new Regent (*wazīr*) Muḥammad Abū Likaylik. The roster gives a large number of places to minor noblemen entitled Arbāb, and reveals that some of these had begun to identify themselves in patrilineal terms; indeed, several of the high court officials may also be seen to have begun to adopt this practice.[2] Noteworthy also is the appearance of cash fines for the violation of sultanic decrees.[3]

This document introduces a complicated and extended series of disputes between the Awlād al-Shaykh Khōjalī and their neighbors over the boundaries of a landholding here called Jundīya Island, including Rafīda and al-Qaṭ`īya.[4] The designation "island" implies that the landholding was low and fertile, within the high and comparatively permanent banks of the Nile and possibly in part subject to innundation during the annual flood. It probably lay along the Nile slightly below al-Ḥalfāya, but the evidence given does not indicate clearly whether the holding was confined to one bank, or may perhaps have extended across the channel of the river to include land on both sides. The latter hypothesis allows the most economical interpretation of the evidence, and will be adopted provisionally in this study.[5] The southern or upstream boundary, marked by a watercourse on the west (bank?) and a *sidr* tree on the east (bank?), was comparatively uncontroversial. Similarly, the northern or downstream boundary was comparatively settled; it consisted of a standard survey line or *fāṣil* that extended to the east and west away from the river, up the slope of the *jarf* and across the flat and fertile *qurayr*, or land irrigable by means of a riverbank *sāqīya*, and as far inland as the beginning of the elevated *kurus*, land equally fertile but too high to be watered by a wheel situated on the riverbank.[6] Both the eastern and western boundaries, or *mirins*, of the landholding were defined in terms of the line between the *qurayr* and the *kurus*, a line sometimes referred to in the documents as the *qayf*.[7]

The *narratio* provides some history of the landholding. The western boundary was first delineated for the local lord Bādī walad Sarīr at the command of Sultan Nōl, who reigned from 1 Sha`bān 1132/8 June 1720 to 1136/1723-1724.[8] Subsequent discussion, however, gave great weight to a later grant by Sultan Bādī IV (16 Shawwāl 1136/8 July 1724 to 2 Ramaḍān 1175/27 March 1762),[9] who also delineated the western boundary: "King Bādī's delineation of the [western] boundary at the *kurus* is valid because he is a king, who has the right to apportion the lands, whether barren or cultivated. Even if he had added a league to that, he would have prevailed at the judgment, for he is the supreme sultan and the shaykhs of the district are his agents" (Doc. 55). At a later point in his reign Bādī also ajudicated a dispute over the eastern boundary, and ruled in favor of the Awlād al-Shaykh Khōjalī. One is told in some detail of the dispatch of his emissaries to demarcate the disputed line, accompanied by a representative of the subordinate lord with immediate authority over the disputed area, the Shaykh of Qarrī or Walad `Ajīb, the governor of the northern province. Relevant also was the presence of a large gathering of the populace, "for by customary law a *mirin* [boundary] is drawn and put into effect only with good witnesses and true, in a general assembly [of the people]" (Doc. 54). At the accession of Sultan Nāṣir, the Awlād Sarīr reopened dispute over the western boundary, laying claim to a tract called the Island of Walad Ḥarīḥīr, the latter being the name of a prominent west-bank family.[10] Nāṣir sent the most eminent emissaries conceivable, the new Hamaj Regent Muḥammad Abū Likaylik and his restored Shaykh of Qarrī, Muḥammad al-Amīn b. Mismār.[11] They concluded that the disputed territory, the Island of Walad Ḥarīḥīr, lay within the boundaries of the Khōjalāb estate according to the terms of Sultan Bādī's grant.[12] On their return, Sultan Nāṣir confirmed his father's grant to the Khōjalāb and issued the present charter.

باسمك يا كريم بسم الله الرحمن الرحيم الحمد لله الذى ايد الشريعة المحمدية بالادله القرءانية و القواطع الحكمية / المنزله على خير البرية صلى الله عليه و سلم الحمد لله الذى بلغ الرسول و نحن ءامنا بما يقول

الواثق بالله و الرسول السلطان
ناصر بن السلطان بادى
ابن السلطان نول ١١٧٥ [13]

حجة سلطانية و وثيقه ملوكية بمدينة سنار المحروسة المحمية اجلها الله تعالى لدا متوليها / و ابن متوليها الحاكم يومئذ بما فيها سلطان الاسلام جامع كلمة الايمان و مدمر اهل البغى و الطغيان سيف الله القاطع / و سهامه اللامع ناشر لواء العدل فى العالمين ناصر شريعة سيد المرسلين احق من ملك تحت الخلافة باستحقاق / و اولى من ولا الولاية فى الافاق و هو الذى وجه عنان العناية لحماية الاسلام بشهادة الاجماع و تلك شهادة / لا يتطرق اليها النزاع و جدد بنيان الهداية بعد ما اندرست ءاثاره و طمست معالمه و مهد بساط العدل / بعد ان لم يوجد الا مظلوم و ظالمه ذو المفاخر الذى شهد بفضله الخاص و العام و المنثر التى ترفع على الثريا و تكاثر / الغمام و الاخلاق التى رام النسيم ان يشتبهوا بها ما يحاكى لطفها فاصبح عليلا و المعالى التى تمنت الملوك ان يشتبهوا / بها فلم يجدوا الى ذالك سبيلا مولانا السلطان بن السلطان السلطان المظفر المعان السلطان ناصر بن السلطان / بادى بن المرحوم السلطان نول نصره الله الرحمن الرحيم بجاه القرءان العظيم و النبى الكريم ءامين ءامين يا رب العالمين / الى حضرت كل من تقف عليه هذه الوثيقة و الناظر لما فيها من الحقيقة و بعد فان السلطان / المبرور المويد المنصور عرضت عليه وثيقة ابيه السلطان بادى بانه تصدق على الشيخ خوجلى بالجزيرة / الجنديه و ما احتوت عليه من رفيده و القطعيه و هى محددة من الاركان الاربعه صعيدا و سافلا و شرقا و غربا اما فاصلها من جهة الصعيد فى الشرق سدرت التويراب و فى الغرب السيالة الكبيرة المقابله قرن الجبل الازرق و فاصلها / من جهة السافل الفاصل الذى بين المحداب و النوفلاب فيخرج هذا الفاصل و يركز فوق كرس الدليباب و

حدها / من جهة الشرق كرس الدانياب و حدها من جهة الغرب كرس المحمداب الذى فصله السلطان نول لى بادى ولد سرير ثم فى ءاخر / ملك السلطان بادى ناس الشرق نازعوا اولاد الشيخ خوجلى فى المرن الشرقى و اشتكوا اولاد الشيخ خوجلى الى السلطان / بادى و ارسل السلطان مراسيله معهم و هم محمد الفقير ولد عمران و البدوى ولد عم الجندى تكتك و الشيخ محمد الامين بن الشيخ / مسمار ارسل معهم الارباب بدوى ولد عمه مالك و قدموا مراسيل السلطان و مرسال ولد عجيب و حضروا من ناس البلد جمع كثير / و الحراث الكبار العارفين الحدود وقفوا فى منجر فوق كرس الدليباب عند الفاصل و اخرجوا المرن بين الكرس و القرير الى جهة الصعيد / و علموه بحجارة و فى دار ولد المشاطه مرقوا المرن فوق الحرازه و اوسموها و اخرجوه فوق حد الكرس الى سدرة التويراب و انقطعوا / ناس منجر و ناس عبد القادر ولد حماد و ناس ولد نعمه و المحمداب من اولاد الشيخ خوجلى و حسبوا مراسيل السلطان بادى بحضرت / الجمع الكثير على ان من يدخل فى هذا الحد شرقا و غربا بشبرا واحدا عليه حسب الملك و فوقه الف للملك و مرسال ولد عجيب كذلك / قال اليدخل فى هذا الحد بشبرا واحدا عليه الحسب و فوقه الف ثم لما تولى بعد السلطان بادى ابنه السلطان ناصر نصره الله / قدموا الى عنده اولاد الشيخ خوجلى و باركوا له فى الدار و طلبوا منه ان يتمم لهم صدقة ابيه و الحال ان اولاد ولد سرير و جرايهم / اولاد رحمه حضروا و نازعوا اولاد الشيخ خوجلى فى الجزيره ولد حريحير و السلطان ناصر مرق لهم الشيخ محمد ابو لكيلك و الشيخ / محمد الامين ولد مسمار و قدموا فى الدانقه و قروا ورقة الملك بادى بحضرت اولاد ولد سرير و جرايهم و تبينت الجزيرة ولد حريحير / فى بطن الحدود الاربعة ليست الجزيره هذه خارجه من الحدود الاربعه و انقطعوا اولاد سرير و جرايهم اولاد رحمه / من جميع الدار ولد حريحير و غيرها لا طالب و لا مطلوب ثم ان السلطان ناصر اثبت صدقة ابيه و اقرها على حدودها الاربعه / المذكوره الذى حصل فيه النزاع و الذى لم يحصل فيه النزاع تمها كلها و امضاها لاولاد الشيخ خوجلى و ذريتهم و ذرية / ذريتهم يتوارثونها بينهم لا ينازعهم فيها منازع الى ان يرث الله الارض و من عليها و هو خير الوارثين هذا كله ابتغاء / لوجه الله تعالى و طلبا للثواب فى دار الماب و ليوم لا ينفع فيه مال و لا بنون الا من اتى الله بقلب سليم سالمه مسلمه / من جميع الشرور و السبل و المضار لا عليها جساره و لا خساره و لا نزول و لا ضيافه و لا علوق و لا كليقه و لا عاده و لا عانه / و لا قل و لا جل و لا شى من السبل العاديه و نوكد عليكم يا جميع الشيوخ و المقاديم و الجراى الذين من تحتهم الى حد ملكى كله / خصوصا اولاد بادى ولد سرير و جرايهم اولاد رحمه و من ياتى بعدهم الى قيام الساعة لا احدا منكم يتعرض لهذه الصدقة / و من تعرض لها بعد كلامى هذا فقد عرض نفسه للهلاك و الحذر ثم الحذر من المخالفة و المخالف لا يلوم الا نفسه

حضر ذلك و شهد به /

الشيخ محمد ابو لكيلك ولد بادى وزير الملك
و الشيخ عزوزه شيخ حوش ناصر خال الملك
و الشيخ محمد الامين ولد مسمار شيخ قرى
و الشيخ / عبد الله ولد عوض شيخ التاكة
و الشيخ بادى ولد حيدر شيخ اتبره
و الشيخ قاسم (شيخ)[14] القربين
و الشيخ عدلان ولد صباحى ولد صقر / شيخ البحر
و الشيخ على كرار ولد عمر شيخ كردفال
و الشيخ ادريس ولد نايل مقدم السواكره
و السلطان بدر ولد السلطان خميس سلطان فور المسبعات /
و السلطان محمد سلطان قمر
و السلطان تكل الله سلطان برقوا
و الشيخ محمد ولد محمود شيخ القواريه
و الشيخ شنبول ولد ولد نوه / شيخ اربجى
و الشيخ عبد القادر ولد كننه
و الشيخ فضل الله ولد شبردل مقدم العده
و الملك عدلان ملك برساج
و الشيخ بادى مقدم السجاده //
و الشيخ عبد العاطى بن الشيخ محمد قيلى شيخ بيله /
و القاضى محمد ولد عبد الحميد
و الارباب ابراهيم / ولد ولد نونو
و الارباب عمار اخيه
و احمد اخيه /
و الارباب سالم ولد الغنامى نسيب الملك
و الارباب عمه / محمد بت القويضى
و الارباب حبيب ولد هنبوا / رفيق الملك
و الارباب محمد الكوفى رفيق الملك ايضا /
و الارباب عبد الكريم كعيك الانسابى
و الارباب / يوسف ولد ابكر ولد احمد علوان

و الارباب / عبد الكريم ولد الحكيم عبد السلام المغربى
و الارباب / على رضوان
و الارباب احمد الشوبرى ولد الفقيه / بلول حميرا
و الشريف سالم ولد السيد جعفر العلوى /
و الشريف احمد ولد المكحل
و الفقيه عثمان
و الحاج / ابراهيم ولد ناصر خياط الملك
و الارباب محمد / ولد الفقيه حسن الطاحونى
و الفقيه تاج الدين / ولد عبد الرازق معتوق الملك
و الفقيه محمد /
و البشير معتوق الملك ايضا
و الفقيه محمد / ولد ابو الحسن ولد تور المتن
و الفقيه / محمد النور ولد صبر
و الفقيه مدنى ترباس / ولد محمد ولد مدنى
و الفقيه محمد الصافى ولد / النور ولد مسيغره
و الفقيه بليل ولد عمار / ولد ابو النقا

و مسطر الحروف فقير الله تعالى / و احوجهم اليه ابراهيم يعقوب عبد الرازق حميرا / شاهد بذلك و كفا بالله شهيدا تحرير ذلك / ضحوة الاربعا و خمسة و عشر فى شهر الله الحرام / ذى القعده من شهور سنة ١١٧٥ / الف و ماية و خمسة و سبعين من الهجرة النبوية / على صاحبه افضل الصلاة و السلام

In Thy name, O Generous One. In the name of God, the Merciful, the Compassionate. Praise be to God, Who has confirmed the Muḥammadan law with Qur'ānic proofs and definitive judgments that descended upon the best of creation. Praise be to God, Who sent the messenger. We believe in what he says.

He who trusts in God and the messenger
Sultan Nāṣir, the son of Sultan Bādī
The son of Sultan Nōl 1175/1761-1762

A sultanic charter and royal document [issued] in the divinely guarded and protected city of Sinnār, may God Most High exalt her, in the presence of her warden, the son of her warden, the governor at the present time of what is in her, the sultan of Islam who consolidates the authority of the faith and destroys the people of wrongdoing and oppression, the sharp sword of God and His flashing arrows, who spreads the banner of justice throughout the universe, protector of the law of the lord of the messengers, the one most deserving to rule as a Caliph, and foremost among those who rule between the horizons. He it is who has guided the reins of solicitude toward the protection of Islam, according to the testimony of a consensus achieved without dispute, who has renewed the edifice of guidance after its traces had been obliterated and its marks effaced, and who has made even the carpet of justice after [a time in which] one could find only the victim and his oppressor. He possesses glory to whose excellence high and low testify, influence which ascends to the Pleiades and gathers in clouds, a character which the breeze would wish to copy to become mild, but could not imitate, and noble traits in the emulation of which kings grow tired and fail to find a way, our lord the sultan, the son of the sultan, the victorious and divinely aided Sultan Nāṣir, the son of Sultan Bādī, the son of the late Sultan Nōl. May God, the Merciful, the Compassionate, make him victorious through the influence of the sublime Qur'ān and the eminent prophet. Amen, amen, O Lord of the Universe.

To the presence of all who read this document and see the truth therein.

Thereafter: The pious, divinely assisted and victorious sultan was shown a document of his father Sultan Bādī, to the effect that he had bestowed as alms upon Shaykh Khōjalī the island of al-Jundīya, including Rafīda and al-Qaṭ`īya. It is bounded on the four corners, south, north, east, and west. As for its *fāṣil* on the southern side, on the east it is the *sidr* tree of the Tuwayrāb, and on the west the big watercourse across from the peak of Jabal Azraq. Its *fāṣil* on the northern side is the *fāṣil* between the Muḥammadāb and the Nōfalāb; this *fāṣil* goes on and is fixed above the *kurus* of the Dolībāb. Its boundary on the eastern side is the *kurus* of the Dāniyāb. Its boundary on the western side is the *kurus* of the Muḥammadāb, which Sultan Nōl delineated for Bādī walad Sarīr. Then, late in the reign of Sultan Bādī, people of the east disputed with the Awlād al-Shaykh Khōjalī concerning the eastern *mirin*, and the Awlād al-Shaykh Khōjalī complained to Sultan Bādī. Sultan Bādī sent his messengers with them; they were Muḥammad al-Faqīr walad `Imrān and al-Badawī the son of the paternal uncle of the *jundī* Taktak. Shaykh Muḥammad al-Amīn b. al-Shaykh Mismār sent with them Arbāb Badawī the son of his paternal uncle Mālik. The messengers of Sultan Bādī and the messenger of Walad `Ajīb came. A great multitude of the people of the land were present, and the old cultivators who knew the boundaries. They stood at the *fāṣil* above the *kurus* of the Dolībāb in Manjar and delineated the *mirin* between the *kurus* and the *qurayr* as far as the southern side, marking it with stones. In Walad al-Mushāṭa they made the *mirin* run above the *ḥarāz* tree, which they marked with a blaze, and they delineated it above the edge of the *kurus* to the *sidr* tree of the Tuwayrāb. The people of Manjar, the people of `Abd al-Qādir walad Ḥammād, the people of Walad Ni`ma, and the Muḥammadāb have been cut off from the Awlād al-Shaykh Khōjalī. The messengers of Sultan Bādī, in the presence of the great multitude, charged whomsoever might trespass this boundary from east or west by even a single hand's breadth with the king's reckoning, and subjected him to [a fine of] one thousand [*qirsh*] to the king. The messenger of Walad `Ajīb likewise said: "He who trespasses this boundary by even a single hand's breadth falls under the reckoning, and he is subject to [a fine of] one thousand [*qirsh*]." Then when Sultan Bādī was succeeded by his son Sultan Nāṣir, may God grant him victory, the Awlād al-Shaykh Khōjalī came before him and blessed him [as the new ruler of] the country. They asked him to confirm for them the gift of alms of his father. The circumstances were that the Awlād Walad Sarīr and their *jarāī* the Awlād Raḥma had presented themselves to dispute with the Awlād al-Shaykh Khōjalī concerning the island of Walad Ḥarīḥīr. Sultan Nāṣir sent to them Shaykh Muḥammad Abū Likaylik and

Shaykh Muḥammad al-Amīn walad Mismār. They sat in the *danga*[15] and examined the document of King Bādī in the presence of the Awlād Walad Sarīr and their *jarāī*. It was established that the island of Walad Ḥarīḥīr was within the four boundaries and that no [part of] this island was outside the four boundaries. The Awlād Sarīr and their *jarāī* the Awlād Raḥma have been cut off from the estate, Walad Ḥarīḥīr and the rest of it. There is neither a claimant nor a claim. Thereupon Sultan Nāṣir corroborated the gift of alms of his father. He confirmed it according to its four said boundaries, [both] that concerning which there had been dispute and that concerning which there had not been [any] dispute. He confirmed and ratified all of it for the Awlād al-Shaykh Khōjalī, their descendants, and their descendants' descendants. They will bequeath it among themselves; let no challenger challenge them in it until God inherits the earth and those upon it, and He is the Best of Heirs. All this is for the sake of God Most High, asking for reward in the life to come, for a day in which neither wealth nor sons suffice, unless one comes to God with a secure heart. It is completely free from all *shurūr*, *subul*, and *maḍārr*. It is not subject to *jusāra*, *khusāra*, *nuzūl*, *ḍiyāfa*, *`ulūq*, *kalīqa*, *`āda*, *`āna*, *qill*, *jill*, nor any of the customary *subul*. We command you peremptorily, all you shaykhs and *muqaddam*s, and the *jarāī* who are under them throughout my kingdom, all, and especially the Awlād Bādī walad Sarīr and their *jarāī* the Awlād Raḥma, and whoever may come after them until the hour of resurrection, let no one of you trouble this gift of alms. He who troubles it after these my words has exposed himself to destruction. Beware, then beware of disobedience, and let the disobedient blame none but himself.

There were present and witnessed to it:

Shaykh Muḥammad Abū Likaylik walad Bādī, the king's *wazīr*
Shaykh `Azūza, shaykh of the compound of Nāṣir, maternal uncle of the king
Shaykh Muḥammad al-Amīn walad Mismār, Shaykh of Qarrī
Shaykh `Abd Allāh walad `Awaḍ, Shaykh of al-Tāka

Shaykh Bādī walad Ḥaydar, Shaykh of Atbara
Shaykh Qāsim, [Shaykh] of al-Qarbīn
Shaykh `Adlān walad Ṣubāḥī walad Ṣaqar, Shaykh of al-Baḥr
Shaykh `Alī Karrār walad `Umar, Shaykh of Kordofāl
Shaykh Idrīs walad Nāyil, *muqaddam al-sawākira*
Sultan Badr walad al-Sultan Khamīs, Sultan Fūr al-Musabba`āt
Sultan Muḥammad, Sultan Qimr
Sultan Takalla Allāh, Sultan Borqū
Shaykh Muḥammad walad Maḥmūd, *shaykh al-quwwārīya*
Shaykh Shanbūl walad Walad Nūh, Shaykh of Arbajī
Shaykh `Abd al-Qādir walad Kananna
Shaykh Faḍl Allāh walad Shabradal, *muqaddam al-`udda*
Malik `Adlān, *malik bursāj*
Shaykh Bādī, *muqaddam al-sajjāda*
Shaykh `Abd al-`Aṭā b. al-Shaykh Muḥammad Qaylī, Shaykh of Bayla
the *qāḍī*, Muḥammad walad `Abd al-Ḥamīd
Arbāb Ibrāhīm walad Walad Nūnū
Arbāb `Ammār, his brother
Aḥmad, his brother
Arbāb Sālim walad al-Ghanāmī, kinsman by marriage of the king
Arbāb Muḥammad Bitt al-Quwayḍī, his paternal uncle
Arbāb Ḥabīb walad Hanbū, a friend of the king
Arbāb Muḥammad al-Kūfī, likewise a friend of the king
Arbāb `Abd al-Karīm Ka`ik al-Unsābī
Arbāb Yūsuf walad Abbakr walad Aḥmad `Alwān
Arbāb `Abd al-Karīm, son of the physician `Abd al-Salām al-Maghribī
Arbāb `Alī Raḍwān
Arbāb Aḥmad al-Shōbarī walad al-Faqīh Balūl Ḥamīran
Sharīf Sālim walad al-Sayyid Ja`far al-`Alawī
Sharīf Aḥmad walad al-Mikḥal
Faqīh `Uthmān

Ḥājj Ibrāhīm walad Nāṣir, the king's tailor
Arbāb Muḥammad walad al-Faqīh Ḥasan al-Ṭaḥūnī
Faqīh Tāj al-Dīn walad `Abd al-Rāziq, a freedman of the king
Faqīh Muḥammad
al-Bashīr, likewise a freedman of the king
Faqīh Muḥammad walad Abu'l-Ḥasan walad Tōr al-Matn
Faqīh Muḥammad al-Nūr walad Ṣabr
Faqīh Madanī Turbās walad Muḥammad walad Madanī
Faqīh Muḥammad al-Ṣāfī walad al-Nūr walad Musayghira
Faqīh Bilayl walad `Ammār walad Abu'l-Naqā

The writer of the letters is the *faqīr* of God Most High, and most in need of Him, Ibrāhīm Ya`qūb `Abd al-Rāziq Ḥamīran. He is a witness to that, and with God, two witnesses suffice. That was written on the morning of Wednesday, the fifteenth of God's holy month of Dhu'l-Qa`da, from the months of the year 1175, one thousand one hundred seventy-five from the *hijra* of the prophet, upon whose master the best of prayers and peace.

[1]For a previously published version see Abū Salīm, *al-Fūnj wa'l-arḍ*, pp. 104-107.

[2]Spaulding, *Heroic Age*, pp. 214-218; 315-317.

[3]Ibid., pp. 231-233.

[4]See Docs. 14, 18, 25, 52, 53, 54, 55, 56, 60, 61.

[5]In support of this interpretation, one may note that disputes over the western border (Docs. 60, 61) involved the west-bank *makk* of the Jamū`īya as the neighbors' overlord.

[6]Anders Björkelo, "From King to Kāshif: Shendī in the Nineteenth Century," Ph.D Diss., University of Bergen, 1983, pp. 102-103.

[7]Probably to be translated here as "edge, dividing higher land from lower." The term *qayf* is more commonly used to designate the edge between the *jarf* and the *qurayr*; see Björkelo, "King to Kāshif," pp. 102-103.

[8]Spaulding, "Nubian Kingship," p. 17.

[9]Ibid., pp. 17-18.

[10]Note the role of `Awāḍa (or `Awūḍa) walad Ibrāhīm walad Ḥarīḥīr in Docs. 60, 61.

[11]For the early career of Muḥammad al-Amīn see Spaulding, *Heroic Age*, pp. 331-333.

[12]The "document of King Bādī" may refer to Doc. 12, where no boundaries are given, or, perhaps more probably, to another grant by Sultan Bādī to the Khōjalāb.

[13]Two impressions of the seal appear here. For a discussion see Abū Salīm, *al-Khatm*, p. 70.

[14]Missing from the original.

[15]Janet Ewald describes the *danga* of the *makk* of Taqalī as "A large, square building at the center of the royal hawsh [*ḥōsh*, "court complex," "royal compound"] where the makk held audience and heard legal cases" ("Leadership and Social Change," Vol. 2, p. 334). The term *danga* was in common use throughout the northern Sudan and probably does not, as she suggests, derive from the languages of Taqalī or Tagoi. In the Nile valley the term *danga* was normally applied to the parts of a packed-earth palace complex that had more than one story; the *danga* was the tower of a Funj castle.

DOCUMENT 15

Document 15 is a confirming charter issued by Sultan Nāṣir b. Bādī to Faqīh Muḥammad walad Dafʿ Allāh in the month of Ṣafar 1177/11 August - 8 September 1763. The text has been taken by the editors from the original.[1] The latter is in fragments; the top lines containing most of the *invocatio* are missing, and a segment containing about five lines of the opening protocols and the beginning of the body is also lacking. Damage to the right margin has removed part of the names and titles of several witnesses. The estate granted was probably located in the northern province, since the original donation was made by the Shaykh of Qarrī, and it probably consisted of a riverbank landholding because two boundaries sufficed to identify it for survey purposes. The beneficiary was a member of the prominent *fuqarā'* family the `Arakiyīn, and it is likely that the land granted lay along the Blue Nile in the vicinity of Abū Ḥarāz, possibly on the eastern bank.

(باسمك يا كريم بسم الله الرحمن الرحيم الحمد لله الذى ايد الشريعه المحمديه
بالادلة القرءانية و القواطع الحكمية المنزلة على خير البرية صلى الله عليه و سلم)[2]
الحمد لله الذى بلغ الرسول و نحن امنا بما يقول

الواثق بالله و الرسول السلطان
ناصر بن السلطان بادى
ابن السلطان نول ١١٧٥[3]

حجة سلطانية و وثيقة ملوكية بمدينة سنار المحروسة المحمية / اجلها الله تعالى لدا
متوليها الذى ايده الله بالنصر و التمكين و الرفع و التحصين / و جعله ظلا ظليلا ياوى

اليه كل مسكين الذى هو فى الدنيا سعيد و فى الاخرة ان شاء الله / شهيد (و من انطوى باطنه على الصفا و ظاهره على الصدق و الوفا الصادق فى قوله / الامين فى فعله الذى اذا قال صدق و اذا تكلم بالحق نطق مولانا / السلطان بن السلطان السلطان ناصر بن السلطان بادى بن المرحوم السلطان نول نصره الله الرحمن الرحيم / بجاه القرءان العظيم و النبى الكريم امين امين يا رب العالمين الى حضرت كل / من تقف عليه هذه الوثيقة و الناظر لما فيها من الحقيقة و بعد فان السلطان المبرور)[4] المويد المنصور السلطان بادى تمم و امضا ما فعله عبده الشيخ محمد الامين / ولد مسمار بصدقة كرومه ولد المعاك الليله الفادنية و هى معلومة / البقعة و الحدود فحدها من جهة الصعيد دار ام (. . .)[5] و من جهة السافل / دار ام (. . .)[5] هذا لوجه الله تعالى و طلبا للثواب فى دار الماب / و ليوم لا ينفع فيه مال الا من اتى الله بقلب سليم و صارت الدار المذكورة / بحدودها (المعلومة ملكا للفقيه محمد ولد دفع الله و لذريته و ذرية ذريته الى ان يرث الله الارض و من عليها)[6] و هو خير الوارثين لا ينازعه فيها منازع و لا يتعرض له فيها متعرض سالمه / مسلمه من جميع السبل و المضار لا عليها جساره و لا خساره و لا نزول / و لا دم و لا حسب و لا (علوق و لا كليقه)[2] و لا عاده و لا عانه و لا قل و لا جل و لا شىء / من السبل العاديه (و نوكد)[2] عليكم يا جميع الشيوخ و القاديم و الجراى الذين / من تحتهم الى حد ملكى خصوصا كرومه ولد المعاك و جرايه و من اتى بعده / الى قيام الساعة (لا احدا)[2] منكم يتعرض للفقيه محمد ولد دفع الله و لا لذريته و لا لذرية / ذريته فى صدقة هذه الدار و من تعرض لها بعد كلامى و وثيقتى هذه فقد / عرض نفسه للهلاك فالحذر ثم الحذر من المخالفه و المخالف لا يلوم الا نفسه

حضر ذلك و شهد به

الشيخ محمد ابو لكيلك ولد بادى وزير الملك
و الشيخ حسب الله ولد يونس /
و الجندى هارون ولد يونس جندى السوق
و الشيخ عزوزه شيخ حوش ناصر خال الملك
و الشيخ / محمد الامين ولد مسمار ولد عجيب شيخ قرى
و الشيخ (ارداب)[7] ولد بدر شيخ اليس
و الشيخ / عبد الله ولد عوض شيخ (التاكة)[2]
و الشيخ على ولد حسن شيخ اتبره

و الشيخ عبد العطى ولد / الشيخ محمد قيلى شيخ (بيله)[2]
و الشيخ بلول ولد بادى ولد كابرشيخ القربين
و الشيخ / عدلان ولد صباحى (شيخ)[2] البحر
و الشيخ على كرار ولد عمر شيخ كردفال
و الشيخ محمد ولد (محمود)[2] شيخ القواريه
و الشيخ شنبول ولد نوه شيخ اربجى
و الشيخ ادريس ولد // ابو فديره مقدم ابو سنون
و (. . .)[5]
و الشيخ / ادريس ولد نايل مقدم السواكره /
و السلطان بدر ولد السلطان خميس سلطان / المسبعات
و السلطان محمد القمراوى (سلطان قمر)[2] /
و الشيخ عبد القادر ولد (كننه)[2] ولد حمدين /
و الشيخ فضل الله ولد شمردل مقدم العده /
و الملك (عدلان)[2] ملك برساج
و الشيخ (بادى شيخ)[2] السجاده /
و القاضى محمد ولد (عبد الحميد)[2] /
و النايب سعودى ولد خيارى
و الفقيه (محمد)[7] / ولد اودقوا الموذن
و الشريف سالم ولد السيد / جعفر العلوى
و الشريف احمد ولد المكحل
و الارباب / سالم ولد احمد ولد ابو (الغنامى)[2] نسيب الملك
و الارباب / (. . .)[5]
و الارباب محمد الكوفى ولد (. . .)[5] رفيق الملك /
و الارباب حبيب ولد (هنبو)[2] رفيق الملك ايضا
و الارباب حسين ولد العوين رفيق الملك ايضا
(. . .)[5] ولد حجازى /
و الارباب (. . .)[5]
و الارباب الصافى ولد بدر رفيق الملك ايضا
(و الارباب عبد الكريم كعيك)[2] الاونسابى
و محمد / عبد السلام المغربى
و الارباب طه (. . .)[5] خياط الملك

و الفقيه (. . .)[5] /
و الفقيه بلول حميرا
و الفقيه محمد ولد بشير معتوق الملك
و الفقيه (. . .)[5]
و الحاج عبد (الرحمن)[8] ولد ابو زيد ولد الشيخ ادريس ولد (الارباب)[9]
و الحاج (مدنى)[2] ولد محمد ولد مدنى
و الفقيه محمد الصافى
و الفقيه بليل ولد عمار (ولد ابو النقا)[2]

و مسطر الحروف فقير الله ابراهيم يعقوب عبد الرازق محمد (كاتب و شاهد و كفا
بالله)[9] شهيدا تحرير ذلك ظهر الا (. . .)[5] صفر من شهور سنة ماية و سبعة
(و سبعين بعد الالف . . .)[9]

[In Thy name, O Generous One. In the name of God, the Merciful, the Compassionate. Praise be to God, Who has confirmed the Muḥammadan law with Qur'ānic proofs and definitive judgments that descended upon the best of creation.] Praise be to God, Who sent the messenger. We believe in what he says.

He who trusts in God and the messenger
Sultan Nāṣir, the son of Sultan Bādī
The son of Sultan Nōl 1175/1761-1762

A sultanic charter and royal document [issued] in the divinely guarded and protected city of Sinnār, may God Most High exalt her, in the presence of her warden, whom God has supported, aided, invested, elevated, and strengthened, and made a protecting shelter with whom every subject may seek refuge. He is happy in this world and, if God wills, in the next will be a martyr. [His interior is purity, his exterior truth and fidelity. Truthful in word and trustworthy in deed, when he speaks he speaks the truth, and when he speaks the truth he has ordained, our lord the sultan, the son of the sultan, Sultan Nāṣir, the son of Sultan Bādī, the son of the late Sultan Nōl. May God, the Merciful, the Compassionate, grant him victory through the influence of the sublime Qur'ān and the eminent prophet. Amen, amen, O Lord of the Universe.

To the presence of all who read this document and see the truth therein.

Thereafter: The pious], divinely assisted and victorious Sultan Nāṣir confirmed and ratified what his slave Shaykh Muḥammad al-Amīn walad Mismār did concerning Karōma walad al-Ma`āk's gift of alms, al-Fādanīya. Its location and boundaries are known. Its boundary on the southern side is the estate of Umm [. . .] and on the northern side the estate of Umm [. . .]. This is for the sake of God Most High, asking for reward in the life to come, for a day in which wealth does not suffice, unless one comes to God with a secure heart. The said estate, its boundaries [known, has become the property of Faqīh Muḥammad walad Daf` Allāh, his descendants and his descendants' descendants, until God inherits the earth and those upon it], and He is the Best of Heirs. Let no challenger challenge him concerning it. Let no troublemaker trouble him concerning it. It is completely free from all *subul* and *maḍārr*. It is not subject to *jusāra*, *khusāra*, *nuzūl*, *damm*, *ḥasab*, [*`ulūq*, *kalīqa*], *`āda*, *`āna*, *qill*, *jill*, nor any of the customary *subul*. [We command] you [peremptorily], all you shaykhs and *muqaddam*s, and the *jarāī* who are under them throughout my kingdom, especially Karōma walad al-Ma`āk and his *jarāī*, and whoever may come after him until the hour of resurrection, let [no one] of you trouble Faqīh Muḥammad walad Daf` Allāh, his descendants or his descendants' descendants concerning the gift of alms of this estate. He who troubles it after my words and this my document has exposed himself to destruction. Beware, then beware of disobedience, and let the disobedient blame none but himself.

There were present and witnessed to it:

Shaykh Muḥammad Abū Likaylik walad Bādī, the *wazīr* of the king
Shaykh Ḥasab Allāh walad Yūnus
the *jundī*, Hārūn walad Yūnus, *jundī* of the market
Shaykh `Azūza, shaykh of the compound of Nāṣir, maternal uncle of the king
Shaykh Muḥammad al-Amīn walad Mismār walad `Ajīb, Shaykh of Qarrī
Shaykh [Irdāb] walad Badr, Shaykh of Alays
Shaykh `Abd Allāh walad `Awaḍ, Shaykh of [al-Tāka]
Shaykh `Alī walad Ḥasan, Shaykh of Atbara
Shaykh `Abd al-`Aṭā walad al-Shaykh Muḥammad Qaylī, Shaykh of [Bayla]
Shaykh Balūl walad Bādī walad Kābir, Shaykh of al-Qarbīn
Shaykh `Adlān walad Ṣubāḥī, [Shaykh] of al-Baḥr
Shaykh `Alī Karrār walad `Umar, Shaykh of Kordofāl
Shaykh Muḥammad walad [Maḥmūd], *shaykh al-quwwārīya*
Shaykh Shanbūl walad Nūh, Shaykh of Arbajī
Shaykh Idrīs walad Abū Fudayra, *muqaddam* of Abū Sunūn
[. . .]
Shaykh Idrīs walad Nāyil, *muqaddam al-sawākira*
Sultan Badr walad al-Sultan Khamīs, Sultan al-Musabba`āt
Sultan Muḥammad al-Qimrāwī, [Sultan of Qimr]
Shaykh `Abd al-Qādir walad [Kananna] walad Ḥammadayn
Shaykh Faḍl Allāh walad Shamradal,[10] *muqaddam al-`udda*
Malik [`Adlān], *malik bursāj*
Shaykh [Bādī, *shaykh*] *al-sajjāda*
the *qāḍī*, Muḥammad walad [`Abd al-Ḥamīd]
the *nāyib*, Su`ūdī walad Khayyārī
Faqīh [Muḥammad] walad Ūdqū, the muezzin
Sharīf Sālim walad al-Sayyid Ja`far al-`Alawī
Sharīf Aḥmad walad al-Mikḥal
Arbāb Sālim walad Aḥmad walad Abu'l-[Ghanāmī], kinsman by marriage of the king
Arbāb [. . .]

Arbāb Muḥammad al-Kūfī walad [. . .], a friend of the king
Arbāb Ḥabīb walad [Hanbū], likewise a friend of the king
[. . .] walad Ḥijāzī
Arbāb [. . .]
Arbāb al-Ṣāfī walad Badr, likewise a friend of the king
[Arbāb `Abd al-Karīm Ka`ik] al-Ūnsābī
Muḥammad `Abd al-Salām al-Maghribī
Arbāb Ṭaha [. . .], the king's tailor
Faqīh [. . .]
Faqīh Balūl Ḥamīran
Faqīh Muḥammad walad Bashīr, freedman of the king
Faqīh [. . .]
Ḥājj `Abd [al-Raḥmān][8] walad Abū Zayd walad al-Shaykh Idrīs walad al-Arbāb
Ḥājj [Madanī] walad Muḥammad walad Madanī
Faqīh Muḥammad al-Ṣāfī
Faqīh Bilayl walad `Ammār [walad Abu'l-Naqā]

The writer of the letters is the *faqīr* of God Ibrāhīm Ya`qūb `Abd al-Rāziq Muḥammad, [scribe and witness. With God], two witnesses [suffice]. That was written at noon on the [. . .] of Ṣafar from the months of the year [one thousand] one hundred [seventy-] seven [. . .]

[1]For a previously published version see Abū Salīm, *al-Fūnj wa'l-arḍ*, pp. 85-87.

[2]Lacuna. A conjectural reading of the missing text has been taken from Doc. 14.

[3]Abū Salīm, *al-Khatm*, p. 70.

[4]Lacuna. A conjectural reading of the missing text has been taken from Docs. 9 and 14.

[5]Lacuna.

[6]Lacuna; for the restored text see Abū Salīm, *al-Fūnj wa'l-arḍ*, p. 86, note 1.

[7]Lacuna. A conjectural reading of the missing text has been taken from Doc. 16.

[8]For `Abd al-Raḥmān see Spaulding, *Heroic Age*, p. 364 and note 62.

[9]Lacuna. A conjectural reading of the missing text has been restored by the editors.

[10]Compare Shabradal, Doc. 14.

DOCUMENT 16

Document 16 is a nullifying charter issued by Sultan Nāṣir for the Awlād al-Shaykh Khōjalī on 7 Jumāda I 1179/22 October 1765 against al-Jallī walad Walad Umm Maryūm. The text has been taken by the editors from a copy written down in 1910 during the course of the land registration program of the Condominium government; only the latter portion of the copy survives.[1] The document introduces the theme of rivalry for preeminence among the community of Maḥas settlers near the Nile confluence on the part of several families of *fuqarā'*. The senior among these aspirants was Faqīh Arbāb al-`Aqāyid (died 1102/1690-1691); his family built up landholdings between the rivers in what is now Khartoum (Doc. 24).[2] The present document concerns a dispute between the descendants of two of the most illustrious of Faqīh Arbāb's legendary 1,000 students, the families of Shaykh Khōjalī (died 1742) and of Shaykh Ḥammad b. Muḥammad (1055/1645-1646 to 1142/1729-1730), known as Umm Maryūm.[3] The present charter concerns the estate, in modern Khartoum North, containing the tomb of Shaykh Khōjalī; it is the property granted to Shaykh Khōjalī's son `Abd al-Raḥmān by Sultan Bādī IV in 1753 according to the terms of Doc. 12. On the strength of evidence internal to the present document, it would seem that when the Hamaj coup of 1762 brought Sultan Nāṣir to the throne, he may have found the Khōjalāb insufficiently supportive toward the new regime. One is told that he issued a written certificate transferring some or all of the Khōjalāb estate to the incumbant leader of the rival *fuqarā'* family of Shaykh Ḥammad, al-Jallī walad [Muḥammad][4] walad Ḥammad Umm Maryūm. At stake, one may infer, was the political allegiance of the wider Maḥas community. Through the issue of the present charter in 1765 Nāṣir reversed himself, and restored the grant on its original terms to the Awlād al-Shaykh

Khōjalī. The Awlād Umm Maryūm persisted, however, and within the next year or two the Khōjalāb presented a new complaint against them to Sultan Nāṣir (Doc. 47). On this occasion, however, the king ordered the case to be ajudicated locally by the *qāḍī* of Qarrī, who in 1767 ruled in favor of the Khōjalāb (Doc. 46).

(. . .)[5] قبر الشيخ خوجلى و هى معلومه (البقعة)[6] و الحدود فحدها من جهة
السافل الزروقاب و من جهة الصعيد / الحاج عالم و قبة الفقيه حمد ولد ام مريوم و
سادر الى فوق بالدرب الطالع الى الضنيقيله و درب الجمل و من جهة الغرب البحر / و
من جهة الصبح درب الجمل المعتاد و قال السلطان ناصر كل ما كتبته انا سابقا للجلى
من هذه الدار دار اولاد الشيخ / خوجلى و جملة جماعة المحس كل ذلك انا ابطلته و
حلة الشيخ خوجلى المدفون هو فيها حكمها عند اولاده حكم العاده / و الشريعة لا على
مقدم فيها حكم و لا قاضى و لا عسكر و صارت الدار المذكورة بحدودها المعلومة صدقة
/ و ملكا لاولاد الشيخ خوجلى و لذريتهم و ذرية ذريتهم يتوارثونها من وارث الى وارث
حتى يرث الله الارض / و من عليها و هو خير الوارثين لا ينازعهم فى صدقة هذه الدار
منازع و لا يتعرض لهم فيها متعرض سالمة مسلمة / من جميع الشرور و السبل و المضار
لا عليها جسارة و لا خساره و لا نار التنباك (تتغرب)[6] فيها و لا عليها نزول / و لا
عليها شى من السبل العاديه و نوكد عليكم يا جميع الشيوخ و المقاديم و الجراى الذين
من تحتهم الى حد ملكى / كله خصوصا الشيخ محمد الامين ولد مسمار و جملة شيوخ
قرى انتم و جرايكم الجميع و من ياتون بعدكم الى قيام الساعة / لا احدا منكم
يتعرض لاولاد الشيخ خوجلى فى صدقة هذه الدار و لا فى حكمها و لا احدا منكم
يتعرض لذريتهم و لا لذرية ذريتهم / فى صدقة هذه الدار و من تعرض لهم بعد كلامى
و وثيقتى هذه فقد عرض نفسه للهلاك الحذر ثم الحذر من المخالفة / و المخالف لا يلوم
الا نفسه /

حضر ذالك و شهد به

الشيخ حسب الله ولد يونس
و الجندى هارون ولد يونس جندى السوق
و الشيخ محمد ابو لكيلك ولد بادى وزير الملك
و الشيخ عزوزه شيخ حوش ناصر خال الملك /
و الشيخ محمد الامين ولد مسمار ولد عجيب شيخ قرى

و الشيخ ارداب ولد بدر شيخ اليس
و الشيخ عبد الله ولد عوض شيخ التاكة
و الشيخ على ولد حسن شيخ اتبرة
و الشيخ عبد العاطى ابن الشيخ محمد قيلى شيخ بيله /
و الشيخ عمر بن الشيخ قاسم شيخ القربين
و الشيخ عدلان ولد صباحى شيخ البحر
و الشيخ النور بن الشيخ عمر شيخ كردفال
و الشيخ محمد ولد محمود شيخ القوارية
و الشيخ شنبول ولد نوه شيخ اربجى /
و الشيخ نايل بن الشيخ ادريس ولد نايل مقدم السواكره
و السلطان بدر ولد السلطان خميس سلطان فور المسبعاتى
و الشيخ حماد ولد دوكه مقدم العده
و الشيخ الضو ولد الفالح مقدم بيت الهدوم
و الشيخ عبد القادر ولد كننه ولد حمدين
و الملك عدلان ملك برساج
و الشيخ بادى مقدم السجاده
و الخطيب عبد السلام ابن الخطيب عبد اللطيف
و الخطيب سعودى ولد خيارى
و الموذن الفقيه محمد ولد اودقوا
و الشريف سالم ولد السيد جعفر العلوى /
و الشريف احمد ولد المكحل
و الارباب محمد الكوفى رفيق الملك
و الارباب حبيب ولد هنبو رفيق الملك
و الارباب حسين ولد العونى رفيق الملك ايضا
و الارباب الصافى ولد بر رفيق الملك ايضا /
و الارباب عبد القادر الحكيم حكيم الملك
و الشريف عبد الله ولد السيد (الشوبرى)[7]
و الارباب احمد (السريرى)[6] ولد (. . .)[8]
و الفقيه عثمان الكبواوى
و الحاج عوض الدنقلاوى
و الشريف (ضياب)[7] ولد على //
و الارباب يوسف ولد ابكر ولد احمد ولد علوان

و الحاج عبد الكريم كعيك الاونسابى
و الحاج عبد الرسول ولد ابو جلال
و الحاج عبد الله ولد امنه بنت بليله الاونسابي
و الحاج ابراهيم ولد نصر الخياط خياط الملك
و الفقيه سليمان ولد قسومه
و الفقيه محمد ولد دفع الله ابن الشيخ محمد ولد الطريفى
و الفقيه حجازى ولد ابو زيد ولد الشيخ ادريس ولد الارباب
و الفقيه تاج الدين ولد عبد الرازق معتوق الملك
و الفقيه محمد ولد بشير معتوق الملك ايضا
و الفقيه عبد الهادى ولد ولد دوليب
و الفقيه مدنى ترباس ولد محمد ولد مدنى

و مسطر الحروف فقير الله و احوجهم اليه ابراهيم يعقوب عبد الرازق حميرا شاهد بذلك و كفى بالله شهيدا تحرير ذلك ضحوة الاربعا و سبعه ايام خلت من شهر الله جمادى الاول من شهور / سنة ١١٧٩ الف و مايه و تسعه و سبعين من الهجرة النبوية على صاحبها افضل الصلاة و السلام

[. . .] the tomb of Shaykh Khōjalī. Its [location] and boundaries are known. Its boundary on the northern side is al-Zurūqāb, and on the southern side al-Ḥājj `Ālim and the *qubba* of Faqīh Ḥammad walad Umm Maryūm; it extends upward to the path, rising to al-Ḍanīqila and the camel path. On the western side [its boundary is] the river, and on the eastern side the usual camel path. Sultan Nāṣir said: "I have nullified all that I wrote previously for al-Jallī concerning this estate, the estate of the Awlād al-Shaykh Khōjalī and the whole community of Maḥas. The administration of the village in which Shaykh Khōjalī is buried belongs to his sons. It is an administration according to [both] customary and Islamic law; neither *muqaddam*, *qāḍī*, nor soldier has any administrative right over it." The said estate, with its known boundaries, has become a gift of alms and the property of the Awlād al-Shaykh Khōjalī, their descendants and their descendants' descendants. They will bequeath it from heir to heir until God inherits the earth and those upon it, and He is the Best of Heirs. Let no challenger challenge them concerning the gift of alms of this estate. Let no troublemaker trouble them in it. It is completely free from all *shurūr*, *subul*, and *maḍārr*. It is not subject to *jusāra* or *khusāra*; let the fire of tobacco not be lit in it.[9] It is not subject to *nuzūl*, nor to any of the customary *subul*. We command you peremptorily, all you shaykhs and *muqaddams*, and the *jarāī* who are under them throughout my realm, all, especially Shaykh Muḥammad al-Amīn walad Mismār and all the Shaykhs of Qarrī, you and your *jarāī*, and whoever may come after you until the hour of resurrection, let no one of you trouble the Awlād al-Shaykh Khōjalī concerning the gift of alms of this estate, nor in its administration. Let no one of you trouble their descendants nor their descendants' descendants concerning the gift of alms of this estate. He who troubles them after my words and this my document has exposed himself to destruction. Beware, then beware of disobedience, and let the disobedient blame none but himself.

There were present and witnessed to it:

Shaykh Ḥasab Allāh walad Yūnus
the *jundī*, Hārūn walad Yūnus, *jundī* of the market
Shaykh Muḥammad Abū Likaylik walad Bādī, the king's *wazīr*
Shaykh `Azūza, shaykh of the compound of Nāṣir, maternal uncle of the king
Shaykh Muḥammad al-Amīn walad Mismār walad `Ajīb, Shaykh of Qarrī
Shaykh Irdāb walad Badr, Shaykh of Alays
Shaykh `Abd Allāh walad `Awaḍ, Shaykh of al-Tāka
Shaykh `Alī walad Ḥasan, Shaykh of Atbara
Shaykh `Abd al-`Aṭā b. al-Shaykh Muḥammad Qaylī, Shaykh of Bayla
Shaykh `Umar b. al-Shaykh Qāsim, Shaykh of al-Qarbīn
Shaykh `Adlān walad Ṣubāḥī, Shaykh of al-Baḥr
Shaykh al-Nūr b. al-Shaykh `Umar, Shaykh of Kordofāl
Shaykh Muḥammad walad Maḥmūd, *shaykh al-quwwārīya*
Shaykh Shanbūl walad Nūḥ, Shaykh of Arbajī

Shaykh Nāyil b. al-Shaykh Idrīs walad Nāyil, *muqaddam al-sawākira*
Sultan Badr b. al-Sultan Khamīs, Sultan Fūr al-Musabba`ātī
Shaykh Ḥammād walad Dōka, *muqaddam al-`udda*
Shaykh al-Ḍaw walad al-Fāliḥ, *muqaddam* of the wardrobe
Shaykh `Abd al-Qādir walad Kananna walad Ḥammadayn
Malik `Adlān, *malik bursāj*
Shaykh Bādī, *muqaddam al-sajjāda*
the *khaṭīb*, Su`ūdī walad Khayyārī
the muezzin, Faqīh Muḥammad walad Ūdqū
Sharīf Sālim walad al-Sayyid Ja`far al-`Alawī
Sharīf Aḥmad walad al-Mikḥal
Arbāb Muḥammad al-Kūfī, a friend of the king
Arbāb Ḥabīb walad Hanbū, a friend of the king
Arbāb Ḥusayn walad al-`Ūnī, likewise a friend of the king
Arbāb al-Ṣāfī walad Badr, likewise a friend of the king
Arbāb `Abd al-Qādir the physician, the king's physician
Sharīf `Abd Allāh walad al-Sayyid [al-Shōbarī]
Arbāb Aḥmad [al-Sarīrī] walad [. . .]
Faqīh `Uthmān al-Kabawāwī
Ḥājj `Awaḍ al-Dongolāwī
Sharīf [Ḍiyāb] walad `Alī
Arbāb Yūsuf walad Abbakr walad Aḥmad walad `Alwān
Ḥājj `Abd al-Karīm Ka`ik al-Unsābī
Ḥājj `Abd al-Rasūl walad Abū Jallāl
Ḥājj `Abd Allāh walad Āmina bint Balīla al-Unsābī
Ḥājj Ibrāhīm walad Naṣr the tailor, the king's tailor
Faqīh Sulaymān walad Qasūma
Faqīh Muḥammad walad Daf` Allāh b. al-Shaykh Muḥammad walad al-Ṭurayfī
Faqīh Ḥijāzī walad Abū Zayd walad al-Shaykh Idrīs walad al-Arbāb
Faqīh Tāj al-Dīn walad `Abd al-Rāziq, a freedman of the king
Faqīh Muḥammad walad Bashīr, likewise a freedman of the king

Faqīh `Abd al-Hādī walad Walad Dōlīb
Faqīh Madanī Turbās walad Muḥammad walad Madanī

The writer of the letters is the *faqīr* of God and most in need of Him, Ibrāhīm Ya`qūb `Abd al-Rāziq Ḥamīran. He is a witness to that, and with God, two witnesses suffice. That was written on the morning of Wednesday, when seven days had passed of God's month of Jumāda I from the months of the year 1179, one thousand one hundred seventy-nine from the *hijra* of the prophet, upon whose master the best of prayers and peace.

[1]For a previously published version see Abū Salīm, *al-Fūnj wa'l-arḍ*, pp. 96-98.

[2]Arbāb b. `Alī b. `Awn b. `Āmir b. Aṣbaḥ, called "al-Khashin;" *Ṭabaqāt*, pp. 99-100.

[3]*Ṭabaqāt*, pp. 173-181.

[4]Ḥammad Umm Maryūm had three sons, all named Muḥammad.

[5]Approximately the first half of the document is missing.

[6]Lacuna. A conjectural reading of the missing text has been restored by the editors.

[7]Lacuna. A conjectural reading of the missing text has been taken from Doc. 18.

[8]Lacuna.

[9]Conjectural translation.

DOCUMENT 17

Document 17 is a letter from the Hamaj Regent Muḥammad Abū Likaylik to Arbāb Bādī b. al-Shaykh `Abd Allāh. The text was taken by the editors from the original, which is damaged around all the margins; fragments bearing the *invocatio* and the seal have been detached from the rest of the document.[1] The letter is not dated, but may be placed within the regency of Abū Likaylik from 1762 to 1774.[2] It is addressed to a nobleman from the ruling family of Qarrī, and probably a son of the late governor `Abd Allāh b. `Ajīb (Docs. 4, 5, 8, 9, 10). The purpose of the letter was to soothe relations between Arbāb Bādī and the *fuqarā'* of the Awlād Dōlīb, apparently ruffled by the intrusion of a party of the Arbāb's soldiers into their community. Noteworthy is the reference to *muḥallaq*, literally "razor," but which may here refer to *muḥallaqāt*, the small indigenous coinage of eighteenth-century Sinnār.[3]

الحمد لوليه / و الصلاة و السلام / على نبيه /

الواثق بالملك الهادى
الشيخ محمد بن المرحوم
الشيخ بادى ١١٦٠[4]

من حضرت من اعزه الكريم و لا يفارقه ان / شا الله الخير و النعيم الذى هو فى الدنيا سعيد / و فى الاخرة ان شا الله شهيد صادقت القبايل / و مشهور الفضايل الصادق فى قوله الامين / فى فعله الذى اذا قال صدق و اذا تكلم بالحق نطق / الواثق بالملك الهادى الديان الشيخ محمد / ابلكيلك وزير السلطان الى عند الارباب بادى / بن الشيخ عبد الله اما بعد فيسلم عليك الشيخ / محمد جزيل السلام و يقول لك سبب الجواب اليك / من جهت دار ناس الفقه السيد الكريده / الفقيه السيد انت عارفه صاحبه و فى بطن بيته / ذالحين قوم بنفسك و امنع الدليباب منها و ا / نكان

اخذوا فيها فرد محلق اخذه منهم و رده / لى سياده و لا تتهاون بامرهم انا ما بلوم
زول (بعدما)[5] اعلمتك و انذرتك من الخلاف // (. . .)[6] (بامركم على امانت)[7]
/ مكتوب سيدى / الملك بادى الفقه السيد فى زمانه / يزيده ما (. . .) / (. . .)[6]
الله الله / لا احد يعارضهم (و المخالف)[5] لكلامى لا يلومن الا / نفسه و السلام
(. . .)

Praise be to His friend. Prayers and peace upon His prophet.

He who trusts in the King, the Guide
Shaykh Muḥammad, son of the late
Shaykh Bādī 1160/1747-1748

From the presence of him whom the Generous has strengthened, whom He will not distance from goodness and felicity, if God wills, who is happy in this world and, if God wills, in the next will be a martyr, the truthful one among the tribes, who is known for excellence, truthful in word and trustworthy in deed. When he speaks he speaks the truth, and when he speaks the truth he has ordained. He who trusts in the King, the Guide, the Judge, Shaykh Muḥammad Abū Likaylik, *wazīr* of the sultan.

To Arbāb Bādī b. al-Shaykh `Abd Allāh.

Thereafter: Shaykh Muḥammad greets you with many greetings and says to you: The reason for this letter to you is al-Karīda, the estate of the people of Faqīh al-Sayyid. You know Faqīh al-Sayyid and are his friend, but at present you are within his abode with a war party. Warn off the Dōlībāb from it, and if they [the soldiers] have taken a single *muḥallaq*, take it from them and return it to its owner. Do not be inhibited by their orders. I am not blaming anyone. [After] I have informed you and warned you against disobedience [. . .] with your order, according to what was written in good faith by my lord King Bādī.

Faqīh al-Sayyid, in his time, increased [. . .]. God, God, let no one trouble them, and let him who disobeys my word blame none but himself. Farewell.

[1]For a previously published version see Abū Salīm, *al-Fūnj wa'l-arḍ*, p. 67.

[2]Spaulding, *Heroic Age*, pp. 305-325.

[3]Ibid., pp. 146-147.

[4]Abū Salīm, *al-Khatm*, p. 67.

[5]Inserted by the editors; see Abū Salīm, *al-Fūnj wa'l-arḍ*, p. 67.

[6]Lacuna.

[7]This passage is difficult to read.

DOCUMENT 18

Document 18 is a confirming charter issued by Sultan Ismā`īl b. Bādī to the Awlād al-Shaykh Khōjalī on 11 Rabī` I 1184/5 July 1770. The text has been taken by the editors from the original, which is intact and easily legible.[1] The charter confirms the rights of the Khōjalāb to Jundīya Island (Doc. 14). The witness roster reflects the situation at court following the killing of Bādī IV on his return from exile and the collapse of Sultan Nāṣir's unsuccessful revolt against the Hamaj that soon followed. The regicide `Alī walad Ḥasan had been replaced as Shaykh of Atbara, Muḥammad al-Amīn had been deposed as Shaykh of Qarrī, and the new, distinctively Hamaj office of "shaykh of the compound of the king's son" had been introduced.[2]

باسمك يا كريم بسم الله الرحمن الرحيم نستفتح باسمه العظيم و نتوكل عليه فى جميع الامور و لا حول و لا قوة الا بالله العلى العظيم الحمد لله الذى شهدت / بوجوده جميع الكاينات و دلت على وحدانيته عجايب المصنوعات و على اله و صحبه و سلم الحمد لله بفضله عاد الامر لاهله و رجع كل شىء لاصله / الحمد لله الذى ايد الشريعة المحمديه بالادلة القرءانية و القواطع الحكمية المنزلة على خير البرية صلى الله عليه و سلم تسليما كبيرا طيبا مباركا رب العالمين / الحمد لله الذى بلغ الرسول و نحن امنا بما يقول

الواثق بالملك الهادى
السلطان اسماعيل بن
السلطان بادى ١١٨٢ [3]

حجة سلطانية و وثيقة ملوكية بمدينة سنار المحروسة المحمية اجلها الله لدا متوليها سلطان / الاسلام جامع كلمة الايمان و مدمر اهل البغى و الطغيان سيف الله القاطع و سهامه اللامع ناشر لواء العدل فى العالمين ناصر شريعة / سيد المرسلين احق من ملك

تحت الخلافة باستحقاق و اولى من ولا الولاية فى الافاق و هو الذى وجد عنان العناية لحماية الاسلام / بشهادة الاجماع و تلك شهادة لا يتطرق اليها النزاع و جددت بنيان الهداية بعد ما اندرست ءاثارته و طمست معالمه / و مهد بساط العدل بعد ان لم يوجد الا مظلوم و ظالمه ذو المفاخر الذى شهد بفضلها الخاص و العام و المئاثر التى ترتفع على / الثريا و تكثر الغمام و الاخلاق التى رام النسيم ان يحاكى لطفها فاصبح عليلا و المعالى التى تمنت الملوك ان يتشبهوا بها فلم يجدوا / الى ذالك سبيلا سلطان المسلمين و خليفة رب العالمين القايم بامور الدنيا و الدين المنتصب لمصالح المسلمين من اصلح / الله به العباد و انار به البلاد و رحمت الله و سبحانه و تعالى للحاضر و الباد مولانا و اولانا و اغلانا و ناصرنا و معيننا على اعدانا / الواثق بالملك الهادى السلطان بن السلطان السلطان المظفر المعان السلطان اسماعيل بن المرحوم السلطان بادى / نصره الله الرحمن الرحيم بجاه القرءان العظيم و النبى الكريم ءامين ءامين يا رب العالمين الى حضرت كل من تقف عليه هذه / الوثيقة و الناظرلما فيها من الحقيقة و بعد فان السلطان المحفوظ المبرور المويد المنصور السلطان اسماعيل / تمم و امضا ما فعله سابقا السلطان بادى ابيه و السلطان ناصر اخيه من الصدقة التى تصدقوا بها على الشيخ خوجلى من الجزيره / الجنديه و ما احتوت عليه من رفيده و القطعيه و هى محدده من الاركان الاربعه صعيدا و سافلا و شرقا / و غربا فاما حدها من جهة الصعيد الفى الشرق سدرت التويراب و من الغرب السياله الكبيرة المقابلة قرن الجبل الازرق / و من جهة السافل الفاصل البين المحمداب و النوفلاب و يخرج هذا الفاصل و يركز فوق ‹ كرس ›[4] الدليباب و حدها / من جهة الشرق كرس الدليباب ايضا فحدها من جهة الغرب كرس المحمداب الذى فصله السلطان نول لى بادى ولد سرير / ثم فى ءاخر ملك السلطان بادى ناس الشرق نازعوا اولاد الشيخ خوجلى فى المرن الشرقى و اشتكوا اولاد الشيخ خوجلى السلطان بادى /[5] و ارسل السلطان بادى مراسيله معاهم و هم محمد الفقير ولد عمران و البدوى ولد عم الجندى تكتك و الشيخ محمد الامين بن الشيخ مسمار / ارسل معهم الارباب بدوى ولد عمه و قدموا مراسيل السلطان بادى و مرسال ولد عجيب و حضروا من ناس البلد جمع كثير و الحراث الكبار / العارفين الحدود وقفوا فى منجر فوق كرس الدليباب عند الفاصل و اخرجوا المرن بين الكرس و القرير الى جهة الصعيد / علموه بحجاره و فى دار ولد المشاطه مرقوا المرن فوق الحرازه و اوسموها و اخرجوه فوق حد الكرس الى سدرت التويراب / و انقطعوا ناس منجر و ناس عبد القادر دلد حماد و ناس ولد نعمه و المحمداب الجميع انقطعوا من اولاد الشيخ خوجلى و حسبوا مراسيل / السلطان بادى بحضرت الجميع الكثير على ان من يدخل فى هذا الحد شرقا و غربا شبرا واحدا عليه حسب الملك و فوقه الف للملك / و مرسل ولد عجيب كذلك قال اليدخل فى هذا الحد شبرا واحد يقع عليه الحسب

و فوقه الف قرش ثم لما تولى ابنه السلطان ناصر قدموا الى عنده اولاد الشيخ خوجلى و باركوا له فى الدار و طلبوا منه ان يتمم لهم صدقت ابيه السلطان بادى و الحال ان اولاد / ولد سرير و جرايهم اولاد رحمه حضروا و نازعوا اولاد الشيخ خوجلى فى جزيره ولد حريحير و السلطان ناصر مرق لهم الشيخ / محمد ابو لكيلك و الشيخ محمد الامين ولد مسمار و قعدوا الجميع فى الدانقه و قروا ورقت الملك بادى بحضرت اولاد ولد سرير و جرايهم / و تبينت الجزيرة ولد حريحير فى بطن الحدود الاربعه ليست الجزيره هذه خارجه من الحدود الاربعه و انقطعوا اولاد / سرير و جرايهم و اولاد رحمه من جميع الدار ولد حريحير و غيرها لا طالب و لا مطلوب ثم ان السلطان اسماعيل بعد / ما نظر فى حكم هذه الوثيقه تمم و امضا ذلك لاولاد الشيخ خوجلى صدقت هذه الجزيرة و اقرها على حدودها / الاربعه المذكوره الذى حصل فيه النزاع و الذى لم يحصل فيه النزاع كلها مقابلها اولاد الشيخ خوجلى و هذا كله فعله / السلطان اسماعيل ابتغاء لوجه الله تعالى و طلبا للثواب فى دار المئاب و ليوم لا ينفع فيه مال و لا بنون الا من اتى / الله بقلب سليم و صارت جملة هذه الجزيره المذكوره صدقة و ملكا لاولاد الشيخ خوجلى لهم و لذريتهم و ذرية / ذريتهم يتوارثونها من وارث الى وارث حتى يرث الله الارض و من عليها و هو خير الوارثين لا ينازعهم فى صدقت / هذه الجزيره منازع و لا يتعرض لهم فيها متعرض سالمة مسلمة من جميع الشرور و السبل و المضار لا عليها هذه الجزيرة / جسارة و لا خسارة و لا نزول فيها و لا ضيافه و لا علوق و لا كليقه و لا عانه و لا عاده و لا قل و لا جل و لا شىء من السبل / العاديه و نوكد عليكم يا جميع الشيوخ و المقاديم و الجراى الذين من تحتهم الى حد ملكى كله خصوصا اولاد بادى / ولد سرير و جرايهم اولاد رحمه و من ياتى بعدهم الى قيام الساعه لا احدا منكم يتعرض لاولاد الشيخ خوجلى فى هذه الصدقة / و لا احدا منكم يتعرض لذريتهم و لا لذرية ذريتهم فى صدقت هذه الجزيره المذكوره و من تعرض لهم بعد كلامى و وثيقتى / هذه فقد عرض نفسه للهلاك و الحذر ثم الحذر من المخالفة و المخالف لا يلوم الا نفسه

حضر ذالك و شهد به

الشيخ / هارون ولد يونس
و الجندى شوال اخيه جندى السوق
و الشيخ محمد ابو لكيلك ولد بادى وزير الملك
و الشيخ جمعه ولد الشيخ عزوزه / شيخ حوش ناصر خال الملك
و الشيخ سبت ولد بدر شيخ اليس

و الشيخ عجيب ولد عبد الله شيخ قرى
و الشيخ عبد الله ولد عوض / شيخ التاكة
و الشيخ الفضيل ولد مسمار ولد حسن شيخ اتبره
و الشيخ عبد العاطى بن الشيخ محمد قيلى شيخ بيله
و الشيخ عمر بن الشيخ قاسم / شيخ القربين
و الشيخ عدلان ولد صباحى ولد صقر شيخ البحر
و الشيخ ادريس ابن الشيخ على كرار ولد عمر شيخ كردفال //
و الشيخ محمد ولد خضر ولد نايل شيخ حوش ولد الملك
و الوكيل بحر / ولد السلطان خميس سلطان فور المسبعاتى
و وكيل الدار / بادى ولد قدا
و الشيخ احمد ولد محمود شيخ القواريه /
و الشيخ شنبول ولد ولد نوه شيخ اربجى
و المنكروكنا / يحيا شيخ قواويد الملك
و الشيخ عبد القادر ولد كننه / ولد حمدين
و الملك عدلان ملك برساج
و الشيخ بادى / مقدم السجاده
و الشيخ حجر بن الشيخ الزين ولد حجر / اليعقبابى
و القاضى و الخطيب الشريف عبد العزيز / المغربى
و الموذن الفقيه محمد ولد اودقوا
و الشريف / سالم ولد السيد جعفر العلوى
و الشريف ضياب ولد على /
و الشريف عبد الله ولد السيد الشوبرى رجل الحمرا /
و الشريف احمد ولد المكحل
و الارباب سالم ولد / الغنامى نسيب الملك بادى
و الارباب محمد ولد على / رضوان نسيب الملك بادى ايضا
و الارباب عمار ولد / عبد الحفيظ
و الارباب احمد ولد عبد الله ولد حليوه /
و الارباب محمد ولد ابو الحسن المشهور بتور المتن /
و الفقيه حسب الله اخيه
و الارباب يوسف ولد ابكر / ولد احمد ولد علوان
و الفقيه تاج الدين ولد عبد الرازق / معتوق الملك بادى
و الفقيه ابراهيم المغربى / البصلى بالملك اسماعيل

و كاتب الوثيقه / فقيرالله تعالى و احوج عباده اليه ابراهيم / يعقوب عبد الرازق محمد حميرا شاهد بذلك و كفا بالله شهيدا تحرير ذلك ظهر / الاربعا و احدا عشر يوم خلت من شهر الله / ربيع الاول من شهور سنة ١١٨٤ الف و مايه و اربعه و ثمانين من الهجرة / النبوية على صاحبها افضل الصلاة و السلام

In Thy name, O Generous One. In the name of God, the Merciful, the Compassionate. We seek the assistance of His mighty name, and rely upon Him in every matter. There is no power and strength save in God the Exalted and Mighty. Praise be to God, to Whose presence all living beings testify, and Whose unity is indicated by the marvels of man's handiwork. Peace be upon the family and companions of [Muḥammad]. Praise be to God for His excellence. Every affair belongs to its own people, and every thing to its own source. Praise be to God, Who has confirmed the Muḥammadan law with Qur'ānic proofs and definitive judgments that descended upon the best of creation. May God, the Lord of the Universe, bless him and grant him complete, great, good, and blessed peace. Praise be to God, Who sent the messenger. We believe in what he says.

He who trusts in the King, the Guide
Sultan Ismā`īl, the son of
Sultan Bādī 1183/1769-1770

A sultanic charter and royal document [issued] in the divinely guarded and protected city of Sinnār, may God exalt her, in the presence of her warden, the sultan of Islam, who consolidates the authority of the faith and destroys the people of wrongdoing and oppression, the sharp sword of God and His flashing arrows, who spreads the banner of justice throughout the universe, protector of the law of the lord of the messengers, the one most deserving to rule as a Caliph, and foremost among those who rule between the horizons. He it is who has guided the reins of solicitude toward the protection of Islam, according to the testimony of a consensus achieved without dispute, who has renewed the edifice of guidance after its traces had been obliterated and its marks effaced, and who has made even the carpet of justice after [a time in which] one could find only the victim and his oppressor. He possesses glory to whose excellence high and low testify, influence which ascends to the Pleiades and gathers in clouds, a character which the breeze would wish to copy to become mild, and noble traits in the emulation of which kings grow tired and fail to find a way, sultan of the Muslims and Caliph of the Lord of the Universe, steadfast in the affairs of this world and of religion, upright in the affairs of the Muslims, through whom God has prospered the worshipers and illuminated the nations, the mercy of God Most High (praise be to Him) upon the quick and the dead, our lord and leader, our most precious helper and aid against our enemies, he who trusts in the King, the Guide, the sultan, the son of the sultan, the victorious and divinely aided Sultan Ismā`īl, son of the late Sultan Bādī. May God, the Merciful, the Compassionate, grant him victory through the influence of the sublime Qur'ān and the eminent prophet. Amen, amen, O Lord of the Universe.

To the presence of all who read this document and see the truth therein.

Thereafter: The divinely protected, pious, divinely assisted and victorious sultan, Sultan Ismā`īl, has confirmed and ratified what his father Sultan Bādī and his brother Sultan Nāṣir had done previously in regard to the gift of alms which they bestowed upon Shaykh Khōjalī, consisting of the island of al-Jundīya, including Rafīda and al-Qaṭ`īya. It is bounded on the four corners; south, north, east, and west. As for its boundary on the southern side, on the east it is the *sidr* tree of the Tuwayrāb, and on the west the big watercourse across from the peak of Jabal Azraq. On the northern side [its boundary is] the *fāṣil* between the Muḥammadāb and the Nōfalāb; this *fāṣil* goes on and is fixed above the *kurus* of the Dōlībāb. Its boundary on the eastern side is again the *kurus* of the Dōlībāb. Its boundary on the west is the *kurus* of the Muḥammadāb, which Sultan Bādī delineated for Bādī walad Sarīr. Then, late in the reign of Sultan Bādī people of the east disputed with the Awlād al-Shaykh

Khōjalī concerning the eastern *mirin*, and the Awlād al-Shaykh Khōjalī complained to Sultan Bādī. Sultan Bādī sent his messengers with them; they were Muḥammad al-Faqīr walad `Imrān and al-Badawī the son of the paternal uncle of the *jundī* Taktak. Shaykh Muḥammad al-Amīn b. al-Shaykh Mismār sent with them Arbāb Badawī, the son of his paternal uncle. The messengers of Sultan Bādī and the messenger of Walad `Ajīb came. A great multitude of the people of the land were present, and the old cultivators who knew the boundaries. They stood at the *fāṣil* above the *kurus* of the Dōlībāb in Manjar and delineated the *mirin* between the *kurus* and the *qurayr* as far as the southern side, marking it with stones. In Walad al-Mushāṭa they made the *mirin* run above the *ḥarāz* tree, which they marked with a blaze, and they delineated it above the edge of the *kurus* to the *sidr* tree of the Tuwayrāb. The people of Manjar, the people of `Abd al-Qādir walad Ḥammād, the people of Walad Ni`ma, and all the Muḥammadāb have been cut off from the Awlād al-Shaykh Khōjalī. The messengers of Sultan Bādī, in the presence of the great multitude, charged whomsoever might trespass this boundary from east or west by even a single hand's breadth with the king's reckoning, and subjected him to [a fine of] one thousand [*qirsh*] to the king. The messenger of Walad `Ajīb likewise said: "He who trespasses this boundary by even a single hand's breadth falls under the reckoning, and he is subject to [a fine of] one thousand *qirsh*." Then, when his son Sultan Nāṣir succeeded, the Awlād al-Shaykh Khōjalī came before him and blessed him [as the new ruler of] the country. They asked him to confirm for them the gift of alms of his father, Sultan Bādī. The circumstances were that the Awlād Walad Sarīr and their *jarāī* the Awlād Raḥma had presented themselves to dispute with the Awlād al-Shaykh Khōjalī concerning the island of Walad Ḥarīḥīr. Sultan Nāṣir sent to them Shaykh Muḥammad Abū Likaylik and Shaykh Muḥammad al-Amīn walad Mismār. They sat in the *danga* and examined the document of King Bādī in the presence of the Awlād Walad Sarīr and their *jarāī*. It was established that the island of Walad Ḥarīḥīr was within the four boundaries and that no [part of] this island lay outside the four boundaries. The Awlād Sarīr and their *jarāī* the Awlād Raḥma have been cut off from all the estate, Walad Ḥarīḥīr and the rest of it. There is neither a claimant nor a claim. Thereupon Sultan Ismā`īl, after he had examined the ruling of this document, confirmed and ratified that to the Awlād al-Shaykh Khōjalī, [namely], the gift of alms of this island. He confirmed it according to its four said boundaries, [both] those concerning which there had been dispute and those concerning which there had not been [any] dispute, all of it, as an award to the Awlād al-Shaykh Khōjalī. All this Sultan Ismā`īl did for the sake of God Most High, asking for reward in the life to come, for a day in which neither wealth nor sons suffice, unless one comes to God with a secure heart. All this said island has become a gift of alms and property of the Awlād al-Shaykh Khōjalī, for them and their descendants, and their descendants' descendants. They shall bequeath it from heir to heir until God inherits the earth and those upon it, and He is the Best of Heirs. Let no challenger challenge them concerning the gift of alms of this island. Let no troublemaker trouble them in it. It is completely free from all *shurūr*, *subul,* and *maḍārr*. This island is not subject to *jusāra*, *khusāra*, *nuzūl*, *ḍiyāfa*, *`ulūq*, *kalīqa*, *`āna*, *`āda*, *qill*, *jill*, nor any of the customary *subul*. We command you peremptorily, all you shaykhs and *muqaddam*s, and the *jarāī* who are under them throughout my kingdom, all, and especially the Awlād Bādī walad Sarīr and their *jarāī* the Awlād Raḥma, and whoever may come ofter them until the hour of resurrection, let no one of you trouble the Awlād al-Shaykh Khōjalī concerning this gift of alms. Let no one of you trouble their descendants, nor their descendants' descendants, concerning the gift of alms of this said island. He who troubles them after these my words and this my document has exposed himself to destruction. Beware, then beware of disobedience, and let the disobedient blame none but himself.

There were present and witnessed to it:

Shaykh Hārūn walad Yūnus
the *jundī*, Shawwāl his brother, *jundī* of the market

Shaykh Muḥammad Abū Likaylik walad Bādī, the *wazīr* of the king
Shaykh Jum`a walad al-Shaykh `Azūza, shaykh of the compound of Nāṣir, maternal uncle of the king
Shaykh Sabat walad Badr, Shaykh of Alays
Shaykh `Ajīb walad `Abd Allāh, Shaykh of Qarrī
Shaykh `Abd Allāh walad `Awaḍ, Shaykh of al-Tāka
Shaykh al-Faḍīl walad Mismār walad Ḥasan, Shaykh of Atbara
Shaykh `Abd al-`Aṭā b. al-Shaykh Muḥammad Qaylī, Shaykh of Bayla
Shaykh `Umar b. al-Shaykh Qāsim, Shaykh of al-Qarbīn
Shaykh `Adlān walad Ṣubāḥī walad Ṣaqar, Shaykh of al-Baḥr
Shaykh Idrīs b. al-Shaykh `Alī Karrār walad `Umar, Shaykh of Kordofāl
Shaykh Muḥammad walad Khiḍr walad Nāyil, shaykh of the compound of the king's son
the *wakīl* Baḥr, son of Sultan Khamīs, Sultan Fūr al-Musabba`ātī
the *wakīl al-dār* Bādī walad Qudā
Shaykh Aḥmad walad Maḥmūd, *shaykh al-quwwārīya*
Shaykh Shanbūl walad Walad Nūh, Shaykh of Arbajī
Mankrōknā Yaḥyā, shaykh of the king's *qawāwīd*
Shaykh `Abd al-Qādir walad Kananna walad Ḥammadayn
Malik `Adlān, *malik bursāj*
Shaykh Bādī, *muqaddam al-sajjāda*
Shaykh Ḥajar b. al-Shaykh al-Zayn walad Ḥajar al-Ya`qūbābī
the *qāḍī* and *khaṭīb*, Sharīf `Abd al-`Azīz al-Maghribī
the muezzin, Faqīh Muḥammad walad Ūdqū
Sharīf Sālim walad al-Sayyid Ja`far al-`Alawī
Sharīf Ḍiyāb walad `Alī
Sharīf `Abd Allāh walad al-Sayyid al-Shōbarī, "The man of al-Ḥamrā"
Sharīf Aḥmad walad al-Mikḥal
Arbāb Sālim walad al-Ghanāmī, King Bādī's kinsman by marriage
Arbāb Muḥammad walad `Alī Raḍwān, also King Bādī's kinsman by marriage
Arbāb `Ammār walad `Abd al-Ḥafīẓ

Arbāb Aḥmad walad `Abd Allāh walad Ḥilyū
Arbāb Muḥammad walad Abu'l-Ḥasan, known as "Tōr al-Matn"
Faqīh Ḥasab Allāh, his brother
Arbāb Yūsuf walad Abbakr walad Aḥmad walad `Alwān
Faqīh Tāj al-Dīn walad `Abd al-Rāziq, a freedman of King Bādī
Faqīh Ibrāhīm al-Maghribī, who prayed with King Bādī[6]

The writer of the document is the *faqīr* of God Most High, and of all His worshipers most in need of him, Ibrāhīm Ya`qūb `Abd al-Rāziq Muḥammad Ḥamīran. He is a witness to that, and with God, two witnesses suffice. That was written at noon on Wednesday, when eleven days had passed from God's month of Rabī` I from the months of the year 1184, one thousand one hundred eighty-four from the *hijra* of the prophet, upon whose master the best of prayers and peace.

[1]For a previously published version see Abū Salīm, *al-Fūnj wa'l-arḍ*, pp. 111-115.

[2]Spaulding, *Heroic Age*, pp. 317-320.

[3]Two impressions of the seal appear here.

[4]This word is consistently written *kursī* in Doc. 18.

[5]The scribe left a blank line in the original document here, perhaps to accommodate folding it; the text continues unbroken.

[6]A conjectural translation.

DOCUMENT 19

Document 19 is a *laissez-passer* issued by Sultan Ismā`īl b. Bādī to the traveler James Bruce in 1772. An English translation was published by Bruce's biographer Alexander Murray, and this is given here.[1] The sultan explained that Bruce, known as "El Hakim Yagoube," came from Ethiopia ("Habbesh") and wanted to go to Upper Egypt ("Rif"); he should be given what he needed for the journey. The letter is addressed to Ibrāhīm walad Musnad, the first leader of the Jamū`īya to be elevated to the status of *makk*, as part of the Hamaj attempt to cripple the Shaykhs of Qarrī by building up their west-bank rivals.[2] Bruce, however, chose to pass along the east bank through the territory of Qarrī; there is no indication that he met the *makk* or presented the letter.

Letter of Ismail, king of Sennaar, recommending Mr Bruce to Shekh Ibrahim Walad Musnad. 1772.

In thy name, O most Gracious.

In the name of God, the merciful, the gracious. Praise be to God, who has sent his prophet, and we believe in what he has said.

[The impression of the royal signet, placed after this, has the words Al Watek bil Mulk al-hadai Assultan Ismail Ben Assultan Bâde. 1183 The truster in the directing king, the Sultan Ismail, son of Sultan Baady.][3]

From the presence of the Sultan of the Moslems, and the Chalife of the Lord of both worlds, upright in spiritual and temporal affairs, the prosperous establisher of the Moslems, the conquering sheriffe, Sayyed al mursalin (prince of those that were sent), the standard-bearer of justice and virtue towards all mankind, the guardian of the country, the conqueror of slaves, the subduer of the people that are infidels and out of the right way, and of the people that are wicked and perverse; may the mercy of the eternal and supreme God be upon the presence and dignity of our lord and chief, and may we conquer and subdue our enemies; Al Watek bil Mulk alhadia, the sultan, who is the son of sultans, the sultan, who is the conqueror of kings, Ismail, son of the renowned sultan Baady, may the most merciful God gave [sic] him victory, and may the august Koran, and the glorious prophet guide him. So be it. So let it be, O Lord of both worlds! -- To the presence of Shekh Ibrahim Wulad Musnud, may great peace be upon you. The cause of our writing is this: If there come to you, with this letter, El Hakim Yagoube, sent to us by the Sultan of Habbesh, with strong recommendations, and besides all these the Sheriffe, the Sultan of Mecca, recommended him to us, and said this man is wise, and a foreigner, and is travelling in your quarter; supply him with necessaries for his journey, and while he stays; and this Hakim has been here, and is gone from our land on his way to you, and towards Rîf. What he asks for his journey, give him, and honour him with true honours, because he is a stranger, and recommended to us by kings. Supply him with necessaries for his stay and journey, and send him forward with his companions in whom he has trust. And, after you have forwarded him, write to us that he is gone, with his people, in health and safety, that the fore-mentioned kings may be informed of it with full certainty. And we rely upon you with full certainty; and let no answer come from you, but with praise and thanksgiving to God. God is over that. Farewell.

[1]Alexander Murray, *Account of the Life and Writings of James Bruce of Kinnaird* (Edinburgh: 1808), pp. 225-226.

[2]Spaulding, *Heroic Age*, pp. 352-353.

[3]Compare the seal of Ismā`īl, Doc. 18.

DOCUMENT 20

Document 20 is a *laissez-passer* written for James Bruce in 1772 by the Shaykh of al-Baḥr, `Adlān walad Ṣubāḥī. The English translation provided by Bruce's biographer Alexander Murray is given here.[1] The document is addressed to the senior leader of the Jamū`īya, Musnad (mentioned in the *sanctio* of Doc. 10); both Musnad's father, and his son and successor (Doc. 19), were named Ibrāhīm. At the time of Bruce's visit to Sinnār, the Regent Abū Likaylik himself was absent on campaign in Kordofan, while his son Ibrāhīm served as governor of the capital city, and his friend Shaykh `Adlān, encamped with his entourage not far from Sinnār, provided a reserve force for emergencies.[2] Bruce was well-advised to seek his recommendation.

The reading of `Adlān's seal given by Murray does not inspire complete confidence. He renders the text in Roman transliteration as follows: "el-watek-billah warrasoul almahi Asseik Adelan ben Asseik Subahi, 1776," that is, "The truster in God and the destroying prophet, Adelan, son of Shekh Subahi," or better, "He who trusts in God [and the prophet], the Effacer, Shaykh `Adlān, the son of Shaykh Ṣubāḥī, 1176." The expression "and the prophet" would seem to be an editorial interpolation, as the epithet Effacer properly appertains to God; perhaps it represents a misreading of *al-marḥūm*, "the late [Shaykh Ṣubāḥī]." Often, when a Sinnār seal employed one of the attributes of Allāh it also employed two, the first being *al-malik*, "the King." Therefore, a conjectural improved reconstruction of the seal text might read:

الواثق بالملك الماحى
الشيخ عدلان بن المرحوم
الشيخ صباحى ١١٧٦

He who trusts in the King, the Effacer
Shaykh `Adlān, son of the late
Shaykh Ṣubāḥī 1176/1762-1763

One may note that the seal is dated to the year of the Hamaj coup which brought Shaykh `Adlān to power. Before that, he had probably not been a person of great prominence; as a chronicler tactfully expressed the situation, "He became famous with Shaykh Muḥammad [Abū Likaylik], but it could never be verified whether or not his family had previously been shaykhs--God knows."[3] Shaykh `Adlān's seal, Murray could not fail to notice, "is much larger than that of the king."[4]

Letter of Shekh Adelan, vizier to the king of Sennaar, recommending Mr Bruce to Shekh Musnad, father of Ibrahim above-mentioned.

In the name of the most merciful God. Praise be to God alone, and Mahommed great is his glory.

[On the seal is el- Watek-billah warrasoul almahi Asseik Adelan ben Asseikh Subahi, 1176].

After the salutation of peace from the most high God with his mercy, blessing, and favour. From the presence of him, who has hope in his virtues, and fortitude under his affliction, endowed with upright counsel and clear judgment, useful among the children of the sword, the liberal warrior, who is fortunate in this world, and, if it please God, shall be happy in the next, Al Watek Billah warrasoul almahi, the Shekh Adelan, son of the renowned Shekh Subahi, may God bless him, Amen. To the presence of Shekh Musnad, Sheikh Adelan salutes you with abundant peace, and will bestow on you more power and honours. What we have to inform you of in this is the coming to you of El Hakim Yagoube, our friend and our companion (sahibna warafikna), and the friend of the king. The Sheriffe of Mecca sent letters with him to us long ago, in which he said to us, Supply him with necessaries, that, accommodated by you on our account, he may pass through all the dominions of the king of the Funge.--Fail not with respect to the traveller, who may be of benefit to thy life, for he is one of the men who are skilled in the cure of diseases; his travelling is for knowledge, and his ornament is his fortitude. Strengthen your heart towards him, and convey him along with his people to Rîf; for he is a man that has not with him money, or a number of people; he has only books and medicines; and his camels loaden [sic] with his books and medicines, and his horse. He has with him nothing else. His camels also are weak: retain them, and forward him with others, in order that you may fulfil what is most just. And that he may go with peace we have written to you.

[1]Murray, *Life and Writings*, pp. 226-227.

[2]Spaulding, *Heroic Age*, pp. 319-325.

[3]*Makhṭūṭa*, p. 82

[4]Murray, *Life and Writings*, p. 226.

DOCUMENT 21

Document 21 is a *laissez-passer* issued for the traveler James Bruce by the Hamaj notable `Adlān walad Ṣubāḥī, Shaykh of al-Baḥr, in 1772. An English translation was given by Bruce's biographer Alexander Murray, and this is offered here.[1] For Shaykh `Adlān's seal, see the introduction to Doc. 20.

Letter of Shekh Adelan to Ali Bey, announcing the departure of Mr Bruce from Sennaar to Egypt. 1772.

In the name of the most merciful God, the Lord of both worlds. Blessing and peace be upon our Lord Mahommed, his family and friends, the supporters, who are majestic, pure, illustrious, and radiant.

[The seal with the inscription on it above-mentioned.]

May it come with the sprinkling of the dew of perfume, scented with ambergris and odours, to the presence excelling in bounty, that speaks virtue and piety, the fountain of excellence and perfections, the spring of honours and favours, the horse that first reaches the goal, the chief of the masters of exalted eloquence, whose way of life increases his power, the drawn sword of God over every commander, and the arrow of prudence over every conqueror. So be it. The resplendent majesty, the chief of the chiefs of Cairo (Messir al Cahira) may God exalt his high rank, and make the backs of his enemies the place of his sword; may the arrows of his troops never forsake his flying enemies, and the armies of his terror be in their dejected hearts; may the bridle of his firm purpose train them to obedience, and the wisdom of his policy tame all their skill. The Shekh super-excellent and illustrious, glorious in his benefits to all mankind, bright in the love of his heart towards the explainers of what is dark, the prince of the city of Cairo the fortified, may God make the tree of peace flourish in his heart--Omir Allawat, the Sanjack, Ali Bey, God is with him--Amen. Your friend, Shekh Adelan, salutes you with exceeding peace, and prays for an increase of your power and honour. Next. What calls us to the intercourse of these letters, and the cause of our composing them is, that your servant, El Hakim Yagoube, came to us from the land of Habbesh with letters from the Sultan of Mecca and Metical Aga, and letters also from the Sultan of Habbesh, that we should treat him with kindness and civilities, and forward him speedily on his way to your presence; and we desired him to stay until we might be beneficent to him, but he refused and would not, fearing blame from you and your authority over all. So he is gone from us to seek you, with friendship and peace, and we hope that he will obtain his desire from those that know what is hid, in order that your friendship may be more fully established towards us, and that you may be joined to us more nearly, and that amity may be between our house and your house; and let us not be deprived of letters from you, for correspondence is half an interview.

[1]Murray, *Life and Writings*, pp. 227-228.

DOCUMENT 22

Document 22 is a charter issued to several notables of the Ḥamrān, among them Shaykh `Alī walad Maḥmūd walad Kuwayn, on 27 Ṣafar 1188/9 May 1774. The text has been taken from the version published by al-Ṭayyib Muḥammad al-Ṭayyib, apparently based upon an imperfect copy of an original document.[1] The opening of the body of the document is missing, so that it may not be established whether it originates or confirms a grant, and several minor infelicities of expression raise small questions about the accuracy in detail of the published text. The land granted may have been located in the territory of the Ḥamrān along the upper Setit, in the province of al-Tāka; before the cession of the province to the Shukrīya (Doc. 28), eastern notables played prominent roles in the affairs of the central government.[2] The witness roster is the earliest from the regency of Bādī walad Rajab, and reflects his brief alliance with Sultan Ismā`īl against his ambitious nephews, the sons of Muḥammad Abū Likaylik.

الواثق بالله و رسوله
السلطان اسماعيل
ابن السلطان بادى[3]

بسم الله الرحمن الرحيم نستعين بالله العظيم و نتوكل عليه فى جميع الامور الحمد لله الذى ايد الشريعة المحمدية بالادلة القرءانيه و القواطع الحكمية المنزلة على خير البرية و سلم تسليما كثيرا طبيعا مباركا يا رب العالمين حجة سلطانية و وثيقة ملوكية بمدينة سنار المحروسة محمية اجلها الله تعالى لدا متوليها سلطان المسلمين و خليفة رب العالمين القايم بامور الدنيا و الدين المنصف لمصالح المسلمين ناصر شريعة سيد المرسلين و ناشر لواء العدل و الفضل على كافة العالمين الواثق بالملك الهادى السلطان اسماعيل بن

السلطان بادى بن السلطان نول نوره الله الرحمن الرحيم بجاه القران العظيم و النبى الكريم امين يا رب العالمين الى حضرت (كل من)[4] تقف عليه (هذه)[4] الوثيقة و الناظر لما فيها من الحقيقة فان السلطان المبرور المويد المنصور السلطان اسماعيل بن السلطان بادى (. . .)[5] قندلاوى و الشيخ على ولدمحمود ولد كوين الشيخ قرن العلج صارت ملكا له بتصرف فيها حيث شاء و اما حدها من الصعيد طينة النور قندلاوى و الصبح و من الغرب درب الجمل و من تال السافل خور عبيدحدا مصامير و الارض هبة لله و رسوله الى يوم لا ينفع مال و لا بنون الا من اتى الله بقلب سليم و لا واحد يتعرض له و لا يبد بينهم من جميع الشرور و السبل و المضار و عليهم خسارة و لا دم و لا حسب و لا قور و لا دينا و لا اعشار و لا افطار و لا شيئا عليهم فى السبيل العادية فنوءكد عليكم ايها الشيوخ و المقاديم و الجنادى و من يتعرض بعد وسقى و كلامى هذا فلا يلوم الا نفسه و قد عرض نفسه لى الهلاك و الحذر ثم الحذر من الخلافة

و استشهدت على كلامى هذا

الامين هارون ولد يونس
و الجندى شوال ولد يونس جندى السوق
و الوزير الشيخ بادى رجب
و الشيخ الضو شيخ حوش ناصر خال الملك
و الشيخ سبت ولد بدر شيخ (اليس)[4]
و الشيخ مسمار شيخ التاكه
و الشيخ الفضل ولد مسمار
و الشيخ (عبد العاطى)[6] شيخ بيله
و الشيخ احمد شيخ البحر
و الشيخ عمر ولد الشيخ قاسم
و الشيخ شنبول شيخ اربجى
و السلطان غرادم ولد السلطان خميس المسبعاوى
و الشيخ محمد خضر شيخ (حوش ولد الملك)[6]
(و) الشيخ بلوله ولد الشيخ بادى
و القاضى احمد ود الارباب الضوا
(و) الارباب يونس ولد الارباب سليمان
و الشيخ الضوا ولد يحيى

و المأذون الفكى عبد الحفيظ
و الشريف عبد الله
و الارباب سالم نسيب الملك
و الارباب حسب الله ولد ابو الحسن
و الارباب محيميد

و قد تمت هذه الوثيقة (بيوم)[7] الخميس سبعة و عشرون يوم خلت من شهر الله صفر سنة الف (و مايه)[8] و ثمانيه و ثمانين بعد الهجرة النبوية صل الله على و سلم

He who trusts in God and His messenger
Sultan Ismā`īl
The son of Sultan Bādī[3]

In the name of God, the Merciful, the Compassionate. We ask help of the Mighty God, and rely upon Him in every matter. Praise be to God, Who has confirmed the Muḥammadan law with Qur'ānic proofs and definitive judgments that descended upon the best of creation. O Lord of the Universe, grant [him] complete, abundant, good, and blessed peace. A sultanic charter and royal document [issued] in the divinely guarded and protected city of Sinnār, may God Most High love her, in the presence of her warden, sultan of the Muslims and Caliph of the Lord of the Universe, steadfast in the affairs of this world and of religion, just in the affairs of the Muslims, protector of the law of the lord of the messengers, who spreads the banner of justice and excellence throughout the whole universe, he who trusts in the King, the Guide, Sultan Ismā`īl, the son of Sultan Bādī, the son of Sultan Nōl. May God, the Merciful, the Compassionate, illuminate him through the influence of the sublime Qur'ān and the eminent prophet. Amen, O Lord of the Universe.

To the presence of [all who] read [this] document and see the truth therein.

The pious, divinely assisted and victorious Sultan Ismā`īl, the son of Sultan Bādī [. . .][5] Qandilāwī, Shaykh `Alī walad Maḥmūd walad Kuwayn, Shaykh Qarn al-`Alaj. It has become his property, from which he may enjoy the usufruct whenever he wishes. As for its southern boundary, it is the cultivated land of al-Nūr Qandilāwī, and [also on] the east. On the west it is the camel path, and on the north it is Khōr `Abīd, a boundary of Maṣāmīr. The land is a gift for [the sake of] God and His messenger, for a day in which neither wealth nor sons suffice, unless one comes to God with a secure heart. Let no one trouble him, nor disperse among them. [They are exempted] from all the *shurūr*, *subul*, and *maḍārr*. They are not subject to *khusāra*, *damm*, *ḥasab*, *quwwār*, *dīnā*, *a`shār*, *afṭār*, nor are they subject to any of the customary *subul*. We command you peremptorily, O shaykhs, *muqaddam*s, and *jundī*s. He who makes trouble after my document and these my words must blame none but himself, for he has exposed himself to destruction. Beware, then beware of disobedience.

I call as witnesses to these my words:

the *amīn*, Hārūn walad Yūnus
the *jundī*, Shawwāl walad Yūnus, *jundī* of the market
the *wazīr*, Shaykh Bādī [walad] Rajab
Shaykh al-Ḍaw, shaykh of the compound of the people of the maternal uncle of the king
Shaykh Sabat walad Badr, Shaykh of [Alays]
Shaykh Mismār, Shaykh of al-Tāka
Shaykh al-Faḍl walad Mismār
Shaykh [`Abd al-`Aṭā], Shaykh of Bayla
Shaykh Aḥmad, Shaykh of al-Baḥr
Shaykh `Umar walad al-Shaykh Qāsim
Shaykh Shanbūl, Shaykh of Arbajī
Sultan Ghurdām, son of Sultan Khamīs al-Musabba`āwī

Shaykh Muḥammad Khiḍr, shaykh [of the compound of the king's son]
Shaykh Balūla walad al-Shaykh Bādī
the *qāḍī*, Aḥmad wad al-Arbāb al-Ḍaw
Arbāb Yūnus walad Arbāb Sulaymān
Shaykh al-Ḍaw walad Yaḥyā
the muezzin, Fikī ʿAbd al-Ḥafīẓ
Sharīf ʿAbd Allāh
Arbāb Sālim, a kinsman by marriage of the king
Arbāb Ḥasab Allāh walad Abu'l-Ḥasan
Arbāb Muḥīmayd

This document was completed on Thursday, when twenty-seven days had passed from God's month of Ṣafar in the year one thousand [one hundred] eighty-eight from the *hijra* of the prophet. May God bless [him] and grant him peace.

[1]al-Ṭayyib Muḥammad al-Ṭayyib, *al-Turāth al-shaʿbī li-qabīlat al-Ḥamrān* (Khartoum: 1970), pp. 4-5.

[2]Spaulding, *Heroic Age*, pp. 319; 333-335; 383.

[3]Contrast with the seal text of Ismāʿīl, Doc. 18.

[4]Restored by the editors.

[5]Several lines of text are missing.

[6]Lacuna. A conjectural reading of the missing text has been taken from Doc. 18.

[7]Reading *mīm* for *nūn*.

[8]In the place of *li-ṭānānīya*.

DOCUMENT 23

Document 23 is a confirming charter issued by the Hamaj Regent Bādī walad Rajab to Shaykh Barakāt walad Maḍuwī on 24 Sha`bān 1192/17 September 1778. The text has been taken by the editors from the original.[1] The document is truncated at the top, and the opening protocols are missing. The charter confirmed the administrative authority of Shaykh Barakāt,[2] *khalīfa* to Shaykh Idrīs walad al-Arbāb,[3] over the lower Blue Nile *fuqarā'* settlement of al-`Aylafūn. The charter also bestowed upon the *faqīh* the right to sponsor a market, a privilege ordinarily reserved to the territorial nobility.[4] The scribe identified the location of the writing of the document as Ghosbīya, probably the village of that name on the east bank of the Blue Nile slightly above the modern Wad Madanī. The witness roster reveals not a court, but the entourage of a high official on the move. Noteworthy by their presence are Bādī's nephews and bitter rivals, the future Regents Rajab and Nāṣir, and also several military officers bearing the Funj title *mankarūkan* (plural and variant, *mankrōknā*).

(. . .)[5] لما فيها من الحقيقه و بعد فان المحفوظ المبرور المويد المنصور الوزير الشيخ
بادى ولد رجب / تمم و امضا ما فعله سابقا السلطان اسماعيل للشيخ بركات ولد
مضوى خليفه الشيخ ادريس / ولد الارباب من حكم الحله العيلفون و السوق و قطع
منها شيوخ القواريه كلهم و جرايهم / و من ياتى بعدهم الى قيام الساعه لانه شيا من
قديم الزمان من السلاطين السابقين قاطعين / القواريه من حكم حله الشيخ ادريس
المذكوره كذالك الوزير الشيخ بادى ولد رجب / تمم و امضا ذلك الحكم للشيخ بركات
ولد مضوى و ملكه حكم حلته و سوقه لا احدا يتعرض / له فى حكم حلته و سوقه لا
شيوخ القواريه و لا غيرهم من العساكر و الجراى هاكذا / فعله الوزير الشيخ بادى ولد

رجب ابتغا لوجه الله تعالى و كرامه للشيخ ادريس / ولد الارباب و لخليفته الشيخ بركات ولد مضوى و طلبا للثواب فى دار الماب و ليوم لا ينفع / فيه مال و لا بنون الا من اتى الله بقلب سليم و صار حكم هذه الحله العيلفون و السوق فى / يدى الخليفه لا احدا منكم يتعرض لهم فى حكم حلتهم و لا لذريتهم و ذريه ذريتهم و من يعرض / لهم بعد جوابى و وثيقتى هذه فقد عرض نفسه للهلاك و الحذر ثم الحذر من الخلاف و من / خالف و تعرض لايلوم الا نفسه

حضر و شهد بذلك

الشيخ هارون ولد يونس الامين
و الشيخ / دكين ولد عمارى سيد خيل الفونج
و الشيخ الضوا ولد مريسه شيخ حوش عزوزه
و الشيخ محمد ولد / خدر شيخ حوش ولد الملك
و الشيخ موسى ولد سنق الوادى مقدم خيل الملك
و الشيخ شنبول / شيخ اربجى
و الشيخ بادى ولد كتوا مقدم عيله الملك
و الشيخ خميس ولد بديرى مقدم / الفرسان
و الشيخ الامين ولد دليبه
و الشيخ عجيب ولد نور
و الشيخ ناصر ولد شبلانى / الدفه
و الارباب بادى ولد قدا
و الارباب محمد ولد كمير
و الارباب رجب بن الشيخ محمد /
و الارباب كتوا بن الشيخ بادى
و الارباب ناصر بن الشيخ محمد
و الارباب رجب بن الشيخ // بادى
و المنكروكن سبت الحماد /
و المنكروكن الضوا ولد حمد
و المنكروكن / كاب
و على ولد حسين
و بلوله

و المنكروكن / سرور
و سعدان اخيه
و فضل الله ولد / دحاله

و من اولاد العرب

الارباب حسب / الله ولد ابوا الحسن
و الارباب سليمان / الراشدابى
و الارباب على ولد عيشه /
و الحاج حمد الشافع

و انا فقير الله على / ابن الفقيه ادم المكنا بالحله غسبيه / كاتب و شاهد و الله خير الشاهدين / تحرير ذلك يوم الاربعا اربعه و عشرين / خلت من شعبان سنة الف و مايه / و اثنين و تسعين بعد الهجره النبويه / على صاحبها افضل الصلاة و ازكى التحيه

[. . .] the truth therein. Thereafter: The divinely preserved, pious, divinely assisted, and victorious *wazīr*, Shaykh Bādī walad Rajab, has confirmed and ratified what Sultan Ismā`īl did previously for Shaykh Barakāt walad Maḍuwī, *khalīfa* to Shaykh Idrīs walad al-Arbāb, in regard to the administration of the village of al-`Aylafūn and the market. All the shaykhs of the *quwwārīya* and their *jarāī* are cut off from it, and whoever may follow after them until the hour of resurrection, for it is a matter longstanding from the previous sultans that the *quwwārīya* be cut off from the administration of the village of the said Shaykh Idrīs. And so likewise the *wazīr*, Shaykh Bādī walad Rajab, has confirmed and ratified that administration to Shaykh Barakāt walad Maḍuwī; the administration of his village and his market belong to him. Let no one trouble him in the administration of his village and his market, neither the shaykhs of the *quwwārīya* nor any of the soldiers or *jarāī*. The *wazīr*, Shaykh Bādī walad Rajab, has done this for the sake of God Most High, and to honor Shaykh Idrīs walad al-Arbāb and his *khalīfa*, Shaykh Barakāt walad Maḍuwī, asking for reward in the life to come, for a day in which neither wealth nor sons suffice, unless one comes to God with a secure heart. The administration of the village of al-`Aylafūn and the market have become the possession of his [Shaykh Idrīs walad al-Arbāb's] *khalīfa*. Let no one trouble them in the administration of their village, nor their descendants, nor their descendants' descendants. He who troubles them after my letter and this my document has exposed himself to destruction. Beware, then beware of disobedience, and let him who disobeys blame none but himself.

There were present and witnessed to it:

Shaykh Hārūn walad Yūnus, the *amīn*
Shaykh Dakīn walad `Ammār, *sīd al-khayl* of the Funj
Shaykh al-Ḍaw walad Murīsa, shaykh of the compound of `Azūza
Shaykh Muḥammad walad Khiḍr, shaykh of the compound of the king's son
Shaykh Mūsā walad Sanaq al-Wādī, *muqaddam al-khayl* of the king
Shaykh Shanbūl, Shaykh of Arbajī
Shaykh Bādī walad Kitū, *muqaddam* of the family of the king
Shaykh Khamīs walad Bidayrī, *muqaddam* of the knights
Shaykh al-Amīn walad Dulayba
Shaykh `Ajīb walad Nūr
Shaykh Nāṣir walad Shiblānī al-Diffa
Arbāb Bādī walad Qudā
Arbāb Muḥammad walad Kamīr
Arbāb Rajab b. al-Shaykh Muḥammad
Arbāb Kitū b. al-Shaykh Bādī
Arbāb Nāṣir b. al-Shaykh Muḥammad
Arbāb Rajab b. al-Shaykh Bādī
Mankarūkan Sabat al-Ḥammād
Mankarūkan al-Ḍaw walad Ḥammad
Mankarūkan Kāb
`Alī walad Ḥusayn

Balūla
Mankarūkan Surūr
Sa`dān, his brother
Faḍl Allāh walad Daḥḥāla

From among the sons of the Arabs:

Arbāb Ḥasab Allāh walad Abu'l-Ḥasan
Arbāb Sulaymān al-Rāshidābī
Arbāb `Alī walad `Aysha
Ḥājj Ḥammad al-Shāfi`

I, the *faqīr* of God Most High, `Alī b. al-Faqīh Adam, located in the village of Ghosbīya, am scribe and witness, and God is the Best of Witnesses. That was written on Wednesday, when 24 [days] had passed of Sha`bān in the year 1192 from the *hijra* of the prophet, upon whose master the best of prayers and purest salutations.

[1]For a previously published version see Jay Spaulding, "A Charter of Bādī b. Rajab, Hamaj Regent of Sinnār," *Sudan Texts Bulletin* 5 (1983): 68-72.

[2]*Ṭabaqāt*, p. 54, note 12.

[3]Ibid., pp. 49-65.

[4]Spaulding, *Heroic Age*, pp. 107-112.

[5]The opening protocols are missing.

DOCUMENT 24

Document 24 is a confirming charter issued by Sultan `Adlān b. Ismā`īl to Faqīh Ismā`īl b. Muḥammad b. Arbāb al-`Aqāyid and his sister Sittinā on 1 Dhu'l-Ḥijja 1194/28 November 1780. The text has been taken by the editors from the original, supplemented by material from an early copy preserved as a companion to the somewhat tattered original by its keepers.[1] The charter confirms a grant to a prominent descendant of the seventeenth-century holy man Arbāb al-`Aqāyid,[2] whose settlement was located at the Nile confluence on the site of modern Khartoum.[3] The terms of the grant are unusually detailed; they include the bestowal of land, slaves, and free subjects (the Marīnāb). Several technical terms appear in this document. *Salūka* land, usually riverbank *jarf* or island land, meant land seasonally innundated by the Nile flood that could be cultivated with a digging stick (*salūka*). A *turus* (plural, *turūs*) was a low ridge built around the low sides of a rainland field to retain runoff moisture; as comparatively fixed features of the landscape, they could be used for survey purposes. The *ḥabl* was a linear unit of measure for rainland common in the Khartoum area but not elsewhere; it consisted of eight cubits.[4] The witness roster reflects the political situation between the fall of the Hamaj Regent Bādī walad Rajab and the revolt against the Hamaj of Sultan `Adlān.[5] Conspicuous was the sole descendant of the old, matrilineal Funj dynasty, the Unsāb; he identified himself as Shaykh `Abd Allāh, the son of his mother Āmina, the daughter of her mother Balīla, the Unsābī.[6] The *malik bursāj* al-Ḍaw also identified himself as the son of his mother for the purpose of witnessing this charter, but by the following year he had followed the prevailing trend toward patrilineal preference (Doc. 25).

[هذه صورة حجة سلطانية و وثيقة ملوكية بمدينة سنار المحروسه المحمية على (. . .)[7]
ختم السلطان عدلان بن السلطان اسماعيل صورة نقش خاتم الواثق بالملك الجليل
السلطان عدلان بن السلطان اسماعيل تاريخ ختمه سنة ١١٩٠ الف و مايه وسبعين[8]
ختمان باعلا الوثيقه على اليمين واحد و على الشمال واحد[9] تاريخها عصر الثلاثا اول
يوم خلا من شهر المحرم[10] الحرام من شهور سنة ١١٩٤ من الهجرة النبوية على
صاحبها ازكى التحية و افضل السلام][11]

الواثق بالملك
الجليل
السلطان عدلان بن
عيل
السلطان اسما ١١٩٠[9]

[بسمك يا كريم بسم الله الرحمن الرحيم الحمد لله الذى شهد بوجوده الكاينات و دلت على][11] حدانيته جميع المصنوعات و على ءاله و صحبه و سلم / [الحمد لله الذى ايد الشريعة المحمدية بالايات][11] القرءانية و القواطع الحكمية المنزلة على خير البريه صلى الله عليه [و سلم تسليما كثيرا طيبا مباركا يا رب العالمين][11] / الحمد لله بفضله عاد الامر لاهله و رجع كل شىء لاصله / [الحمد لله الذى بلغ الرسول / و نحن ءامنا][11] بما يقول / حجة [سلطانية و وثيقة][11] ملوكية بمدينة سنار المحروسة المحمية / اجلها الله تعالى لدا [متوليها سلطان][11] الاسلام جامع كلمة الايمان و مدمر اهل البغى و الطغيان سيف الله القاطع / و سهامه اللامع [ناشر لواء العدل فى][11] العالمين ناصر شريعة سيد المرسلين و احق من ملك تحت الخلافة / [باستحقاق و اولى من ولى الولاية فى الافاق][11] و هو الذى وجه عنان العناية لحماية الاسلام بشهادة الاجماع / و تلك شهادة لا يتطرق [اليه النزاع][11] و جدد بنيان الهداية بعد ما اندرست اثاره و طمست معالمه / [و مهد][11] بساطه [بعد ان لم][11] يوجد الا مظلوم و ظالمه ذو المفاخر الذى شهد بفضله الخاص و العام / و الماثر التى التى[10] ترتفع على [الثريا و تكاثر الغمام][11] و الاخلاق التى رام النسيم ان يحكى لطفها فاصبح عليلا و المعالى التى / تمنت الملوك ان [يتشبهوا بها][11] فلم يجدوا الى ذلك سبيلا سلطان المسلمين و خليفة رب العالمين / القايم بامور الدنيا و الدين [المنتصر لمصالح][11] المسلمين [من اصلح الله به][11] العباد و انار به البلاد و رحمه الله / سبحانه و تعالى للحاضر و الباد مولانا و اولانا و اعلانا و ناصرنا و معيننا على اعدانا الواثق بالملك الجليل / السلطان بن السلطان السلطان المظفر المعان السلطان عدلان بن

المرحوم السلطان اسماعيل / زيدت ايام عدله و [جددت ليالى][11] سعده بجاه القران العظيم و النبى الكريم امين امين يا رب العالمين / [الى][11] حضرة كل من تقف [عليه هذه][11] الوثيقه و الناظر لما فيها من الحقيقه و بعد فان السلطان / [المحفوظ المويد المبرور المنصور][11] السلطان عدلان تمم و امضى ما فعلوه السلاطين السابقين و هو ما فعله / جده السلطان بادى بن المرحوم السلطان نول و عمه السلطان ناصر و ابيه السلطان اسماعيل / من جميع الجاه القديم و الجديد للفقيه محمد سابقا و انا ذالحين لاحقا عرض على هذه الجاه و تممته و امضيته / للفقيه اسماعيل بن محمدبن ارباب العقايد جميع جاهه القديم و الجديد و حلته و مشرعها فهذا المشرع من / جيهه الصبح [الداداب لليل فقر و من][11] الغرب خور ولد العيسيلى و من تحت تتبع البحر اينما توجه و من فوق درب الجمل / و ايضا السلطان عدلان تمم و امضى جاه [ستنا][11] بنت الفقيه محمد المريناب كلهم رقبتهم و سلوكتهم ظهره و بحر حضريه / و رفاعيه و ايضا السلطان عدلان تمم و امضا له جاه اولاد طه و هم محمد ابو قرن و اولاده جبر الله و سعيد / و الامين و محمد ولد رحيم و اولاد بنت الفقيه بساطى و هم محمد و على و اولاد ايوب الثلاثه و هم محمد و ابراهيم و النور / [و مختار الفزارى و ايضا][11] السلطان عدلان تمم و امضا له دار الفقيه محمد القديمه و هى ترس ولد بلو / [و ترس الحفير و ترس احمد ولد حامد الفى][11] رفاع و ترس قراصه الخمسه و هن معلومات البقعه و الحدود فحدهن / [من جيه الصبح ترس وداع الله و من جيهه][11] الغرب ركن ترس الفقيه محمد العند فاطمه بنت الحاج و ترس الفقيه يس / الليال قلاده [و ترس احمد ولد الفقه و ترس قرشى][11] ولد حمد و ترس ولد البصيرى و ترس عبد القادر ولد حمد و ترس اولاد الحاج / و ترس ولد بدوى و ترس طه ولد سعد و ترس ولد زياده و تروس الفقيه بساطى ولد ارباب الاثنين [ثبن][11] و لميض / و تروس الحاج مدنى الاثنين و تروس اسماعيل ولد الفقيه الاثنين ترس ولد المعمرى و ترس ولد عيسى العند يس ولد طه / و سلوكه عشه بنت طه ظهره و بحر حضريه و رفاعيه و ترس محمد ولد عشه و دار المريناب الليل الموقف / و من جيهه السافل سبعين عود الثلاث الفقيه محمد ولد ارباب و عشرين [الليلات][11] احمد ولد الفقيه بساطى و ترس على ولد بكر القدام ترس وداعه الله و تروس الفقيه ارباب ولد فرح الاثنين / و من جيهه الجزيره ثلاثين عود الليلات الفقيه محمد ولد ارباب خافسا من الشرق للهوى و الكبره الليله احمد ولد الفقيه و عشرين احمد ولد / الفقيه و عشره حلو و عشرين محمد ولد عشه و جرف محمد نور ولد بكرى الفى الخرطوم و دار ارباب ولد فرح الفى الجزيره / و ثمانيه عشره [حبل خافسه من][11] الهوى للشرق و جرف الهوى الليل ارباب و ثلاثين عود

فى جرف فقر و من / جيهه دار الفقيه ارباب الليله المقرن القويطع و هى سته و
[عشرون عود و عشره][11] الفقيه على ولد ارباب خافسه / من البحر للبحر و ساقيه
ارباب ولد فرح الفى الخرطوم و ايضان ساقيه [ارباب ولد فرح][11] الفى ام مقد و
ترس ولد الفوسى / و اولاد الحاج و هذا كله فعله السلطان عدلان ابتغا لوجه الله تعالى
و [طالبا للثواب][11] فى دار الماءب و ليوم لا ينفع فيه مال / و لا بنون الا من اتى
الله بقلب سليم و صارت الحله و مشرعها و الرجال المذكورين و الدار المذكوره
[الحضريه و الرفاعيه / الفى الضهره و الفى البحر الجميع جاه لله و لرسوله و جاه][11]
السلاطين السابقين و [جاهته][11] انا السلطان / [للفقه اسماعيل بن الفقه] [11] محمد
ولد ارباب العقايد لا عليهم الجميع بجساره و لا خساره و لا دم و لا حسب / [و لا
قوار و لا نار و لا زريبه و لا رغم و لا][11] متورت و لا رباط و لا حجر قش و لا فى
البشاقره و لا فى ابو مقد و لا حلاس / و [لا يواشي و لا يدخل حلتهم و لا عليهم][11]
نزول و لا ضيافه و حكم حلتهم و جميع ديارهم كله فى ايدهم و لا عليهم عاده // [و
لا قل و لا جل و لا شىء من السبل العاديه و نوكد عليكم يا جميع الشيوخ و المقاديم
و الجراين الذين من تحتهم الى حد ملكى كله خصوصا انتم][11] يا شيوخ /
[القواريه][11] الوقت هذا الذى فى الدار الشيخ محمد تكتك ولد الشيخ النور
قندلاوى و الوقت هذا فى دار / اليس الشيخ سبت ولد بدر و ولد قدوره انتم يا
هذه / الشيوخ المذكورين و جراكم الجميع و من ياتى بعدكم / الى قيام الساعه لا احد
منكم يتعرض لاولاد الفقيه / ارباب العقايد و لا احد منكم يتعرض لذريتهم / و لا
لذريه ذريتهم فى هذا الجاه القديم من الرقبه / و الطين و من تعرض لهم بعد هذه
الوثيقه / السابقه و اللاحقه و بعد كلام السلطنيه / السابقين و بعد كلامى هذ و وثيقتى
هذه / فقد عرض نفسه للهلاك الحذر ثم الحذر / من المخالفه و المخالف لا يلوم الا
نفسه /

حضر ذلك و شهد به

الشيخ هرون ولد يونس / امين السلطان
و الجندى شوال اخيه جندى السوق /
و الشيخ رجب بن الشيخ محمد [ابوا لكيلك وزير الملك عدلان][11] /
و الشيخ الضو ولد مريسه شيخ [حوش ناصر خال الملك][11] /
و الشيخ محمد الامين ولد مسمار ولد عجيب شيخ قرى /
و الشيخ سبت ولد بدر شيخ اليس

و الشيخ مسمار / ولد حمد الزير شيخ التكه
و الشيخ الفضيل ولد مسمار / شيخ اتبره
و الشيخ عبد العاطى بن الشيخ محمد قيلى شيخ بيله /
و الشيخ احمد ولد على شيخ البحر
و الشيخ عمر بن الشيخ / قاسم شيخ القربين
و الشيخ محمد تكتك ولد الشيخ / النور قندلاوى
و الشيخ قاسم بن الشيخ ادريس / ولد نايل مقدم السواكره
و الشيخ محمد ولد خضر ولد / نايل مقدم حوش ناصر ولد الملك
و الملك الضو ولد / [حوى] [11] ملك برساج
و الشيخ بلوله بن الشيخ بادى / شيخ السجاده
و القاضى عبد العزيز المغربى المراكشى /
و الخطيب احمد بن الخطيب عبد الحفيظ ولد نونو /
و الارباب عمار اخيه
و الشيخ حجر بن الشيخ الزين / اليعقبابى
و الارباب الضو ولد قنبيلى
و الارباب / حسين ولد [العونى][11] رفيق السلطنه السابقين /
و الارباب يوسف ولد ابكر ولد احمد ولد علوان /
و الفقيه حجازى ولد ابو زيد [ولد الشيخ ادريس][11] / ولد الارباب
و [الفقه حسب الله ولد ابو الحسن][11] / المشهور [بتور المتن][11] /
[و الشيخ][11] عبد الله ولد / [امنه][11] بنت بليله الانسابى /
و الفقيه / محمد ولد بشير معتوق الملك بادى
و الحاج / مركز معتوق الشيخ جمع كاكاوى /
و الا بن خضر

و كاتب الوثيقه فقير الله تعالى / و احوجهم [لدى الله][11] ابراهيم يعقوب عبد الرازق / محمد حميرا شاهد به و كفانا الله بشهيدا / تحرير ذلك عصر الثلاثا و اول يوم خلا / من شهر الله ذى الحجه الحرام من شهور / سنه ١١٩٤ / الف و مايه و اربعه و تسعين من الهجره / النبويه على صاحبها [ازكى / التحيه و افضل السلام][11]

[This is a copy of a sultanic charter and royal document (issued) in the divinely guarded and protected city of Sinnār (. . .). The seal of Sultan `Adlān b. al-Sultan Ismā`īl: a copy of the seal impression (is), "He who trusts in the Sublime King, Sultan `Adlān the son of Sultan Ismā`īl." The date of the seal is 1190/1776-1777, one thousand one hundred seventy (sic). There are two seals at the top of the document, one on the right and one on the left. Its date is the afternoon of Tuesday, the first day of the holy month of Muḥarram (sic) from the months of the year 1194 from the *hijra* of the prophet, upon whose master the purest of salutations and best of peace].

He who trusts in the Sublime King
Sultan `Adlān, the son of Sultan
Ismā`īl 1190/1776-1777

In Thy name, O Generous One. In the name of God, the Merciful, the Compassionate. Praise be to God, to Whose presence all living beings testify, and Whose unity is indicated by man's handiwork. Peace be upon the family and Companions of [Muḥammad]. Praise be to God, Who has confirmed the Muḥammadan law with Qur'ānic verses and definitive judgments that descended upon the best of creation. May God bless him and grant him complete, abundant, good, and blessed peace. O Lord of the Universe! Praise be to God for His excellence. Every affair belongs to its own people, and every thing to its own source. Praise be to God, Who sent the messenger. We believe in what he says.

A sultanic charter and royal document [issued] in the divinely guarded and protected city of Sinnār, may God Most High exalt her, in the presence of her warden, the sultan of Islam, who consolidates the authority of the faith and destroys the people of wrongdoing and oppression, the sharp sword of God and His flashing arrows, who spreads the banner of justice throughout the universe, protector of the law of the lord of the messengers, the one most deserving to rule as a Caliph, and foremost among those who rule between the horizons. He it is who has guided the reins of solicitude toward the protection of Islam, according to the testimony of a consensus achieved without dispute, who has renewed the edifice of guidance after its traces had been obliterated and its marks effaced, and who has made even the carpet [of justice] after [a time in which] one could find only the victim and his oppressor. He possesses glory to whose excellence high and low testify, influence which ascends to the Pleiades and gathers in clouds, a character which the breeze would wish to copy to become mild, and noble traits in the emulation of which kings grow tired and fail to find a way, sultan of the Muslims and Lord of the Universe, steadfast in the affairs of this world and of religion, just in the affairs of the Muslims, through whom God has prospered the worshipers and illuminated the nations. May God Most High (praise be to Him) be merciful to him in this life and the hereafter, our lord and leader, our most eminent protector and aid against our enemies, he who trusts in the Sublime King, the sultan, the son of the sultan, the victorious and divinely aided Sultan `Adlān, son of the late Sultan Ismā`īl. May the days of his justice be increased, and the nights of his good fortune be renewed through the influence of the sublime Qur'ān and the eminent prophet. Amen, amen, O Lord of the Universe.

To the presence of all who read this document and see the truth therein.

Thereafter: The divinely preserved and assisted, pious, and victorious Sultan `Adlān has confirmed and ratified what the previous sultans did; that is, what his grandfather Sultan Bādī, son the the late Sultan Nōl, his paternal uncle Sultan Nāṣir, and his father Sultan Ismā`īl, did previously concerning the grant to Faqīh Muḥammad--all of it, old and new. Now I subsequently have been presented with this grant. I have confirmed and ratified it for Faqīh Ismā`īl b. Muḥammad b. Arbāb al-`Aqāyid--all of his grant, old and new, his village and its watering place. This watering place is on the eastern side al-Dādāb as far as Faqr and on the west Khōr walad `Isaylī. Below, it follows the river wherever it goes, and above, the camel path. Furthermore, Sultan `Adlān has confirmed and ratified the grant to Sittinā bint al-Faqīh Muḥammad of the Marīnāb--all of them, their slaves and *salūka* land, rainland and riverain land, sedentaries and pastoralists. Furthermore, Sultan `Adlān has confirmed and ratified for him the grant of the Awlād Ṭaha, they being Muḥammad Abū Qurun and his sons Jabr Allāh, Sa`īd, al-Amīn, and Muḥammad walad Raḥīm, the Awlād Bint al-Faqīh Busāṭī, they being Muḥammad and `Alī, the three Awlād Ayyūb, they being Muḥammad, Ibrāhīm, and al-Nūr, and Mukhtār al-Fazārī. Furthermore, Sultan `Adlān has confirmed and ratified for him the old estate of the Faqīh Muḥammad, consisting of the *turus* of Walad Balū, the *turus* of the reservoir, the *turus* of Aḥmad walad Ḥāmid which is in the pastoral lands, and the *turus* [called] "Qurāṣa al-Khamsa." The location and boundaries of these are known. Their boundary on the eastern side is the *turus* of Widā` Allāh. On the western side the *turus* of the Faqīh Muḥammad is set at Fāṭima bint al-Ḥājj and the *turus* of the Faqīh Yāsīn as far as Qullāda, [then at] the *turus* of Aḥmad walad al-Faqīh, the *turus* of Qurashī walad Ḥammad, the *turus* of the Awlād al-Ḥājj, the *turus* of Walad Badawī, the *turus* of Ṭaha walad Sa`d, the *turus* of Walad Ziyāda, the two *turūs* of the Faqīh Busāṭī walad Arbāb, "Thibn" and "Lamīḍ," the two *turūs* of al-Ḥājj Madanī, the two *turūs* of Ismā`īl walad al-Faqīh, *turus* "Walad al-Mu`ammarī" and *turus* "Walad `Īsā" as far as Yāsīn walad Ṭaha, the *salūka* land of `Asha bint Ṭaha, rainland and river land, sedentary and pastoral, and the *turus* of Muḥammad walad `Asha, and the estate of the Marīnāb as far as the halting place. On the northern side [it extends] seventy rods, [including] the three of Faqīh Muḥammad walad Arbāb and twenty as far as Aḥmad walad al-Faqīh Busāṭī, the *turus* of `Alī walad Bakr in front of the *turus* of Widā`at Allāh and the two *turūs* of Faqīh Arbāb walad Faraḥ. On the side of the island [it extends] thirty rods as far as Faqīh Muḥammad walad Arbāb extending from the east to al-Hawā and al-Kubra as far as Aḥmad walad al-Faqīh, and twenty [rods] of Aḥmad walad al-Faqīh, ten of Ḥilū, twenty of Muḥammad walad `Asha, and the *jarf* of Muḥammad Nūr walad Bakrī which is in Khartoum, and the estate of Arbāb walad Faraḥ which is on the island, and eighteen *ḥabl* extending from al-Hawā to the east, and the *jarf* of al-Hawā as far as Arbāb, and thirty rods in the *jarf* of Faqr. On the side of the estate of Faqīh Arbāb [it extends] as far as the dividing *muqran*;[12] it is twenty-six rods and the ten of Faqīh `Alī walad Arbāb, extending from the river to the river, and the *sāqīya* of Arbāb walad Faraḥ which is in Khartoum, and likewise the *sāqīya* of Arbāb walad Faraḥ which is in Umm Maqad and the *turus* of Walad al-Fūs and the Awlād al-Ḥājj. All this Sultan `Adlān has done for the sake of God Most High, asking for reward in the life to come, for a day in which neither wealth nor sons suffice, unless one comes to God with a secure heart. The village and its watering place, the men mentioned, and the said estate both sedentary and pastoral, that which is in the rainlands and that which is in the riverain lands, all of it is a grant for the sake of God and His messenger, a grant of the previous sultans. I the sultan have granted it to Faqīh Ismā`īl b. al-Faqīh Muḥammad walad Arbāb al-`Aqāyid. All of them are not subject to *jusāra, khusāra, damm, ḥasab, quwwār, nār, zarība, raghm, matūrāt, rubāṭ, ḥajr al-qashsh*, neither in al-Bushāqara nor in Abū Maqad, not in settling and not in pasturing. Let no one enter their village. They are subject neither to *nuzūl* nor to *ḍiyāfa*. The administration of their village and of all their estates is in their hands. They are not subject to *`āda, qill, jill*, nor any of the customary *subul*. We command you peremptorily, all you shaykhs and *muqaddam*s, and the *jarāī* who are under them throughout my kingdom, all, but especially you, O shaykhs of the *quwwārīya* who are presently in the estate, Shaykh Muḥammad Taktak walad al-Shaykh al-Nūr Qandilāwī, and presently in the province of Alays, Shaykh Sabat walad Badr and Walad Qadūra, you the aforementioned shaykhs and all your *jarāī*, and whoever may come after you until the hour of resurrection, let no one of you trouble the Awlād al-Faqīh Arbāb al-`Aqāyid, and let no one of you trouble their descendants or their descendants' descendants concerning this old grant of slaves and land. He who troubles them after this documentation previous and present, and after the word of the previous sultans, and after this my word and my document, has exposed himself to destruction. Beware, then beware of disobedience, and let the disobedient blame none but himself.

There were present and witnessed to it:

Shaykh Hārūn walad Yūnus, the *amīn* of the sultan
the *jundī*, Shawwāl his brother, *jundī* of the market
Shaykh Rajab b. al-Shaykh Muḥammad Abū Likaylik, *wazīr* of King `Adlān
Shaykh al-Ḍaw walad Murīsa, shaykh of the compound of Nāṣir, maternal uncle of the king
Shaykh Muḥammad al-Amīn walad Mismār walad `Ajīb, Shaykh of Qarrī
Shaykh Sabat walad Badr, Shaykh of Alays
Shaykh Mismār walad Ḥammad al-Zīr, Shaykh of al-Tāka
Shaykh al-Faḍīl walad Mismār, Shaykh of Atbara
Shaykh `Abd al-`Aṭā b. al-Shaykh Muḥammad Qaylī, Shaykh of Bayla
Shaykh Aḥmad walad `Alī, Shaykh of al-Baḥr
Shaykh `Umar walad al-Shaykh Qāsim, Shaykh of al-Qarbīn
Shaykh Muḥammad Taktak walad al-Shaykh al-Nūr Qandilāwī
Shaykh Qāsim b. al-Shaykh Idrīs walad Nāyil, *muqaddam al-sawākira*
Shaykh Muḥammad walad Khiḍr walad Nāyil, shaykh of the compound of Nāṣir, the king's son
Malik al-Ḍaw walad Ḥawā, *malik bursāj*
Shaykh Balūla b. al-Shaykh Bādī, *shaykh al-sajjāda*
the *qāḍī*, `Abd al-`Azīz al-Maghribī al-Marākashī
the *khaṭīb*, Aḥmad the son of the *khaṭīb* `Abd al-Ḥafīẓ walad Nūnū
Arbāb `Ammār, his brother
Shaykh Ḥajar b. al-Shaykh al-Zayn al-Ya`qubābī
Arbāb al-Ḍaw walad Qanbaylī
Arbāb Ḥusayn walad al-`Ūnī, companion of the previous sultans
Arbāb Yūsuf walad Abbakr walad Aḥmad walad `Alwān
Faqīh Ḥijāzī walad Abū Zayd walad al-Shaykh Idrīs walad al-Arbāb
Faqīh Ḥasab Allāh walad Abu'l-Ḥasan, known as "Tōr al-Matn"
Shaykh `Abd Allāh walad Āmina bint Balīla al-Unsābī

Faqīh Muḥammad walad Bashir, a freedman of King Bādī
Ḥājj Markaz, a freedman of Shaykh Jum`a Kākāwī
Ulla b. Khiḍr

The writer of the document, the *faqīr* of God Most High and the most in need of God, Ibrāhīm Ya`qūb `Abd al-Rāziq Muḥammad Ḥamīran, is a witness to it, and God suffices us with two witnesses. That was written on the afternoon of Tuesday, the first day of God's holy month of Dhu'l-Ḥijja, from the months of the year 1194, one thousand one hundred ninety-four from the *hijra* of the prophet, upon whose master the purest of salutations and best of peace.

[1]For a previously published version see Jay Spaulding, "A Confirming Charter of Sultan `Adlān b. Ismā`īl of Sinnār," *Sudan Texts Bulletin* 3 (1981): 20-37. The original is filed in the National Records Office as Miscellaneous 1/41/869, and the copy as 1/41/868.

[2]*Ṭabaqāt*, pp. 99-100; see the introduction to Doc. 16.

[3]The present document seems to supply the first reference to the place-name "Khartoum."

[4]Brocchi, *Giornale*, Vol. 5, pp. 260, 429.

[5]Spaulding, *Heroic Age*, pp. 338-339.

[6]See also Doc. 16.

[7]Lacuna.

[8]Error in original

[9]For the seal of `Adlān see Abū Salīm, *al-Khatm*, p. 65.

[10]Dittography in original.

[11]Restored from NRO Miscellaneous 1/41/868.

[12]The *muqran* is the tip of the peninsula between the Blue and White Niles.

DOCUMENT 25

Document 25 is a confirming charter issued by Sultan `Adlān b. Ismā`īl to the Awlād al-Shaykh Khōjalī on 17 Dhu'l-Ḥijja 1195/4 December 1781. The text has been taken by the editors from the original, which is easily legible and intact except for minor fraying with loss of a few letters along the right edge.[1] The charter confirms the grant of Jundīya Island to the Awlād al-Shaykh Khōjalī. After a review of previous litigation (Docs. 14, 18), the document describes the rejection of a new challenge along the eastern boundary of the estate. The witness roster reflects the relative tranquility of the early rule of the Hamaj Regent Rajab b. Muḥammad Abū Likaylik. Noteworthy is the brief appearance of a court faction identified as "the Funj" and associated with the family of the king; they were soon to follow Sultan `Adlān into revolt against the Hamaj.[2] In this witness roster the fashion for claiming several generations of ancestors through the male line reached an apogee perhaps best personified by the scribe.[3]

باسمك يا كريم بسم الله الرحمن الرحيم نستفتح باسمك العظيم و نتوكل عليه فى جميع
الامور و لا حول و لا قوة الا بالله العلى العظيم / الحمد لله الذى شهدت بوجوده جميع
الكاينات و دلت على وحدانيته عجايب المصنوعات الحمد لله ايد الشريعة المحمدية
بالادلة القرءانية / و القواطع الحكمية المنزلة على خير البرية صلى الله عليه و سلم تسليما
كثيرا طيبا مباركا رب العالمين الحمد لله الذى بلغ الرسول و نحن ءامنا بما / يقول

الواثق بالملك
الجليل
السلطان عدلان بن
عيل
السلطان اسما ١١٩٠[4]

حجة سلطانية و وثيقة ملوكية بمدينة سنار المحروسة المحمية اجلها الله تعالى لدا متوليها فوق الموالى و بجهة الايام و الليالى من زالت به غبن / المحس و الضلالة و زالت بوجوده اهل المكر و الجهالة و استجلب العدل لى البلاد و زال به اهل العناد و الفساد فهو كهفا لكل ملتجى و عونا لكل مرتجى / صاحب اللب المذكور و الكف المنصور و المقام المخبور الذى له فى كل الرام الاصابة و فى كل الوقايع المهابة من ورث المملكة من اجداده و اختص بالملك / و الشرف دون اضداده السلطان المكين و فى دين الله صادق و امين فباسمه طاب الملك و النظام و انقادت لهيئته جميع العسلر على التمام فبملكه / زال الاسر عن المغلوب و الهم عن الموهوب فتكاملت له الفضايل كلها و السجايا و ازاح الله به المحس و البلايا شجاع همام و فارس درغام هازم الالوف / و كاسرالصفوف وافر السجيه و ملاطف للرعيه اصيل الجد حسين الخد بهجة الملوك شرارة للخصيم مبدى لصاحبه البشرى و التسليم كلامه كالدر / المنظوم و لفظه كالخط المرسوم فارس النجابة و سريع الاجابة بيت الامانه السالم من الكذب و الخيانة الفارس اللبيب و البطل النجيب الواثق بالملك / الجليل السلطان بن السلطان السلطان المظفر المعان السلطان عدلان بن المرحوم السلطان اسماعيل نصره الله الرحمن الرحيم بجاه القران / العظيم و النبى الكريم ءامين ءامين يا رب العالمين الى حضرت كل من تقف عليه هذه الوثيقة و الناظر لما فيها من الحقيقه و بعد فان السلطان / المحفوظ المبرور الموید المنصور السلطان عدلان تمم و امضا ما فعلوه السلاطين السابقين السلطان بادى جده و السلطان ناصر عمه / و السلطان اسماعيل ابيه من الصدقة التى تصدقوا بها على الشيخ خوجلى و هى الجزيرة الجنديه و ما احتوت عليه من رفيده و القطعيه و هى محدده / من الاركان الاربعة صعيدا و سافلا و شرقا و غربا فاما حدها من جهة الصعيد الفى الشرق سدرت التويراب و من الغرب السياله الكبيرة المقابلا / قرن الجبل الازرق و من جهة السافل الفاصل البين المحداب و النوفلاب و يخرج هذا الفاصل قبله و يركز فوق (كرس)[5] الدليباب و حدها من جهة / المشرق كرس الدليباب ايضا فحدها من جهة الغرب كرس المحداب الذى فصله السلطان نول لبادى ولد سرير ثم فى ءاخر ملك السلطان بادى / ناس الشرق نازعوا اولاد الشيخ خوجلى فى المرن الشرقى و اشتكوا اولاد الشيخ خوجلى للسلطان بادى و ارسل السلطان بادى مراسيله[6] / معاهم و هم محمد الفقير ولد عمران و البدوى ولد عم الجندى تكتك و الشيخ محمد الامين بن الشيخ مسمار / ارسل معهم الارباب بدوى ولد عمه و قدموا مراسيل / السلطان بادى و مرسال ولد عجيب و حضروا من ناس البلد جمع كثير و الحراث الكبار العارفين الحدود وقعوا فى منجر فوق كرس الدليباب / عند الفاصل و اخرجوا المرن بين الكرس و القرير الى جهة الصعيد علموه بحجارة و فى دار ولد المشاطه مرقوا المرن فوق الحرازة و اوسموها و اخرجوه / فوق حد الكرس الى سدرت التويراب و انقطعوا ناس منجرو ناس عبد

القادر ولد حماد و ناس ولد نعمه و المحمداب الجميع انقطعوا من اولادالشيخ / خوجلى
و حسبوا مراسيل السلطان بادى بحضرت الجمع الكثير على ان من يدخل فى هذا
الحد شرقا و غربا عليه حسب الملك و فوقه الف للملك و مرسال / ولد عجيب كذلك
قال اليدخل فى هذا الحد شبرا واحدا يقع عليه الحسب و فوقه الف قرش ثم لما
تولى ابنه السلطان ناصر قدموا الى عنده اولاد الشيخ خوجلى / و باركوا له فى الدار و
طلبوا منه ان يتمم لهم صدقة ابيه السلطان بادى و الحال ان اولاد سرير و جرايهم
اولاد رحمه حضروا و نازعوا اولاد الشيخ خوجلى فى الجزيره ولد / حريحير و السلطان
ناصر مرق لهم الشيخ محمد ابو لكيلك و الشيخ محمد الامين ولد مسمار وقعوا الجميع
فى الدانقه و قروا ورقت الملك بادى بحضرت اولاد ولد سرير / و جرايهم و تبينت
الجزيره ولد حريحير فى بطن الحدود الاربعة ليست الجزيرة هذه خارجه من الحدود
الاربعه و انقطعوا اولاد سرير و جرايهم و اولاد رحمه من جميع / الدار ولد حريحير و
غيرها لا طالب و لا مطلوب ثم ان السلطان اسماعيل بعدما نظر فى حكم هذه الوثيقه
تمم و امضا ذلك كله لاولاد الشيخ خوجلى و اقرها على حدودها / الاربعه المذكوره الذى
حصل فيه نزاع و الذى لم يحصل فيه نزاع كله مقابلا اولاد الشيخ خوجلى ثم لما تولى
ابنه السلطان عدلان نازعوهم اولادعبد الهادى / عبد الحافظ و اخوانه من جهة الحد
الشرقى فى الاقانين و شكوهم للسلطان عدلان و السلطان عدلان ارسل لاولاد الشيخ
خوجلى و حضروا اولاد / [7] اولاد الشيخ خوجلى مع اولاد عبد الهادى فى وجه الوزير
الشيخ رجب بن الشيخ محمد ابو لكيلك و الشيخ رجب حضر الفونج و عيلة الملك و
اتكلموا اولاد / عبدالهادى مع اولاد الشيخ خوجلى و الشيخ رجب قال لهم عرضوا
مكاتيبكم و عرضوا مكاتيبهم الفريقين و انقطعوا اولاد عبد الهادى من دعويهم / فى
الاقانين و غيرها و بقى الحق لاولاد الشيخ خوجلى و صاروا اولادعبد الهادى مقطوعين
النزاع لا لهم دعوى و لا طلب و انا السلطان عدلان / تممت صدقة الجزيره لاولاد
الشيخ خوجلى و حكمت بانقطاع اولاد عبد الهادى و قررت الجزيره على حدودها
المعلومه شرقا و غربا و سافلا / و صعيدا الذى حصل فيه نزاع و الذى لم يحصل فيه
نزاع كلها مقابلا اولاد الشيخ خوجلى و هذا كله فعله السلطان عدلان ابتغاء لوجه الله
تعالى / و طلبا للثواب فى دار الماب و ليوم لا ينفع فيه مال و لا بنون الا من اتى الله
بقلب سليم و صارت جملة هذه الجزيره صدقة و ملكا لاولادالشيخ خوجلى / لهم و
لذريتهم و ذرية ذريتهم يتوارثونها من وارث لوارث حتى يرث الله الارض و من عليها
و هو خير الوارثين لا ينازعهم فى صدقة هذه الجزيره / منازع و لا يتعرض لهم فيها
متعرض ساله مسلمه من جميع الشرور و السبل و المضار لا عليها هذه الجزيره جساره و
لا خساره و لا نزول فيها و لا ضيافه / و لا علوق و لا كليقه و لا عاده و لا عانه و لا
قل و لا جل و لا شىء من السبل العاديه و نوكد عليكم يا جميع الشيوخ و المقاديم و

الجراى الذين من تحتهم الى / حد ملكى كله خصوصا اولاد بادى ولد سرير و جرايهم اولاد رحمه و من ياتى بعدهم الى قيام الساعة لا احدا منكم يتعرض لاولاد الشيخ خوجلى / فى هذه الصدقه و لا احدا منكم يتعرض لذريتهم و لا لذرية ذريتهم فى صدقة هذه الجزيره المذكوره و من تعرض لها بعد كلامى و وثيقتى هذه فقد عرض / نفسه للهلاك و الحذر ثم الحذر من المخالفه و المخالف لا يلوم الا نفسه

حضر ذلك و شهد به

الشيخ هارون ولد يونس
و الجندى شوال / اخيه جندى السوق
و الوزير الشيخ رجب ولد الشيخ محمدابو لكيلك
و الشيخ الضو ولد مريسه شيخ حوش خال الملك
و الشيخ محمد الامين ولد مسمار شيخ / قرى
و الشيخ دكين شيخ اليس
و الشيخ مسمار ولد حمد الزير شيخ التاكه
و الشيخ الفضيل ولد مسمار شيخ اتبره
و الشيخ عبد العاطى // بن الشيخ محمد قيلى شيخ بيله
و الشيخ عمر ولد الشيخ قاسم / شيخ القربين
و الشيخ احمد ولد على شيخ البحر
و الشيخ / قاسم ولد الشيخ ادريس ولد نايل مقدم السواكره /
و السلطان ءادم ولد السلطان خميس سلطان فور / المسبعاتى
و الشيخ محمد تكتك ولد الشيخ النور قندلاوى / شيخ القواريه
و الشيخ محمد ولد خضر شيخ حوش ولد / الملك
و الشيخ اونسه ولد قدا شيخ الراو
و الشيخ محمد / ولد ناصر شيخ بيت الهدوم
و الملك الضو ولد جميل / ملك برساج
و الشيخ بلوله ولد الشيخ بادى شيخ السجاده /
و القاضى الشريف عبد العزيز
و الخطيب احمد ولد / عبد الحفيظ ولد نونو
و الارباب عمار اخيه
و الارباب / الضو ولد يحيا ولد شنبلى
و الارباب سليمان /

و الارباب حسين ولد العونى
و الارباب (يوسف)[8] / ولد ابكر
و الشريف محمد الساسى
(و الحاج مركز)[8] / معتوق جمعه
و الفقيه محمد ولد (بشير)[8] معتوق الملك
و الفقيه مدنى ترباس ولد محمد / ولد مدنى

و مسطر الحروف خضر ابراهيم يعقوب / عبد الرازق محمد حميرا شاهد بذلك و كفى بالله / شهيدا تحرير ذلك عصر الثلاثا و سبعة عشر يوم خلت من شهر ذو الحجة الحرام من شهور / سنة ١١٩٥ الف و ماية و خمسة و تسعين من الهجرة النبوية على صاحبها / افضل الصلاة و ازكى السلام

In Thy name, O Generous One. In the name of God, the Merciful, the Compassionate. We seek the assistance of Thy mighty name, and rely upon Him in every matter. There is no power and no strength save in God the Exalted and Mighty. Praise be to God, to Whose presence all living beings testify, and Whose unity is indicated by the marvels of man's handiwork. Praise be to God, [Who] has confirmed the Muḥammadan law with Qur'ānic proofs and definitive judgments that descended upon the best of creation. May God, the Lord of the Universe, bless him and grant him complete, abundant, good, and blessed peace. Praise be to God, Who sent the messenger. We believe in what he says.

He who trusts in the Sublime King
Sultan `Adlān, the son of Sultan
Ismā`īl 1190/1776-1777

A sultanic charter and royal document [issued] in the divinely guarded and protected city of Sinnār, may God Most High exalt her, in the presence of her warden, [who stands] over the subjects by day and by night, with whom the wrong of tribulation and error ceased, and with whose presence the people of deceit and ignorance vanished, who procured justice for the nations, with whom the people of opposition and corruption vanished. He is a cave to every refugee, and an aid to all who aspire. Celebrated of intellect, victorious of hand and renowned of rank, he has the answer to every desire, and dignity for every occasion. He inherited the kingdom from his forefathers, and he alone enjoys the distinction of rule without opposition. The powerful sultan, who is true and faithful in the religion of God. With his name, rule and order became pleasant, and all the soldiers of his corps obey him precisely. In his reign the fetter has fallen from the captive, and anxiety from the fortunate. All the virtues are perfected in his character, and through him God has banished trials and tribulations. A gallant hero and knight, the lion, the vanquisher of thousands and shatterer of the ranks, abounding in character and kindly to the subjects, noble of ancestry and handsome of face, resplendence of the kings, a spark to the adversary but a source of good tidings and cheer to his friend. His speech is like strung pearls, and his words like drawn calligraphy, a knight of nobility, swift in reply, abode of fidelity, safe from lies and treachery, the intelligent knight and well-born hero. He who trusts in the Sublime King, the sultan, the son of the sultan, the victorious and divinely aided Sultan `Adlān, son of the late Sultan Ismā`īl. May God, the Merciful, the Compassionate, grant him victory through the influence of the sublime Qur'ān and the eminent prophet. Amen, amen, O Lord of the Universe.

To the presence of all who read this document and see the truth therein.

Thereafter: The divinely preserved, pious, divinely assisted and victorious Sultan `Adlān has confirmed and ratified what the previous sultans--Sultan Bādī his grandfather, Sultan Nāṣir his paternal uncle, and Sultan Ismā`īl his father--have done in regard to the gift of alms they bestowed upon Shaykh

Khōjalī. It is the island of al-Jundīya, including Rafīda and al-Qaṭ`īya. It is bounded on the four corners; south, north, east, and west. As for its boundary on the southern side, on the east it is the *sidr* tree of the Tuwayrāb and on the west the big watercourse across from the peak of Jabal Azraq. On the northern side [its boundary is] the *fāṣil* between the Muḥammadāb and the Nōfalāb; this *fāṣil* goes on beyond that, and is fixed above the *kurus* of the Dōlībāb. Its boundary on the western side is the *kurus* of the Muḥammadāb, which Sultan Nōl delineated for Bādī walad Sarīr. Then, late in the reign of Sultan Bādī people of the east disputed with the Awlād al-Shaykh Khōjalī concerning the eastern *mirin*, and the Awlād al-Shaykh Khōjalī complained to Sultan Bādī. Sultan Bādī sent his messengers with them; they were Muḥammad al-Faqīr walad `Imrān and al-Badawī the son of the paternal uncle of the *jundī* Taktak. Shaykh Muḥammad al-Amīn b. al-Shaykh Mismār sent with them Arbāb Badawī, the son of his paternal uncle. The messengers of Sultan Bādī and the messenger of Walad `Ajīb came. A great multitude of the people of the land were present, and the old cultivators who knew the boundaries. They stood at the *fāṣil* above the *kurus* of the Dōlībāb in Manjar and delineated the *mirin* between the *kurus* and the *qurayr* as far as the southern side, marking it with stones. In Walad al-Mushāṭa they made the *mirin* run above the *ḥarāz* tree, which they marked with a blaze, and they delineated it above the edge of the *kurus* to the *sidr* tree of the Tuwayrāb. The people of Manjar, the people of `Abd al-Qādir walad Ḥammād, the people of Walad Ni`ma, and all the Muḥammadāb, have been cut off from the Awlād al-Shaykh Khōjalī. The messengers of Sultan Bādī, in the presence of the great multitude, charged whomsoever might trespass this boundary from east or west with the king's reckoning, and subjected him to [a fine of] one thousand [*qirsh*] to the king. The messenger of Walad `Ajīb likewise said: "He who trespasses this boundary by even a single hand's breadth falls under the reckoning, and he is subject to [a fine of] one thousand *qirsh*." Then when his son Sultan Nāṣir succeeded, the Awlād al-Shaykh Khōjalī came before him and blessed him [as the new ruler of] the country. They asked him to confirm for them the gift of alms of his father, Sultan Bādī. The circumstances were that the Awlād Sarīr and their *jarāī* the Awlād Raḥma had presented themselves to dispute with the Awlād al-Shaykh Khōjalī concerning the island of Walad Ḥarīḥīr. Sultan Nāṣir sent to them Shaykh Muḥammad Abū Likaylik and Shaykh Muḥammad al-Amīn walad Mismār. They all sat in the *danga* and examined the document of King Bādī in the presence of the Awlād Walad Sarīr and their *jarāī*. It was established that the island of Walad Ḥarīḥīr was within the four boundaries and that no [part of] this island was outside the four boundaries. The Awlād Sarīr and their *jarāī* and the Awlād Raḥma have been cut off from all the estate, Walad Ḥarīḥīr and the rest of it. There is neither a claimant nor a claim. Thereupon Sultan Ismā`īl, after he had examined the ruling of the document, confirmed and ratified all that to the Awlād al-Shaykh Khōjalī. He confirmed it according to its four said boundaries, [both] those concerning which there had been dispute and those concerning which there had not been [any] dispute, all of it, as an award to the Awlād al-Shaykh Khōjalī. Then, when his son Sultan `Adlān succeeded, the Awlād `Abd al-Hādī--`Abd al-Ḥāfiẓ and his brothers--disputed with them [the Awlād al-Shaykh Khōjalī] concerning the eastern boundary in al-Aqānīn, and complained about them to Sultan `Adlān. Sultan `Adlān sent for the Awlād al-Shaykh Khōjalī, and the sons of the Awlād al-Shaykh Khōjalī appeared before the *wazīr* Shaykh Rajab b. al-Shaykh Muḥammad Abū Likaylik together with the Awlād `Abd al-Hādī. Shaykh Rajab summoned into his presence the Funj and the family of the king, and the Awlād `Abd al-Hādī spoke with the Awlād al-Shaykh Khōjalī. Shaykh Rajab said to them: "Present your documents." The two parties presented their documents. The Awlād `Abd al-Hādī were cut off in their claim to al-Aqānīn and so forth, for the right to it belonged to the Awlād al-Shaykh Khōjalī. The Awlād `Abd al-Hādī were cut off in their dispute, having neither a plea nor a claim. I, Sultan `Adlān, have confirmed the gift of alms of the island to the Awlād al-Shaykh Khōjalī. I have ruled that the Awlād `Abd al-Hādī be cut off. I have confirmed the island according to its well-known boundaries, east, west, north, and south, [both] those concerning which there had been dispute and those concerning which there had not been [any] dispute, all of it, as an award to the Awlād al-Shaykh Khōjalī. All this Sultan `Adlān has done for the sake of God Most High, asking for reward in the life to come, for a day in which neither wealth nor sons suffice, unless one comes to God with a secure heart. All this island has become a gift of alms and property of the Awlād al-Shaykh Khōjalī; it is for them, their descendants and their descendants' descendants. They shall bequeath it from heir to heir until God inherits the earth and those upon it, and He is the Best of Heirs. Let no challenger challenge them concerning the gift of alms of this island. Let no troublemaker trouble them in it. It is completely free from all *shurūr*, *subul*, and *maḍārr*. This island is not subject to *jusāra*, *khusāra*, *nuzūl*, *ḍiyāfa*, *`ulūq*, *kalīqa*, *`āda*, *`āna*, *qill*, *jill*, nor any of the customary *subul*. We command you peremptorily, all you shaykhs and *muqaddam*s, and the *jarāī* who are under them throughout my kingdom, all, and especially the Awlād Bādī walad Sarīr and their *jarāī* the Awlād Raḥma, and whoever may come after them until the hour of resurrection, let no one of you trouble the Awlād al-Shaykh Khōjalī in this gift of alms, and let no one of you trouble their descendants or their descendants' descendants concerning the gift of alms of this said island. He who troubles it after my words and this my document has exposed himself to destruction. Beware, then beware of disobedience, and let the disobedient blame none but himself.

There were present and witnessed to it:

Shaykh Hārūn walad Yūnus
the *jundī*, Shawwāl his brother, *jundī* of the market
the *wazīr*, Shaykh Rajab walad al-Shaykh Muḥammad Abū Likaylik
Shaykh al-Ḍaw walad Murīsa, shaykh of the compound of the maternal uncle of the king
Shaykh Muḥammad al-Amīn walad Mismār, Shaykh of Qarrī
Shaykh Dakīn, Shaykh of Alays

Shaykh Mismār walad Ḥammad al-Zīr, Shaykh of al-Tāka
Shaykh al-Faḍīl walad Mismār, Shaykh of Atbara
Shaykh `Abd al-`Aṭā b. al-Shaykh Muḥammad Qaylī, Shaykh of Bayla
Shaykh `Umar walad al-Shaykh Qāsim, Shaykh of al-Qarbīn
Shaykh Aḥmad walad `Alī, Shaykh of al-Baḥr
Shaykh Qāsim walad al-Shaykh Idrīs walad Nāyil, *muqaddam al-sawākira*
Sultan Adam walad al-Sultan Khamīs, Sultan Fūr al-Musabba`ātī
Shaykh Muḥammad Taktak walad al-Shaykh al-Nūr Qandilāwī, *shaykh al-quwwārīya*
Shaykh Muḥammad walad Khiḍr, shaykh of the compound of the king's son
Shaykh Unsa walad Qudā, *shaykh al-rāw*[9]
Shaykh Muḥammad walad Nāṣir, shaykh of the wardrobe
Malik al-Ḍaw walad Jamīl, *malik bursāj*
Shaykh Balūla walad al-Shaykh Bādī, *shaykh al-sajjāda*
the *qāḍī*, Sharīf `Abd al-`Azīz
the *khaṭīb*, Aḥmad walad `Abd al-Ḥafīẓ walad Nūnū
Arbāb `Ammār, his brother
Arbāb al-Ḍaw walad Yaḥyā walad Shanbalī
Arbāb Sulaymān
Arbāb Ḥusayn walad al-`Ūnī
Arbāb [Yūsuf] walad Abbakr
Sharīf Muḥammad al-Sāsī
[Ḥājj Markaz], a freedman of Jum`a
Faqīh Muḥammad walad Bashīr, a freedman of the king
Faqīh Madanī Turbās walad Muḥammad walad Madanī

The writer of the letters, Khiḍr Ibrāhīm Ya`qūb `Abd al-Rāziq Muḥammad Ḥamīran, is a witness to that, and with God, two witnesses suffice. That was written on the afternoon of Tuesday, when seventeen days had passed from the holy month of Dhu'l-Ḥijja from the months of the year 1195, one thousand one hundred ninety-five from the *hijra* of the prophet, upon whose master the best of prayers and purest peace.

[1]For a previously published version see Abū Salīm, *al-Fūnj wa'l-arḍ*, pp. 116-120.

[2]Spaulding, *Heroic Age*, pp. 326-347.

[3]Ibid., pp. 215-217.

[4]Two impressions of the seal appear here; see Abū Salīm, *al-Khatm*, p. 65.

[5]The scribe consistently writes *kursī*.

[6]A blank line follows, perhaps to accommodate the folding of the document; the text continues without interruption.

[7]Dittography in original.

[8]Lacuna. A conjectural reading of the missing text has been taken from Doc. 24.

[9]In Taqalī, Ewald found the *rāw* to be "A two story building incorporated into the royal hawsh's fence which housed the royal drum and where the arbab al-thamaniya meet" ("Leadership and Social Change," Vol. 2, p. 342). The term is in general use throughout the northern Sudan for an elevated, fortified, governmental structure and probably does not, as she suggests, derive from the languages of Taqalī or Tagoi.

DOCUMENT 26

Document 26 is a charter issued by Ibrāhīm b. Muḥammad Abū Likaylik concerning a dispute over land between Ḥājj Ḥāmid walad `Awūḍa and `Ubayd walad Idrīs. The text has been taken by the editors from a photocopy of the original.[1] The document is truncated at the bottom; only the opening protocols and the beginning of the body are present. The charter was written after the death of Abū Likaylik in about 1188/1774-1775 and before the execution of Ibrāhīm at the beginning of 1200/1785; it was probably issued between 1782 and 1785, when Ibrāhīm governed the town of Sinnār on behalf of the Regent Rajab while the latter was absent on campaign in Kordofan.[2] The present document is the first of a pair, with Doc. 62, concerning the rival claims of the two litigants. Both stages in the dispute were ajudicated in al-Tumayd, which is identified as a trading center or *bandar*. The land in dispute probably lay on the west bank of the Blue Nile slightly below modern Hassaheisa. Document 26 concerns the land itself (*dār*), while Doc. 62 addresses the question of enduring original residual rights (*aṣl*); from the latter one may infer that Ḥājj Ḥāmid was the successful litigant on both occasions. Noteworthy is Ibrāhīm's use of an *inscriptio* typical of, and appropriate to, a private legal document of the period rather than the formula common to most public documents of Sinnār.

بسم الله الرحمن الرحيم / الحمد لله و الصلاة و السلام على سيدنا رسول الله / صلى
الله عليه و سلم / حجة سلطانية و وثيقة ملوكية واقعة / ببندر التميد المحروسة المحمية
اجلها الله تعالى / لدا متوليها و الحاكم (يوميذ)[3] بما فيها مالك اعنة قاصيها / و
دانيها و حاضرها و باديها فذاك الشيخ ابراهيم ابن / المرحوم الشيخ محمد ابو لكيلك
نصره الله امين و بعد مما احتيج اليه و وجب الاشهاد عليه فان الحاج / حامد ولد
عوضة و عبيد ولد ادريس تنازعوا / فى دار ولد كبوكنى و سيف الدين و الحاج
قال الدار / هذه (. . .)[4]

In the name of God, the Merciful, the Compassionate. Praise be to God, and prayers and peace upon our lord the messenger of God. May God bless him and grant him peace.

A sultanic charter and royal document issued in the *bandar* of al-Tumayd, the divinely guarded and protected, may God Most High exalt her, in the presence of her warden, the governor [at the present time] of what is in her, master of the reins of her far places and near, her sedentaries and pastoralists, that is, Shaykh Ibrāhīm, son of the late Shaykh Muḥammad Abū Likaylik. May God grant him victory. Amen. According to what is necessary for it, as written certification requires: Ḥājj Ḥāmid walad `Awūḍa and `Ubayd walad Idrīs disputed concerning the estate of Kabūknī and Sayf al-Dīn. Ḥājj said: "This estate (. . .)."

[1]For previously published versions see Sadik Nur, "Land Tenure," pp. 51-52 and Plate VIa, and Abū Salīm, *al-Fūnj wa'l-arḍ*, p. 142.

[2]Spaulding, *Heroic Age*, pp. 325, 339-343.

[3]Restored by Dr. Abū Salīm.

[4]The balance of the document is missing.

DOCUMENT 27

Document 27 is a charter issued on 6 Jumāda II 1203/4 March 1789 to Faqīh Muḥammad walad Dā'ūd of Kitra, confirming his right to lands his family had held under sultanic grant since the reign of Bādī II. The text has been taken by the editors from Neil McHugh's study of a nineteenth-century copy.[1] The beneficiary was a member of the Ya`qūbāb community of the `Abbūd area, and a prominent personal supporter of the late Muḥammad Abū Likaylik.[2] It is noteworthy that neither the name of the charter-issuing benefactor (presumably the incumbent Regent Nāṣir b. Muḥammad Abū Likaylik) nor the reigning sultan is mentioned. This may be a copyist's oversight, but it may also reflect troubled conditions at the capital at the time the charter was issued; it is quite possible that as of March 1789 no successor to the late Sultan `Adlān had yet been chosen, nor had Nāṣir yet been formally invested as Regent.[3]

بسمك يا كريم انه من سليمان و انه بسم الله الرحمن الرحيم الا تعلوا على واتونى /
مسلمين[4] الحمد لله الذى بلغ الرسول و نحن امنا بما يقول /
حجة و وثيقه مملوكيه بمملكه سنار المحميه اعلى الله تعالى لمتوليها السلطان المكين و فى
دين الله / صادق و امين و باسمه طاب الملك و النظام و انقادة جميع العساكر (على
التمام)[5] فبملكه ذل الاسر على / المغلوب و الهم عن المهموم فنطقه المشاهد كلها بان
السلطان قد تمم و امضى ما فعلوه السلطين / السابقين من صدقة الدار التى تصدق بها
السلطان بادى ولد ارتبات للشيخ حمدان البطران / و (قال)[6] الشيخ محمد ابو
لكيلك قد تصدقت بها و امضيتها الى الشيخ محمد ولد داوود صدقة لله و لرسوله / له
و لذريته لا يعارضه فيها معارض و الدار المذكوره معلومة البقعة و الحدود فحدها من

جيهة / الصعيد حفيرات المحمديه و من جيهة الصبح ترس الامين الكاملى و التب ابوا عشيره و دبة / رحوم و دار ام الك و من السافل الموالح التومات و درب السنط الذى يروح الى الشبيك / و من جيهة الغرب عن الحجيرات العاقبات قوز الطوالى عند الميكح ام ساق فهنا انتهت الحدود / و صارت الدار المذكوره بحدودها المعلومه صدقة و ملك للشيخ محمدولدداوود له و لذريته يتوارثها / من وارث الى وارث حتى يرث الله الارض و من عليها و هو خير الوارثين لا ينازعه فى هذه الصدقة / منازع و لا يتعرض لهم فيها متعرض سالمة من جميع الشرور و السبل و المضار لا عليها جسارة و لا / خسارة و لا عادة و لا عنادة و لا ربط و لا حل و لا شى من السبل العاديه و ناكد عليكم يا جميع / الشيوخ و المقاديم و الجراى الى حد ملكى كله لا احد منكم يتعرض الى الشيخ محمد ولد داوود له و لا لذريته / (فى هذه) الصدقه و من تعرض بعد هذا فقد عرض نفسه للهلاك و الحذر ثم الحذر من الخلاف و المخالف (لا يلوم الى نفسه)[7] //

الشهدا على ذالك

الشيخ هارون ولد يونس / امين السلطان
و الجندى على ولد شوال / جندى السوق
و الشيخ ناصر بن محمد لكيلك /
و الشيخ سباب ولد عبد الرازق شيخ حوش ناصر /
و الشيخ عبد الله ولد محمد الامين
و الشيخ عمر جور / ولد حمد دريش
و الشيخ عجيب ولد هاكيت /
و الشيخ محمد كمتور
و الشيخ احمد ولد سليم
و الشيخ ابراهيم / ولد دريش
و الشيخ عمر ولد قاسم شيخ الغرب /
و الشيخ قاسم ولد ادريس مقدم
(و) السلطان محمد ولد بدر /
و الشيخ على ولد مرزوق
و السلطان (. . .)[8] /
(و) دفع الله ولد حسن
و الملك احمد ولد عدلان /

و كان ذلك بيوم الخميس سادس يوم / من شهر الله جماد الثانى سنة ١٢٠٣ الف / و مايتين و ثلاثه من هجرته صلى الله عليه و سلم /

هذه الصوره طبق الاصل حرفا بحرف فيه (. . .)[8]

"In Thy Name, O Generous One. 'Surely it is from Sulaymān and surely it is in the name of God, the Beneficent, the Merciful: That exalt not yourselves against Me and come to me in submission.'"[9] Praise be to God, Who sent the messenger. We believe in what he says.

A charter and royal document [issued] in the divinely protected kingdom of Sinnār. May God Most High exalt her warden the powerful sultan, faithful and true in the religion of God. In his name the domain and order are good, and all the soldiers [obey completely]. Under his rule the bonds of the vanquished are loosened and the downhearted receive inspiration. All the witnesses say that the sultan has confirmed and ratified what the previous sultans did concerning the gift of alms of the estate which Sultan Bādī walad Irtibāṭ bestowed upon Shaykh Ḥamdān al-Baṭrān. Shaykh Muḥammad Abū Likaylik [said]: "I have bestowed it as alms and ratified it for Shaykh Muḥammad walad Dā'ūd." It is a gift of alms for [the sake of] God and His messenger, for him [Muḥammad walad Dā'ūd] and his descendants. Let no troublemaker trouble him in it. The location and boundaries of the said estate are known. Its boundary on the southern side are the reservoirs of the Muḥammadāb; on the eastern side the *turus* of al-Amīn al-Kāmilī, al-Tabb Abū `Ushayra, the *dabba* of Raḥūm, and the estate of the king's mother; on the north al-Mawāliḥ al-Tūmāt and the path of al-Sunuṭ which goes to al-Shibayk; on the west [it is] at the stony ground of Gōz al-Ṭuwālī at al-Maykiḥ Umm Sāq. Here the boundaries end. The said estate, its boundaries known, has become a gift of alms and the property of Shaykh Muḥammad walad Dā'ūd, for him and his descendants. They shall bequeath it from heir to heir until God inherits the earth and those upon it, and He is the Best of Heirs. Let no challenger challenge him concerning this gift of alms. Let no troublemaker trouble them concerning it. It is free from all the *shurūr*, *subul*, and *maḍārr*. It is not subject to *jusāra*, *khusāra*, *`āda*, *`anāda*, *rabṭ*, *ḥall*, nor any of the customary *subul*. We command you peremptorily, all you shaykhs and *muqaddam*s, and the *jarāī* throughout my kingdom, all [of you]. Let no one of you trouble Shaykh Muḥammad walad Dā'ūd or his descendants [concerning this] gift of alms. He who troubles after this has exposed himself to destruction. Beware, then beware of disobedience, and let the disobedient [blame none but himself].

The witnesses to that are:

Shaykh Hārūn walad Yūnus, the *amīn* of the sultan
the *jundī*, `Alī walad Shawwāl, *jundī* of the market
Shaykh Nāṣir b. Muḥammad Abū Likaylik
Shaykh Sabbāb walad `Abd al-Rāziq, shaykh of the compound of Nāṣir
Shaykh `Abd Allāh walad Muḥammad al-Amīn
Shaykh `Umar Jūr walad Ḥammad Darīsh
Shaykh `Ajīb walad Hākīt
Shaykh Muḥammad Kamtūr
Shaykh Aḥmad walad Salīm
Shaykh Ibrāhīm walad Darīsh
Shaykh `Umar walad Qāsim, Shaykh of [al-Qarbīn][10]
Shaykh Qāsim walad Idrīs, *muqaddam*
Shaykh `Alī walad Marzūq
Sultan (. . .)
Daf` Allāh walad Ḥasan
Malik Aḥmad walad `Adlān

That was on Thursday, the sixth day of God's month of Jumāda II in the year 1203, one thousand two hundred three from his [Muḥammad's] *hijra*. May God bless him and grant him peace.

This copy follows the original letter by letter (. . .)

[1]Neil McHugh, "Land, Lords and Holy Men in Eighteenth-Century Sinnār: Two Documents," *Fontes Historiae Africanae: Bulletin d'Information* Nos. 7/8 (1982/1983): 12-32; a photocopy is on p. 31. Dr. McHugh provides numerous corrections to show how this Sudanese text of the late nineteenth century could be transformed into Classical Arabic.

[2]*Ṭabaqāt*, pp. 109-110. For the Ya`qūbāb, see McHugh, "Land, Lords and Holy Men," p. 14 and "Holymen of the Blue Nile."

[3]Jay Spaulding, "Two Documents from the days of Nāṣir b. Muḥammad Abū Likaylik, Hamaj Regent of Sinnār," *Fontes Historiae Africanae: Bulletin d'Information*, Nos. 7/8 (1982-1983): 33-37; see also *Heroic Age*, pp. 344-352.

[4]Qur'ān 27:30.

[5]Omitted from McHugh's text; but see photocopy, p. 31.

[6]McHugh ("Land, Lords and Holy Men, p. 16, note 1), "One word illegible." The present editors have restored this conjectural reading.

[7]The present editors follow McHugh in this conjectural reconstruction.

[8]Lacuna.

[9]The scriptural translation is supplied by McHugh.

[10]The copyist errs in writing *al-gharb*. Copyists omitted many titles, probably because they no longer understood their meaning.

DOCUMENT 28

Document 28 is an originating charter issued by Sultan Bādī V to `Awaḍ al-Karīm "Abū Sinn," Shaykh of the Shukrīya, on 12 Rabī` I 1206/9 November 1791. The text has been taken by the editors from a photocopy of the original, which is intact and easily legible.[1] The grant, probably ordered by the incumbant Regent, Nāṣir b. Muḥammad Abū Likaylik, followed by some years the successful revolt of the Shukrīya against the Hamaj in 1193/1779-1780, and acknowledged their *de facto* independence by bestowing their tribal *dār* upon the rebel leader. The grant, much larger than any other recorded, included a sizeable portion of the Buṭāna, from about the latitude of the confluence (Wad Ḥasūna and Abū Dulayq) southward to al-Luwayqa on the Rahad, between the Blue Nile and the Rahad in the west and the Atbara in the east. The eastern Funj province of al-Tāka hereafter vanished from governmental records, and the claims of the northern provincial governor, the Shaykh of Qarrī or Walad `Ajīb, to Dabarkī on the Dinder and other southeastern territories was rendered very tenuous.[2]

باسمك يا كريم بسم الله الرحمن الرحيم الحمد لله الذى بلغ الرسول و نحن ءامنا بما يقول /

الواثق بالملك
الهادى بن دكين
السلطان بن بادى

حجة سلطانية و وثيقة ملوكية بمدينة سنار المحروسة المحمية اجلها تعالى لدا متوليها سلطان المسلمين و خليفة / رب العالمين القايم بامور الدنيا و الدين المنتصب لمصالح

المسلمين و ناصر شريعة سيد المرسلين و ناشر لواء العدل و الفضل / على كافة العالمين من اصلح الله به العباد و انار به البلاد و قامع اهل الكفر و المكر و العناد و اهل الظلم و الفساد و رحمه الله سبحانه و تعالى / (للحاضر)[3] و الباد الواثق بالملك الهادى السلطان ابن السلطان المظفر المعان السلطان بادى بن المرحوم دكين بن السلطان بادى نصره الله الرحمن الرحيم بجاه القران العظيم و النبى الكريم ءامين ءامين يا رب العالمين الى حضرت كل من تقف عليه / هذه الوثيقة و الناظر لما فيها من الحقيقة و بعد فان السلطان المحفوظ المبرور المويد المنصور السلطان بادى اعطى / و امضا امضاء تاما للشيخ عوض الكريم ابى سن بن على بن ابى على بن محمد الاديقم شيخ قبيلة الشكرية اطيان مطرية / و بحرية بشرق بحر العاديك و شرق الرهد و هى ارض واسعة حدودها من الصعيد عين اللويقة و من الصباح بحر اتبره لغاية / الشريف حسب الله و من السافل اطيان الشيخ الصالح على ابو دليق و الشيخ الصالح حسن ولد حسونه و من الغرب السحل الشرقى من بحر العاديك و بحر الرهدليعمر فيها قبيلة الشكرية و غيرهم ممن يختارهم و ينتفع باخذ خراجها منهم و يخرج / من داخل تلك الحدود طين العبدلاب فقط عطاء ناجزا له و لذريته و لذرية ذريته الى ما شاء الله لا ينازعهم فيها منازع / و لا يعارضهم فيها معارض و من يتعرض له بعد وثيقتى هذه فقد عرض نفسه للهلاك و الحذر ثم الحذرمن المخالفة و المخالف / لا يلوم الا نفسه

حضر ذلك و شهد به

الوزير الشيخ ناصر بن الشيخ محمد ابو لكيلك
و الامين الشيخ هارون ولد / يونس
و الجندى على ولد شوال جندى السوق
و الشيخ صباب ولد عبد الرازق شيخ حوش خال الملك
و الشيخ بادى / ولد مسمار شيخ قرى
و الشيخ عمر جور ولد حمد الزير شيخ التاكة
و الشيخ عجيب ولد هاكيت شيخ اتبرة
و الشيخ / ابراهيم ولد عبدالعاطى شيخ بيله
و الشيخ صباحى ولد عدلان شيخ البحر
و الشيخ و الشيخ [4] على ولد النور / شيخ كردفال
و الشيخ قاسم ولد ادريس ولد نايل مقدم السواكرة

و السلطان عبد الله ولد السلطان بادى سلطان / فور المسبعات
و الملك احمد ولد عدلان ملك برساج
(. . .)[5] شيخ السجاده
و الشيخ مدنى ولد شنبول شيخ اربجى
و الشيخ / على ولد محمود شيخ القوارية
و الموذن عثمان ولد بلى
و القاضى الشريف عمر
و الخطيب نوار ولد عمار

و مسطر / الحروف فقير الله خضر ابراهيم يعقوب حميرا و كفى بالله شهيدا
(تحرير)[6] ذلك ظهر الاثنين و اثنا عشر ليلة / خلت من شهر الله ربيع الاول الاول[4] من
شهور سنة ١٢٠٦ بعد المايتين و الالف من الهجرة النبوية / على صاحبها افضل
الصلاة و ازكى السلام

In Thy name, O Generous One. In the name of God, the Merciful, the Compassionate. Praise be to God, Who sent the messenger. We believe in what he says.

He who trusts in the King,
the Guide, the son of Dakīn,
Sultan Bādī

A sultanic charter and royal document [issued] in the divinely guarded and protected city of Sinnār, may God Most High exalt her, in the presence of her warden, the sultan of the Muslims and Caliph of the Lord of the Universe, steadfast in the affairs of this world and of religion, just in the affairs of the Muslims, protector of the law of the lord of the messengers, who spreads the banner of justice and excellence throughout all the universe, through whom God has prospered the worshipers and illuminated the nations, who destroys the people of unbelief, deceit, and opposition, the people of tyranny and corruption.

May God Most High (praise be to Him) be merciful to him in this life and the hereafter. He who trusts in the King, the Guide, the sultan, the son of the sultan, the victorious and divinely aided Sultan Bādī, the son of the late Dakīn, the son of Sultan Bādī. May God, the Merciful, the Compassionate, grant him victory through the influence of the sublime Qur'ān and the eminent prophet. Amen, amen, O Lord of the Universe.

To the presence of all who read this document and see the truth therein.

Thereafter: The divinely protected, pious, divinely assisted and victorious Sultan Bādī has given and ratified completely to Shaykh `Awaḍ al-Karīm Abū Sinn b. `Alī b. Abū `Alī b. Muḥammad al-Idayqim, Shaykh of the Shukrīya tribe, rainland and riverain land east of the Blue Nile and the Rahad. It is a wide land. Its boundary on the southern side is the spring of al-Luwayqa, on the east the Atbara river as far as Sharīf Ḥasab Allāh, on the northern side the lands of the good Shaykh `Alī Abū Dulayq and the good Shaykh Ḥasan walad Ḥasūna, and on the west, the east bank of the Blue Nile and the Rahad. [He has given it] so that the Shukrīya tribe may live in it, along with others whom he may choose, and so that he may benefit through collecting its land tax from them. The land of the `Abdallāb is totally outside what lies within these boundaries. It is a gift, executed for him, his descendants and his descendants' descendants, for as long as God wills. Let no challenger challenge them concerning it. Let no troublemaker trouble them in it. He who troubles it after this my document has exposed himself to destruction. Beware, then beware of disobedience, and let the disobedient blame none but himself.

There were present and witnessed to it:

the *wazīr*, Shaykh Nāṣir b. al-Shaykh Muḥammad Abū Likaylik
the *amīn*, Shaykh Hārūn walad Yūnus
the *jundī*, `Alī walad Shawwāl, *jundī* of the market

Shaykh Ṣabbāb walad ʿAbd al-Rāziq, shaykh of the compound of the maternal uncle of the king
Shaykh Bādī walad Mismār, Shaykh of Qarrī
Shaykh ʿUmar Jūr walad Ḥammad al-Zīr, Shaykh of al-Tāka
Shaykh ʿAjīb walad Hākīt, Shaykh of Atbara
Shaykh Ibrāhīm walad ʿAbd al-ʿAṭā, Shaykh of Bayla
Shaykh Ṣubāḥī walad ʿAdlān, Shaykh of al-Baḥr
Shaykh ʿAlī walad al-Nūr, Shaykh of Kordofāl
Shaykh Qāsim walad Idrīs walad Nāyil, *muqaddam al-sawākira*
Sultan ʿAbd Allāh walad al-Sultan Bādī, Sultan Fūr al-Musabbaʿāt
Malik Aḥmad walad ʿAdlān, *malik bursāj*
[. . .], *shaykh al-sajjāda*
Shaykh Madanī walad Shanbūl, Shaykh of Arbajī
the muezzin, ʿUthmān walad Balla
the *qāḍī*, Sharīf ʿUmar
the *khaṭīb*, Nuwwār walad ʿAmmār

The writer of the letters is the *faqīr* of God, Khiḍr Ibrāhīm Yaʿqūb Ḥamīran. With God, two witnesses suffice. That was written at noon on Monday, when twelve nights had passed from God's month of Rabīʿ I from the months of the year 1206, [six] after the one thousand two hundredth from the *hijra* of the prophet, upon whose master the best of prayers and purest peace.

[1]Sadik Nur, "Land Tenure," Plate 3. For a previously published version see Abū Salīm, *al-Fūnj wa'l-arḍ*, pp. 135-136.

[2]Spaulding, *Heroic Age*, pp. 333-335, 383-391.

[3]Lacuna. A conjectural reading of the missing text has been taken from Doc. 40.

[4]Dittography in original.

[5]It would seem that a name has been omitted here.

[6]Lacuna. The last two letters of this word have been restored by the editors.

DOCUMENT 29

Document 29 is a letter from the Regent Nāṣir b. Muḥammad Abū Likaylik to his governor of the northern province, Bādī b. Mismār. The text has been taken by the editors from the original, which is damaged around all the margins with some loss of text.[1] The letter warned Bādī against tolerating transgressions against the island of al-Karīda, land of the Awlād Dōlīb; a similar warning concerning the same property had been issued by Abū Likaylik himself (Doc. 17). Since Bādī seems to have issued Doc. 51 late in 1794 in response to this request, it is probable that the present document was written earlier in the same year.[2]

الحمد لوليه و الصلاة / و السلام على نبيه /

الوزير الشيخ ناصر
ابن الوزير الشيخ محمد
ابن الشيخ بادى ١٢٠٤[3]

من حضرت المحترم المكرم المهاب المعظم قنديل الزمان و سراج / البلدان و مدمر اهل المكرى و البغى و الطغيان و امين جيش السلطان / افخر الامرا و عمدت الوزرا سيف الله القاطع و سهامه اللامع المعتصم بالله الصمد الوزير الشيخ ناصر ابن المرحوم الشيخ محمد ابلكيلك / نصره الله الرحمن الرحيم امين الى حضرت الشيخ بادى ابن المرحوم الشيخ / مسمار يسلم عليك الوزير الشيخ ناصر كثير السلام و يقول لك ان الذى نعرفك / من جهة الفقرا الدواليب معاكم بالبلد اهل وصالا قديم من جدك الشيخ / عجيب معا جدهم الشيخ محمد ولد دوليب اخوان فى الله و الفقيه السيد / و الفقيه دوليب حضروا وقت جدك الشيخ عبد الله و ابوك الشيخ مسمار / و فى زمنهم ما هم

معاينين احد بعين حرمه فى المراتب ما لا هم و الحاصل / ان السلطان بادى ملك
الفونج تصدق على الفقيه محمد السيد و الفقيه / دوليب بجزيرة الكريده صدقتا لله و
لرسوله و اوقفها عليهم وقفا / راجيا تظلب فى دار الاخر صدقتا قديمة عندهم بلغت
مقدار (ستين)[4] / عام اولاد حسب النبى تخليهم يعارضوهم فيها ليش انت لا
(تعاينهم)[5] بقراهم لكم و لا تعاينهم كونهم اصحاب لنا من ابونا الشيخ (. . .)[6]
/ (. . .)[6] ناسكم ما لهم طريق على الطين // (. . .)[6] / (. . .)[6] / و تقطع
منهم (. . .)[6] / الماله وجه و لا (. . .)[6] الدار هذه بلغت فى ايد / الفقرا مقدار
ستين / عام لا فى الشيوخ اولاد / عجيب القبلك و لا الوكلا / ما فى من عارضهم فيها
/ ذالحين ترا جوابى جاك / بعد الفات لا تحصل / معارضه و لا نزاع فى دار / الفقرا
امنع ناسك اولاد / اخوك اولاد العجيل و جرايهم لا يتعرضوهم ماهم الازرق / لا يشربوه
حبلهم المرمى / لا يشيلوه و ما فعله الملك لهم من الصدق و الشى (الفى)[5] مكتوبهم
ماضى الله الله من الخلاف و نوكد / عليك غاية التاكيد // و القادم اليكم بجوابى حسن
/ انت و الفقه زين العابدين الشيخ // هل يمرق معكم / فى اخوانه واحد كان ماشى
من / خاتم الملك / امرق (منه)[7]

Praise be to His friend, and prayers and peace upon His prophet.

The *wazīr* Shaykh Nāṣir
The son of the *wazīr* Shaykh Muḥammad
The son of Shaykh Bādī 1204/1789-1790

From the presence of the honored, revered, respected, and exalted, candlestick of the age and lamp unto the nations, who destroys the people of deceit, wrongdoing, and oppression, *amīn* of the army of the sultan, the most glorious of commanders and support of the ministers, the sharp sword of God and His flashing arrows, he who relies upon God the Eternal, the *wazīr* Shaykh Nāṣir, son of the late Shaykh Muḥammad Abū Likaylik. May God, the Merciful, the Compassionate, grant him victory. Amen.

To the presence of Shaykh Bādī, son of the late Shaykh Mismār.

The *wazīr* Shaykh Nāṣir greets you with many greetings and says to you: That of which we inform you concerns the *fuqarā'* of the Dōwālīb, a people living together with you in the land as brethern in God from of old, from [the time of] your forefather Shaykh `Ajīb, [who lived] with their forefather Shaykh Muḥammad walad Dōlīb. Faqīh al-Sayyid and Faqīh Dōlīb were present in the time of your grandfather Shaykh `Abd Allāh and your father Shaykh Mismār, and in their times no one was held in higher dignity or esteem than they. It came to pass that Sultan Bādī, King of the Funj, bestowed the island of al-Karīda as alms upon Faqīh Muḥammad al-Sayyid and Faqīh Dōlīb as a gift of alms for the sake of God and His messenger. We gave it to them as a *waqf*,[8] desiring protection in the hereafter; it is theirs as an old gift of alms, and has been for an interval of sixty years. Make the Awlād Ḥasab al-Nabī desist from troubling them concerning it. Why do you not have regard for their recitation of the Qur'ān for you, nor for their being our friends from [the time of] our father Shaykh [Muḥammad Abū Likaylik]? Your people have no access to the cultivated lands [. . .]. This estate has been in the possession of the *fuqarā'* for an interval of sixty years, and none of the shaykhs of the Awlād `Ajīb before you, nor any agent, troubled them in it. Now you see my letter which has come to you. After that, let there be no trouble or dispute concerning the estate of the *fuqarā'*. Forbid your people the Awlād Ḥasab al-Nabī, and forbid the sons of your brother the Awlād al-`Ajayl and their *jarāī* to trouble them. Let them not drink of their blue water, nor carry off [so much as] a rope they have thrown away. What the king did for them concerning the gift of alms and that which is in their documents is valid. God, God, [protect you] against disobedience. We command you most emphatically. Ḥasan is coming to you with my letter. If Faqīh Zayn al-`Abdīn al-Shaykh is going with you, there is one of his brethern who was [also] going on the authority of the king's seal; stay away from him.[9]

[1]For a previously published version see Abū Salīm, *al-Fūnj wa'l-arḍ*, pp. 77-78.

[2]Spaulding, *Heroic Age*, p. 357.

[3]Abū Salīm, *al-Khatm*, p. 69.

[4]Lacuna. Word inserted by the editors on the basis of what follows.

[5]Conjectural reading.

[6]Lacuna.

[7]The *mīm* only is visible. Dr. Abū Salīm (*al-Fūnj wa'l-arḍ*, p. 78) proposes completing the word thus. An alternative reading would be *ma`hū*, which would approximately reverse the meaning of this phrase.

[8]This is one of a very few examples of the designation of land bestowed as alms as being *waqf*; Sinnār did not have a centrally administered *waqf* institution as found in some other Islamic lands.

[9]Or: "Go with him."

DOCUMENT 30

Document 30 is a confirming charter issued by `Adlān b. Muḥammad Abū Likaylik to Faqīh Muḥammad walad Dā'ūd of Kitra on 26 Muḥarram 1210/12 August 1795. The text has been taken by the editors from Neil McHugh's study of a nineteenth-century copy.[1] The document confirms the rights of the Faqīh Muḥammad to ancestral lands, probably those described in greater detail in Doc. 27. It rejects the claim of challenging litigants, who had previously and unsuccessfully pressed their suit before the *qāḍī* Sharīf `Abd al-`Azīz. At the time `Adlān issued this charter he was not yet Regent, but the litigants may have turned to him as a likely successor to the faltering incumbant Nāṣir. In the event, however, `Adlān's brief tenure as Regent would be postponed until the death of his brother Idrīs, who succeeded to the office at Nāṣir's fall.[2]

بسمك يا كريم انه من سليمان و انه بسم الله الرحمن الرحيم الا تعلوا على و اتونى /
(مسلمين)[3] /
فهذه حجة قطعية و وثيقة عادية محررت مرضيه عادليه بالديار الفنجيه بمدينة / سنار المحروسه المحمية اجلها الله لدا متوليها و مالك اعنة قاصيها و دانيها / و حاضرها و باديها و الحاكم يوميذ عليها و ما فيها المحترم المكرم المهاب المعظم الليث / الادهم و الملاذ الافخم مالك العصر امين جيش الملك السلطان افخر الامرا / و عمدة الوزرا سيف الله القاطع اللامع المعتصم بالملك الصمد الشيخ عدلان بن المرحوم / الشيخ محمد وزير المملكة الفنجيه الى حضرة من تقف عليه الوثيقه و الناظر لما فيه / من الحقيقه ان الرجل العاقل البالغ الرشيد فى صحة بدنه من الموانع الشرعيه / شرع الشيخ محمد ولد داوود دعواه فى دار الشيخ حمدان التى كانت صدقة / مشهوره بوثايق من زمن

السلطان بادى ولد ارباط الى السلطان اسماعيل / و الى هذا زمان الوزير بن الشيخ محمد ابو لكيلك و كانوا المدعين هم موسى ولد / نورين و الهادى ولد يعقوب و موسى و اولاد عيسى مرزوق و محمد واولاد الهادى / كلا منهم ان يتكلم بدعوته و تكلما الرجال المذكورين موسى ولد نورين و الهادى / ولد يعقوب فى اصل الدار المذكورة ثم قال لهم الشيخ محمد بن الشيخ داوود مقيمين عليها / من حياة ابونا الشيخ داوود و ابواتكم الفقه الزين و ضو النور و عيسى و اولاد / نورين منقطعين مننا ما لكم فيها دعوة و لا طلب و انا بالبينة العديله و كان / الشيخ محمد بن الشيخ داوود قد عرض وثيقه من عبد العزيز ظهرها على انقطاعهم من اباءهم / و قروا الوثيقه فى وجه الشيخ عدلان بن الشيخ محمد بحضرة جميع غفير و الشيخ محمد بن الشيخ / داوود بالوجه المبين و الشيخ عدلان بن الشيخ محمد قطعها بانقطاع مانع و صارة / (وثيقه)[4] الدار المذكورة بحدودها المعلومه ملكا للشيخ محمد ولد داوود يتوارثونها من / وارث الى وارث الى يرث الله الارض و من عليها و هو خير الوارثين و كان / الشريف عبد العزيز قد تمم و امضا ورقة السلطان ارتباط و السلطان / اسماعيل تمم لورقة السلطان بادى ولد ارتباط و كان المحفوظ المبرور المويد / المنصور الشيخ عدلان بن الشيخ محمد ابو لكيلك قد تمم و امضا ما فعلوه السلاطين / بالحق المبين و على حكم القاضى الشريف عبد العزيز ما فعله بشريعة سيد المرسلين // و قد اثبتت الدار الدار المذكورة دار الفراش / بحدودها المعلومه ملكا للشيخ محمد بن الشيخ / داود لا يعارضه فيها معارض و لا ينازعه / فيها منازع الى ذريته و من تعرض لهم / فى هذه الدار فقد عرض نفسه للهلاك و ذلك / بحضرة جماعة من المسلمين و الحمد لله رب / العالمين

و شهد بذلك

صالح ولد رحمه / (مقدم)[5] فرسان التاكا
و الشيخ قنجارى
و محمد / (. . .)[6]
و احمد ولد كابوا
و ساوى اخيه /
و الفقه احمد بن القاضى نصير
و الفقه احمد / الكامل
و الفقه الضو ولد ابو دليق
و الفقيه / الزين ولد زهرا

و الفقه البشير ولد الترابى /
و الفقه مدنى ولد نجد
و محمد ولد نايل
و ابراهيم / ولد عويضه
و فضل ولد احمد نور
و سناد / و احمد ولد الضو
و مضوى ولد عبد الله /
و فزارى ولد رحمة الله
و الشيخ محمود / ولد ادريس
و المانكروكنا ولد فرج /
و (المانكروكنا)[7] ولد عبد الله

و مسطر الاحرف / محمد ولد على كاتب و شاهد و كفى بالله / شهيدا تحرير ذلك ضحوت / السبت نهار سته و عشرين / يوما خلت من شهر الله عاشور سنة / سنة ١٢١٠ الف و مايتين و عشره سنين بعد هجرة سيد المرسلين عليه افضل الصلاة / و التسليم /

و قد صارت مقابلة هذه الصوره على اصل الصوره المنسوخه منها و بعد التصفح لها حرفا بحرف (وجدت)[7] طبق الاصل من الوثيقة العتيقة و الاعتماد / تصدق منها عليها فيعمل بها كاصلها و السلام /

قاضى الاسلام احمد على

وكيل المحكمة سليمان (حجاز)[7]

"In Thy Name, O Generous One. 'Surely it is from Sulaymān and surely it is in the name of God, the Beneficent, the Merciful: That exalt not yourselves against me and come to me [in submission].'"[9] This is a definitive charter and customary document, equitably written and approved in the Funj territories, in the divinely guarded and protected city of Sinnār, may God Most High exalt her, in the presence of her warden, master of the reins of her far places and near, her sedentaries and pastoralists, the governor at the present time of her and what is in her, the honored, the revered, respected, and exalted, the dark lion, the most splendid refuge, master of the age, *amīn* of the army of the king, the sultan, the most glorious of commanders and support of the ministers, the sharp and flashing sword of God, he who relies upon God the Eternal, Shaykh `Adlān, son of the late Shaykh Muḥammad, *wazīr* of the Funj kingdom.

To the presence of him who reads the document and sees the truth therein.

Shaykh Muḥammad walad Dā'ūd, a man of sound mind, mature, of good reputation, his body free from the canonical impediments, has testified in his plea concerning the estate of Shaykh Ḥamdān, well known to be a gift of alms through documents from the time of Sultan Bādī walad Irbāṭ down to Sultan Ismā`īl, and to this time of the *wazīr* [Nāṣir], son of Shaykh Muḥammad Abū Likaylik. The plaintiffs were Mūsā walad Nūrayn, al-Hādī walad Ya`qūb, Mūsā, the Awlād `Īsā, Marzūq and Muḥammad, and the Awlād al-Hādī; each spoke for his claim. The two men mentioned, Mūsā walad Nūrayn and al-Hādī walad Ya`qūb, each spoke concerning the origin of the said estate. Then Shaykh Muḥammad b. al-Shaykh Dā'ūd said to them: "[We] have been occupying it since the lifetime of our father Shaykh Dā'ūd, whereas your forefathers Faqīh al-Zayn, Ḍaw al-Nūr, `Īsā, and the Awlād Nūrayn have been cut off from us. You have neither a plea nor a claim to it. I bring evidence to that effect." Shaykh Muḥammad walad Dā'ūd presented a document of [the *qāḍī*] `Abd al-`Azīz in which it appeared that they [the plaintiffs] had been cut off from [the time of] their forefathers. The document was read before Shaykh `Adlān b. al-Shaykh Muḥammad, in the presence of a great multitude; Shaykh Muḥammad b. al-Shaykh Dā'ūd had clear proof. Shaykh `Adlān b. al-Shaykh Muḥammad cut it off with a prohibiting severance. The [document of the] said estate, its boundaries known, has become the property of Shaykh Muḥammad walad Dā'ūd. They shall bequeath it from heir to heir until God inherits the earth and those upon it, and He is the Best of Heirs. Sharīf `Abd al-`Azīz had confirmed and ratified the document of Sultan Irtibāṭ, and Sultan Ismā`īl had confirmed the document of Sultan Bādī walad Irtibāṭ. The divinely protected, pious, divinely assisted, and victorious Shaykh `Adlān b. al-Shaykh Muḥammad Abū Likaylik has confirmed and ratified what the sultans did, by clear right and according to the ruling of the *qāḍī*, Sharīf `Abd al-`Azīz, which he had made according to the law of the lord of the messengers. I have confirmed the estate, the said estate, the estate of al-Firāsh, according to its well known boundaries, as the property of Muḥammad b. al-Shaykh Dā'ūd. Let no troublemaker trouble him concerning it, and let no challenger challenge him concerning it--nor his descendants. He who troubles them concerning this estate has exposed himself to destruction. That was in the presence of a gathering of Muslims. Praise be to God, the Lord of the Universe.

There witnessed to that:

Ṣāliḥ walad Raḥma, *muqaddam* of the knights of al-Tāka
Shaykh Qanjārī
Muḥammad [. . .]
Aḥmad walad Kābū
Sāwī, his brother
Faqīh Aḥmad, son of the *qāḍī* Nuṣayyir
Faqīh Aḥmad al-Kāmili
Faqīh al-Ḍaw walad Abū Dulayq
Faqīh al-Zayn walad Zahrā
Faqīh al-Bashīr walad al-Turābī
Faqīh Madanī walad Najdi
Muḥammad walad Nāyil
Ibrāhīm walad `Uwayḍa

Faḍl walad Aḥmad Nūr

Sannād

Aḥmad walad al-Ḍaw

Maḍuwī walad `Abd Allāh

Fazārī walad Raḥmat Allāh

Shaykh Maḥmūd walad Idrīs

Mankrōknā Walad Faraj

Mankrōknā Walad `Abd Allāh

The writer of the letters is Muḥammad walad `Alī, scribe and witness. With God, two witnesses suffice. That was written on the morning of Saturday, when twenty-six days had passed of God's month of `Āshūrā in the year 1210, one thousand two hundred ten years after the *hijra* of the lord of the messengers, upon whom be the best of prayers and peace. This copy was composed with the original of the copy, from which it was copied. After an examination letter by letter [it was found to be] exactly the same as the old document. We have authenticated it so that it may be used as if it were the original. Farewell.

The *qāḍī al-Islām* Aḥmad `Alī

The *wakīl al-maḥkama* Sulaymān [al-Ḥajjāz][10]

[1]McHugh, Land, Lords and Holy Men," pp. 12-32; a photocopy is on p. 32.

[2]Spaulding, "Two documents," pp. 33-37; see also *Heroic Age*, pp. 361-365.

[3]Qur'ān 27:30.

[4]Probably inserted in error by the copyist.

[5]Inserted by Dr. McHugh.

[6]Lacuna.

[7]Conjectural reading.

[8]Dittography in original.

[9]Scriptural translation supplied by Dr. McHugh.

[10]For these Mahdist officials see McHugh, "Land, Lords and Holy Men," p. 30, note 5.

DOCUMENT 31

Document 31 is a letter from the Regent Nāṣir b. Muḥammad Abū Likaylik to Faqīh al-Amīn al-Majdhūb of al-Dāmir. The text has been taken by the editors from the original, which is truncated at the top; the seal and part of the opening protocols are missing.[1] The letter is not dated, but it may probably be placed in the year 1797, when the faltering Nāṣir made an appeal for support to leading holy men of the kingdom.[2]

(. . .)[3] من حضرت المحترم المكرم المهاب المعظم (قنديل الزمان)[4] / و سراج البلدان و مدمر اهل المكرى و البغى و الطغيان / و امين جيش السلطان افخر الامرا و عمدت الوزرا سيف / الله القاطع و سهامه اللامع المعتصم بالله الصمد الوزير / الشيخ ناصر ابن المرحوم الشيخ محمد ابلكيلك نصره الله الرحمن / الرحيم امين الى حضرت الفقيه الامين يسلم عليك الوزير / الشيخ ناصر كثير السلام و الذى نعرفك به ان سابق / جوابنا جاك معا الحاج عبد الجبار و ما جانا منك نظر / و لا خبر قطعت النظر مننا ليش لعل المانع خير / ذالحين ترا ثانى جوابنا جاك لا تسمع كلام الناس / امان الله امان الله البينى و بينك معمره ما فيها / نقص و لا زايده ناقص الله الله على ذالك / و بعد الفات نظرك لا ينقطع مننا و زولك فى / الوقت هذا / هل يقدم الى / عندنا و بعده / السلام عليك الف الف

[. . .] From the presence of the honored, revered, respected, and exalted, [candlestick of the age] and lamp unto the nations, who destroys the people of deceit, wrongdoing, and oppression, *amīn* of the army of the sultan, the most glorious of commanders and support of the ministers, the sharp sword of God and His flashing arrows, he who relies upon God the Eternal, the *wazīr* Shaykh Nāṣir, son of the late Shaykh Muḥammad Abū Likaylik. May God, the Merciful, the Compassionate, grant him victory. Amen.

To the presence of Faqīh al-Amīn.

The *wazīr* Shaykh Nāṣir greets you with many greetings. That of which we inform you is, that previously our letter came to you with al-Ḥājj `Abd al-Jabbār, but we have had neither sight nor news of you. Why is the sight of you denied us? Perhaps there is a hindrance? Now it is good for you to see our letter which has come to you again. Do not listen to what people say. The *amān* of God, the *amān* of God is firmly established between us and you. There is no breach in it, nor has any flaw been added to it. God, God upon that! After that has been left behind, the sight of you will not be denied us. Will not your messenger come to us at this very time? After that, one thousand thousand farewells.

[1]For a previously published version see [M. I. Abū Salīm], *Sādat al-Majādhīb* [Khartoum: no date], Vol. I [no pagination]; hereafter cited as *Sādat al-Majādhīb.*

[2]Spaulding, *Heroic Age*, pp. 365-367.

[3]Lacuna.

[4]Lacuna. A conjectural reading of the missing text has been taken from Doc. 29.

DOCUMENT 32

Document 32 is a confirming charter issued by Sultan Ranfā b. Bādī to the Awlād Dōlīb during 1213/1798-1799. The document has been taken by the editors from the original, which is damaged around the margins with some loss of text.[1] The charter reflects the compromise arranged during 1798-1799 by the new Regent Idrīs b. Muḥammad Abū Likaylik with the rebel Muḥammad Kamtūr, a powerful claimant to the office of Shaykh al-Baḥr. Kamtūr had advanced Ranfā as an anti-sultan to Idrīs's incumbent, Bādī VI; to make peace, Idrīs deposed Bādī, invested Ranfā, and appointed Kamtūr Shaykh of al-Baḥr. One beneficiary of the present grant was a personal *wazīr* to Idrīs. The present document also confirms orally-preserved accounts from the northern province that a Shaykh `Umar held office there in 1193-1194/1779-1780 between `Ajīb b. `Abd Allāh and the restoration of Muḥammad al-Amīn b. Mismār, late in the tenure of the Regent Bādī b. Rajab (Doc. 23).[2]

باسمك يا كريم بسم الله الرحمن الرحيم الحمد لله الذى بلغ الرسول و نحن ءامنا بما (يقول)[3]

الواثق بالملك الهادى
السلطان رانفى ابن
السلطان بادى ١٢١٢

حجة سلطانية و وثيقة ملوكية بمدينة سنار المحروسة المحمية اجلها الله تعالى لدا متوليها سلطان / الاسلام و جامع كلمة الايمان و مدمر اهل البغى و الطغيان سيف الله القاطع و سهامه اللامع / ناشر الوية العدل فى العالمين ناصر شريعة سيد المرسلين احق من ملك تحت الخلافة باستحقاق و اولى / من ولى الولية فى الافاق و هو الذى وجه عنان العناية لحماية الاسلام بشهادة الاجماع و تلك الشهادة / لا يتطرق اليها النزاع و جددت بيان

الهداية بعد ما اندرست ءاثاره و طمست معالمه و مهد بساطه / بعد ان لم يوجد الا مظلوم و ظالمه ذو المفاخر الذى شهد به الخاص و العام و المئاثر التى ترتفع على / الثريا و تكاثر الغمام و الاخلاق التى رام النسيم ان يحاكى لطفها فاصبح عليلا و المعالى التى تمنت / الملوك ان يتشبهوا بها فلم يجدوا الى ذلك سبيلا مولانا السلطان بن السلطان السلطان المظفر المعان السلطان رانفى بن المرحوم السلطان بادى نصره الله الرحمن الرحيم بجاه القرءان / العظيم و النبى الكريم ءامين ءامين يا رب العالمين اما بعد ان المحفوظ المبرور المويد المنصور / السلطان رانفى عرض عليه وثيقة من اولاد عجيب بصدقة العشرللفقه السيد / ابن الفقه عبد الهادى بن الشيخ محمد دوليب التى فى مرن ولد عبوده و الصدقة ناجزة / من الشيخ محمد الامين و الشيخ عجيب و اخيه الشيخ عمر و الشيخ ناصر فلما را السلطان ما فى تلك الوثايق تمم تلك الصدقة و امضاها لله و لرسوله فحدها من جهة الصعيد / بقيت امها و من جهة السافل ام حجوبه و من الصبح مرن النابر و من الغرب الناصراب و ذراعها بابو ثمانية اذرع و ايضا عرضت وثيقة من طه شيخ الدانياب صدقة الفقه السيد باربعة عود فى الطلوح فحدها من جهة (. . .)[4] / من جهة السافل (. . .)[4] / (. . .)[4] / (. . .)[4]

(و الشيخ كنان)[3] // ولد الفضيل شيخ (اتبرة)[3] /
(و الشيخ ابراهيم ولد عبد العاطى شيخ بيله)[5] /
(و الشيخ محمد)[3] كمتور ولد الشيخ احمد شيخ (البحر)[3] /
و الشيخ سعيد ولد على شيخ كردفال /
و الشيخ عمر ولد قاسم شيخ القربين /
و الشيخ موسى ولد ادريس مقدم / السواكره
و الشيخ بادى ولد النور / شيخ القواريه
و الشيخ عدلان / ولد شنبول شيخ اربجى
و الشيخ / محمود ولد محمد شيخ (حوش خال)[5] / الملك
و الشيخ رجب ولد بادى /
و السلطان ءادم البرقاوى
و الشيخ عبد الله ولد جابر مقدم قواويد (الملك)[3] /
و الملك احمد ولد عدلان (ملك برساج)[3] /
و جماعة ولد بادى شيخ (السجادة)[4] /
(و القاضى)[5] الشريف عمر
و الخطيب (نوار)[5]

(و الموذن)[5] / عثمان ولد بلى
و الشيخ (الزين)[5] /
و الفقيه محمد بان بيه ولد ابراهيم

(و الكاتب)[5] خضر ابراهيم تحرير ذلك ضحوت الاربعاء (. . .)[4] / من شهور سنه ١٢١٣ ثلاثة عشر بعد (المايتين)[6] / و الالف من الهجرة النبوية على صاحبها افضل (الصلاة)[6] / و ازكى السلام

In Thy name, O Generous One. In the name of God, the Merciful, the Compassionate. Praise be to God, Who sent the messenger. We believe in what [he says].

He who trusts in the King, the Guide
Sultan Ranfā, the son of
Sultan Bādī 1213/1798-1799

A sultanic charter and royal document [issued] in the divinely guarded and protected city of Sinnār, may God Most High exalt her, in the presence of her warden, the sultan of Islam, who consolidates the authority of the faith and destroys the people of wrongdoing and oppression, the sharp sword of God and His flashing arrows, who spreads the banners of justice throughout the universe, protector of the law of the lord of the messengers, the one most deserving to rule as a Caliph, and foremost among those who rule between the horizons. He it is who has guided the reins of solicitude toward the protection of Islam, according to the testimony of a consensus achieved without dispute, who has renewed the evidence of guidance after its traces had been obliterated and its marks effaced, and who has made even his carpet [of justice] after [a time in which] one could find only the victim and his oppressor. He possesses glory to whose excellence high and low testify, influence which ascends to the Pleiades and gathers in clouds, a character which the breeze would wish to copy to become mild, and noble traits in the emulation of which kings grow tired and fail to find a way, our lord the sultan, the son of the sultan, Sultan Ranfā, the son of the late Sultan Bādī. May God, the Merciful, the Compassionate, grant him victory through the influence of the sublime Qur'ān and the eminent prophet. Amen, amen, O Lord of the Universe.

Thereafter: The divinely protected, pious, divinely assisted and victorious Sultan Ranfā was shown a document from the Awlād `Ajīb concerning the gift of alms of al-`Ushr to Faqīh al-Sayyid b. al-Faqīh `Abd al-Hādī b. al-Shaykh Muḥammad Dōlīb. It is in the *mirin* of Walad `Abūda. The gift of alms is executed by Shaykh Muḥammad al-Amīn, Shaykh `Ajīb, his brother Shaykh `Umar, and Shaykh Nāṣir. When the sultan saw what is in these documents, he confirmed this gift of alms and ratified it for the sake of God and His messenger. Its boundary on the southern side is the remainder of the tract from which it was demarcated,[7] on the northern side Umm Ḥajūba, on the east the *mirin* of al-Nāyir, and on the west the Nāṣirāb. Its cubit is eight cubits [per rod]. Furthermore: I was shown a document from Ṭaha, Shaykh of the Dāniyāb, of a gift of alms to Faqīh al-Sayyid of four rods in al-Ṭulūḥ. Its boundary on the [southern] side is [. . .], on the northern side [. . .].

[There were present and witnessed to it:]

[. . .]
[Shaykh Kannān] walad al-Faḍīl, Shaykh of [Atbara]
[Shaykh Ibrāhīm walad `Abd al-`Aṭā, Shaykh of Bayla]
[Shaykh Muḥammad] Kamtūr walad al-Shaykh Aḥmad, Shaykh of [al-Baḥr]
Shaykh Sa`īd walad `Alī, Shaykh of [Kordofāl]
Shaykh `Umar walad Qāsim, Shaykh of al-Qarbīn
Shaykh Mūsā walad Idrīs, *muqaddam al-sawākira*
Shaykh Bādī walad al-Nūr, *shaykh al-quwwārīya*
Shaykh `Adlān walad Shanbūl, Shaykh of Arbajī
Shaykh Maḥmūd walad Muḥammad, shaykh of the [compound of the maternal uncle] of the king

Shaykh Rajab walad Bādī
Sultan Adam al-Borqāwī
Shaykh `Abd Allāh walad Jābir, *muqaddam* [of the king's] *qawāwīd*
Malik Aḥmad walad `Adlān, [*malik bursāj*]
Jammā`a walad Bādī, *shaykh* [*al-sajjāda*][6]
[the *qāḍī*], Sharīf `Umar
the *khaṭīb*, Nuwwār
[the muezzin], `Uthmān walad Balla
Shaykh [al-Zayn]
Faqīh Muḥammad Bān Bihi walad Ibrāhīm

[The writer is] Khiḍr Ibrāhīm. That was written in the morning on Wednesday [. . .] from the months of the year 1213/1798-1799, one thousand [two hundred] thirteen from the *hijra* of the prophet, upon whose master the best of [prayers] and purest peace.

[1]For a previously published version see Abū Salīm, *al-Fūnj wa'l-arḍ*, pp. 82-84.

[2]Spaulding, *Heroic Age*, pp. 330-335 and 369-371.

[3]Lacuna. A conjectural reading of the missing text has been restored from Doc. 40.

[4]Lacuna.

[5]Lacuna. A conjectural reading of the missing text has been restored from Doc. 28.

[6]Lacuna. A conjectural reading has been restored by the editors.

[7]Literally, "the remainder of its mother."

DOCUMENT 33

Document 33 is a charter issued by the *qāḍī* Sharīf `Umar b. Ibrāhīm on 16 Muḥarram 1214/20 June 1799. The text has been taken by the editors from a miniscule copy of the original preserved in the photographic collection of the Sudanese Ministry of Culture and Information; when enlarged the photograph reveals an intact and easily legible document.[1] The charter records the foreclosure by the judge on a mortgage held by Arbāb Faraḥ walad Muḥammad, possibly Faraḥ walad Abū Ẓahr, some of whose private business papers are also found in the Ministry's photographic collection.[2] The land mortgaged was agricultural rainland and probably lay east of the Blue Nile in the vicinity of the capital city; it consisted of 28 *jada`a*. The present document may be compared to Doc. 4 in that it records the extinction of the landholding rights of a woman, in this case named Bakhīta bint Ḥassān, through action by a *qāḍī* according to the *sharī`a*, in favor of a male businessman.[3] Significant is the judge's evaluation of the mortgaged land in terms of specie; under the prevailing system of measurement, two *qism* of of gold equalled one *mithqāl*, and four *mithqāl* were equivalent to one *waqīya*.[4]

الحمد لله و الصلاه و السلام / على رسول الله صلى الله عليه و سلم /

الله
حق معتبر
عبده القاضى
الشريف عمر
١٢٠٢
سنه

حجه شرعيه محرره مرضيه قاطعه سنيه جاريه على منهج المالكيه / واقعه بالديار الفنجيه
نازله بمدينه سنار المحروسه المحميه اجلها الله / تعالى لدى متوليها و الحاكم يوميذ بما
فيها مالك اعنه قاصيها و دانيها و حاضرها / و باديها و فاصل خصوماتها و دعاويها
القاضى الاكبر و الحاكم الاقهر و البرهان / الاظهر حاكم الاقليم والبندر قاضى المسلمين
بسنار و ما والاها من النواحي و الا / قطار الواثق بالله العزيز الرحيم القاضى المالكى
الشريف عمر بن المرحوم الشريف / ابراهيم لطف الله به ءامين و بعد فقد حضر
مجلس الشرع الشريف و محفل لدين / المنيف السالم من الجور و التحريف الرجل
العاقل الرشيد الارباب فرح ولد محمد / و المره الحرمه العاقله الرشيده بخيته بنت
حسان فلما ان حضروا جميعا مجلس / القضا بين يدى الحاكم الشرعى ادعى الارباب
فرح ان له على بخيته المذكوره وقيتين / و سبعه قسم و نصف قسمه ذهب و ارهنته فى
مقابله ذلك طين زراعه ارض / مطر كاينها فى الشرق ثم بعد مضى الاجل طلب منها
الخلاص فباعت عليه من / الطين اربعه عشر جدعه بوقيه و مثقال ذهب و انقطع له عليها
وقيه / و خمسه قسم و نصف قسمه ذهب و طلبت من الحاكم الشرعى ان يمهلها مدت
/ سبعه ايام لنوفيه ذلك القدر المذكور فامهلها الحاكم سبعه ايام فلم تات / و لم توفيه
حقه فتلوم لها الحاكم سبعه ايام اخر فلم توفه فامر الحاكم / الحاكم الشرعى ببيع الطين
المرهون و ارسل اليه رسوله فحدده و ذرعه فوجده / ثمانيه و عشرين جدعه بالعود
الرباع منها الاربعه عشر جدعه التى باعتها / بخيته بنت حسان على الارباب فرح سابقا
بوقيه و مثقال و الباقى لها من / الطين المرهون تحت يدى الارباب فرح فى مقابله الوقيه
و خمسه قسم و نصف / قسمه ذهب فقيمها الحاكم الشرعى بجماعه المسلمين فى القدر
المترتب عليها / و هى الوقيه و خمسه قسم ذهب و نصف قسمه و صارالطين المذكور
الثمانيه / و عشرين جدعه بحدوده و جميع ما فيه ملكا للارباب فرح فحده من جهه
السافل / فزع زينب و من جهه الصعيد فوق عابد و من الصبح فوق الققيد / ضياب و
من جهه الغرب فوق حاه جبر الله و خميس ولد حماد فهذه بيان حدود / الطين
المذكور و قد وقع التحديد بحضرت موجد القاضى عبد الرحمن بن الفقيه / رحمه
الحمتويابى و جماعه المسلمين من اهل جيرت الطين و ديرته منهم ادريس / ولد
الشايب و ادريس ولد نفره و عوض الله ولد حسن و احمد ولد نصر و ابزيد / ولد
المونه و محمد ولد حمدين و حسين ولد ابعاج و ابراهيم و الفقيه قسم الله / ولد
ابراهيم و قد حكم الحاكم الشرعى بصحه جميع ذلك بدليل قول الشيخ خليل رحمه
الله تعالى و باع الحاكم ان امتنع او غاب ببعد فهذا // ما حكم به حكما انفذه و
امضيه / و اوجب العمل بمقتضاه بمقضا / ه و سيضع خطه و مهره الكريم / اعلاه
تغويه لما حكم (. . .)[5] / و ارتضاه

حضر ذلك و شهد / به

الفقيه الامين ولد العشاب /
و الشريف ياسين البغداد /
و عبد الرحمن بن الشريف / عبد العزيز
و الفقيه ادريس / حوار الفقيه الجنيد
و الارباب / يعقوب ولد ابكر
و الفقيه ابراهيم ولد الفقيه ولد صبر /

و انا احمد الوراق كاتب / و شاهد و الله تعالى خير / الشاهدين حرر ذلك يوم /
الخميس سته عشر يوم خلت / من شهر الله المحرم الحرام / عاشوراء الذى هو من
شهور / سنه الف و مايتين / و اربعه عشر سنه / من هجرته صلى الله عليه و سلم //6

الامر كما ذكر و الشان كما / كتب و سطر
و انا القاضى / الشريف عمر و هذا خطى / بيدى

Praise be to God, and prayers and peace upon the messenger of God. May God bless him and grant him peace.

He who reveres God's law
His servant, the *Qāḍī*
Sharīf 'Umar
Year 1203/1788-1789

A charter according to Islamic law, definitive and legitimate, written and approved according to Mālikī procedure, taking place in the Funj territories in the city of Sinnār, the divinely guarded and protected, may God Most High exalt her, in the presence of her warden, at that time the governor of what is in her, master of the reins over her far and near places, her sedentaries and pastoralists, resolver of her quarrels and disputations, the greatest *qāḍī* and most potent judge, the most evident proof, judge of the countryside and city, *qāḍī* of the Muslims in Sinnār and in the provinces and districts under his protection, he who trusts in God the Powerful, the Compassionate, the Mālikī *qāḍī* Sharīf `Umar, son of the late Sharīf Ibrāhīm. May God be pleased with him. Amen.

Thereafter: There came before the court of noble law, assembly for the sublime religion, safe from injustice and corruption, the man of sound mind and good character, Arbāb Faraḥ walad Muḥammad, and the free woman of sound mind and good character, Bakhīta bint Ḥassān. When they came together before the court of justice, into the presence of the lawful judge, Arbāb Faraḥ claimed that the said Bakhīta owed him two *waqīya*, seven and one-half *qism* of gold, and that she had given him as security in return for that cultivable land, rainland located in the east. Then after the expiration of the appointed term he demanded from her the payment. She sold him fourteen *jada`a* of the land for a *waqīya* and a *mithqāl* of gold, so he cancelled it; she owes one *waqīya*, five and one-half *qism* of gold. She asked the judge for a delay of seven days to pay the said amount, so the judge granted her a delay of seven days. But she did not come, and did not satisfy his right. The judge postponed her [case] for seven additional days, but she did not pay. So the judge, the lawful judge, ordered the sale of the mortgaged land. He sent to it his messenger, who demarcated it and measured it. He found it to be twenty-eight *jada`a* with a four-[cubit] rod, of which Bakhīta bint Ḥassān had previously sold to Arbāb Faraḥ fourteen *jada`a* for a *waqīya* and a *mithqāl*, the remainder of the mortgaged land being in the possession of Arbāb Faraḥ as security for the *waqīya*, five and one-half *qism* of gold. The judge, with a gathering of Muslims, appraised it at the value of what she owed, and that is a *waqīya*, five and one-half *qism* of gold. The said land, the twenty-eight *jada`a*, with its boundaries and everything that is in it, has passed as private property to Arbāb Faraḥ. Its boundary on the northern side is Faza` and Zaynab, on the southern side above `Abīd, on the east above al-Quqayd Ḍiyāb, and on the western side above the village of Jabr Allāh and Khamīs walad Ḥammād. This is a declaration of the boundaries of the said land. The demarcation took place in the presence of the representative of the *qāḍī*, `Abd al-Raḥmān b. al-Faqīh Raḥma al-Ḥamtuwiyābī, and an assembly of the Muslims from the people neighboring the land and thereabouts, among them Idrīs walad al-Shāyib, Idrīs walad Nufra, `Awaḍ Allāh walad Ḥasan, Aḥmad walad Naṣr, Abzayd walad al-Mūna, Muḥammad walad Ḥammadayn, Ḥusayn walad Ab`āj, Ibrāhīm, and Faqīh Qism Allāh walad Ibrāhīm. The lawful judge ruled that all that was valid, with the guidance of the words of Shaykh Khalīl, may God Most High be merciful to him: "The judge shall sell if he [the debtor] avoids [payment] by being absent at a distance." This is the principle according to which he ruled, and he carried out the ruling and executed it, and made the matter binding according to his settlement. He shall put his signature and noble seal upon it. May God raise him above temptation and be pleased with him when he has ruled [. . .].

There were present and witnessed to it:

Faqīh al-Amīn walad al-`Ishāb
Sharīf Yāsīn al-Baghdādi
`Abd al-Raḥmān b. al-Sharīf `Abd al-`Azīz
Faqīh Idrīs, disciple of Faqīh al-Junayd
Arbāb Ya`qūb walad Abbakr
Faqīh Ibrāhīm walad al-Faqīh Walad Ṣabr

I, Aḥmad al-Warrāq, am scribe and witness, and God Most High is the Best of Witnesses. This was written on Thursday, when sixteen days had passed in God's holy month, al-Muḥarram of the `Āshūrā', from the months of the year 1214 from his *hijra*, may God bless him and grant him peace.

The matter is as mentioned, and the affair as written and recorded. I am the *qāḍī* Sharīf `Umar, and this is written in my hand.

[1]Sudan Government Ministry of Culture and Information, photograph IND 283. For a previously published version see Jay Spaulding, "A Mortgage Foreclosure from Sinnār," *Sudan Texts Bulletin*, Vol. 1 (1979): 26-31.

[2]Spaulding, *Heroic Age*, pp. 201-202; "Two Credit Documents from Sinnār," *Sudan Texts Bulletin*, Vol. 2 (1980): 59-61.

[3]For an extended treatment see Spaulding, "Land-Sales by Women in Sinnār."

[4]Spaulding, "Mortgage Foreclosure," p. 26.

[5]Lacuna.

[6]Handwriting changes; what follows is in the upper margin.

DOCUMENT 34

Document 34 is a letter from the Regent Idrīs b. Muḥammad Abū Likaylik to the leaders of the Majādhīb community of al-Dāmir. The text has been taken by the editors from the original, which is truncated at the top; the seal and most of the opening protocols are missing.[1] The document is not dated, but circumstantial evidence strongly suggests that it was issued during Idrīs's northern campaign,[2] and probably in 1216/1801-1802.[3] The members of the defeated war party are described as "Kunjāra," certainly meaning Fūr-speaking westerners, but probably followers of Hāshim of the Kordofan Musabba`āt rather than men under the Dār Fūr sultan.

(. . .)[4] / الشيخ محمد نصره الله امين الى حضرت الفقه احمد بن الفقه / حمد
محمد المجذوب و الفقه عبد الله اخيه و الفقه الامين اخيه / و الفقه مدنى ولد الفقه
احمد يسلم عليكم الوزير الشيخ ادريس / كثير السلام و الذى نعرفكم به نحن روحنا
من السافل خليانين / و الجماعة تعبانه و مرقنا عدلان مع الحرمة على جهة الغرب /
للرعية الهناك قلنا يجيب شيا يعد فى يومين ثلاثه / و الحاصل عرضوا له كنجاره فوق
الدرب ناس عيساوى / و اتلاقوا معاهم و بفضل رب العلمين ان نصروا عليهم / و
قتلوهم اشر قتله و اسروا ملكهم عيساوى و المقتول / فى الملوك الاخرين اثنين و عشرين
مك و اخلاط الناس / كثير جملت المقتول و الماسور من الاحرار بلا / العبيد مايتين زول
// و حربتنا الحمد لله سالمة و خيلنا / سالمات و ما مرق من كنجارة بلا اربعة / رجال

[. . . Idrīs b.] al-Shaykh Muḥammad, may God grant him victory. Amen.

To the presence of Faqīh Aḥmad b. al-Faqīh Ḥammad Muḥammad al-Majdhūb, Faqīh `Abd Allāh his brother, Faqīh al-Amīn his brother, and Faqīh Madanī walad al-Faqīh Aḥmad.

The *wazīr* Shaykh Idrīs greets you with many greetings. That of which we inform you is, that we set out to withdraw from the north. The party was exhausted, so we sent out `Adlān with the warriors to the west [bank] to the subjects who are there, saying he should bring [back] something [provisions] in two or three days. Briefly, [some] Kunjāra, the people of `Īsāwī, encountered him on the road; they closed with them and by the grace of the Lord of the Universe, were victorious over them. They killed them with a great slaughter and captured their *malik*, `Īsāwī. The dead among their other *malik*s were twenty-two *makk*s, and a great crowd of the common people were killed. Captured from among the free men, without [not counting] the slaves, were two hundred. Our warriors, God be Praised, are safe, and our horses are safe. Only four men of the Kunjāra escaped.

[1]For previously published versions see *Sādat al-Majādhīb*, Vol. 2 and R.S. O'Fahey and Jay Spaulding, "A Sudanese Battle in About 1800," *Sudan Texts Bulletin*, Vol. 2 (1980): 42-46.

[2]Spaulding, *Heroic Age*, pp. 371-380.

[3]Ibid., pp. 404-405.

[4]Lacuna. The document is truncated at the top. Enough of the lower parts of the letters of the last omitted line are visible toward the left to make possible the identification of the issuing authority as Idrīs b. Muḥammad Abū Likaylik.

DOCUMENT 35

Document 35 is an originating charter issued by Muḥammad b. `Adlān b. Muḥammad Abū Likaylik; the text has been taken by the editors from the original, which is intact and easily legible.[1] The document records a grant to Faqīh Aḥmad b. `Īsā of the estate of Umm Ḥawāya, located on the west bank of the Blue Nile adjoining the village cemetery of Altī, near the modern al-Masīd. The beneficiary held the unusual office of *al-faqīh al-kabīr*, or "Great Faqīh" of Sinnār.[2] Document 42 is an originating charter issued by Ḥusayn b. Muḥammad Abū Likaylik; it records his grant of the same estate, Umm Ḥawāya, and also to Aḥmad b. `Īsā. No other example is known of two originating charters, both of which claim to dispose of precisely the same property.

The editors suggest that this anomaly should be interpreted in terms of rivalry between Ḥusayn, the last titular Hamaj Regent, and his nephew Muḥammad `Adlān, the *de facto* strongman of the period, who was known by the improvised title *al-mānjil al-kabīr*, "Great Mānjil" or "Generalissimo."[3] One may hypothesize that the beneficiary wanted written confirmation of his rights from both Hamaj authorities, but found that the man he asked second refused to confirm the charter issued by the man he had asked first, insisting rather upon producing a second originating charter issued by himself, conveying rights to the same property. The salient question would thus be, which of the two Hamaj lords issued the first charter, and which the second?

Document 42 is dated 27 Rabī` II 1235/12 February 1820, and no internal discrepancies seem to challenge this claim. The present document is dated 17 Rabī` II 1225/22 May 1810, and would thus seem to antedate Doc. 42 by a decade; for this reason it has been given its present place in the chronological sequence of documents issued by officials of the central government. However, Doc. 35 also bears the seal of Muḥammad `Adlān (compare Doc. 43), and the seal is inscribed with the date 1231/1815-1816, several years after the ostensible date of the issue of Doc. 35. Moreover, the scribe who wrote Doc. 35 was himself aware that something was wrong with the sealing of the document, and included a statement to that effect as an integral part of the text and before reaching his conclusion. That might seem to exclude the possibility that Doc. 35 was really issued in 1810, but that Muḥammad `Adlān's seal was added several years later. Was Doc. 42 in fact the first grant, and Doc. 35 the second, issued in reality in 1820 or even early 1821, but clumsily falsified to make it appear to have chronological priority? This possibility cannot be entirely excluded.

Yet the question is further complicated by the presence of a second seal, that of Sultan Bādī VI (compare Doc. 40). It is therefore entirely possible that Doc. 35 was indeed written in 1810, but that the sultan's seal was wrongly affixed to it during the drafting process, that the scribe took note of this state of affairs in the text, and that the seal of Muḥammad `Adlān was added several years later--the "right" seal, to be sure, but by then bearing a "wrong" date.[4] This second interpretation is given some support by the fact that when Muḥammad `Adlān issued Doc. 35, ostensibly in 1810, he had not yet elevated loyal slave supporters such as Tayfara from *Mankarūkān* to Shaykh; this he had done by 1813, when he issued Doc. 38.[5] These promotions were never recognized by Ḥusayn (see Doc. 42), and were therefore an expression of the rivalry between the two men, and probably a matter taken seriously by both. If Muḥammad `Adlān had made a shaykh of Tayfara by 1813, he would have been unlikely to demote him to *Mankarūkān* again in 1820 or 1821; it is more likely that Doc. 35 was in fact issued in 1810 before the elevation of Tayfara and his comrades.

بسم الله الرحمن الرحيم

الواثق بالملك العدل
السلطان بادى بن السلطان
طبل سنه ١٢٢٠

الشيخ محمد بن
الوزير الشيخ عدلان
١٢٢١

حجه سلطانيه و (وثيقه ملوكيه)[6] بديار الفنجيه بمدينه سنار المحروسه المحميه لدا متوليها و ابن متوليها مالك اعنه قاصيها و دانيها و حاضرها و باديها سيف الله القاطع و سهامه اللامع سعد من حلاه و ندم من عاداه من تهابه الرجال و تخشى من صولته الابطال يوم الحرب و النزال المتوكل على الله الديان الشيخ محمد بن المرحوم الوزير الشيخ عدلان كان الله له حيث كان الى حضرت كل من تقف عليه هذه الوثيقه و الناظر لما فيها من الحقيقه و بعد ان المحفوظ المبرور المويد المنصور الشيخ محمد بن الشيخ عدلان تصدق على الفقه احمد بن الفقه عيسى الانصاريابى جميع الرفاعيه فى دار ام حوايه و من يليها صدقه لله و لرسوله و ليوم لا ينفع فيه مال و لا بنون الا من اتى الله بقلب سليم و الدار المذكوره معلومه البقعه و الحدود حدها من جهه القبله مقبره التى و من جهه الغرب المشرع توتاوا و من جهه البحر موج بحر الصيف و من جهه الخلا درب الجمل فهناك انتهت الحدود و صارت الدار المذكوره بحدودها المعلومه ملكا و حوزا للفقه احمد بن عيسى لا ينازعه فيها منازع و لا يتعرض له فيها متعرض و خصوصا رحمه ولد فضل الله و جرايه و من تعرض له بعد كلامى هذا فقد عرض نفسه للهلاك و الحذر ثم الحذر من الخلاف و قوه الراس و هى ساله مسلمه من جميع السبل و المضار لا عليها جساره و لا خساره و لا حسب و لا قوار و لا نار و لا علوق و لا منوره و لا كياب و لا دم و لا شى من جميع السبل العاديه

حضر و شهد بذلك

الارباب قاسم بن الشيخ محمد ابلكيلك
و الارباب موسى بن الشيخ بادى
و الارباب محمد بن الشيخ حسين
و الارباب حسن اخيه

و الارباب عدلان اخيهم
و الارباب حسن بن الشيخ رجب
و الارباب على اخيه
و الارباب رجب
و الارباب ادريس
و الارباب على
و الارباب حسن
و الارباب ادهم
و الارباب ابراهيم
ابناء الشيخ عدلان
و الارباب عدلان بن الشيخ محمد
و الارباب محمد بن الارباب دفع الله
و الارباب عدلان اخيه
و الارباب دفع الله بن الارباب احمد
و الارباب محمد بن الارباب دفع الله سليمان
و الارباب ابراهيم ولد عويضه
و الفقه محمد بن الفقه عبد الجليل
و الفقه محمد ولد حسين
و خوجلى ولد منا الله
و المنكروكن محمد بن فرج الله
و المنكروكن تيفر
و المنكروكن فضل الله ولد سكوت
و المنكروكن محمد ولد كاب
و المنكروكن بخيت ابو سليمه
و المنكروكن محمد ولد جمع الله
و المنكروكن ادريس ولد الصاموته
و المنكروكن حسان مقدم العكليته
و المنكروكن فضل الله ولد (مفريول)[6]
و حمد
و ادريس
ابنا ابش

تحرير ذلك بيوم الخميس فى شهر الله ربيع الثانى نهار سبعه عشر خلون منه تاريخ
ذلك (سنه)[6] الف و مايتين و خمسه و عشرين من هجره مسك الختام(. . .)[6] الظلام
عليه افضل الصلاة و السلام و انا دفع الله بن برى كاتب و شاهد

In the name of God, the Merciful, the Compassionate.

He who trusts in the Impartial King
Sultan Bādī, the son of Sultan
Ṭabl Year 1220/1805-1806

Shaykh Muḥammad, the son of
The *wazīr* Shaykh `Adlān
1231/1815-1816

A sultanic charter and royal document [issued] in the Funj territories, in the divinely guarded and protected city of Sinnār, in the presence of her warden, the son of her warden, master of the reins of her far places and near, her sedentaries and pastoralists, the sharp sword of God and His flashing arrows. Happy is he who pleases him, while he who earns his enmity will repent. He inspires awe in men, and on the day of war and strife heroes quail at his assault. He who trusts in God the Judge, Shaykh Muḥammad, son of the late *wazīr* Shaykh `Adlān. May God be with him wherever he is.

To the presence of all who read this document and see the truth therein.

Thereafter: The divinely protected, pious, divinely assisted and victorious Shaykh Muḥammad b. al-Shaykh `Adlān has bestowed as alms upon Faqīh Aḥmad b. al-Faqīh `Īsā al-Anṣāriyābī all the pastoral lands in the estate of Umm Ḥawāya and that which adjoins it. It is a gift of alms for God and His messenger, for a day in which neither wealth nor sons suffice, unless one comes to God with a secure heart. The location and boundaries of the said estate are known. Its boundary on the eastern side is the cemetery of Altī; on the western side the watering place of Tūtāwā; on the side of the river the summer water level, and on the side of the waste land the camel path. There the boundaries end. The said estate, its boundaries known, has become the property and possession of Faqīh Aḥmad b. ʿĪsā. Let no challenger challenge him concerning it. Let no troublemaker trouble him concerning it, especially Raḥma walad Faḍl Allāh and his *jarāī*. He who troubles it after these my words has exposed himself to destruction. Beware, then beware of disobedience and hardheadedness. It is completely free from all the *subul* and *maḍārr*. It is not subject to *jusāra*, *khusāra*, *ḥasab*, *quwwār*, *nār*, *ʿulūq*, *munawwara*, *kiyāb*, *damm*, nor any of the customary *subul*.

There were present and witnessed to it:

Arbāb Qāsim b. al-Shaykh Muḥammad Abū Likaylik
Arbāb Mūsā b. al-Shaykh Bādī
Arbāb Muḥammad b. al-Shaykh Ḥusayn
Arbāb Ḥasan, his brother
Arbāb ʿAdlān, their brother
Arbāb Ḥasan b. al-Shaykh Rajab
Arbāb ʿAlī, his brother
Arbāb Rajab, Arbāb Idrīs, Arbāb ʿAlī, Arbāb Ḥasan, Arbāb Adham, and Arbāb Ibrāhīm, sons of Shaykh ʿAdlān
Arbāb ʿAdlān b. al-Shaykh Muḥammad
Arbāb Muḥammad b. al-Arbāb Dafʿ Allāh
Arbāb ʿAdlān, his brother
Arbāb Dafʿ Allāh b. al-Arbāb Aḥmad
Arbāb Muḥammad b. al-Arbāb Dafʿ Allāh Sulaymān
Arbāb Ibrāhīm walad ʿUwayḍa

Faqīh Muḥammad b. al-Faqīh `Abd al-Jalīl
Faqīh Muḥammad walad Ḥusayn
Khōjalī walad Manā Allāh
Mankarūkan Muḥammad walad Faraj Allāh
Mankarūkan Tayfara
Mankarūkan Faḍl Allāh walad Sukūt
Mankarūkan Muḥammad walad Kāb
Mankarūkan Bakhīt Abū Salīma
Mankarūkan Muḥammad walad Jama` Allāh
Mankarūkan Idrīs walad al-Ṣāmūta
Mankarūkan Ḥassān, *muqaddam al-`akalīta*
Mankarūkan Faḍl Allāh walad Mafriyūl
Ḥammad and Idrīs, the sons of Ibish

That was written on Thursday in God's month of Rabī` II in the daytime, when seventeen days had passed of it. The date of that is the year one thousand two hundred twenty-five from his *hijra*. Incorrect sealing was put upon it. The best of prayers and peace [be upon Muḥammad]. I, Daf` Allāh b. Barrī, am scribe and witness.

[1]NRO Miscellaneous 1/92/1480. For a previously published version see Jay Spaulding, "A Grant by the 'Great Mānjil' to the 'Great Faqīh' of Sinnār," *Sudan Texts Bulletin,* Vol. 4 (1982): 20-28.

[2]Spaulding, *Heroic Age*, pp. 234-235.

[3]Ibid., pp. 440-451.

[4]Compare Doc. 46, to which a seal was added long after its date of issue.

[5]Spaulding, *Heroic Age*, pp. 412-439.

[6]Lacuna. A conjectural reading of the missing text has been supplied by the editors.

DOCUMENT 36

Document 36 purports to be a grant by a Hamaj authority to Aḥmad al-Baṣīr, the last independent Shaykh of the Ḥalāwiyīn, consisting of land where he lived. A very imperfect English version was recorded by G.B. Tame.[1] The charter is not dated. The issuing authority was not the sultan, nor was it "Mohammed Likeilik." As Tame's informants elsewhere made clear, the Hamaj authority contemporary to Shaykh Aḥmad was Muḥammad b. `Adlān b. Muḥammad Abū Likaylik.[2] The object of the grant was apparently Shaykh Aḥmad's village, which probably lay in the Ḥalāwī *dār*, along the Blue Nile near al-Tumayd.

"This title deed from the Sultan is written in the land of the Fung, in the City of Sennar the fortified, governed by her ruler and her ruler's son the lord of far and near. The lord the Sultan ibn El Sultan Mohammed Likeilik has made over to the Sheikh Ahmed el Basir, the Halawi, the *Dar* of his village, be it in rainland or by the river, to the honour of God and his Prophet, as indulgence for that last day when money and sons will be of no avail except to those who have a pure heart. And this village shall have no taxes levied upon it neither *Matura* nor *Mukhlaya* nor *Kersha* nor any of the customary tributes. Take notice of this O soldiers: do not encroach on these rights: for he who does so shall be stricken and die. Peace be upon you. From the Sultan ibn El Sultan Mohammed Likeilik."

[1]G.B. Tame, "Legends of the Halawin of Blue Nile Province," *Sudan Notes and Records*, Vol. 17, No. 2 (1934): 201-216. The charter is on p. 216.

[2]Ibid., p. 206.

DOCUMENT 37

Document 37 is the text of a seal of the court official Wāwrit b. Hārūn, recorded by G.B. Brocchi and dated 1218/1803-1804.[1] In his diary entry for 25 February 1826, Brocchi wrote: "I have seen today an iron seal of Wāwrit Hārūn, of the race of the Funj, secretary to the King of Sinnār. In the Plates is given an impression taken from the original."[2] Wāwrit was the last serving member of the family who had dominated the offices of *amīn* and *jundī* throughout the eighteenth century. Brocchi was told correctly that the seal itself dated from the reign of Sultan Ranfā, but Wāwrit appears in witness rosters only from the period 1813-1820 (Docs. 39, 40, 42). The seal text and a translation are as follows:

الواثق بالملك الديان
واورت هارون
الشيخ بن الشيخ امين
السلطان سنه ١٢١٨

He who trusts in the King, the Judge
Wāwrit Hārūn
The Shaykh, the son of the Shaykh, *amīn*
of the Sultan. Year 1218/1803-1804

[1]Brocchi, *Giornale*, Vol. 5, Plate II, Figure 2. For a previously published version see Jay Spaulding and Abdel Ghaffar Muhammad Ahmed, "A Seal from Nineteenth-Century Sinnār," *Sudan Notes and Records*, Vol. 55 (1974): 175-176; the discussion presented there is flawed by the acceptance of P.M. Holt's incorrect dates for the regency of Ḥusayn b. Muḥammad Abū Likaylik (see Doc. 39).

[2]Brocchi, *Giornale*, Vol. 5, p. 580.

DOCUMENT 38

Document 38 is an originating charter issued by Muḥammad b. \`Adlān b. Muḥammad Abū Likaylik to Faqīh Muḥammad \`Alī walad al-\`Abbās on 10 Muḥarram 1228/13 January 1813. The text is based upon a copy preserved in the papers of A.J. Arkell.[1] The charter conveys rights to land near the modern village of Wad al-\`Abbās, in the southern territories of the Walad \`Ajīb between the Blue Nile and the Dinder about fifteen miles north of the capital. The Regent Ḥusayn confirmed this grant through the issue of Doc. 39 a few days later. The two charters reflect the relatively tranquil conditions in the vicinity of the capital following the restoration of order by the Great *Mānjil* Muḥammad \`Adlān in 1808, under the titular regency of Ḥusayn.[2] For an unnecessary controversy concerning the date of these two documents, see the introduction to Doc. 39. Many witnesses to Doc. 38 are military officers; several are slaves who identify themselves as "sons of the house."[3]

هاذه صورة وثيقه سلطانيه / باسمك يا كريم بسم الله الرحمن الرحيم الحمد لله و
الصلاة و السلام على خاتم رسل الله الكرام /
حجة سلطانية محررة مرضية بديار الفنجية بمدينة سنار المحروسة المحمية اجلها الله تعالى
لدى متوليها و ابن متوليها / مالك اعنتها و قاصيها و دانيها و حاضرها و باديها و
الحاكم يوميذ بمن عليها و من فيها من تهابه الرجال و تخشى من صولته الابطال / يوم
الحرب و النزال المعتصم بالله الديان الشيخ محمد ابن المرحوم الوزير الشيخ عدلان
نصره الله امين الى حضرت كل من تقف عليه / هذه الوثيقة و الناظر لما فيها من
الحقيقه و بعد ان المحفوظ المبرور المويد المنصور الشيخ محمد تصدق على الفقه محمد
على ولد / العباس بدار من طين عجيب ارض مطر موات صدقة لله و لرسوله و ليوم لا
ينفع فيه مال و لا بنون الا من اتى الله بقلب سليم و الدار معلومة / البقعه و الحدود
فحدها من جيهت الصبح دار الشيخ الطريفى ولد الشيخ يوسف و من جيهت السافل

فوق الطنضب و ولد / محمود و من جيهت الغرب عد مليحه و فوق جبين و فوق شرف الدين ولد دوره و حسين ولد دوره و فوق فولت شميم / و من جيهت الصعيد فوق دار فور و دار خميس ولد جنقل هناك انتهت الحدود و صارت الدار المذكورة بحدودها / المعلومة للفقيه محمد على ولد العباس ملكا و حوزا و تصرفا له و لذريته و ذريت ذريته يتوارثونها من وارث الى وارث / حتى يرث الله الارض و من عليها و هو خير الوارثين لا ينازعه فيها منازع و لا يتعرض له فيها متعرض سالمة مسلمة / من جميع الشرور و السبل و المضار لا عليها جسارة و لا خسارة و لا عظم و لا عانه و لا رغم و لا زريبه و لا ضيافة و لا حسب و لا دم و لا نار / و لا قوار و لا نزول و لا مخلاة و لا متورت و لا كليقه و لا قل و لا جل و نوكد عليكم يا جميع الشيوخ و المقاديم و خصوصا حسان و من تبعه و كل / من ياتى بعده انتم و جرايكم و من ياتى من وراءيكم الى قيام الساعة لا احد منكم يتعرض للفقيه محمد على فى هذه و لا احد منكم يتعرض / لذريته و لا ذريت ذريته و من يتعرض له بعد كلامى و وثيقتى هذه فقد عرض نفسه للهلاك و الحذر ثم الحذر من الخلاف / و المخالف لا يلوم الا نفسه و السلام

و قد حضر ذلك و شهد به

الشيخ احمد ولد النور شيخ الفوارى
و الشيخ عدلان ولد شنبول / شيخ اربجى
و الارباب قاسم ولد الشيخ محمد
و الارباب نصر اخيه
و الارباب ادريس ولد بادى
و الارباب موسى اخيه
و الارباب محمد ولد حسين /
و الارباب حسن اخيه
و الارباب محمد ولد ادريس
و الارباب على اخيه
و الارباب حسن ولد رجب
و الارباب ابراهيم اخيه
و الارباب ناصر ولد الارباب / رجب
و الارباب ادريس
و الارباب ابراهيم

و الارباب حسن
و الارباب عيساوى
و الارباب على
ابناء المرحوم الوزير الشيخ عدلان
و الارباب / دفع الله احمد
و الارباب دفع الله محمد
و الارباب ابراهيم عويضة
و الارباب على ولد محمد
و الارباب خوجلى ولد خالد
و الارباب احمد ابن الحاج سليمان /
و حسن ولد عوض الله
و حسين اخيه
و الشيخ فرج الله
و الشيخ تيفره
و الارباب عبد الله ولد سكوت
و الارباب / محمد ولد جميل الله
و الارباب محمد ولد كاب
و المنكروكن بخيت
و المنكروكن كرومه
و على ابوا زوير
و عدلان ولد محجوب
و فضل كرن دوس
و عبد الراضى / ولد البيت
و عيد ولد البيت
و حامد ولد البيت
و احمد ولد البقره

و الكاتب احمد المكى و كفى بالله شهيدا وقع ذلك يوم الخميس نهار عشره / ايام من شهر الله المحرم سنة ١٢٢٨ الف و مايتين و ثمانية و عشرين من هجرت سيد المرسلين صلى الله عليه و سلم و ارضى الله اصحابه اجمعين و السلام

This is a copy of a sultanic document. In Thy name, O Generous One. In the name of God, the Merciful, the Compassionate. Praise be to God, and prayers and peace upon the seal of the eminent messengers of God. A sultanic charter written and approved in the Funj territories in the divinely guarded and protected city of Sinnār, may God Most High exalt her, in the presence of her warden, the son of her warden, master of her reins, her far places and near, her sedentaries and pastoralists, the governor at the present time of those over her and within her, who inspires awe in men, and on the day of war and battle heroes quail at his assault. He who trusts in God the Judge, Shaykh Muḥammad, son of the late *wazīr* Shaykh `Adlān. May God grant him victory. Amen.

To the presence of all who read this document and see the truth therein.

Thereafter: The divinely protected, pious, divinely assisted and victorious Shaykh Muḥammad has bestowed as alms upon Faqīh Muḥammad `Alī walad al-`Abbās an estate from the cultivable land of [the Walad] `Ajīb, virgin rainland. It is a gift of alms for God and His messenger, for a day in which neither wealth nor sons suffice, unless one comes to God with a secure heart. The location and boundaries of the estate are known. Its boundary on the eastern side is the estate of Shaykh al-Ṭurayfī walad al-Shaykh Yūsuf; on the north above al-Ṭanāḍīb and Walad Maḥmūd; on the west `Idd Mulayḥa and above Jannīn, Sharaf al-Dīn walad Dawra, Ḥusayn walad Dawra, and the rain pool of Shammīm; on the south above the estates of the Fūr and of Khamīs walad Janqal. There the boundaries end. The said estate, its boundaries known, has become the property, possession, and usufruct of Faqīh Muḥammad `Alī walad al-`Abbās, his descendants, and his descendants' descendants. They shall bequeath it from heir to heir until God inherits the earth and those upon it, and He is the Best of Heirs. Let no challenger challenge him concerning it. Let no troublemaker trouble him concerning it. It is completely free from all *shurūr*, *subul*, and *maḍārr*. It is not subject to *jusāra*, *khusāra*, *`aẓm*, *`āna*, *raghm*, *zarība*, *ḍiyāfa*, *ḥasab*, *damm*, *nār*, *quwwār*, *nuzūl*, *mukhlā*, *matūrat*, *kalīqa*, *qill*, or *jill*. We command you peremptorily, all you shaykhs and *muqaddams*, especially Ḥassān and his followers, and whoever may come after him, you and your *jarāī*, and whoever may come after you until the hour of resurrection. Let no one of you trouble Faqīh Muḥammad `Alī concerning this, and let no one of you trouble his descendants or his descendants' descendants. He who troubles him after my words and this my document has exposed himself to destruction. Beware, then beware of disobedience, and let the disobedient blame none but himself. Farewell.

There were present and witnessed to it:

Shaykh Aḥmad walad al-Nūr, *shaykh* [*al-quwwārīya*][4]
Shaykh `Adlān walad Shanbūl, Shaykh of Arbajī
Arbāb Qāsim walad al-Shaykh Muḥammad
Arbāb Naṣr, his brother
Arbāb Idrīs walad Bādī
Arbāb Mūsā, his brother
Arbāb Muḥammad walad Ḥusayn
Arbāb Ḥasan, his brother
Arbāb Muḥammad walad Idrīs
Arbāb `Alī, his brother
Arbāb Ḥasan walad Rajab
Arbāb Ibrāhīm, his brother
Arbāb Nāṣir walad al-Arbāb Rajab
Arbāb Idrīs, Arbāb Ibrāhīm, Arbāb Ḥasan, Arbāb `Īsāwī, and Arbāb `Alī, sons of the late *wazīr* Shaykh `Adlān
Arbāb Daf` Allāh Aḥmad
Arbāb Daf` Allāh Muḥammad
Arbāb Ibrāhīm `Uwayḍa
Arbāb `Alī Ilyās
Arbāb `Alī walad Muḥammad

Arbāb Aḥmad b. al-Ḥājj Sulaymān
Arbāb Khōjalī walad Khālid
Ḥasan walad `Awaḍ Allāh
Ḥusayn, his brother
Shaykh Faraj Allāh
Shaykh Tayfara
Arbāb `Abd Allāh walad Sukūt
Arbāb Muḥammad walad Jamīl Allāh
Arbāb Muḥammad walad Kāb
Mankarūkan Bakhīt
Mankarūkan Karūma
`Alī Abū Zuwayyir
`Adlān walad Maḥjūb
Faḍl Karan Dūs
`Abd al-Rāḍī, son of the house
`Īd, son of the house
Ḥāmid, son of the house
Aḥmad walad al-Baqara
the scribe, Aḥmad al-Makkī

With God, two witnesses suffice. That took place on Thursday, on the tenth day of God's month of Muḥarram in the year 1228, one thousand two hundred twenty-eight from the *hijra* of the lord of the messengers. May God bless him and grant him peace. May God be pleased with all his companions. Farewell.

[1]School of Oriental and African Studies, University of London, Arkell Papers, Box 1, File 5, Piece 72. A photocopy and English translation have been published in Holt, "Land-Charters," Plate III and pp. 107-108.

[2]Spaulding, *Heroic Age*, pp. 439-451.

[3]Ibid., pp. 217-218.

DOCUMENT 39

Document 39 is a confirming charter issued by the Regent Ḥusayn b. Muḥammad Abū Likaylik to Faqīh Muḥammad `Alī al-`Abbāsī on 12 Muḥarram 1228/15 January 1813. The text is based upon a copy preserved in the papers of A.J. Arkell.[1] Document 39 confirms the grant of Muḥammad `Adlān recorded in Doc. 38.

P.M. Holt has adduced arguments to the effect that Docs. 38 and 39 must have been issued not in 1813, but in 1808, firstly because he believed that "three of the persons mentioned (Ḥassān and Farajallāh in [Docs. 38 and 39], Ḥusayn w. `Iwaḍallāh in [Doc. 38] only) are identifiable as having died before 1228/1813; secondly, that the political situation in which Shaykh Ḥusayn b. Muḥammad Abī Likaylik was regent obtained only for a few months in 1223/1808."[2]

Both arguments are to be questioned. Since Holt gives no evidence for his belief that the three individuals mentioned were dead in 1813, one may simply respond that the fact that they served as witnesses to government documents in that year may be taken as reasonably firm proof that they were not deceased at the time. More serious is Holt's claim that Ḥusayn b. Muḥammad Abū Likaylik stood at the head of the government only for "a few months in 1223/1808." Firstly, contrary to Holt's mistranslation of Doc. 39, Ḥusayn was never a "sultan;" this may be verified through examination of his own photocopy.[3] However, Ḥusayn was invested as Regent as early as 1806 by the Hamaj strongman of that day, Muḥammad b. Nāṣir b. Muḥammad Abū Likaylik,[4] and he remained Regent until the fall of Sinnār (see Docs. 40, 42), a period not of "a few months," but of almost fifteen years.

Holt's misapprehensions in regard to the regency of Ḥusayn may derive in part from his equally false supposition that Muḥammad b. `Adlān b. Muḥammad Abū Likaylik became Regent after Ḥusayn, allegedly following the fall of Muḥammad b. Ibrāhīm b. Muḥammad Abū Likaylik on 16 August 1808.[5] With the exception of Doc. 39, which wrongly attributes to Muḥammad `Adlān the title of "sultan," probably through the copyist's error, no document from Sinnār even suggests that Muḥammad `Adlān ever bore a title other than "Shaykh" or "Arbāb," or identified himself in any other way than as the son of the Regent `Adlān (Docs. 35, 40, 42, 43). It is from the account of G.B. Brocchi that one learns of his *ad hoc* title of *al-mānjil al-kabīr*; "he was only a general," as one of Brocchi's informants put it, "but a person of great authority, who in a government in such disarray in many cases counted for more than the *wazīr* [the Regent Ḥusayn]."[6] In short, Holt's dating of Docs. 38 and 39 to the year 1808 does not survive serious scrutiny, and no reason remains to challenge the dates given by the documents themselves.

هاذه صورة وثيقه سلطانيه / باسمك يا كريم بسم الله الرحمن الرحيم الحمد لله و
الصلاة و السلام على خاتم رسل الله الكرام /

حجة سلطانيه محررة مرضيه بديار الفنجيه بمدينة سنار المحروسة المحميه اجلها الله تعالى لدا متوليها و ابن متوليها مالك اعنتها / و قاصيها و دانيها و حاضرها و باديها و الحاكم يوميذ بمن عليها و من فيها قنديل الزمان و سراج البلدان و مدمر اهل المكرى و البغى / و الطغيان امين جيش السلطان الواثق بالملك الصمد الوزير الشيخ حسين ابن المرحوم الوزير الشيخ محمد ابو لكيلك نصره الله / امين الى حضرت كل من تقف عليه هذه الوثيقة و الناظر لما فيها من الحقيقه و بعد ان المحفوظ المبرور المويد المنصور الوزير / الشيخ حسين تمم و اعطى ما فعله السلطان محمد عدلان الى الفقيه محمد على العباسى من طين دار عجيب ارض مطر موات / و انا الوزير حسين تممت و اعطيت للفقيه محمد على العباسى ابتغاء مرضات الله تعالى و طلبا للثواب فى دار الماب و ليوم / لا ينفع فيه مال و لا بنون الا من اتى الله بقلب سليم و الدار معلومة البقعه و الحدود فحدها من جيهة الصبح / دار الشيخ الطريفى ولد الشيخ يوسف و من جيهة السافل فوق الطناضب و ولد محمود و من الغرب عد مليحه / و فوق جنين و فوق شرف الدين ولد دوره و حسين ولد دوره و فوق فولت شميم و من جيهة الصعيد فوق دار فور / و دار خميس ولد جنقل هناك انتهت الحدود و صارت الدار المذكورة بحدودها

المعلومة ملكا للفقيه محمد على العباسى له / و لذريته و ذريت ذريته يتوارثونها من وارث الى وارث حتى يرث الله الارض و من عليها و هو خير الوارثين لا ينازعه / فيها منازع و لا يتعرض له فيها متعرض سالمة مسلمة من جميع الشرور و السبل و المضار لا عليها جسارة و لا خسارة / و لا عظم و لا عانة و لا حسب و لا دم و لا نار و لا قوار و لا نزول و لا رغم و لا زريبة و لا ضيافه و لا علوق و لا مخلاة و لا متورت و لا قل و لا جل / و نوكد عليكم ايها الشيوخ و المقاديم و الجراي لا احد منكم يتعرض للفقيه محمد على العباسى خصوصا حسان انت و جماعتك / الى قيام الساعة لا احد منكم يتعرض له و من تعرض له بعد كلامى و وثيقتى هذه فقد عرض نفسه للهلاك و الحذر ثم الحذر من الخلاف / و المخالف لا يلوم الا نفسه

حضر ذلك و شهد به

الشيخ واورت ولد هارون امين السلطان
و الجندى كتفاوا جند السوق
و الشيخ / ناصر ولد الامين شيخ قرى
و الشيخ محمد ولد بدر شيخ اليس
و الشيخ كنان ولد الفضيل شيخ اتبره
و الشيخ كمتور ولد احمد / شيخ البحر
و الشيخ احمد العركى شيخ بيله
و الشيخ النور ولد محمد شيخ القربين
و الشيخ محمد ولد ادريس شيخ حوش ولد الملك /
و الشيخ عدلان ولد شنبول شيخ اربجى
و الارباب حمد ابن المرحوم الوزير الشيخ عدلان
و قاسم ولد محمد
و نصر ولد محمد
و الارباب / دفع الله محمد
و الارباب ابراهيم عويضه
و احمد ولد محمد ابو القاسم
و المنكروكن فرج الله
و المنكروكن تيفره
و المنكروكن / عبد الله ولد سكوت

و المنكروكن فضل الله ولد سلامة
و المنكروكن عبد البين
و المنكروكن حمد السيد
و فضل ولد قاسم / مقدم المهر

و الكاتب احمد المكى و كفى بالله شهيدا وقع ذلك يوم السبت نهار اثنا عشر من شهر الله المحرم سنة ١٢٢٨ / الف و مايتين و ثمانيه و عشرين من هجرت سيد المرسلين صلى الله عليه و سلم و ارضى الله عن اصحابه اجمعين

This is a copy of a sultanic document. In Thy name, O Generous One. In the name of God, the Merciful, the Compassionate. Praise be to God, and prayers and peace upon the seal of the eminent messengers of God. A sultanic charter written and approved in the Funj territories in the divinely guarded and protected city of Sinnār, may God Most High exalt her, in the presence of her warden, the son of her warden, master of her reins, her far places and near, her sedentaries and pastoralists, the governor at the present time of those over her and within her, candlestick of the age and lamp unto the nations, who destroys the people of deceit, wrongdoing, and oppression, *amīn* of the army of the sultan, he who trusts in God the Eternal, the *wazīr* Shaykh Ḥusayn, son of the late *wazīr* Shaykh Muḥammad Abū Likaylik. May God grant him victory. Amen.

To the presence of all who read this document and see the truth therein.

Thereafter: The divinely protected, pious, divinely assisted, and victorious *wazīr* Shaykh Ḥusayn has confirmed and given that which Sultan[7] Muḥammad `Adlān did for Faqīh Muḥammad `Alī al-`Abbāsī concerning the cultivable land of [the Walad] `Ajīb, virgin rainland. I, the *wazīr* Ḥusayn, have confirmed and given [it] to Faqīh Muḥammad `Alī al-`Abbāsī, asking for the acceptance of God Most High, and for reward in the life to come, for a day in which neither wealth nor sons suffice, unless one comes to God with a secure heart. Its location and boundaries are known. Its boundary on the eastern side is the estate of Shaykh al-Ṭurayfī walad al-Shaykh Yūsuf; on the northern side above al-Ṭanāḍib and Walad Maḥmūd; on the west `Idd Mulayḥa and above Jannīn, Sharaf al-Dīn walad Dawra, Ḥusayn walad Dawra, and the rain pool of Shammīm; on the southern side, above the estates of the Fūr and of Khamīs walad Janqal. There the boundaries end. The said estate, its boundaries known, has become the property of Faqīh Muḥammad `Alī al-`Abbāsī, his descendants and his descendants' descendants; they shall bequeath it from heir to heir until God inherits the earth and those upon it. He is the Best of Heirs. Let no challenger challenge him concerning it. Let no troublemaker trouble him concerning it. It is completely free from all *shurūr*, *subul*, and *maḍārr*. It is not subject to *jusāra*, *khusāra*, *`aẓm*, *`āna*, *ḥasab*, *damm*, *nār*, *quwwār*, *nuzūl*, *raghm*, *zarība*, *ḍiyāfa*, *`ulūq*, *mukhlā*, *matūrat*, *qill*, or *jill*. We command you peremptorily, O shaykhs, *muqaddams*, and *jarāī*; let no one of you trouble Faqīh Muḥammad `Alī al-`Abbāsī, especially Ḥassān, you and your followers, until the hour of resurrection. Let no one trouble him. He who troubles him after my words and this my document has exposed himself to destruction. Beware, then beware of disobedience, and let the disobedient blame none but himself.

There were present and witnessed to it:

Shaykh Wawrit walad Hārūn, *amīn* of the sultan
the *jundī*, Kitfāwī, *jundī* of the market
Shaykh Nāṣir walad al-Amīn, Shaykh of Qarrī
Shaykh Muḥammad walad Badr, Shaykh of Alays
Shaykh Kannān walad al-Faḍīl, Shaykh of Atbara
Shaykh Kamtūr walad Aḥmad, Shaykh of al-Baḥr
Shaykh Aḥmad al-`Arakī, Shaykh of Bayla
Shaykh al-Nūr walad Muḥammad, Shaykh of al-Qarbīn
Shaykh Muḥammad walad Idrīs, shaykh of the compound of the king's son
Shaykh `Adlān walad Shanbūl, Shaykh of Arbajī

Arbāb Ḥammad,[8] son of the late *wazīr* Shaykh `Adlān

Qāsim walad Muḥammad

Naṣr walad Muḥammad

Arbāb Daf` Allāh Muḥammad

Arbāb Ibrāhīm `Uwayḍa

Aḥmad walad Muḥammad Abu'l-Qāsim

Mankarūkan Faraj Allāh

Mankarūkan Tayfara

Mankarūkan `Abd Allāh walad Sukūt

Mankarūkan Faḍl Allāh walad Salāma

Mankarūkan `Abd al-Bayyin

Mankarūkan Ḥammad al-Sayyid

Faḍl walad Qāsim, *muqaddam al-mahr*[9]

The scribe is Aḥmad al-Makkī. With God, two witnesses suffice. That took place on Saturday, on the twelfth day of God's month of Muḥarram, in the year 1228, one thousand two hundred twenty-eight from the *hijra* of the lord of the messengers. May God bless him and grant him peace. May God be pleased with all his companions.

[1]School of Oriental and African Studies, University of London, Arkell Papers, Box 1, File 5, Piece 73. A photocopy and English translation have been published by Holt, "Land Charters," Plate IV and pp. 108-110.

[2]Holt, "Land-Charters," p. 116.

[3]Ibid., p. 109 (mistranslation) and Plate IV.

[4]*Makhṭūṭa*, p. 57.

[5]Holt, "Land-Charters," p. 117.

[6]Brocchi, *Giornale*, Vol. 5, p. 443; for the title *al-mānjil al-kabīr*, see pp. 546-547.

[7]This title is not correct; Bādī VI was sultan when Doc. 39 was issued.

[8]Possibly a copyist's error for Muḥammad [`Adlān].

[9]See Jay Spaulding, "*Kora*: A Theme in Nubian Cultural History," *Africa Today*, Vol. 28, No. 2 (1981): 61-68, and *Heroic Age*, pp. 105-107.

DOCUMENT 40

Document 40 is a confirming charter issued by Sultan Bādī VI to Madanī walad Faraḥ on 13 Dhu'l-Qa`da 1230/17 October 1815. The text has been taken by the editors from a miniscule copy of the original preserved in the photographic collection of the Sudanese Ministry of Culture and Information; when enlarged, the photograph reveals an intact and easily legible document.[1] The land conveyed was riverbank property, probably in the vicinity of the capital. The purpose of the grant was to exclude the brothers of the beneficiary from landholding rights they might otherwise have obtained through inheritance. The witness roster reflects the temporary fall from favor of the northern provincial governor Nāṣir b. Muḥammad al-Amīn.[2]

باسمك يا كريم بسم الله الرحمن الرحيم الحمد لله الذى بلغ الرسول و نحن ءامنا بما يقول

الواثق بالملك العدل
السلطان بادى بن السلطان
طبل سنه ١٢٢٠

حجة سلطانية و وثيقة ملوكية بمدينة سنار المحروسة المحمية اجلها الله تعالى لدا متوليها / سلطان المسلمين و خليفة رب العالمين القايم بامور الدنيا و الدين المنتصب لمصالح المسلمين و ناصر شريعة / سيد المرسلين و ناشر لواء العدل و العقل على كافة العالمين من اصلح الله به العباد و انار به البلاد / و قامع اهل الكفر و المكر و العناد و اهل الظلم و الفساد و رحمه الله سبحانه و تعالى للحاضر و الباد / الواثق بالملك العدل السلطان بن السلطان السلطان المظفر المعان السلطان بادى بن المرحوم / السلطان طبل نصره الله الرحمن الرحيم بجاه القران العظيم و النبى الكريم ءامين ءامين يا رب /

العالمين الى حضرت كل من تقف عليه هذه الوثيقة و الناظر لما فيها من الحقيقة و بعد فان المحفوظ / المبرور الموید المنصور السلطان بادى تمم و امضا ما فعله وزيره الشيخ حسين من صدقة / الجرف الذى كان بيد فرح لمدنى ولد فرح و خصه به دون اخوانه لانه لم يكن سابقا اصلا / لهم و لا تصدقت سلطنه لوالدهم فرح و الان الوزير تصدق به لمدنى و انا السلطان / بادى تممت ذلك الصدقة و امضيتها لمدنى ولد فرح ابتغاء مرضات الله تعالى و طلبا / للثواب في دار الماب و ليوم لا ينفع فيه مال و لا بنون الا من اتى الله بقلب سليم و ازلفت الجنة / للمتقين و برزت الجحيم للغاوين[3] و هو الجرف المذكور معلوم البقعة و الحدود فحده من جهة / الصبح جرف ولد فلاله العند شكر الله و من جهة السافل مرن الملك و من جهة الغرب الشلاتيت / القيف و من جهة الصعيد جرف احمد ولد هجو العند شكر الله المقابل مشرع جاره هناك انتها / الحدود و صار الجرف المذكور بحدوده المعلومة صدقة و ملكا لمدنى ولد فرح و لذريته و ذرية / ذريته لا ينازعه في صدقة هذا الجرف المذكور منازع و من يعرض له بعد كلامى و وثيقتى هذه فقد عرض بعد كلامى / و وثيقتى هذه[4] فقد عرض نفسه للهلاك يتوارثونه من وارث الى وارث حتى يرث الله الارض / و من عليها و هو خير الوارثين لا ينازعه فيه منازع و لا يتعرض له فيه متعرض سالم مسلمه / من جميع الشرور و السبل و المضار لا عليه جساره و لا خساره و لا عاده و لا عانه و لا قل و لا / جل و لا شي من السبل العادية و نوكد عليكم يا جميع الشيوخ و المقاديم و الجراي الذين من تحتهم / الى حد ملكى كله خصوصا الوزير الشيخ حسين انت و جرايك و من ياتى بعدكم الى قيام الساعه / لا احد منكم يتعرض منكم يتعرض[4] لذريته و لا لذرية ذريته فى صدقه هذا الجرف / و من تعرض له بعد كلامى و وثيقتى هذه فقد عرض نفسه للهلاك و الحذر ثم الحذر من المخالفة و المخالف / لا يلوم الا نفسه

حضر ذلك و شهد به

الوزير الشيخ حسين بن الشيخ محمد ابو لكيلك
و الشيخ واورت بن الشيخ / هارون امين السلطان
و الجندى كتفاو بن الجندى محمد تكتك جندى السوق
و الشيخ بادى بن ضياب شيخ حوش خال الملك //
و الشيخ شمام ولد الشيخ الامين شيخ قرى /
و الشيخ محمد ولد بدر شيخ اليس
و الشيخ كنان / ولد الفضيل شيخ اتبرة
و الشيخ محمد العركى / ولد عبد العلى شيخ بيله

و الشيخ محمد كمتور ولد احمد / شيخ البحر
و الشيخ محمد ولد النور شيخ القرابين /
و الشيخ قاسم ولد رباط مقدم السواكره
و السلطان / ابكير سلطان فور المسبعات
و الشيخ احمد / ولد النور شيخ القواريه
و الشيخ عدلان ولد / شنبول شيخ اربجى
و الشيخ محمد ولد ادريس / شيخ حوش ولد الملك
و الشيخ على ولد عمر / مقدم الشلاتيت
و السلطان ادم سلطان / برقو
و الشيخ احمد ولد بان النقا مقدم قواويد / الملك
و الملك محمد ولد عدلان ملك برساج /
و الارباب محمد ولد عدلان
و الارباب / دفع الله ولد احمد
و الارباب دفع الله / ولد محمد
و القاضى الشريف عبد الرحمن /
و الخطيب نوار
و الموذن الفقيه محمد / بان بيه
و الفقيه عدلان ولد ولد العونى /
و الفقيه مزمل ولد ولد الشرقاوى
و الفقيه / حسن ولد ولد عشيب
و الفقيه احمد ولد / ضياب معتوق الملك

و كاتب الوثيقه / خضر ابراهيم يعقوب حميرا تحرير ذلك ضحوه / الثلاثا و ثلاثه عشر ليلت خلت من شهر ذى / القعده الحرام من شهور سنه ١٢٣٠ / ثلاثين بعد المايتين و الالف من الهجره / النبويه على صاحبها افضل الصلاه / و ازكى السلام

In Thy name, O Generous One. In the name of God, the Merciful, the Compassionate. Praise be to God, Who sent the messenger. We believe in what he says.

He who trusts in the Impartial King
Sultan Bādī, the son of Sultan
Ṭabl Year 1220/1805-1806

A sultanic charter and royal document [issued] in the divinely guarded and protected city of Sinnār, may God Most High exalt her, in the presence of her warden, the sultan of the Muslims and Caliph of the Lord of the Universe, steadfast in the affairs of this world and of religion, just in the affairs of the Muslims, protector of the law of the lord of the messengers, who spreads the banner of justice and wisdom throughout all the universe, through whom God has prospered the worshipers and illuminated the nations, who subdues the people of unbelief, deceit, and opposition, the people of tyranny and corruption. May God Most High (praise be to Him) be merciful to him in this life and the hereafter. He who trusts in the Impartial King, the sultan, the son of the sultan, the victorious and divinely aided Sultan Bādī, son of the late Sultan Ṭabl. May God, the Merciful, the Compassionate, grant him victory through the influence of the sublime Qur'ān and the eminent prophet. Amen, amen, O Lord of the Universe.

To the presence of all who read this document and see the truth therein.

Thereafter: The divinely protected, pious, divinely assisted and victorious Sultan Bādī has confirmed and ratified what his *wazīr*, Shaykh Ḥusayn, has done in regard to the gift of alms of the *jarf* which was in the possession of Faraḥ, to Madanī walad Faraḥ. He has conferred it upon him alone, without his brothers, for it was not theirs previously by origin nor did I grant authority over it to their father Faraḥ. Now the *wazīr* has given it as alms to Madanī, and I, Sultan Bādī, have confirmed this gift of alms and ratified it for Madanī walad Faraḥ, for the acceptance of God Most High, asking for reward in the life to come, for a day in which neither wealth nor sons suffice, unless one comes to God with a secure heart. "Paradise shall be brought forward for the Godfearing, and Hell advanced for the perverse."[5] The location and boundaries of the said *jarf* are known. Its boundary on the eastern side is the *jarf* of Walad Falāla, belonging to Shukr Allāh, on the northern side the *mirin* of the king, on the western side al-Shalātīt al-Qayf, and on the southern side the *jarf* of Aḥmad walad Hājū, belonging to Shukr Allāh and facing the watering place of his neighbor. There the boundaries end. The said *jarf*, its boundaries known, has become the gift of alms and property of Madanī walad Faraḥ, his descendants and his descendants' descendants. Let no challenger challenge him in regard to the gift of alms of the said *jarf*. He who troubles him after my words and this my document has exposed himself to destruction. They shall inherit it from heir to heir until God inherits the earth and those upon it, and He is the Best of Heirs. Let no challenger challenge him concerning it. Let no troublemaker trouble him concerning it. It is completely free from all *shurūr*, *subul*, and *maḍārr*. It is not subject to *jusāra*, *khusāra*, *`āda*, *`āna*, *qill*, *jill*, nor any of the customary *subul*. We command you peremptorily, all you shaykhs and *muqaddams*, and the *jarāī* who are under them throughout my kingdom, all, and especially the *wazīr* Shaykh Ḥusayn, you and your *jarāī*, and whoever may come after you until the hour of resurrection, let no one of you trouble his descendants or his descendants' descendants in the gift of alms of this *jarf*. He who troubles him after my words and this my document has exposed himself to destruction. Beware, then beware of disobedience, and let the disobedient blame none but himself.

There were present and witnessed to it:

the *wazīr*, Shaykh Ḥusayn b. al-Shaykh Muḥammad Abū Likaylik
Shaykh Wāwrit b. al-Shaykh Hārūn, *amīn* of the sultan
the *jundī*, Kitfāwi the son of the *jundī* Muḥammad Taktak, *jundī* of the market
Shaykh Bādī b. Diyāb, shaykh of the compound of the king's maternal uncle
Shaykh Shammām walad al-Shaykh al-Amīn, Shaykh of Qarrī
Shaykh Muḥammad walad Badr, Shaykh of Alays
Shaykh Kannān walad al-Faḍīl, Shaykh of Atbara
Shaykh Muḥammad al-`Arakī walad `Abd al-`Alī, Shaykh of Bayla
Shaykh Muḥammad Kamtūr walad Aḥmad, Shaykh of al-Baḥr
Shaykh Muḥammad walad al-Nūr, Shaykh of al-Qarbīn

Shaykh Qāsim walad Rubāṭ, *muqaddam al-sawākira*
Sultan Abkīr, Sultan Fūr al-Musabba`āt
Shaykh Aḥmad walad al-Nūr, *shaykh al-quwwārīya*
Shaykh `Adlān walad Shanbūl, Shaykh of Arbajī
Shaykh Muḥammad walad Idrīs, shaykh of the compound of the king's son
Shaykh `Alī walad `Umar, *muqaddam* of the Shalātīt
Sultan Adam, Sultan of Borqū
Shaykh Aḥmad walad Bān al-Naqā, *muqaddam* of the king's *qawāwīd*
Malik Muḥammad walad `Adlān, *malik bursāj*
Arbāb Muḥammad walad `Adlān
Arbāb Daf` Allāh walad Aḥmad
Arbāb Daf` Allāh walad Muḥammad
the *qāḍī*, Sharīf `Abd al-Raḥmān
the *khaṭīb*, Nuwwār
the muezzin, Faqīh Muḥammad Bān Bihi
Faqīh `Adlān walad Walad al-`Ūnī
Faqīh Muzammil walad Walad al-Sharqāwī
Faqīh Ḥasan walad Walad `Ushayb
Faqīh Aḥmad walad Diyāb, a freedman of the king

The writer of the document is Khiḍr Ibrāhīm Ya`qūb b. Ḥamīran. That was written on the morning of Tuesday, when thirteen nights had passed from the holy month of Dhu'l-Qa`da from the months of the year 1230, one thousand two hundred thirty from the *hijra* of the prophet, upon whose master the best of prayers and purest peace.

[1]Sudan Government, Ministry of Culture and Information, photograph IND 288. For a previously published version see Jay Spaulding, "A Confirming Charter of Sultan Bādī b. Ṭabl of Sinnār," *Sudan Texts Bulletin*, Vol. 1 (1979): 18-25.

[2]Spaulding, *Heroic Age*, pp. 445-446.

[3]Qur'ān 26:90-91.

[4]Dittography in original.

[5]Scriptural translation supplied by the editors.

DOCUMENT 41

Document 41 is confirming charter issued by Sultan Bādī VI to Muḥammad al-`Arakī walad `Abd al-`Alī, his Shaykh of Bayla (Doc. 40). The land conveyed probably lay east of the Blue Nile and north of the capital along the lower course of the Rahad. The original document was sent by Shaykh Muḥammad Zayn b. al-Shaykh al-Rayyiḥ al-`Arakī to Samuel Hillelson for photocopying in Khartoum, probably in 1928, but neither the original nor the photocopy has been located. The version given here is an English translation preserved in "The Arakiin," by `Abd Allah Effendī El Shafie, 8 August 1928.[1] The material in parentheses was included by the translator; brackets enclose additions by the present editors.

"A royal wasigha [document] written in Sennar during the reign of Sultan Bade, the Just, the Powerful and the Protector of the Muslims against the enemies of Islam. Following the good example of his ancestors the Sultan granted to Fiki Mohammed walad Ali all that Sultan Range [Ranfā] had already gifted to Sheikh Mohammed Abdel Rahman Ebn Sheikh Badr Malik El Gin (who is said to be buried at Hafayer village) i.e. all the land in Dar Wad El Garrad, Dar Wad Seyyid & Hafayer. The sultan hereby declares that this is a sound and genuine gift for the sake of God. In virtue of this Wasigha [document] the owner and his descendants are exempted from the following taxes:

1 Guar [*quwwār*] (Market Fees)

2 Nar [*nār*] (In the days of the Blue Sultanate [the Funj Kingdom] when

grazing or one of the houses of the royal family caught fire the custom was that the natives paid 'nar' tax to make good the loss.)

3 Matara [*maṭāra*] (derived from the well of a saqia [*sāqīya*] not on the river, paid to the royal family)

4 Mukhlaya [*mukhlā*] (Forage for the sultan's animals)

5 Nuzool [*nuzūl*] (diafa [*ḍiyāfa*, "hospitality"] collected for the sultan from natives of villages visited by him)

All Sheikhs, Arbabs & subjects of the Blue Sultanate, especially those who live opposite "Hosh Um el Melik" ["the compound of the mother of the king"] are hereby warned not to interfere with the property gifted by the Sultan to Sheikh Mohammed walad Ali and his descendants and everybody [who] disobeys this order will be liable to the severest punishment."

[1]NRO Dakhlia 112/5/28 "Arakiin."

DOCUMENT 42

Document 42 is an originating charter issued by the Regent Ḥusayn b. Muḥammad Abū Likaylik to Faqīh Aḥmad b. `Īsā on 27 Rabī` II 1235/12 February 1820, bestowing upon him the estate of Umm Ḥawāya. For the controversial relationship between Doc. 42 and another grant of the same property by Muḥammad b. `Adlān b. Muḥammad Abū Likaylik, see the introduction to Doc. 35. The text has been taken by Dr. Abū Salīm from a copy in the handwriting of the early twentieth-century Sudanese historian Muḥammad `Abd al-Raḥīm.[1] The copyist has omitted some of the opening protocols. The witness roster bears examination as the last evidence concerning the state of government in Sinnār on the eve of the Turkish conquest.[2]

حجة سلطانية و وثيقة ملوكية محررة مرضية بالديار الفنجية بمدينة سنار المحروسة المحمية اجلها الله تعالى لدا متوليها مالك قاصيها و دانيها الحاكم يوميذ بمن عليها و ما فيها المحترم المكرم المهاب المعظم الليث الادهم و الملاذ الافخم قنديل الزمان و سراج البلدان و مدمر اهل المكر و البغى و الطغيان و امين جيش السلطان الواثق بالملك الصمد الوزير الشيخ حسين بن الشيخ محمد ابو لكيلك نصره الله امين (. . .) الى حضرت كل من تقف عليه هذه الوثيقة و الناظر لما فيها من الحقيقة و بعد فان المحفوظ المبرور الموید المنصور الوزير الشيخ حسين تصدق على الفقيه احمد بن الفقيه عيسى بجميع الرفاعية فى دار ام حواية و من يليها صدقة لله و لرسوله و للثواب فى دار المئاب و ليوم لا ينفع فيه مال و لا بنون الا من اتى الله بقلب سليم له و لذريته و لذرية ذريته يتوارثونها من وارث الى وارث الى ان يرث الله الارض و ما عليها و هو خير الوارثين و الدار معلومة البقعة و الحدود فحدها من جهة القبلة مقبرة حلة التى و من جهة الغرب المشرع توتاو و من جهة السافل من بحر الصيف و من جهة الصعيد

درب الجمل فهناك انتهت الحدود و صارت الدار المذكورة بحدودها المعلومة ملكا و حوزا للفقيه احمد بن الفقيه عيسى سالمة مسلمة من جميع الشرور و السبل العادية و نوكد عليكم يا جميع الشيوخ و المقاديم و الجراى و خصوصا رحمة ولد فضل الله و جرايه و من ياتى من بعده الى قيام الساعة لا احد منكم يتعرض لهذه الصدقة و من تعرض لها بعد كلامى هذا و وثيقتى هذه فقد عرض نفسه للهلاك و الحذر ثم الحذر من المخالفة و المخالف لا يلومن الا نفسه

حضر و شهد بذلك

الشيخ واورت ولد هارون امين السلطان و جند السوق
و الشيخ ناصر ولد الامين شيخ قرى
و الشيخ سليمان ولد بدر شيخ اليس
و الشيخ كنان شيخ اتبرة
و الشيخ كمتور شيخ البحر
و الشيخ محمد العركى شيخ بيله
و الشيخ محمد ولد النور (شيخ القربين)
و الشيخ محمد ود ادريس شيخ ود الملك
و الشيخ عدلان ولد شنبول شيخ اربجى
و الارباب محمد عدلان
و قاسم ولد الشيخ محمد
و الارباب موسى ود بادى
و الارباب محمد الشيخ حسين
و الارباب رجب
و الارباب ادريس
ابناء الشيخ عدلان
و الارباب دفع الله
و الارباب محمد ابراهيم عويضة
و المنكروكن تيفرة
و فضل حمد ولد شمام
و عبد الباقى عبد البين

و الكاتب الفقيه محمد الحاج كاتب و شاهد و كفى بالله شهيدا تحرير ذلك نهار السبت لسبع و عشرين خلون من شهر ربيع الثانى من شهور سنه ١٢٣٥ من هجرة المكرم صلى الله عليه و سلم

A sultanic charter and royal document, written and approved in the Funj territories, in the divinely guarded and protected city of Sinnār, may God Most High exalt her, in the presence of her warden, the master of her far places and near, the governor at the present time of those over her and within her, the honored, revered, respected, and exalted, the dark lion, the most splendid refuge, candlestick of the age and lamp unto the nations, who destroys the people of deceit, wrongdoing, and oppression, *amīn* of the army of the sultan, he who trusts in God the Eternal, the *wazīr* Shaykh Ḥusayn b. al-Shaykh Muḥammad Abū Likaylik. May God grant him victory. Amen.

To the presence of all who read this document and see the truth therein.

Thereafter: The divinely protected, pious, divinely assisted, and victorious *wazīr* Shaykh Ḥusayn has bestowed as alms upon Faqīh Aḥmad b. al-Faqīh `Īsā all the pastoral lands in the estate of Umm Ḥawāya and that which adjoins it. It is a gift of alms for [the sake of] God and His messenger, for reward in the life to come, for a day in which neither wealth nor sons suffice, unless one comes to God with a secure heart. It is for him, his descendants, and his descendants' descendants. They shall bequeath it from heir to heir until God inherits the earth and those upon it, and He is the Best of Heirs. The location and boundaries of the estate are known. Its boundary on the eastern side is the cemetery of the village of Altī; on the western side the watering place of Tūtāwā; on the northern side the summer water level, and on the southern side the camel path. There the boundaries end. The said estate, its boundaries known, has become the property and possession of Faqīh Aḥmad b. al-Faqīh `Īsā. It is completely free from all *shurūr* and customary *subul*. We command you peremptorily, all you shaykhs, *muqaddams*, and *jarāī*, especially Raḥma walad

Faḍl Allāh and his *jarāī*, and he who comes after him until the hour of resurrection, let no one of you trouble this gift of alms. He who troubles it after these my words and this my document has exposed himself to destruction. Beware, then beware of disobedience, and let the disobedient blame none but himself.

There were present and witnessed to it:

Shaykh Wāwrit walad Hārūn, *amīn* of the sultan and *jundī* of the market
Shaykh Nāṣir walad al-Amīn, Shaykh of Qarrī
Shaykh Sulaymān walad Badr, Shaykh of Alays
Shaykh Kannān, Shaykh of Atbara
Shaykh Kamtūr, Shaykh of al-Baḥr
Shaykh Muḥammad al-`Arakī, Shaykh of Bayla
Shaykh Muḥammad walad al-Nūr, [Shaykh of] al-Qarbīn
Shaykh Muḥammad wad Idrīs, shaykh of the king's son
Shaykh `Adlān walad Shanbūl, Shaykh of Arbajī
Arbāb Muḥammad `Adlān
Qāsim walad al-Shaykh Muḥammad
Arbāb Mūsā wad Bādī
Arbāb Muḥammad al-Shaykh Ḥusayn
Arbāb Rajab and Arbāb Idrīs, sons of Shaykh `Adlān
Arbāb Daf` Allāh
Arbāb Muḥammad Ibrāhīm `Uwayḍa
Mankarūkan Tayfara
Faḍl Ḥammad walad Shammām
`Abd al-Bāqī `Abd al-Bayyin

The scribe is Faqīh Muḥammad al-Ḥājj, scribe and witness. With God, two witnesses suffice. That was written on Saturday, on the day when twenty-seven had passed from the month of Rabī` II of the months of the year 1235 from the *hijra* of the most noble one. May God bless him and grant him peace.

[1]NRO Miscellaneous 1/92/1480.

[2]Spaulding, *Heroic Age*, pp. 446-447.

DOCUMENT 43

Document 43 is a letter issued by Muḥammad b. `Adlān b. Muḥammad Abū Likaylik late in 1820 or early in 1821 during the course of the Turkish invasion of Sinnār. The text has been taken by the editors from a photocopy published by al-Shāṭir Buṣaylī `Abd al-Jalīl.[1] The present letter, probably one of many similar calls to resistance issued by the Great *Mānjil* at this moment of crisis, was directed to the leader of a community of holy men of the north-central Gezira.[2]

بسم الله الرحمن الرحيم / الحمد لله وحده / محمد لا نبى بعده

الشيخ محمد بن
الوزير الشيخ عدلان
١٢٣١

من حضرت من تهابه الرجال و تخشى من صولته الابطال / يوم الحرب و النزال الواثق بالله الديان الشيخ محمد بن / المرحوم الوزير الشيخ عدلان نصره الله امين الى حضرت / الفقيه احمد ولد الفقيه ابراهيم الفرضى و كافة الفقرا / الفرضيين يسلم عليكم جزيل السلام فالذى نعرفكم به / نحن زماننا هذا كله ما طلبنا القبايل قاعدين فى الجزيرة / و عمارها تعبوا و يعسوا نظرنا فى حالهم رفقا بهم / و الوقت هذا قطعنا بقينا فى الدندر طالبين / قبايل الشرق و العربان و انتم اياكم مرتبتنا و فقرانا / و اسباب دعوتنا الصالحة و شركانا فى الخير و الشر / بعد وصول جوابى انتم و جملة فقراكم // جدوا و اجتهدوا و اتعبوا بسوال الله / على نية قضا حاجتنا بهمة عالية / و نية صادقة لا يكون منكم غفلة و لا تهاون / و لا فترة و ان سالتم عن الترك سلطنة / مصر بلغنا خبر قدومهم فى ماية و ثمانين و / الف و هذا شيا قاسى على كافة

المسلمين / اتركوا جميع اموركم و اصرفوا همتكم بالسؤال / ان شاء الله ربنا يبطل سفرهم و يرجعهم / الى محلهم كونهم ما يعرفوا مرتبة و لا غيره / و لا عندهم اعتبار في خاص و لا عام لا تتهاونوا / بذلك

In the name of God, The Merciful, the Compassionate. Praise be to God alone. There is no prophet after Muḥammad.

Shaykh Muḥammad, the son of
The *wazīr* Shaykh `Adlān
1231/1815-1816

From the presence of him who inspires awe in men, while on the day of war and strife heroes quail at his assault, he who trusts in God the Judge, Shaykh Muḥammad, son of the late *wazīr* `Adlān. May God grant him victory. Amen.

To the presence of Faqīh Aḥmad walad al-Faqīh Ibrāhīm al-Farḍī and all the *fuqarā'* of the Farḍiyīn.

He greets you with many greetings. That of which we inform you is, that in all our days we have never demanded anything from the tribes living in the Gezira, nor from their cultivation, in stress or in peace, but, I believe, have regarded them in their condition as friends. At present we have come to the Dinder to mobilize the tribes of the east and the nomads. As for you, our distinguished *fuqarā'*, the reason for our truthful appeal and our common cause together through thick and thin, is that after receiving my letter which has come to you, you and all your *fuqarā'* should exert yourselves anew and to the utmost in the affair of God and toward attending to our very important needs. [We ask] a true determination, without neglect, or scorn, or half-hearted treatment. As you ask about the Turks of the sultanate of Egypt, we [first] heard that they were coming [back] in 1180/1766-1767. This is an outrage to all Muslims, so leave all your affairs and direct your attention to the matter. If God wills, Our Lord will thwart their expedition and send them back to their place. They understand neither social rank nor the absence of it. They have no conception of high class and none of low. Do not fail in that.

[1]al-Shāṭir Buṣaylī `Abd al-Jalīl, *Ma`ālim ta'rīkh Sūdān wādī al-Nīl* (Cairo: 1955), p. 267. A flawed printed version may be found on p. 268.

[2]The biography of the father of the recipient, Ibrāhīm b. `Abūdī, is included in the *Ṭabaqāt* (p. 79). His burial place, and the probable residence of the recipient of Doc. 43, was at al-Ghabīya; see *Ṭabaqāt*, p. 79, note 6.

DOCUMENT 44

Document 44 is an originating charter issued by the northern provincial governor Ḥammad b. `Alī, nicknamed "al-Simayḥ,"[1] to Faqīh Khōjalī. The text has been taken by the editors from the original.[2] The grant conveyed rights to two riverbank properties, probably near the Nile confluence, and it also released the community of Maḥas settlers on Tūtī Island from obligations to the government. Document 44 is not dated, but may be the earliest extant charter from Sinnār. It may be placed with certainty within the lifetime of Shaykh Khōjalī, who died in 1155/1742-1743.[3] It probably antedates the earliest extant charter issued by the central government, Doc. 2 of 1729, for by that date Shaykh Ḥammad had already been succeeded by `Ajīb b. Muḥammad al-`Ajayl,[4] and he in turn by his son Bādī and his grandson Ḍiyāb, the incumbant Shaykh of Qarrī who witnessed Doc. 2.[5] The *arenga* of Doc. 44 asks that spiritual rewards go to "Sultan Bādī," presumably the reigning monarch at the time of the issue of the charter. Sultan Bādī IV became king on 8 July 1724;[6] if one were to assume that he was the ruler mentioned, it would follow that not only Ḥammad, but also `Ajīb, Bādī, and Ḍiyāb all must have governed between 1724 and 1729. The editors regard this as unlikely, and prefer to believe that the "Sultan Bādī" referred to was Bādī III; Doc. 44 must therefore have been issued before his death in 1128/1715-1716.[7] The only fixed date in the career of Ḥammad b. `Alī is that of his memorable attack upon Shandī in 1118/1706-1707,[8] probably during his retreat from Qarrī after the failure of the revolt of 1705-1706.[9] If this assumption is correct, the present document was probably issued before 1118/1706-1707. Consistent with this interpretation is the almost complete turnover in courtiers between the witness roster of Doc. 44 and that of its nearest dated successor, Doc. 47.

الواثق برب الناس
الشيخ حمد

الحمد لوليه و الصلاة / و السلام على نبيه من حضرت الصدر الاجل عالى القدر و المحل / المحفوظ من الخطايا و الزلل من ترجا فضايله و اومن قوايله / الصادق فى قوله الطيب فى فعله الواثق بالملك الوالى الشيخ / حمد بن المرحوم الشيخ على زيدت ليالى مجده و جددت ليالى سعده / بجاه القرءان العظيم و النبى الكريم امين اما بعد فان الشيخ حمد/ تصدق على الفقه خوجلى بساقية عبد الكريم و هو عشره / (اعواد بابو)[10] ثمانية اذرع لوجه الله الكريم للسلطان بادى تكون / ذخيرة له يوم القيامه ليوم لا ينفع فيه مال و لا بنون الى من / اتى الله بقلب سليم حديدها من جهة الصعيد حجاز و من جهت / السافل اولاد سره انها سالمه مسلمه من جميع الشرور و الخدم لا / علوق و لا غيره

و الشهدا على ذلك

الفقه بلوله
و الفقه عبد الرحمن القاضى
و الفقه عبد الصمد
و من العسكر
كنينى و اخيه ابو القاسم
و عبد الله / ولد سيد القوم
و تمام سيد القوم
و دفع الله ولد ولد / نمر و اخيه عبد القادر /
و نمر
و حسن ولد دليل
و عبد الله ولد حميده
و فضل الله ولد شند /
و حماد ولد الكنب
و حمد ولد ابو زقيبير
و عنتار ولد على
و وديد / سيد الخيل

و سرير ولد ولد سرير و عبد الله اخيه
و قرن ولد / سرير
و زراع

و كاتب الاحرف الفقير الى الله تعالى (. . .)[11] الدين كاتب و شاهد (. . .)[12] //

و ايضا تصدق الشيخ حمد بن المرحوم على على الفقه خوجل بعشره اعواد بابو ثمانيه و هى عشرت اخيه عامر الصعيدية من البحر الغرب الى الشرق تلى الجموعيه بشهادات هوءلاء المذكورين هذه الصدقه بعد الاولى التى فى داخل الوثيقة و ايضا المحس السكان معكم بتوب كسرنا لكم عظمهم و جوهناهم (. . .)[11] اعانت للدين بشهدت الشهود المعلومين

He who trusts in the Lord of the People

Shaykh Ḥammad

Praise be to His friend, and prayers and peace upon His prophet.

From the presence of the illustrious commander, high of rank and station, divinely protected from transgression and error, who hopes for His favor and trusts in His word, truthful in word and kindly in deed, who trusts in the King, the Ruler, Shaykh Ḥammad, son of the late Shaykh `Alī. May the nights of his splendor be increased and the nights of his good fortune renewed through the influence of the sublime Qur'ān and the eminent prophet. Amen.

Thereafter: Shaykh Ḥammad has bestowed as alms upon Faqīh Khōjalī the *sāqīya* "`Abd al-Karīm," having ten rods of eight cubits [each], for the sake of God the Generous, and for Sultan Bādī. It will be a treasure for him on the day of resurrection, for a day in which neither wealth nor sons suffice, unless one comes to God with a secure heart. Its boundaries are on the southern side Ḥijāzī and on the northern side the Awlād Surra. It is completely free from all *shurūr* and service dues; [it is not subject to] *`ulūq*, nor to anything else.

The witnesses to that are:

Faqīh Balūla
Faqīh `Abd al-Raḥmān, the *qāḍī*
Faqīh `Abd al-Ṣamad

From among the soldiers:

Kanīnī and his brother Abu'l-Qāsim
`Abd Allāh, son of the *sīd al-qūm*
Tammām, *sīd al-qūm*
Daf` Allāh walad Walad Nimr and his brother `Abd al-Qādir
Nimr
Ḥasan walad Dalīl
`Abd Allāh walad Ḥumayda
Faḍl Allāh walad Shanad
Ḥammād walad al-Kanbu
Ḥammad walad Abū Zaqībīr
`Antār walad `Alī
Wadīd, *sīd al-khayl*
Sarīr walad Walad Sarīr and `Abd Allāh his brother
Qurun walad Sarīr
Zirā`

The writer of the letters is the *faqīr* of God Most High [. . .] al-Dīn, scribe and witness.

Furthermore: Shaykh Ḥammad, son of the late `Alī, has bestowed as alms upon Faqīh Khōjalī ten rods of eight [cubits]. These are the ten of his brother `Āmir, [bounded] on the south by the river, and from west to east following [the border of] the Jamū`īya. [This was done] with the witness of the aforementioned, this [second] gift of alms after the first which is within the document. Furthermore, for your sake I have broken for you the obligation of the Maḥas who live with you on Tūtī [Island]; we have granted them [. . .] to aid the religion. [This was done] with the witness of the known witnesses.

[1]*Ṭabaqāt*, pp. 203-204.

[2]For a previously published version see Abū Salīm, *al-Fūnj wa'l-arḍ*, pp. 88-89.

[3]*Ṭabaqāt*, p. 201.

[4]It is reasonably certain that `Ajīb b. Muḥammad al-`Ajayl succeeded Ḥammad al-Simayḥ directly, for among holy men this transition became the archtypical example of a "bad" ruler followed by a "good" one; see *Ṭabaqāt*, p. 98.

[5]For the succession of Bādī and Ḍiyāb see NRO Miscellaneous 1/20/232; Ḥasan b. Shāwir, "Wāḍiḥ al-bayyān fī mulūk al-`Arab bi'l-Sūdān wa-mulūk al-`Abdallāb min al-Shaykh `Ajīb al-Awwil ilā ta'rīkhihī;" the tenure of Ḍiyāb in 1729 is confirmed by Doc. 2. The NRO collection also contains an unclassified fragment of an authentic but faded and truncated letter from "Shaykh Diyāb, son of the late Bādī" to Faqīh Madlūl b. al-Faqīh `Abd al-Jabbār, thanking him for his blessing, soliciting his prayers, and informing him of his own appointment as governor of the northern province: "Praise be to God! God's will came to pass. The king, may God prolong his life, did not leave me wanting for anything; he gave me the land of my father."

[6]Spaulding, "Nubian Kingship," p. 17.

[7]O'Fahey and Spaulding, *Kingdoms*, p. 57.

[8]*Ṭabaqāt*, pp. 123, 239-240, 243.

[9]O'Fahey and Spaulding, *Kingdoms*, pp. 74-77.

[10]Conjectural reading.

[11]Lacuna.

[12]Lacuna. What follows is in the margin in a different handwriting.

DOCUMENT 45

Document 45 is a letter from Ḥammād b. \`Ajīb to Faqīh Khōjalī. The text has been taken by the editors from the original.[1] Ḥammād, nicknamed *ẓilf al-\`ijl* or "Calf's Foot," was remembered in later years as a successful general in the service of his father, \`Ajīb b. Muḥammad al-\`Ajayl; however, the present document provides some indication that he may also have succeeded \`Ajīb as governor of the northern province, as did his brothers Bādī and \`Abd Allāh,[2] though perhaps his tenure was brief. Document 45 was written before the death of Shaykh Khōjalī in 1155/1742-1743.[3] Since \`Abd Allāh, on the strength of the witness rosters of the central government, would seem to have governed throughout the period from 1733 to 1744,[4] it is probable that Ḥammād held office before 1733. If the tradition is correct that \`Abd Allāh ousted Ḍiyāb because of the latter's miserliness and other undesirable qualities, then Ḥammād must have served before 1729, when Ḍiyāb held office.[5] Ḥammād's brother Shammām, mentioned in Doc. 45, accompanied the governor \`Abd Allāh to Kordofan, where both perished at the hands of the Musabba\`āt in 1747.[6] The letter provides evidence of the limitations placed by the Funj government upon even the most eminent of holy men early in the eighteenth century, before the age of collapse.

من حضرت الصدر الاجل عالى القدر و المحل المحفوظ من الخطايا و الزلل المختص
بمزيد / عناية الله عز و جل المحفوظ بعين عناية الملك المجيب الشيخ حماد ابن المرحوم
الشيخ عجيب حفظه الله امين الى حضرت سيدى و مسندى و من على الله و عليه
اعتمادى فذاك الحاج / خوجلى حفظه الله امين اما بعد فان الشيخ حماد يخصك منه

بجزيل السلام و ابرد التحيه / و الاكرام و يقول لك الذى نعرفك به عرضك الله
(. . .)[7] بكل خيرانى انا مقتدى بقولك و مستبارك بسورتك لانى جربتها و حصل لى
فيها خير ببركتك و اتباع السنه و انا و الله و الله ثم و الله اذا كان امر اقسا من هذا
و يبقا انا بديته من تلقا نفسى و انت منعتنى منه امتنع و نفسى / راضيه لاكن هذا بقى
امرا سلطانى و انا ما لى فيه اختيار فالمطلوب من الله ثم منك لا تاخذ علينا / (. . .)[7]
وصيتك السابقة و ذالحين جاتنى وصيتك مع ناس شمام اخوى و ذكرت ان الناس من
/ فيهم فقرا و نحن لا نعلم بحالهم فالذى نطلبه من فضلك و احسانك انت يا سيدى /
تتفصل علينا و تعرفنا باسمايهم و نحن نكتب لهم بامان الله و رسوله مثل ما ذكرت /
لنا اما انهم يرحلوا علينا و عليهم امان الله او يزحفوا من العرب و يعرفونا به مكانهم /
و عليهم الامان الحقيقه هذا ما نطلبه منك و الفضل من الله ثم منك لا سبيل لنا على
اقربا / الفقرا و اهل الضلام اللهم اعنا عليهم و انك لا تنسانا من الدعا اناء الليل و
اطراف / النهار و ما كان لنا فيه خير الى هذا الان فكرنا عليه فى ما يصلح حالنا و
يكشف / منا هذه الغمه و جوابك خل يجينا بمعرفة اسماء الناس بعجله مع حامل
الورقه و ان / كان يمتنعوا من الرحيل انت تكون لنا شاهد اننا خصيناهم بالامان و
امتنعوا و خالفوا / نريدك ان تسل لنا الله ان يعيننا عليهم بعد الخلاف و نظرك خل
يجينا بعجلة / و جوابك ايضا انت خلى يجى من عندك الى عندهم خاصه مع زولك ان
سمعوا كلامنا و كلامك / زحفوا و اعلمونا مكانهم امان الله نحن ما نخالف قولك و لا
نقدر امان الله و ان ابوا خالفوا قولك و قولنا و ابوا امان الله الله يعين عليهم و انت
شهدت الخلاف

From the presence of the most illustrious commander, high of rank and station, divinely protected from transgression and error, authorized through an abundance of solicitude by God Most Mighty and Great, protected by the solicitous eye of the Mighty King, Shaykh Ḥammād, son of the late Shaykh `Ajīb. May God protect him. Amen.

To the presence of my lord and support, upon whom, along with God, I rely, and that is al-Ḥājj Khōjalī. May God protect him. Amen.

Thereafter: Shaykh Ḥammād bestows upon you many greetings from him, and the coolest of salutations and respects, and says to you: That of which we inform you is, may God show you [. . .] with all my good deeds, I am emulating your word and fathoming your counsel. I have attempted it, and goodness has come to this through your blessing and compliance with the *sunna.* O God, O God, and then, O God! Were it only a matter farthest removed from this, that I might pay his wergild on my own account. You have bidden me, [saying]: "Cease!" As for myself, I accept that, but this remains an order of my sultan and I have no choice. The demand is from God, and then from you. Do not blame us [. . .] your previous order. Now your order has come to me with the people of my brother Shammām. You have mentioned that among the people there are *fuqarā'*, but we do not know their condition. What we are asking of your generosity and kindness, O my lord, is that you would do us the favor of telling us their names. We will write to them with the *amān* of God and His messenger, just as you have mentioned to us. If they are travelling toward us, they have the *amān* of God; if they are going about with the nomads, let us know where they are, and they shall have a true *amān.* This is what we are asking of you. Grace is from God, and then from you. We have no access to the associates of the *fuqarā'.* O God, aid us against the people of tyranny! Do not forget us in prayer by fall of night or break of day, for to this very moment we are considering every good possibility for improving our situation and removing this distress from ourselves. Let your letter come to us quickly via the bearer of [this] sheet with information about the names of the people. If they refuse to set out, you are our witness that we have extended to them the *amān*, but that they have refused and disobeyed. We want you to ask God to help us against them after the disobedience. Let view of you come to us quickly. Also, have a letter come from you to them; send it with your messenger. If they obey my words and yours and get under way, let us know their location [and they will have] the *amān* of God; we will not and cannot disobey your word [that they should have] the *amān* of God. But if they refuse, and disobey your word and ours, and refuse the *amān* of God, may God help [us] against them, and you have witnessed the disobedience.

[1]For a previously published version see Abū Salīm, *al-Fūnj wa'l-arḍ*, pp. 90-91.

[2]Ḥasan b. Shāwir, "Wāḍiḥ al-bayyān;" Docs. 4, 5, 8, 9, and 10.

[3]*Ṭabaqāt*, p. 201.

[4]Docs. 4, 5, 8, 9 and 10.

[5]Doc. 2; Ḥasan b. Shāwir, "Wāḍiḥ al-bayyān."

[6]R.S. O'Fahey and J.L. Spaulding, "Hāshim and the Musabba`āt," *Bulletin of the School of Oriental and African Studies*, Vol. 35, No. 2 (1972): 316-333.

[7]Lacuna.

DOCUMENT 46

Document 46 is a charter issued by Faqīh Ḍayf Allāh, the *qāḍī* of Shaykh `Ajīb b. `Abd Allāh of Qarrī, on 4 Rabī` II 1181/30 August 1767. The text has been taken by the editors from the original, which is frayed at the bottom and along a fold through the middle of the document.[1] The charter contains the judge's ruling concerning a longstanding dispute between the Awlād al-Shaykh Khōjalī and their neighbors the Awlād Walad Umm Maryūm (Docs. 12, 16). The circumstances in which this litigation took place, and which occasioned the subsequent addition of the personal endorsements found at the end of the charter, are described in Doc. 47. The social and political situation delineated by the charter raises questions about the interrelationship between royal and Islamic justice, and between customary law and the *sharī`a* in Qarrī in the late 1760s.[2]

بسم الله الرحمن الرحيم / و الصلاة و السلام على نبينا الامين / الحمد لله الذى ايد
الشريعه المحمدية بالقواطع القرانيه و الادلة الشرعية التى نزلت على خير البريه / محمد
صاحب النفس الرضية و الخلق العلية و على اله بكرة و عشية فهذه حجة شرعية قاطعة
مالكية / محررة مرضية بالديار الفنجية بنواحى قرى المحروسة المحمية اجلها الله تعالى
لدا متوليها و الحاكم بما فيها الفقه / ضيف الله اما بعد فقد حضر لديه تخاصم بين
يديه بمجلس الشرع الشريف السالم من الزيغ و التحريف / الرشيدان العاقلان خوجلى
و الجلى متنازعين عنده بامر من السلطان ناصر بن السلطان بادى للشيخ عجيب / بن
الشيخ عبد الله و الشيخ عجيب كتب الى عبده مرناتى ان يقعدهم الشرع عند الفقه
ضيف الله و من / امتنع منهم فليحكم عليه باللدد و حين حضروا بين يديه فادعا كل
منهما الملك و الحوز فى الدار التى كانت / بيد عطية الله عبد اولاد عجيب بعد ثبوت
الوكالة المفوضة بالبينه الشرعية خوجلى بوكالة من / ابايه اولاد الفقه خوجلى و الجلى

بوكالة من ابيه الفقيه مقبول و اخوانه و اولاد اعمه[3] حاضرين معه / فى مجلس الشرع و امر الحاكم كلا منهما بالبينة على صحة دعواه بالحوز لان الصدقة بلا حوز باطلة / بدليل قول المصنف و حيز و ان بلا اذن قال بن عبد السلام القبول و الحيازة معتبران الا ان القبول ركن / و الحيازة شرط نص عليه عبد الباقى و الخراشى و تت[4] قال الشيخ عبد الباقى عند قول المصنف و باقطاع الامام / الارض فهو تمليك فله بيعه و هبته و يورث عنه و يفتقر الى حيازة على المشهور كساير العطايا و مثله ايضا / الخراشى و اقام خوجلى البينة المدلة على ان الدار من زمن حماد ولد عجيب فى يد السواكره وظايف السلطنة / عليها اولاد الفقه حمد ما حازها الى ان ملكها و حازها اولاد الفقه خوجلى فى زمن مسمار فارتفعت / الوظايف و تصرفوا فيها التصرف التام بالملك و الحوز و البينة المذكورة منهم الفقه عبد الدافع بنقل / عدلين منه شرف الدين الزروقابى و الفقه محمد ولد راد الله و الفقه جميل الله ولد مكى / و الفقه الصافى ولد بشاره و الشيخ بركات خليفة الشيخ ادريس و الشيخ ادريس ولد ناصر و الشيخ / ادريس ولد نصار و الفقيه السيد ولد حمد السيد و الحاج محمد القنبو و الفقه محمد ولد مضوى ولد ابراهيم / و الفقه سليمان ولد النور و سنوسى ولد حمدان و الفقه مضوى المشهور بى ولد الشيخ ادريس و محمد / بربر و حموده ولد سرور و جمع كثير من الركابية و المحس و غيرهم و البينة التى شهدت لاولاد الفقه خوجلى / منهم من زكى و منهم من استند فيه الحاكم لعلمه بدليل قول المصنف و لا يستند لعلمه الا فى التعديل فيستند له / و لو شهدت بينة بجرح لان عمله اقوى من البينه نص عليه الشيخ عبد الباقى و ادعى الجلى الحوز فى زمن / حماد و امره الحاكم بالبينة على ثبوت حوزه و انظره لها باجتهاده كما قال صاحب المختصر قال الخراشى ما لهم يتبين / لدده و الا حكم عليه من الان ثم اتى ببينة لم يقبلها الشرع ثم اعذر له ثانيا باجتهاده و الحال انه تغيب / و هرب من حكم الشرع بعد استيفا الحجة و ثبت تغيبه و هروبه بالبينة العدلة قال الشيخ عبد الباقى / اذا تغيب المدعى عليه بعد استيفا الحجة و هرب من القضا فانه يقضى عليه و يعجزه و لا يكون له اذا / قدم ان يقوم بحجته بمنزلة ما لو قضى عليه و هو حاضر ثم بعد ثبوت التغيب و الهروب و العجز عن البينة / و انقضا مدة التلوم حكم لاولاد الفقه خوجلى بالدار المذكورة بحدودها المعلومة فحدها من جهة الصعيد / الحاج عالم يمر على الدرب السافل القوز الطالع الى الضنيقيلة و من جهة السافل دار الزروقاب و من جهة / الصبح درب الجمل المعتاد و من جهة الغرب البحر و عجز الجلى و قطع نزاعه هو و اخوانه و اولاد اعمه المخاصمين / معه عن كل حجة يقومون بها فى ما سجل و سطر لعجز الجميع عن البينة بدليل قول المصنف و يعجزه و بدليل قول الشيخ / عبد الباقى المتقدم فى هذه المسالة و بدليل قول الخراشى عند قول المصنف و انظره

لها باجتهاده ما لهم يتبين لدده / و الا حكم عليه من الان و وقع / هذا الحكم بحضرة العلما منهم الفقيه محمد بن الفقه حمد السيد و الفقه محمد ولد السلمه / و بمشورة الفقه اسماعيل خليفه الشيخ صغيرون شيخ القوز

حضر ذلك الحكم و شهد به

الفقه ابوا ادريس خليفة الفقه / عبد الدافع
و الشيخ اخيه
و الفقه احمد ابن عيسى
و الفقه محمد بن على بساطى ارباب
و الفقه محمد ولد حاج
و الفقه ابراهيم / ابن الحاج قرش
و الفقه صالح ولد الزين
و الفقه الخليل ولد الزين
و الفقه بشير ولد كبوشيه
و الفقه مدنى ولد موسى /
و الفقه الامين ولد الحاج
و الفقه (محمد)[5] بن الفقه عبد المحمود
و الفقه محمد ولد الحاج عشير

و مسطر الاحرف الحاج السيد / رحمه كاتب و شاهد بذلك و الله خير الشاهدين تحرير ذلك بيوم الاحد اربعة خلة من ربيع الثانى من شهور سنة ١١٨١ احدى و ثمانين بعد المائة و الالف من الهجرة النبوية على صاحبها عليه افضل الصلاة و السلام //[6]

نعم انا فقير الله احمد / نظرت هذا الحكم فوجدته صحيح لا خلل فيه و لا / ينقض حكم الحاكم الا فى مخالفه / الكتاب و السنة و الاجماع / كما قال المصنف ما خالف قاطع / او جلى قياس (. . .)[7] /[6]

لا شك انى نظرت فى هذا الحكم / فوجدته صحيحا لا خلل فيه بدليل / قول الشيخ خليل و لا ينقضه (. . .)[7] / العدل العالم قال الشيخ (التاتاى)[5] / لا ينظر فيه ليلا (. . .)[7] / و الخصام و تفاقم الحال و انا حامد[5] / ابوا مونه و هذا خطى بيدى /[6]

فانا فقير الله تعالى يوسف ابن / محمد الطريفى نظرت / فى هذا الحكم فوجدته / صحيحا و هذا خطى / بيدى /[6]

نعم انا فقير الله عبد الله ابى بكر / سبط الشيخ محمد نظرت / فى هذا الحكم فوجدته صحيحا / و هذا خطى بيدى /[6]

و ايضا ان حكم العلما عرض علينا و نظرنا / ما فيه و علمنا انه على حق بدليل / المتن و الشرح و انا فقير الله مدن بن / محمد[6]

نعم انا فقير الله احمد حمد السيد / نظرت هذا الحكم فوجدته صحيحا لا خلل فيه و هذا خطى /[6]

و ايضا ان هذا الامر عرض على الفقيه / احمد ولد المايدى و رءاه و امضاه / و قال نعم على الحق و هذا خطى بيدى /[6]

نعم هذا الحكم صحيح و انا فقير الله / احمد بن الفقه سالم الماجدى /[6]

فانا فقير الله محمد ابن ابو امنه نظرت فى هذا الحكم فوجدته صحيحا و هذا خطى بيدى /[6]

(. . .)[7]

نعم ان الامر كما ذكر / و الشان كما سطر / و حكمت بذلك و انا / فقير الله ضيف الله / ابن الفقه محمد (. . .)[7] /[6]

(. . .)[7] فقير الله محمد بن الفقه / حمد السيد حضر هذا / الحكم و اتممته و هذا / خطى بيدى[6]

نعم انا فقير الله / محمد بن عبد الكافى حضرت هذا / الحكم و تممت و هذا خطى بيدى /[8]

تصفحت الحكم فوجدته / صحيحا و امضيت العمل بموجبه[9]

الواثق (. . .)[7]
العبد القاضى
عبد العزيز بن الشريف
محمد الهدى
١١٨٣

In the name of God, the Merciful, the Compassionate, and prayers and peace upon our trustworthy prophet. Praise be to God, Who has supported the Muḥammadan law with decisive Qur'ānic [evidence] and legal proofs, which descended upon the best of creation, Muḥammad, whose soul is acceptable and whose nature supreme. [Prayers and peace be] upon his family morning and evening.

This is a definitive Mālikī legal charter written and approved in the Funj territory, in the regions of Qarrī, the divinely guarded and protected, may God Most High exalt her, in the presence of her warden, the governor of what is in her, Faqīh Ḍayf Allāh.

Thereafter: There came into his presence to litigate before him at the noble court of law, secure from deviation and corruption, the two men of good character and sound mind, Khōjalī and al-Jallī. They were disputing before him at the order of Sultan Nāṣir, son of Sultan Bādī, to Shaykh `Ajīb b. al-Shaykh `Abd Allāh. Shaykh `Ajīb wrote to his slave Marnātī to submit them to the judgment of Faqīh Ḍayf Allāh; should either of them refuse, he would rule against him with great vehemence. When they came before him, both claimed the ownership and possession of the estate which had been in the possession of `Aṭīyat Allāh, a slave of the Awlād `Ajīb. After the establishment of [their] authorization to represent in the giving of legal testimony--Khōjalī representing his fathers the Awlād al-Faqīh Khōjalī and al-Jallī representing his father Faqīh Maqbūl, his brothers, and his paternal cousins (who were present with him at the court of law)--the judge ordered both of them to prove the validity of the claim to possession, for a gift of alms without possession is invalid. According to the words of The Author [Khalīl b. Isḥāq]: "So take possession, even without [specifically expressed] permission." Ibn `Abd al-Salām said: "Acceptance and possession are both inherent qualities [of a gift of alms], though acceptance is a basic principle and possession a condition." `Abd al-Bāqī, al-Khurāshī, and [al-Tatā'ī also] specified [that]. Shaykh `Abd al-Bāqī said, on the word of The Author: "Apportionment of the land lies with the *imām*, for he owns it and has the right to sell it, give it away, or inherit it." That requires possession, as is generally understood in regard to other gifts. Al-Khurāshī [said] the same. Khōjalī gave evidence proving that up to the time of Ḥammād walad `Ajīb[10] the estate had been in possession of the *sawākira*; the government had administered it. The Awlād al-Faqīh Ḥammad had never possessed it before the Awlād al-Faqīh Khōjalī assumed rights of ownership and possession over it in the time of Mismār. The administration [of the government] was lifted, and they [the Awlād Khōjalī] enjoyed full rights of usufruct over it, including both ownership and possession.

The said evidence included [the testimony of]:

Faqīh `Abd al-Dāfi`, according to the two authorized witnesses Sharaf al-Dīn al-Zurūqābī and Faqīh Muḥammad Rād Allāh
Faqīh Jamīl Allāh walad Makkī
Faqīh al-Ṣāfī walad Bishāra
Shaykh Barakāt, *khalīfa* to Shaykh Idrīs
Shaykh Idrīs walad Nāṣir
Shaykh Idrīs walad Naṣṣār
Faqīh al-Sayyid walad Ḥammad al-Sayyid
Ḥājj Muḥammad al-Qanbū
Faqīh Muḥammad walad Maḍuwī walad Ibrāhīm

Faqīh Sulaymān walad al-Nūr
Sanūsī walad Ḥamdān
Faqīh Maḍuwī, known as Walad al-Shaykh Idrīs
Muḥammad Barbar
Ḥamūda walad Surūr
and a large gathering of the Rikābīya, the Maḥas, and others.

Some of these testified for the Awlād al-Faqīh Khōjalī [in person], while the judge accepted testimony concerning the knowledge of others in writing, according to the words of The Author: "Do not accept written testimony concerning his knowledge except in witnessing; then you may accept it in writing unless it is testimony under constraint, for his deed is stronger than the testimony." Shaykh `Abd al-Bāqī [also] specified [that]. Al-Jallī claimed to have had possession in the time of Ḥammād. The judge ordered him to produce evidence to establish his possession, and through his judicial discretion, granted him a delay as The Author of the *Mukhtaṣar* said [he might do]. Al-Khurāshī said: "They do not have to give evidence in the midst of a vehement dispute unless he [the judge] rules that he [a witness] must do so at once." Then he brought evidence that the court did not accept, so again [the judge] excused him through his judicial discretion. The fact was that he was deliberately absenting himself and fleeing from the judgment of the court. After the completion of the argumentation he [the judge] established the fact of his [al-Jallī's] deliberate absence and flight by the evidence of authorized witnesses. Shaykh `Abd al-Bāqī said: "If the defendant absents himself after the completion of the argumentation and flees from judgment, he [the judge] shall rule against him and void [his claim]. If he should come [later], he has no choice but to take his case as it stands, just as if [the judge] had ruled against him in his presence."

Thereupon, after the establishment of [al-Jallī's] deliberate absence, flight [from judgment] and lack of evidence, and the elapse of a period of censure, he [the judge] ruled in favor of the Awlād al-Faqīh Khōjalī concerning the said estate, its boundaries known. Its boundary on the southern side is al-Ḥājj `Ālim, and it runs along the path north of the *qōz* up to al-Ḍanīqīla. On the northern side [its boundary is] the estate of the Zurūqāb, on the eastern side the customary camel track, and on the west the river. He [the judge] voided and cut off al-Jallī's suit--his, and his brothers', and that of the sons of his paternal uncles litigating with him--from any argument remaining to them concerning what has been recorded and written, for all failed to give proof. [He acted] according to the word of The Author and voided it, and according to the word of Shaykh `Abd al-Bāqī cited previously in this case, and according to the word of al-Khurāshī on that of The Author: "He [the judge] may grant a delay at his discretion; they do not have to give evidence in the midst of a vehement dispute unless he rules that he [a witness] must do so at once." This ruling took place in the presence of the *`ulamā'*, among them Faqīh Muḥammad b. al-Faqīh Ḥammad al-Sayyid and Faqīh Muḥammad walad al-Sallama, with the consultation of Faqīh Ismā`īl, *khalīfa* to Shaykh Ṣughayyirūn and Shaykh of al-Qōz.

There were present at that ruling and witnessed to it:

Faqīh Abū Idrīs, *khalīfa* to Faqīh `Abd al-Dāfi`
Shaykh, his brother
Faqīh Aḥmad b. `Īsā
Faqīh Muḥammad b. `Alī Busāṭī, Arbāb
Faqīh Muḥammad walad Ḥājj
Faqīh Ibrāhīm b. al-Ḥājj Qurashī
Faqīh Ṣāliḥ walad al-Zayn
Faqīh al-Khalīl walad al-Zayn
Faqīh Bashīr walad Kabushīya
Faqīh Madanī walad Mūsā
Faqīh al-Amīn walad al-Ḥājj
Faqīh Muḥammad b. al-Faqīh `Abd al-Maḥmūd
Faqīh Muḥammad walad al-Ḥājj `Ushayr

The writer of the letters, al-Ḥājj al-Sayyid Raḥma, is scribe and witness, and God is the Best of Witnesses. That was written on Sunday, four days having passed of Rabī` II from the months of the year 1181, one thousand one hundred eighty-one from the *hijra* of the prophet, upon whose master the best of prayers and peace.

Yes. I, *faqīr* of God Aḥmad [b. `Īsā] have examined this ruling and found it sound. There are no flaws in it, and the ruling of the judge may not be infringed upon except in violation of The Book, the *sunna*, and the consensus. As The Author said: "Do not oppose a decisive [ruling] or remove an analogy [. . .]."

There is no doubt. I have examined this ruling and found it sound. There are no flaws in it. According to the word of Shaykh Khalīl: "Do not oppose [the ruling of] the just *`ālim.*" Shaykh [al-Tatā'ī] said: "Do not examine it [. . .] the litigation and the situation becomes aggravated." I am Ḥāmid Abū Mūna, and this is written in my hand.

I, *faqīr* of God Most High Yūsuf b. Muḥammad al-Ṭurayfī, have examined this ruling and found it sound. This is written in my hand.

Yes. I, *faqīr* of God `Abd Allāh Abū Bakr, grandson of Shaykh Muḥammad, have examined this ruling and found it sound. This is written in my hand.

Furthermore, the ruling of the *`ulamā'* was shown to us. We have examined it and found that it is legally correct according to the text and the commentary. I am *faqīr* of God Madanī b. Muḥammad.

Yes. I, *faqīr* of God Aḥmad Ḥammad al-Sayyid have examined this ruling and found it sound. There are no flaws in it. This is my handwriting.

Furthermore, this matter was laid before Faqīh Aḥmad walad al-Māyidī. He examined it and approved it, saying yes to [the ruling's] legal correctness. This is written in my hand.

Yes. This ruling is sound. I am *faqīr* of God Aḥmad b. al-Faqīh Sālim al-Mājidī.

I, *faqīr* of God Muḥammad b. Abū Āmina have examined this ruling and found it sound. This is written in my hand.

[. . .]

Yes. The affair is as mentioned and the matter as written. I have ruled in favor of that. I, *faqīr* of God Ḍayf Allāh b. al-Faqīh Muḥammad [. . .].

[I], *faqīr* of God Muḥammad b. al-Faqīh b. al-Faqīh Ḥammad al-Sayyid was present at this ruling, and I confirmed it. This is written in my hand.

Yes. I, *faqīr* of God Muḥammad b. `Abd al-Kāfī was present at this ruling, and I confirmed [it]. This is written in my hand.

I have studied the ruling and found it sound, and endorsed the act with an affirmative judgment.

He who trusts in [. . .]
The worshiper, the judge
`Abd al-`Azīz b. al-Sharīf
Muḥammad al-Mahdī
1183/1769-1770

[1]For a previously published version see Abū Salīm, *al-Fūnj wa'l-arḍ*, pp. 92-95. The editors have also consulted a copy preserved by the keepers of the original.

[2]Spaulding, *Heroic Age*, pp. 183-187.

[3]Spelled as shown.

[4]Lacuna. A conjectural reading of the missing text has been restored from what follows.

[5]Conjectural reading.

[6]Handwriting changes.

[7]Lacuna.

[8]Handwriting changes. This endorsement has been taken from the copy, on the assumption that the copyist may have been able to read a portion of the original now faded beyond accurate decipherment.

[9]Handwriting changes. It is probable that the first part of this endorsement is missing, but this may not be verified through the configuration of the original document nor ammended through reference to the copy.

[10]Probably the Shaykh of Qarrī Ḥammād b. `Ajīb b. Muḥammad al-`Ajayl; see Doc. 45.

DOCUMENT 47

Document 47 is a confirming charter issued by the Shaykh of Qarrī `Ajīb b. `Abd Allāh to the Awlād al-Shaykh Khōjalī on 19 Sha`bān 1181/10 January 1768. The text has been taken by the editors from the original, which is intact and easily legible.[1] The charter confirms the ruling of the judge Ḍayf Allāh recorded in Doc. 46, and explains why additional endorsements were added following the original ruling; one may note that the seal of `Abd al-`Azīz, the *qāḍī* of Sinnār, must have been added at an even later date than the present document of 1181, for the judge's seal is dated 1183.

When Shaykh `Abd Allāh joined the ill-fated expedition to Kordofan that culminated in the disaster of 1747 (Doc. 45), he left Qarrī in the hands of his brother Mismār, who served briefly as Shaykh of Qarrī following the death of `Abd Allāh.[2] Mismār was succeeded by his son Muḥammad al-Amīn, a gifted leader and, following the coup of 1762, a stalwart supporter of the sultans against the Hamaj.[3] Muḥammad Abū Likaylik succeeded in ousting Muḥammad al-Amīn between 1765 and 1768, and appointed `Ajīb b. `Abd Allāh in his place; the present document illustrates `Ajīb's close obedience to his superiors in the capital. By 1772, he had been driven from Qarrī by Muḥammad al-Amīn. The second Hamaj regent Bādī walad Rajab ousted Muḥammad al-Amīn again shortly after coming to power in about 1774. After a brief and unsuccessful interlude during which he entrusted Qarrī to a shaykh named Nāṣir, Bādī reappointed `Ajīb, who governed Qarrī a second time until his death at the hands of the Shukrīya in 1193/1779-1780.[4]

الحمد لوليه و الصلاة و السلام على نبيه

المتوكل على الله
الشيخ عجيب بن المرحوم الشيخ
عبد الله سنه ١١٨٠[5]

فهذه حجة قطعية و وثيقة [6] مرضية اجلها الله تعالى لدى متوليها / شيخ قرى المحروسة المحمية صاحب المقامات العلية و الاقوال / الصادقه الوفيه المامون على دينه و الرعيه المتمسك بالشريعة / المحمديه المتوكل على الله الشيخ عجيب بن المرحوم الشيخ عبد الله / زيدت ايام عدله و جددت ليالى سعده بجاه محمد و اله / امين و بعد فان اولاد الفقيه خوجلى شكوا الى السلطان / ناصر طول الله عمره من جهة غلاطهم فى الدار مع ناس الجلى ولد / ولد ام مريوم و الملك مدهم الى عندى و قال لى اعطيهم الشريعه / عند العلما كل من له حق ياخذ حقه و مديتهم الى عند / الفقيه ضيف الله ابطل دعوا الجلى و ثبت الدار لى / اولاد الفقيه خوجلى بحكم الشرع و بعد الانقطاع الجلى / نازع و غالط فى الانقطاعة ثانيا بحضرة الفقرا ناس ولد / الماجدى و امثالهم و رجعناهم الى الفقيه ضيف الله يصح / حكم الانقطاع و الفقيه ضيف الله احضر العلما و كل واحد / منهم كتب خطه بصحة حكمه و انقطاعة الجلى من الدار بالشرع / المحمدى و انا تميت و امضيت حكم الشرع و ملكت الدار لاولاد / الفقيه خوجلى و الدار المذكورة حدها من جهة الصعيد / الحد الفى ورقة الشيخ مسمار[7] و من جهة السافل دار / الزروقاب

حضر و شهد بذلك

محمد سيد القوم
و تمام / سيد القوم
و خوجلى سيد القوم
و عجيب ولد محمد ولد دقيس //
و البشير ولد الفقيه / دفع الله شيخ المساعيد /
و عميرى ولد حمد ولد نايل / سيد الخيل
و قنديل / ولد محمد ولد قبرت / شيخ دبركى
و بلال / شيخ السواكره /
و عبد الله ولد مكاوى / شيخ السلطيه

و / وديدى ولد ضياب / شيخ العبوداب /
و مرناتى ولد على شيخ / الحلفاية
و مرناتى ولد / سليمان
و حماد ولد / عربى
و الارباب بادى / و الارباب عمر اولاد الشيخ / عبد الله
و عجيب ولد / شمام و محمد نور اخيه /
و الفقيه عبد الحليم بن / الفقيه انوار
و الحاج احمد / البدوى

و ابو بكر بن محمد كاتب / و كفى بالله شهيدا تحرير ذلك ضحا / الاحد ١٩ من شعبان من شهور / سنه ١١٨١ بعد الهجرة النبويه / على صاحبها افضل الصلاة و ازكى / التحيه

Praise be to His friend, and prayers and peace upon His prophet.

He who trusts in God
Shaykh `Ajīb, son of the late Shaykh
`Abd Allāh Year 1180/1766-1767

This is a definitive charter and document, approved [and written in Qarrī], may God Most High exalt her, in the presence of her warden, the Shaykh of Qarrī, the divinely guarded and protected, the lord of high station, truthful and veracious in word, who is faithful to his religion and to the subjects, who holds fast to the Muḥammadan law, he who trusts in God, Shaykh `Ajīb, son of the late Shaykh `Abd Allāh. May the days of his justice be increased and the nights of his good fortune be renewed through the influence of Muḥammad and his family. Amen.

Thereafter: The Awlād al-Faqīh Khōjalī complained to Sultan Nāṣir, may God lengthen his life, in regard to their dispute concerning land with the people of al-Jallī walad Walad Umm Maryūm. The king referred them to me and said to me: "Apply the *sharī'a* to them before the *'ulamā'*, and he who has a right should get his right." So I referred them to Faqīh Ḍayf Allāh. He nullified the claim of al-Jallī and confirmed the estate to the Awlād al-Shaykh Khōjalī by a legal judgment. After the decision al-Jallī again disputed it and raised objections to it before some of the *fuqarā'*, the people of Walad al-Mājidī and their like, so we returned them to Faqīh Ḍayf Allāh to verify the ruling judgment. Faqīh Ḍayf Allāh summoned the *'ulamā'*, and each one of them wrote in his own hand to verify the ruling that cut off al-Jallī from the estate according to Muḥammadan law. I have confirmed and ratified the legal ruling, and have made the estate the property of the Awlād Khōjalī. The boundary of the said estate on the southern side is that which is in the document of Shaykh Mismār, and on the northern side the estate of the Zurūqāb.

There were present and witnessed to that:

Muḥammad, *sīd al-qūm*
Tammām, *sīd al-qūm*
Khōjalī, *sīd al-qūm*
'Ajīb walad Muḥammad walad Duqays
al-Bashīr walad al-Faqīh Daf' Allāh, *shaykh al-musā'īd*
'Umayrī walad Ḥammad walad Nāyil, *sīd al-khayl*
Qandīl walad Muḥammad walad Qabrat, Shaykh of al-Dabarkī
Bilāl, *shaykh al-sawākira*
'Abd Allāh walad Makkāwī, *shaykh al-salaṭīya*
Wadīdī walad Ḍiyāb, Shaykh of al-'Abūdāb
Marnātī walad 'Alī, Shaykh of al-Ḥalfāya
Marnātī walad Sulaymān
Ḥammād walad 'Arabī
Arbāb Bādī and Arbāb 'Umar, sons of Shaykh 'Abd Allāh
'Ajīb walad Shammām and Muḥammad Nūr his brother

Faqīh `Abd al-Ḥalīm b. al-Faqīh Anwār
Ḥājj Aḥmad al-Badawī
Abū Bakr Muḥammad, scribe.

With God, two witnesses suffice. That was written on the morning of Sunday, the nineteenth of Sha`bān, from the months of the year 1181 from the *hijra* of the prophet, upon whose master the best of prayers and purest salutations.

[1]For a previously published version see Abū Salīm, *al-Fūnj wa'l-arḍ*, pp. 99-100; a photocopy is reproduced on p. 143.

[2]For the descent of Mismār, see Doc. 24; Ḥasan b. Shāwir, "Wāḍiḥ al-bayyān," believed that Mismār was the son of `Abd Allāh, but this is not confirmed by contemporary documents. The NRO collection contains an unclassified charter issued by Mismār as Shaykh of Qarrī; it is authentic and sealed, but heavily damaged, perhaps by water, which has caused the ink to run. The editors have only been able to read scattered phrases near the end of the *intitulatio* and part of the seal.

[3]Spaulding, *Heroic Age*, pp. 331-347; 351-355.

[4]Ibid., pp. 331-333.

[5]Abū Salīm, *al-Khatm*, p. 66.

[6]The scribe has left out the expected reference to the document's place of issue, to which the following conventional formulas apply.

[7]The document of Mismār described above names other parties and is probably not the document mentioned here.

DOCUMENT 48

Document 48 is an originating charter issued by Ḥammād b. `Arabī, Shaykh of the Dāniyāb, to Faqīh al-Sayyid b. `Abd al-Hādī b. Muḥammad walad Dōlīb. The text has been taken by the editors from the original, which is frayed across the bottom with some loss of text. An unusual feature are the characters used in lieu of a seal.[1] The land conveyed probably lay in the vicinity of the settlement of the Awlād Dōlīb at Kadarū, though not on the riverbank. Document 48 was issued before Doc. 49, which confirms it, and therefore dates to the tenure of Shaykh `Ajīb b. `Abd Allāh (Doc. 47). Since Ḥammād b. `Arabī appears only once in the witness rosters of Qarrī, and that in Doc. 47 of 1768, it is perhaps more likely that both Docs. 48 and 49 originated during `Ajīb's first period of rule (possibly about 1766-1772) than his second. Both documents were almost certainly issued after 1180/1766-1767, the date of `Ajīb's seal, and definitely before his death in 1193/1779-1780.

الحمد لوليه / و الصلاة و السلام على / نبيه /

٨٦٤٢[2]

٥

فرغل الجيلى

م ع ر و ف ش ق ى ق / ا ل ن ع م ا نى

حجة قطعية و وثيقة عرفية محررة مرضية بالديار الفنجية / لدا متوليها و الحاكم عليها و ما فيها شيخ الدانياب الشيخ حماد بن المرحوم / الشيخ عربى حفظه الله و تولاه و

نصره على جميع اعداه اما بعد ان الشيخ / حماد المذكور تصدق على الفقه السيد بن الفقه عبد الهادى بن الشيخ / محمد ولد دوليب بارضا موات و بور ليس فيها عمار و تلك الدار معلومة / الحدود و البقعة و المكان حدها من جهة الصبح سيال العنتاراب فوق غدير مازن و من / جهة المغرب غدير فروع و من جهة الصعيد القلع و من جهة السافل الهبجة / صدقه ناجزة لوجه الله الكريم و طلبا للثواب فى دار الماب و ليوم لا ينفع / فيه مال و لا بنون الا من اتى الله بقلب سليم و صارت الدار المذكورة بحدودها / المعلومة صدقة و ملكا للفقه السيد بن الفقه عبد الهادى بن الشيخ محمد / ولد دوليب له و لذريته و ذرية ذريته الى ان يرث الله الارض و من عليها / و هو خير الوارثين سالمة مسلمة من جميع السبل العاديه و المضار العرفية / لا خدمة و لا جباية و لا علوق و لا نزول و لا عادة و لا عانه و حكمها فى ايد سيدها /

حضر ذالك و شهد به

الشيخ مرناتى ولد سليمان
و الشيخ مرناتى / ولد على
و احمد ولد حسن
و الصافى و الزاكى اولاد على ولد حسن
و مسمار / و بخيت اولاد سليمان
و مسمار و عيسى اولاد سليمان
و حامد ولد الشيخ / طه
و طه ولد احمد
و دانى ولد الشيخ مسمار
و الجيلى ولد حسن /
و خوجلى و هجو اولاد الشيخ بادى

و مسطر الاحرف فقير الله / (. . .)[3] الفقه النور بن الفقه عبيد كاتب و شاهد و الله خير الشاهدين / (. . .)[3] نهار عشرة ايام فى شهر المحرم (. . .)[3]

Praise be to His friend, and prayers and peace upon His prophet.

[Characters]

A definitive charter and customary document, written and approved in the Funj territories, in the presence of her warden, the governor over her and what is in her, the Shaykh of the Dāniyāb, Shaykh Ḥammād, son of the late Shaykh `Arabī, may God preserve and care for him, and grant him victory over all his enemies.

Thereafter: The said Shaykh Ḥammād has bestowed as alms upon Faqīh al-Sayyid b. al-Faqīh `Abd al-Hādī b. al-Shaykh Muḥammad walad Dōlīb [an estate of] barren wasteland with no cultivation on it. The boundaries, location and place of this estate are known. Its boundary on the eastern side is the watercourse of al-`Antāriyāb above Ghadīr Māzin, on the western side Ghadīr Furū`, on the southern side al-Qala`, and on the northern side al-Habaja. It is a free gift of alms for the sake of God the Generous, asking for reward in the life to come, for a day in which neither wealth nor sons suffice, unless one comes to God with a secure heart. The said estate, its boundaries known, has become a gift of alms and property of Faqīh al-Sayyid b. al-Faqīh `Abd al-Hādī b. al-Shaykh Muḥammad walad Dōlīb, for him, his descendants and his descendants' descendants, until God inherits the earth and those upon it, and He is the Best of Heirs. It is completely free from all customary *subul* and *maḍārr*. [It is not subject to] *khidma*, *jubāya*, *`ulūq*, *nuzūl*, *`āda,* nor *`āna*. Its governance belongs to its owner.

There were present and witnessed to that:

Shaykh Marnātī walad Sulaymān
Shaykh Marnātī walad `Alī
Aḥmad walad Ḥasan
al-Ṣāfī and al-Zākī, sons of `Alī walad Ḥasan
Mismār and Bakhīt, sons of Sulaymān
Mismār and `Īsā, sons of Sulaymān
Ḥāmid walad Shaykh Ṭaha

Ṭaha walad Aḥmad
Dānī walad Shaykh Mismār
al-Jaylī walad Ḥasan
Khōjalī and Hājū, sons of Shaykh Bādī

The writer of the letters, the *faqīr* of God [. . .] Faqīh al-Nūr b. al-Faqīh `Ubayd, is scribe and witness, and God is the Best of Witnesses. [. . .] in the daytime, ten days in the month of al-Muḥarram [. . .].

[1]For a previously published version see Abū Salīm, *al-Fūnj wa'l-arḍ*, pp. 68-69.

[2]The precise meaning of these characters is not known to the editors.

[3]Lacuna.

DOCUMENT 49

Document 49 is a confirming charter issued by the Shaykh of Qarrī `Ajīb b. `Abd Allāh to Faqīh al-Sayyid b. `Abd al-Hādī b. Muḥammad Dōlīb, ratifying the grant of his subordinate Ḥammād b. `Arabī (Doc. 48). The text has been taken by the editors from the original, which is frayed across the bottom with some loss of material.[1] Circumstances suggest that Doc. 49 may have been issued during `Ajīb's first period of rule in Qarrī rather than his second (Docs. 47, 48).

الحمد لوليه و الصلاة و السلام على نبيه /

المتوكل على الله
الشيخ عجيب بن المرحوم الشيخ
عبد الله سنه ١١٨٠[2]

فهذه حجة فرعية و وثيقة ملوكيه محررة مرضية بالديار الفنجية ببندر قرى المحروسة (المحمية)[3] من حضرت صاحب المقامات العلية و الاقوال الصادقة الوفيه / المامون على دينه و الرعية المتمسك بالشريعة المحمدية المتوكل على الله الشيخ / عجيب بن المرحوم الشيخ عبد الله زيدت ايام عدله و جددت ليالى / سعده بجاه القرءان العظيم و النبى الكريم امين و بعد فان المحفوظ / المبرور المويد المنصور الشيخ عجيب بن المرحوم عبد الله تمم و امضا / ما فعله حماد ولد عربى شيخ الدانياب للفقيه السيد بن الشيخ عبد الها / دى بن الشيخ محمد ولد دوليب من جهة صدقة دار موات و بور / ليس فيها عمار و تلك الدار معلومة الحدود و البقعة حدها من / جهة الصعيد (القلع)[4] و من جهة السافل الهجبة و من جهة الصبح غدير مازن / و سيال العنتاراب و من جهة المغرب غدير فروع صدقة ناجزة لوجه / الله الكريم و طلبا للثواب فى دار الماب و

ليوم لا ينفع فيه مال و لا / بنون الا من اتى الله بقلب سليم و صارت الدار المذكورة
بحدودها / المعلومة صدقة و ملكا لوجه الله الكريم للفقيه السيد ولد الشيخ عبد الهادى
/ له و لذريته و ذرية ذريته الا ان يرث الله الارض و من عليه و هو خير / الوارثين
سالمة مسلمة من جميع الشرور و السبل العادية لا عليها (عادة و لا)[5] / عانه و لا
نزول و لا تورات و لا (. . .)[6]

Praise be to His friend, and prayers and peace upon His prophet.

He who trusts in God
Shaykh `Ajīb, son of the late Shaykh
`Abd Allāh Year 1180/1766-1767

This is a subsidiary charter and royal document written and approved in the Funj territories, in the *bandar* of Qarrī, the divinely guarded and protected, in the presence of the lord of high station, truthful and veracious in word, who is faithful to his religion and to the subjects, who holds fast to the Muḥammadan law, he who trusts in God, Shaykh `Ajīb, son of the late Shaykh `Abd Allāh. May the days of his justice be increased and the nights of his good fortune renewed through the influence of the mighty Qur'ān and the noble prophet. Amen.

Thereafter: The divinely preserved, pious, divinely assisted and victorious Shaykh `Ajīb, son of the late Shaykh `Abd Allāh, has confirmed and ratified what Ḥammād walad `Arabī, Shaykh of the Dāniyāb, has done for Faqīh al-Sayyid b. al-Shaykh `Abd al-Hādī b. al-Shaykh Muḥammad walad Dōlīb in regard to the gift of alms of an estate of barren wasteland with no cultivation on it. The boundaries and location of this estate are known. Its boundary on the southern side is al-Qala`, on the northern side al-Habaja, on the eastern side Ghadīr Māzin and the watercourse of al-`Antāriyāb, and on the western side Ghadīr Furū`. It is a free gift of alms for the sake of God the Generous, asking for reward in the life to come, for a day in which neither wealth nor sons suffice, unless one comes to God with a secure heart. The said estate, its boundaries known, has become a gift of alms and property for the sake of God the Generous for Faqīh al-Sayyid walad al-Shaykh `Abd al-Hādī, for him, his descendants and his descendants' descendants, until God inherits the earth and those upon it, and He is the Best of Heirs. It is completely free from all *shurūr* and the customary *subul.* It is not subject to [*`āda*], *`āna*, *nuzūl*, *tūrāt*, [. . .].

[1]For a previously published version see Abū Salīm, *al-Fūnj wa'l-arḍ*, pp. 70-71.

[2]Abū Salīm, *al-Khatm*, p. 66. This reading supercedes his previous interpretations (*al-Fūnj wa'l-arḍ*, pp. 70, 99).

[3]Written vertically in the left margin.

[4]Parts of each letter of this word are missing.

[5]Conjectural reading.

[6]Lacuna.

DOCUMENT 50

Document 50 is an originating charter issued by the Shaykh of Qarrī Muḥammad al-Amīn b. Mismār to Faqīh Muḥammad b. al-Sayyid walad Dōlīb. The text has been taken by the editors from the original, which is frayed across the bottom with some loss of text.[1] The property bestowed was island land on the west bank of the Nile a short distance below the confluence. The date of the charter is lost; however, since the roster of provincial courtiers closely resembles that of 1768 (Doc. 47), it is likely that the document was issued not long thereafter.[2] Document 58 confirmed this grant.

الواثق بالله
العزيز الجبار الشيخ محمد
الامين بن المرحوم الشيخ
مسمار سنه ١١٨٤

فهذه حجة قطعية و وثيقة عرفية محررة مرضية لدا شيخ / قرى المحروسة المحمية اجلها الله تعالى لدا متوليها و بن متوليها / و الحاكم يوميذ عليها و ما فيها صاحب الهيبة و الوقار و مالك ازمة / المجد و الافتخار و امين السلطان على سر الاسرار و منفذ احكامه على / (فى)[3]ساير الاقطار و عامله على جميع الديار و حامى حمايته باليل و النهار المتوكل / على العزيز الجبار الشيخ محمد الامين بن المرحوم الشيخ مسمار نصره الله الرحمن / الرحيم بجاه القرءان العظيم و النبى الكريم امين يا رب العالمين اما بعد فان المحفوظ المبرور المويد المنصور الشيخ محمد الامين تصدق على الفقيه / محمد بن الفقيه السيد ولد دوليب فى ثلاثين عود فى مرن الدناجلة فى الجزيرة / فى دار التى بيد الشوشى و هى معلومة الحدود و البقعة و المكان فحدها من جهة / السافل دار جماع و من جهة الصعيد بقية امها و من حهة الصبح البحر و من جهة الغرب / المرن المعلوم الليل

الكرس و ذراعها ابو ثمانية صدقة ناجزة لله و لرسوله ابتغا للثواب فى دار الماب و ليوم لا ينفع فيه مال و لا بنون الا من اتى الله بقلب سليم / و صارت الدار المذكورة بحدودها المعلومة صدقة و ملكا للفقيه محمد الى ان يرث / الله الارض و من عليها و هو خير الوارثين

حضر و شهد بذلك

محمد سيد القوم
و / و[4] عجيب ولد دقيس
و البشير ولد النعيم شيخ المساعيد
و وديدى ولد الكنجه
و عبد الله ولد مكاوى (ما)[3] مقدم السلطيه
و قنديل ولد قبرت
و حسب الله ولد / نايل مقدم الخيل
و مرناتى ولد سليمان
و عجيب مقدم السواكره
و عباس شيخ / القوز
و محمد ولد شرندول
و محمد ولد ابو اكويكير
و تمام سيد القوم
و الجندى / حماد
و العقيد مر الجواب
و العقيد جاد الله ولد متيسه
و العقيد امين
و العقيد / ادريس ولد الصنيب
و عاصى القد مقدم خيل الشيخ الداخل
و بلال مقدم القواويد /
و اولاد الشيخ مسمار منهم
الارباب على
و الارباب عثمان
و الارباب شمام

و الارباب / ناصر
و الارباب دياب
و الارباب ابكر
و الارباب الاسيد
و الارباب شاور /
و الارباب اونسه
و الارباب حسن
و الارباب بادى
و اولاد الشيخ محمد الامين /
الوكيل الارباب عبد الله
و الارباب محمد العجيل
و اولاد الارباب شمام
محمد نور /
و بشير
و الارباب محمد بن الشيخ حمد السميح
و الارباب عبد القادر ولد ءامنه /
و مصطفى ولد قليمه
و حمد ولد محمود
و حسن سيد بيت العده
و العجب /
و البشير زيات الشيخ
و الارباب على عجيلاوى

و من الاصحاب

الفقيه عمار / و بلال اخيه اولاد عبد الحفيظ
و حسب القوى بن الحاج عوض
و الفقيه / حامد المصلى بالشيخ
و الفقيه كير معلم اولاد الشيخ

و مسطر الاحرف فقير الله / (. . .)[5] بن الخطيب عبد اللطيف يشهد بذلك /
(. . .)[5] سمعه فانما اثمه على الذين (. . .)[5] / (. . .)[5] الاثنين و عشرين

(. . .)[5] / (. . .)[5] // النبوية صلى الله على صاحبها بكرة / و عشية عليه افضل الصلاة / و ازكى السلام

و انها سالمة (مسلمة)[6] / من جميع الشرور و السبل و المضار / العادية لا عليها شي قل او جل و نوكد / عليكم يا جميع العمال و الجراى الذين هم تحت / ملكي شرقا و غربا برا و بحرا لا احد يدنى / و يتعرض للفقيه محمد في ذلك فمن تعرض / فقد عرض نفسه للهلاك الحذر (ثم الحذر)[6] / من المخالفة و المخالف لا يلوم الا (نفسه)[6] / و خصوصا الشوشي و من (يقوم)[6] / مقامه الله الله على ذلك

He who trusts in God
The Mighty, the Omnipotent, Shaykh Muḥammad
al-Amīn, son of the late Shaykh
Mismār Year 1184/1770-1771

This is a definitive charter and customary document, written and approved in the presence of the Shaykh of Qarrī, the divinely guarded and protected, may God Most High exalt her, in the presence of her warden and the son of her warden, the governor at the present time over her and what is in her, who inspires awe and conveys dignity, possessed of the utmost glory and splendor, entrusted by the sultan with the secret of secrets, a gateway for his commands throughout the country and his agent over all the land, his protector by night and by day, he who trusts in the Mighty, the Omnipotent, Shaykh Muḥammad al-Amīn, son of the late Shaykh Mismār. May God, the Merciful, the Compassionate, grant him victory through the influence of the mighty Qur'ān and the noble prophet. Amen, O Lord of the Universe.

Thereafter: The divinely preserved, pious, divinely assisted and victorious Shaykh Muḥammad al-Amīn has bestowed as alms upon Faqīh Muḥammad b. al-Faqīh al-Sayyid walad Dōlīb thirty rods in the *mirin* of al-Danājla, on the island in the estate in the possession of al-Shūshī. Its boundaries, location, and place are known. Its boundary on the northern side is Dār Jimmā`, and on the southern side the balance of the tract from which it was delineated,[7] on the eastern side the river, and on the western side the well-known *mirin* as far as the *kurus*. Its cubits are eight [per rod]. It is a free gift of alms for the sake of God and His messenger, asking for reward in the life to come, for a day in which neither wealth nor sons suffice, unless one comes to God with a secure heart. The said estate, its boundaries known, has become a gift of alms and the property of Faqīh Muḥammad, until God inherits the earth and those upon it, and He is the Best of Heirs.

There were present and witnessed to that:

Muḥammad, *sīd al-qūm*
`Ajīb walad Duqays
al-Bashīr walad al-Na`īm, *shaykh al-musā`īd*
Wadīdī walad al-Kanja
`Abd Allāh walad Makkāwī, *muqaddam al-salaṭīya*
Qandīl walad Qabrat
Ḥasab Allāh walad Nāyil, *muqaddam al-khayl*
Marnātī walad Sulaymān
`Ajīb, *muqaddam al-sawākira*
`Abbās, Shaykh of al-Qōz
Muḥammad walad Sharnadūl
Muḥammad walad Abū Ikwīkīr
Tammām, *sīd al-qūm*
the *jundī*, Ḥammād
`Aqīd Jād Allāh walad Mutaysa
`Aqīd Amīn
`Aqīd Idrīs walad al-Ṣunayb
`Āṣī al-Qad, *muqaddam al-khayl* to the Shaykh of al-Dākhila
Bilāl, *muqaddam al-qawāwīd*

Sons of Shaykh Mismār, among them: Arbāb `Alī, Arbāb `Uthmān, Arbāb Shammām, Arbāb Nāṣir, Arbāb Diyāb, Arbāb Abbakr, Arbāb al-Asīd, Arbāb Shāwir, Arbāb Unsa, Arbāb Ḥasan, and Arbāb Bādī

Sons of Shaykh Muḥammad al-Amīn: the *wakīl*, Arbāb `Abd Allāh and Arbāb Muḥammad al-`Ajayl

Sons of Arbāb Shammām, Muḥammad Nūr and Bashīr

Arbāb Muḥammad, son of Shaykh Muḥammad al-Simayḥ

Arbāb `Abd al-Qādir walad Āmina

Muṣṭafā walad Qalīma

Ḥammad walad Maḥmūd

Ḥasan, *sīd bayt al-`udda*

al-`Ajab

al-Bashīr, *zayyāt al-shaykh*

Arbāb `Alī `Ajaylāwī

From the friends:

Faqīh `Ammār and Bilāl his brother, sons of `Abd al-Ḥafīẓ

Ḥasab al-Qawwī b. al-Ḥājj `Awaḍ

Faqīh Ḥāmid, who prays with the shaykh

Faqīh Kīr, tutor to the sons of the shaykh

The writer of the letters, the *faqīr* of God [`Abd al-Salām[6]], son of the *khaṭīb* `Abd al-Laṭif, is a witness to that [. . .] he heard it. For in as much as he erred against those who [. . .] twenty-two [. . . after the *hijra*[6]] of the prophet, may God bless its master morning and evening, and upon him the best of prayers and purest peace.

It is completely free from all customary *shurūr*, *subul*, and *maḍārr*. It is not subject to anything, neither *qill* nor *jill*. We command you peremptorily, all you *`ummāl* and the *jarāī* who are under them and who are under my authority, whether east or west, by land or by river, let no one draw near to or trouble Faqīh Muḥammad in that [gift of alms]. He who makes trouble has exposed himself to destruction. Beware, [then beware] of disobedience, and let the disobedient blame none but [himself], especially al-Shūshī, and whoever may take his place. God, God upon that.

[1]For a previously published version see Abū Salīm, *al-Fūnj wa'l-arḍ*, pp. 72-74.

[2]Spaulding, *Heroic Age*, pp. 331-333.

[3]This word appears here, but is not properly part of the text.

[4]Dittography in original.

[5]Lacuna.

[6]Conjectural reading.

[7]Literally, "the remainder of its mother."

DOCUMENT 51

Document 51 is a confirming charter issued by the Shaykh of Qarrī Bādī b. Mismār for the Awlād Dōlīb on 2 Jumāda II 1209/25 December 1794. The text has been taken by the editors from the original, which is damaged at the lower right corner with some loss of text.[1] The document was issued in response to a command of the Regent Nāṣir b. Muḥammad Abū Likaylik (Doc. 29), and struck down the claims of rival litigants. Several of the latter represented contending branches of the maturing and rapidly segmenting new princely patrilineage of late eighteenth-century Qarrī, whose rivalries kept the provincial capital in turmoil from about 1788 to 1800.[2]

الواثق بالملك الجبار
الشيخ بادى بن المرحوم الشيخ
مسمار بن بادى ١٢٠٦

فهذه حجة قطعيه و وثيقه عرفيه محرره مرضية بنواحي قرى المحروسة [3] المحمية / اجلها الله تعالى (لدا)[4] متوليها و ابن متوليها و الحاكم يوميذ عليها و ما فيها صاحب الهيبه و الوقار / و مالك ازمة المجد و الافتخار و امين السلطان على سر الاسرار و منفذ احكام فى ساير / الاقطار و عامله على جميع الديار و حامى حمايته باليل و النهار المتوكل على العزيز الجبار الشيخ بادى / بن المرحوم الشيخ مسمار نصره الرحمن الرحيم ءامين يا رب العالمين زيدت ايام عدله و جددت ليالى سعده / بجاه القرءان (العظيم)[5] و النبى الكريم ءامين الى حضرت من تقف عليه هذه الوثيقه و الناظر لما فيها / من الحقيقة اما بعد فقد حصل النزاع من الشيخ عمر بن المرحوم الشيخ عبد الله و اولاد (عجيب بن)[6] الشيخ مسمار و اولاد حسب النبى فى راس الجزيرة الكريدة من جهة السافل و الفقه (محمد)[6] / بن الفقه السيد قال لهم الدار هذه هى

لنا متصدق بها الملك ملك الفونج السلطان بادى / على ابويه الفقه السيد و الفقه دوليب
صدقة قديمه بلغت فى ايدنا من الملكية مقدار (ستين)[6] / عام حايزين لها و
متصرفين فيها لنفسنا و لمن نزرعه [7] تصرف الملاك ما نازعنا فيها منازع / و لا عارضنا
فيها معارض و دعواكم هذه باطل ليس لكم هنا اصلا معانا فى طين الملك / نحن ما نا
قاعدين فوقها الا بالحقيقه من ملك الفونج ثم ان المحفوظ المبرور المويد / المنصور
الشيخ بادى بن المرحوم الشيخ مسمار امر الفقه محمد ان ياتيه بمكتوب الملك / بادى و
الفقه محمد اتا بمكتوب المرحوم السلطان الملك بادى و عرضه على الشيخ بادى / و نظر
ما فيها فوجده محتويا الما اددعوه الجماعة فى مسطور الملك بادى و الحد المشرع /
الذى هو على سافل قرن الحلة فلما نظر الشيخ بادى ما فى مكتوب ملك الفونج
السلطان / الملك بادى فوجده صحيحا و حكم على الجماعه بالانقطاعه و بطل دعويهم و
تمم / و امضى ما فعله السلطان الملك بادى للفقرا الدواليب و مرق اخيه (شاور)[8]
/ للحد و مرقه على ما فى مكتوب الملك السلطان بادى و ملك الفقرا دارهم / (. . .)[9]
و لا ينازعهم فيها (منازع)[8] و انها سالمة مسلمه من جميع السبل (العاديه)[8] /
(. . .)[9] و لا تورات و لا مخلا و لا كليقه و لا قلة و / (. . .)[9] و حربتهم (. . .)[9]
مكتوب الملك بادى / (. . .)[9]

و الشيخ البشير (. . .)[9] // (. . .)[9] / (. . .)[9] / (. . .)[9]
و الارباب (. . .)[9] / جماع
و الارباب شمام (ولد)[8] / الاسيد
و الارباب بادى
و الا / رباب عثمان (. . .)[9] /
و الارباب على كر (. . .)[9] / حسن
و الارباب (. . .)[9] / مسمار
و الاولاد الارباب (. . .)[9]/
و مسمار
و عبد الله
و حماد
(و)[8] / الامين
و مسمار ولد (. . .)[9] /
احمد جبت /

و عثمان ولد فاطر
و عجيب /
(و)[8] فضل الله ولد نصير
و (. . .)[9] / دكام
و التوم
و عبدان /
و بطران
و حمد ولد (شاور مقدم)[8] / القواويد

حرر ذلك / الظهر بيوم الاثنين / من جماد الثان عام (تسعه)[8] / بعد مضى الالف
و المايتين (بعد الهجرة)[8] / النبوية صلى الله عليه (بكرة)[8] / و عشية عليه
افضل (الصلاة و)[8] / التحية و الكاتب لاصلها (و المحرر)[8] / لفصلها فقير
الله (عوض الله بن الحاج)[8] ضحوى يشهد (بذلك)[8] / (و كفى)[8] بالله شهيدا

He who trusts in the Omnipotent King
Shaykh Bādī, son of the late Shaykh
Mismār 1206/1791-1792

This is a definitive charter and customary document written and approved in the regions of Qarrī, the divinely guarded and protected, may God Most High exalt her, in the presence of her warden, the son of her warden, the governor at the present time over her and what is in her, who inspires awe and conveys dignity, possessed of the utmost glory and splendor, entrusted by the sultan with the secret of secrets, a gateway for his commands throughout the country and his agent over all the land, his protector by night and by day, he who trusts in the Mighty, the Omnipotent, Shaykh Bādī, son of the late Shaykh Mismār. May the Merciful and Compassionate grant him victory. Amen, O Lord of the Universe. May the days of his justice be increased and the nights of his good fortune renewed through the influence of the mighty Qur'ān and the noble prophet. Amen.

To the presence of him who reads this document and sees the truth therein.

Thereafter: There occurred a dispute among Shaykh `Umar, son of the late Shaykh `Abd Allāh, the Awlād [al-Asīd[10]] b. al-Shaykh Mismār, and the Awlād Ḥasab al-Nabī concerning the tip of the island of al-Karīda on the northern side. Faqīh [Muḥammad], son of Faqīh al-Sayyid, said to them: "This estate belongs to us. It was given as alms by the king, the king of the Funj, Sultan Bādī, to my forefathers Faqīh al-Sayyid and Faqīh Dōlīb. It is an old gift of alms from the monarchy, and has remained in our possession for an interval of sixty years. We have possessed it and enjoyed its usufruct for ourselves, the one of us who cultivated it enjoying the right of usufruct. No challenger disputed with us about it, and no troublemaker troubled us in it. This claim of yours is groundless; you have no right here with us as far as the king's land is concerned, for we are only occupying it by rights derived from the king of the Funj." Thereupon the divinely preserved, pious, divinely assisted and victorious Shaykh Bādī, son of the late Shaykh Mismār, ordered Faqīh Muḥammad to bring the document of King Bādī. So Faqīh Muḥammad brought the document of the late sultan, King Bādī, and he showed it to Shaykh Bādī. He examined what was in it, and found it to contain, in the writing of King Bādī, that which the [opposing] party had challenged; the boundary is the watering place which is at the northern tip of the village. When Shaykh Bādī had examined what was in the document of the king of the Funj, the sultan, King Bādī, and had found it to be sound, he ruled against the [opposing] party and nullified its claims. He confirmed and ratified what the sultan, King Bādī, had done for the *fuqarā'* of the Dowālīb. He sent his brother Shāwir to delineate the boundary according to what was in the document of the king, Sultan Bādī. He made the *fuqarā'* the owners of their estate as private property. [. . .] Let no [challenger] challenge them in it. It is completely free from all [customary] *subul* [. . . It is not subject to . . .] *tūrāt*, *mukhlā*, *kalīqa*, *qill* [. . .] and their troops [. . .] the document of King Bādī.

[There were present and witnessed to it:]

[. . .]
Shaykh al-Bashīr [. . .]
[. . .]
Arbāb [. . .]
Arbāb Jammā`
Arbāb Shammām walad al-Asīd
Arbāb Bādī
Arbāb `Uthmān [. . .]
Arbāb `Alī [. . .] Ḥasan
Arbāb [. . .] Mismār
[. . .], Mismār, `Abd Allāh, Ḥammād, and al-Amīn, sons of Arbāb [. . .]
Mismār walad [. . .]
Aḥmad Jabat
`Uthmān walad Fāṭir
`Ajīb
Faḍl Allāh walad Nuṣayyir
[. . .] Dukkām
al-Tōm
`Abdān
Baṭrān
Ḥammad walad Shāwir, *muqaddam al-qawāwīd*

That was written at noon on the second day of Jumāda II in the year one thousand two hundred nine from the *hijra* of the prophet, may God bless him morning and evening, and upon him be the best of prayers and salutations. The writer of the original and composer of its parts is the *faqīr* of God `Awaḍ Allāh b. al-Ḥājj Ḍaḥawī. He is a witness to that, and with God two witnesses suffice.

[1]For a previously published version see Abū Salīm, *al-Fūnj wa'l-arḍ*, pp. 79-81.

[2]Spaulding, *Heroic Age*, pp. 352-357, 371-374.

[3]Written *al-marūsa*.

[4]Word omitted; restored by the editors.

[5]Written *al-'īm*.

[6]Lacuna. A conjectural reading has been restored by the editors.

[7]A correction by the scribe has been incorporated into the text.

[8]Conjectural reading.

[9]Lacuna.

[10]Lacuna; only the letters *al-* are visible. The only known son of Mismār whose name began thus was al-Asīd, and the editors have restored this reading on a conjectural basis.

DOCUMENT 52

Document 52 is a confirming charter issued by Arbāb Abū Bakr b. Sulaymān, Malik of the Jamū`īya, to the Awlād al-Shaykh Khōjalī. The text has been taken by the editors from the original, which is damaged across the bottom with some loss of characters.[1] The charter is not dated, but may be assigned to the reign of Arbāb Abū Bakr; this had not yet begun in 1206/1791-1792 and was over by 1798.[2] It is likely that Abū Bakr died in battle with Hāshim of the Musabba`āt in 1796, and that Doc. 52 was issued during the period 1206/1791-1792 to 1796.[3] The charter records one episode in the long dispute between the Awlād al-Shaykh Khōjalī and their neighbors introduced in Doc. 14. Noteworthy is the assessment of a penalty in kind.

الحمد لله و الصلاة و السلام على رسول الله / فهذه حجة فرعية و وثيقة ملوكيه محررة مرضية بالديار الفنجية / على يدى ملك الجمواعيه[4] اجلها الله تعالى لدا متوليها و ابن متوليها الارباب / الملك ابا بكر ابن المرحوم الملك سليمان حفظه الله و رعاه و نصره و تولاه بجاه / محمد خير انبياه اما بعد فان المحفوظ المبرور الارباب[5] الملك ابابكر عرضوا عليه[5] اولاد / الشيخ خوجلى حكم السلطان فى العادة و حكم الشريعة فى دار الشيخ خوجلى من جهة الطين المرق من جهة العرب[4] و المحمداب نازعوا اولاد الشيخ خوجلى فيه و شكوا على / الملك ابا بكر و قطع المحمداب من دار الشيخ خوجلى ما لهم فى القرب[4] تحت القيف و لو / شبرا واحدا و انقطعوا المحمداب بالعاده و الشريعة ثم ان الملك ابا بكر تم و امضا لا / ولاد الشيخ خوجل[4] حكم الشريع و حكم العاده و قطع نزاع المحمداب من دار الشيخ خوجل[4]/ ما لهم تحت القيف و لو شبر و ملك الدار لاولاد الشيخ خوجل لا يعارضهم فيها معارض / و لا ينازعهم فيها منازع و من تعرض لهم بعد ذلك عليه الحسب و ان نازع / فيها واحد او اثنين و اكثر كل واحد ادبته جمل الحذر ثم الحذر من الخلاف / و المخالف لا يلومن الا (نفسه)[5]

حضر و شهد بذالك
اخوانه اولاد الملك (سليمان)[5] (. . .)[6]
و حامد ولد احمد قا (. . .)[6]

Praise be to God, and prayers and peace upon the messenger of God.

This is a subsidiary charter and royal document written and approved in the Funj territories in the presence of the Malik of the Jamū`īya, may God Most High exalt them, in the presence of their warden, the son of their warden, Arbāb al-Malik Abū Bakr, son of the late Malik Sulaymān. May God preserve and guard him, grant him victory, and care for him through the influence of Muḥammad, the best of His prophets.

Thereafter: The Awlād al-Shaykh Khōjalī showed the divinely preserved and pious Arbāb Malik Abū Bakr a ruling of the sultans at customary law and a ruling at Islamic law concerning cultivable land in the estate of Shaykh Khōjalī along the western side. The Muḥammadāb challenged the Awlād al-Shaykh Khōjalī concerning it and complained to Makk Abū Bakr, but he cut off the Muḥammadāb from the estate of Shaykh Khōjalī; they have nothing on the west below the *qayf*, not even a hand's breadth. The Muḥammadāb were cut off by both customary law and Islamic law. Thereupon Makk Abū Bakr confirmed and ratified for the Awlād al-Shaykh Khōjalī the ruling at customary law and the ruling at Islamic law. He cut off the claim of the Muḥammadāb to the estate of Shaykh Khōjalī; they have nothing below the *qayf*, not even a hand's breadth. He made the estate the property of the Awlād al-Shaykh Khōjalī. Let no troublemaker trouble them concerning it. Let no challenger challenge them concerning it. He who troubles them after that is subject to the reckoning; whoever challenges [them] concerning it, be they one, two, or more, I will fine each a camel. Beware, then beware of disobedience, and let the disobedient blame none but himself.

There were present and witnessed to that:

his brothers, the sons of Makk [Sulaymān]

[. . .]

Ḥāmid walad Aḥmad Qā [. . .]

[1]For a previously published version see Abū Salīm, *al-Fūnj wa'l-arḍ*, p. 134.

[2]Spaulding, *Heroic Age*, pp. 399-400; Doc. 53.

[3]Ibid., p. 401.

[4]Spelled as shown.

[5]Conjectural reading.

[6]The document is truncated here.

DOCUMENT 53

Document 53 is a confirming charter issued by the Shaykh of Qarrī `Abd Allāh b. `Ajīb to the Awlād al-Shaykh Khōjalī on 7 Muḥarram 1213/21 June 1798. The text has been taken by the editors from the original.[1] The charter records one episode in the longstanding dispute between the Khōjalāb and their neighbors introduced in Doc. 14.

الحمد لله بلغ الرسول و نحن امنا بما يقول /

الواثق بالله
المجيب الشيخ عبد الله
ابن المرحوم الشيخ
عجيب ١٢٠٥[2]

حجة فرعية و وثيقه مرضية بالديار الفنجية بنواحي قرى المحروسة المحمية اجلها / الله تعالى لدا متوليها و ابن متوليها و الحاكم يوميذ عليها و ما فيها صاحب المقامات / العالية و الاقوال الصادقة الوفية المامون على دينه و الرعية المتمسك بالشريعة / المحمدية الواثق بالله المجيب الشيخ عبد الله بن المرحوم الشيخ عجيب زيدت ايامه / و جددت ليالى سعده بجاه محمد و اله امين الى حضرت كل من تقف عليه هذه / الوثيقة و الناظر لما فيها من الحقيقة و بعد فان المحفوظ المبرور المويد المنصور الشيخ عبد الله قدموا اليه الفقرا اولاد الشيخ خوجلى و شكوا له الدانياب و المحمداب فى طينهم المرق فى راس المارحة فى الغرب و حضر الملك ادريس ملك الجموعيه و شيوخه / ضو البيت و حمودة و حضر مبدا شيخ الدانياب و على ولد فضل الله و من معه من (اهله)[3] / من الدانياب و امر اولاد الشيخ خوجلى باحضار مكاتيبهم على ما زعموا فاتوا بوثيقة / من الملك بادى و الملك ناصر على تحديد دارهم شرقا و غربا و صعيدا و سافل الكرس / من القرير و ثبت ذلك الطين المرق المتنازعين فيه فى بطن المكاتيب / و الشيخ عبد الله

كلم المحمداب و الدانياب هل لكم دعوة فاقروا و اعترفوا على انفسهم / من غير جبر و لا اكراه ما لنا عند اولاد الشيخ خوجلى دعوة حدهم على ما فى مكاتيبهم / حد الكرس من القرير و صاروا مقطوعين و المحفوظ المبرور المويد المنصور حكم / لاولاد الشيخ خوجلى بالطين على ما فى مكاتيبهم و قطع نزاع المحمداب و الدانياب / من الطين و حرض عليهم ان من تعدا بعد جوابى هذا و لو بشبر عليه الحسب و فوقه / الف و صارت الدار ملك اولاد الشيخ خوجلى الى ان يرث الله الارض و من عليها و هو خير / الوارثين

حضر ذلك و شهد به

صالح سيد القوم
و بشير سيد القوم
و عجيب // ولد دقيس
و مبدا شيخ الدانياب
و عثمان / ولد فاطر شيخ المساعيد
و المبارك شيخ / الحلفاية
و احمد ولد الرضى شيخ دبركى /
و النور مقدم السواكرة
و ولد بشاره سيد الخيل /
و عسيلى مقدم السلطية
و دفع الله جندى / قرى
و شمام ولد عبد الله شيخ حلة حمد
و الو / كيل ضياب
و الوكيل عبد الله بن الشيخ عمر /
و اولاد الشيخ عجيب
مالك
و حسن
و مسمار /
و اولاد الارباب بادى
عبد الله
و عجيب
و محمد ولد / العجيل ولد الشيخ مسمار بن الشيخ عمر

و عبد الله /
و عجيب
اولاد الارباب على
و محمد ولد مسمار
و / عجيب ولد ابكر
و اللطيف ولد عثمان و اولاده /
عثمان
و حماد
و اونس
و على ولد ابكر
و الاسيد/ ولد ضياب
و على ولد محمد ولد السميح
و احمد /
و ابوا حنه
اولاد ابكر
و عمر ولد الاسيد
و محمد / ولد عجيب ولد مكاوى

و من الفقرا

الارباب محمد / بن الارباب عبد الحليم
و الفقه محمد ولد حسنه /
و الفقيه عبد الرحمن محيميد
و محمد ولد البدوى /
و مدنى ولد العباس

و الكاتب لاصلها و المحرر / لفصلها فقير الله ادريس بن الحاج محمد ابو المعالى / و كفى بالله شهيدا تحرير ذلك ضحوة / الثلاثا نهار سبعه خلون من المحرم سنة الف و مايتين / و ثلاثه عشر من هجرة خير البريه عليه افضل / السلام و ازكى التحية

Praise be to God. He sent the messenger, and we believe in what he says.

He who trusts in God
the Cause, Shaykh `Abd Allāh
son of the late Shaykh
`Ajīb 1205/1790-1791

A subsidiary charter and document approved in the Funj territories, in the regions of Qarrī, the divinely guarded and protected, may God Most High exalt her, in the presence of her warden, the son of her warden, the governor at the present time over her and what is in her, the lord of high station, truthful and veracious in word, who is faithful to his religion and to the subjects, who holds fast to the Muḥammadan law, he who trusts in God the Cause, Shaykh `Abd Allāh, son of the late Shaykh `Ajīb. May his days be increased and the nights of his good fortune renewed through the influence of Muḥammad and his family. Amen.

To the presence of all who read this document and see the truth therein.

Thereafter: The *fuqarā'*, Awlād al-Shaykh Khōjalī, came to the divinely preserved, pious, divinely assisted and victorious Shaykh `Abd Allāh and complained to him against the Dāniyāb and the Muḥammadāb concerning their land which runs from the tip of al-Māriḥa on the west. King Idrīs, Makk of the Jamū`īya came, and his shaykhs Ḍaw al-Bayt and Ḥamūda. Mubdā, Shaykh of the Dāniyāb came, and `Alī walad Faḍl Allāh and some of his people from among the Dāniyāb. [Shaykh `Abd Allāh] ordered the Awlād al-Shaykh Khōjalī to present their documents concerning that which they claimed. They brought a document from King Bādī and [one from] King Nāṣir concerning the boundaries of their estate, east, west, south, and north; [the boundary runs between] the *kurus* and the *qurayr*. [Shaykh `Abd Allāh] established that the land concerning whose course the disputants were disputing was [named] in the body of the documents. Shaykh `Abd Allāh said to the Muḥammadāb and the Dāniyāb: "Do you have a claim?" They themselves admitted and acknowledged, without compulsion or coercion: "We have no claim against the Awlād al-Shaykh Khōjalī. Their boundary is according to that which is in their documents; [it runs between] the *kurus* and the *qurayr*." They were cut off. The divinely preserved, pious, divinely assisted and victorious [Shaykh `Abd Allāh] ruled in favor of the Awlād al-Shaykh Khōjalī concerning the land, according to what was in their documents. He cut off the dispute of the Muḥammadāb and the Dāniyāb from the land, and he charged them: "Whoever trespasses after this my document, even by a hand's breadth, is subject to the reckoning, and he is subject to [a fine of] one thousand [*qirsh*]." The estate has become the property of the Awlād al-Shaykh Khōjalī until God inherits the earth and those upon it, and He is the Best of Heirs.

There were present and witnessed to that:

Ṣāliḥ, *sīd al-qūm*
Bashīr, *sīd al-qūm*
`Ajīb walad Duqays
Mubdā, Shaykh of the Dāniyāb
`Uthmān walad Fāṭir, *shaykh al-musā`īd*
al-Mubārak, Shaykh of al-Ḥalfāya
Aḥmad walad al-Raḍī, Shaykh of Dabarkī
al-Nūr, *muqaddam al-sawākira*
Walad Bishāra, *sīd al-khayl*
`Isaylī, *muqaddam al-salaṭīya*
Daf` Allāh, the *jundī* of Qarrī
Shammām walad `Abd Allāh, Shaykh of Ḥillat Ḥammad
the *wakīl*, Ḍiyāb
the *wakīl*, `Abd Allāh b. al-Shaykh `Umar
sons of Shaykh `Ajīb: Mālik, Ḥasan, and Mismār
sons of Arbāb Bādī: `Abd Allāh and `Ajīb
Muḥammad walad al-`Ajayl walad al-Shaykh Mismār b. al-Shaykh `Umar

`Abd Allāh and `Ajīb, sons of Arbāb `Alī
Muḥammad walad Mismār
`Ajīb walad Abbakr
al-Laṭīf walad `Uthmān and his sons `Uthmān, Ḥammād, and Unsa
`Alī walad Abbakr
al-Asīd walad Ḍiyāb
`Alī walad Muḥammad walad al-Simayḥ
Aḥmad and Abū Ḥinna, sons of Abbakr
`Umar walad al-Asīd
Muḥammad walad `Ajīb walad Makkāwī

From among the *fuqarā'*:

Arbāb Muḥammad b. al-Arbāb `Abd al-Ḥalīm
Faqīh Muḥammad walad Ḥusna
Faqīh `Abd al-Raḥmān Muḥaymīd
Muḥammad walad al-Badawī
Madanī walad al-`Abbās

The writer of the original and composer of its parts is the *faqīr* of God Idrīs b. al-Ḥājj Muḥammad Abu'l-Ma`ālī. With God, two witnesses suffice. That was written on the morning of Tuesday, when seven days had passed of al-Muḥarram in the year one thousand two hundred thirteen from the *hijra* of the best of creation, upon whom the best of peace and purest salutations.

[1]For a previously published version see Abū Salīm, *al-Fūnj wa'l-arḍ*, pp. 132-133.

[2]Abū Salīm, *al-Khatm*, p. 71.

[3]Conjectural reading.

DOCUMENT 54

Document 54 is a confirming charter issued by the northern provincial governor `Abd Allāh b. `Ajīb to the Awlād al-Shaykh Khōjalī on 18 Ramaḍān 1214/13 February 1800. The text has been taken by the editors from the original.[1] The charter documents one episode in the longstanding dispute between the Khōjalāb and their neighbors introduced in Doc. 14. The present document raises important questions about contemporary legal procedure in Qarrī. It is a charter at customary law, issued by the secular ruler, but it is paired with a parallel and corresponding Islamic document issued by Shaykh `Abd Allāh's *qāḍī*, Muḥammad walad Ḍayf Allāh (Doc. 55).[2] Both documents' treatment of the case will be examined here.

The governor's charter offers some review of previous litigation in the case, including mention of the previously issued sultanic rulings and an account of `Abd Allāh's own previous judgment as recorded in Doc. 53; at that time the Khōjalāb had been plaintiffs, and the evidence contained in the sultanic documents decisive. In the sequel described here, however, the Khōjalāb were placed in the role of defendants, an Islamic judge was summoned by the prince, and the outcome of the case rested upon the testimony of living witnesses rather than written documents. Given the prevailing assumption by the *sharī`a* that the testimony of witnesses rather than written documents should be considered binding, the suit described in Docs. 54 and 55 may be interpreted as a challenge to customary law by plaintiffs who expected to be able to overturn sultanic charters with the sworn testimony of living men. Seen from this perspective, it is most interesting to observe that the governor's document emphasizes the importance of witnesses in customary law, while the *qāḍī*'s charter emphasizes the right of a sultan to allocate lands and to record such acts in written charters. It would seem that the prince and his judge, both intending to uphold the tenure of the Khōjalāb, each attempted to deflect the plaintiffs' arguments, grounded in the *sharī`a*, by defending precisely those principles of legal authority and proof most characteristic of the legal code of the other.

The initial claim of the plaintiffs was based upon *mirin* and *hadim*. The former apparently meant an assertion that a boundary line existed below the *qayf* of the *kurus*, giving the plaintiffs rights in the *qurayr*. The meaning of *hadim* (literally "wrecking" or "destruction") is not certain in the present context, but may have meant a claim based on changes in the configuration of the land due to the action of the Nile flood. It would seem that the two claims were inherently incompatible, and it may be significant that according to the judge's record it was he, the *qāḍī*, who obliged the plaintiffs to select one claim or the other. When the plaintiffs chose the plea based on *mirin*, they were then obliged to choose between a claim resting upon the alleged existence of an old *mirin* or a new. Presumably the claim to an "old *mirin*" would have been more vulnerable to the evidence of the sultanic charters of the Khōjalāb; therefore the plaintiffs chose to plead on the basis of a "new *mirin*," whose existence could be substantiated by living witnesses.

Having appealed to an Islamic judge and chosen a plea likely to stand or fall on sworn testimony, the plaintiffs now had to acknowledge that those individuals likely to swear in their favor did not enjoy the status of *`udūl*, or authorized witnesses according to the conventions of Islamic jurisprudence. If the *qāḍī*s of Qarrī had in fact established a standing panel of *`udūl* (this is possible but unsubstantiated), the judge in this instance excused the plaintiffs from relying upon them; rather, he allowed them to appeal to the testimony of other men. When the plaintiffs presented their witnesses, however, the governor disqualified them on the basis of customary law; he held them to be partisan advocates for the plaintiffs rather than disinterested representatives of the wider community--whose presence, according to customary law, would have been necessary for the creation of a "new *mirin*."

With that, the case of the plaintiffs collapsed, and they conceded defeat by pronouncing the customary formula of submission. Through formally accepting the views of a respected member of the opposing faction, they would seem to have freed themselves from penalty for having wrongfully troubled the tenure of the victors. Since no mention of the concession ritual is found in the *qāḍī*'s document, it should probably be interpreted as a procedure according to customary law, and at this point in the trial the governor, on the evidence of his document, was ready to rule against the plaintiffs. The *qāḍī*'s charter, however, indicates that the defendants were then allowed to present their written evidence for consideration by the judge, and that the political overlords of the plaintiffs were allowed to testify against their subjects; on this basis, the judge then ruled against the plaintiffs. The charter of the *qāḍī* was witnessed by prominent holy men of the area, and that of the Shaykh of Qarrī by members of the provincial court.[3]

الحمد لله الذى بلغ الرسول / و نحن شهدا بما يقول /

الواثق بالله
المجيب الشيخ عبد الله
ابن المرحوم الشيخ
عجيب ١٢٠٥[4]

حجة عادية و وثيقة مرضية بالديار الفنجية بنواحى مدينة قرى المحروسة المحمية اجلها
الله تعالى / لدا متوليها الحاكم عليها يوميذ و ما فيها صاحب المقامات العليه و الاقوال
الصادقة الوفية المامون على دينه و الرعية / المتمسك بالشريعة المحمدية الواثق بالله
المجيب الشيخ عبد الله بن المرحوم الشيخ عجيب زيدت / ايام عدله و جددت ليالى
سعده بجاه محمد و ءاله امين يا رب العالمين الى حضرت كل من تقف عليه / هذه
الوثيقة و الناظر لما فيها من الحقيقة و بعد فان الفقرا اولاد الشيخ خوجلى قد قدموا /
الى حضرت الشيخ عبد الله و شكوا له المحمداب و الدانياب فى طينهم المرق فى
الغرب و المحفوظ / المبرور المويد المنصور احضر ملك الجموعيه ادريس و شيوخه الذين
من تحته حموده و ضو البيت / و احضر مبد شيخ الدانياب و على ولد فضل الله و

من معه من اهله من الدانياب و امر اولاد الشيخ خوجل باحضار / مكاتيبهم فاتوا بمكاتيب الملوك السلطان بادى و السلطان ناصر و السلطان اسماعيل على تحديد دارهم / شرقا و غربا حد الكرس من القرير و ثبت ذلك الطين المتنازعين فيه فى بطن المكاتيب و الشيخ عبد الله / كلم المحمداب و الدانياب هل لكم دعوة فاقروا و اعترفوا على انفسهم و شهدوا على غيرهم من غير جبر و لا اكراه ما لنا / فى دار الشيخ خوجلى دعوة مقطوعين منها حدهم على ما فى مكاتيبهم حد الكرس من القرير و المحفوظ المبرور الشيخ عبد الله حكم لاولاد الشيخ خوجلى بالطين على ما فى مكاتيبهم و قطع نزاع المحمداب و الدانياب / منهم و حدد عليهم ان من تعدا بعد جوابى هذا عليه الحسب و فوقه الف و صارت الدار ملكا لاولاد الشيخ خوجل لا يعارضهم فيها معارض و لا ينازعهم فيها منازع ثم بعد حكم ولد عجيب و تحديده عليهم بعد ما (. . .)[5] / (. . .)[5] الشيخ عبد الله و تور معاهم حسن اخيه و مبدا شيخ الدانياب / من الطين و زراعتهم الزرعوها و قدموا جو لى الشيخ عبد الله برجالهم و نسايهم و شيوخهم جباره ولد عبود و اخوه (. . .)[5] / و اولاد عمه و ابراهيم ولد محمد احيمر و اولاد عمه و ولد عبد العزيز و احمد بن على ولد ضياب و على ولد محمد اخوه / و قالوا لنا حق فى الطين انهم لنا اولاد خوجلى و الشيخ عبد الله حضر لهم اولاد الشيخ خوجلى و احضر لهم / كبار البلد و عماره و كبار قرى و العساكر و احضر قاضيه الفقيه محمد ولد ضيف الله و فقرا الحلفايه و قعد لهم / ديوان فى ساقيته الليلت الليمونه و نهم المحمداب و قال لهم اتكلم بدعواكم و قالوا المحمداب لنا فى الطين / مرن و هدم و قالوا لهم اولاد الشيخ خوجلى امسكوا لكم كلاما واحد هل نحادثكم فيه ثم بعد ذلك ابطلوا / دعوى الهدم و تكلموا بالمرن و قالوا لهم اولاد خوجل هل هو مرنا قديم او جديد قالوا لهم فعلوه ابواتنا و ابواتكم جديد و امرهم الشيخ عبد الله بالبينة على ما ادعوه و (جبوا)[6] له ناس الغرب و اولاد الشيخ خوجل / قالوا ليهم ناس الغرب محاميين معكم ما بناخذهم و امرهم الشيخ ان يجيبوا الطيبين من اهل الشرق و / الغرب يختاروا منهم لان المرن فى العادة ما بيمرق و لا بنجز الا بالطيبين العدول و الجمع الكثير و عجزوا / عن ذلك ثم بعد ذلك تكلموا بالسنتهم و قالوا صحا جا و كذبا راح ما عندنا بينة غير اولاد الشيخ خوجلى / و رضينا بهم و الشيخ عبد الله قال لهم اختاروا فيهم قالوا رضينا و اكتفينا بذمة الفقه الماحى بن الفقه احمد و جابوا لهم الفقه الماحى و سالوه عما فى ذمته و قالوا لهم ما بعرف لكم مرن و لا زراعة و لا / سمعت به و انكسر المحمداب و الدانياب من اولاد الشيخ خوجل و بقى الطين المرن ملكا لاولاد / الشيخ خوجل على حدهم الفى مكاتيبهم من عند الفاصل السيالة التى مقابلة قرن الجبل الازرق الى عند حجر ولد / الحليوه الفاصل

الذى بين النوفلاب و المحداب ما لى الدانياب و لا المحداب شبر و لا ذراع فى القرير تحت / القيف الغربى و المحفوظ المبرور المويد المنصور الشيخ عبد الله حكم على الدانياب / و المحداب بالانقطاعه و ملك الدار لاولاد الشيخ خوجلى و صارت ملكا لهم و لذريتهم الى ان / يرث الله الارض و من عليها و هو خير الوارثين لا يعارضهم فيها معارض و لا ينازعهم فيها منازع / الحذر ثم الحذر من الخلاف و المخالف لا يلومن الا نفسه

حضر و شهد بذلك

صالح سيد القوم
و بشيرى / سيد القوم
و عجيب ولد دقيس
و عثمان ولد محمد فاطر شيخ المساعيد
و مبد شيخ الدانياب /
و المبارك // شيخ / الحلفايه
و احمد ولد / الرضا شيخ دبركى
و نور مقدم / السواكره
و ولد بشاره سيد الخيل /
و عسيلى مقدم السلطية
و دفع الله جندى قرى /
و شمام ولد عبد الله شيخ حلة حمد
و الوكيل ضياب / بن الارباب بادى
و الوكيل عبد الله بن الشيخ عمر /
و مالك
و حسن
و مسمار
اولاد الشيخ عجيب
و عجيب بن الارباب بادى
و عبد الله / اخيه
و محمد ولد العجيل ولد الشيخ عبد الله
و اولاد الارباب على / ولد بادى

عبد الله
و عجيب
و مسمار بن الشيخ عمر
و اللطيف ولد / عثمان و اولاده
عثمان
و حماد
و اونسه
و على ولد ابكر
و الاسيد ولد ضياب
و اولاد ابكر
احمد
و ابو حنه
و عمر ولد الاسيد /
و محمد ولد عجيب ولد مكاوى
و على ولد الاسيد
و سند ولد محمد ولد / جماع
و جماع اخيه
و الارباب محمد بن الفقيه عبد الحليم انوار
و محمد / بن الحاج البدوى
و عبد الكريم ولد محمد ولد بله
و مدنى ولد / العباس
و الحاج زروق ولد محمد نصر
و عبد الواحد ولد السيد

و من الفقرا

الفقه محمد ولد ضيف الله
و الفقه دفع الله اخيه /
و الفقه محمد بن الحاج عمارة
و الحاج ضحوى بن مكوار
و عوض الله / ولده

و محمد نور بن الحاج عبد الرحمن
و الحاج ادريس بن الحاج محمد / ابو المعالى

و الكاتب لاصلها و المحرر لفصلها محمد بن الحاج عماره / يشهد بذلك و الله خير الشاهدين تحرير ذلك عصر الجمعه / ثمانية عشر خلون من رمضان المبارك تاسع شهور سنة / (اربة)[6] عشر بعد الالف و المايتين من هجرة سيدنا / و مولانا محمد صلى الله عليه و سلم

Praise be to God, Who sent the messenger. We are witnesses to what he says.

He who trusts in God
the Cause, Shaykh `Abd Allāh
son of the late Shaykh
`Ajīb 1205/1790-1791

A customary charter and document approved in the Funj territories, in the regions of the city of Qarrī, the divinely guarded and protected, may God Most High exalt her, in the presence of her warden, the governor at the present time over her and what is in her, the lord of high station, truthful and veracious in word, who is faithful to his religion and to the subjects, who holds fast to the Muḥammadan law, he who trusts in God the Cause, Shaykh `Abd Allāh, son of the late Shaykh `Ajīb. May the days of his justice be increased and the nights of his good fortune renewed through the influence of Muḥammad and his family. Amen, O Lord of the Universe.

To the presence of all who read this document and see the truth therein.

Thereafter: The *fuqarā'*, Awlād al-Shaykh Khōjalī, came into the presence of Shaykh `Abd Allāh and complained to him against the Muḥammadāb and the Dāniyāb concerning their land, which runs on the west. The divinely preserved, pious, divinely assisted and victorious [Shaykh `Abd Allāh] summoned the Malik of the Jamū`īya, Idrīs, and his shaykhs who were under him, Ḥamūda and Ḍaw al-Bayt. He also summoned Mubdā, Shaykh of the Dāniyāb, and `Alī walad Faḍl Allāh and some of his people from among the Dāniyāb. [Shaykh `Abd Allāh] ordered the Awlād al-Shaykh Khōjalī to present their documents. They brought documents of the kings, Sultan Bādī, Sultan Nāṣir, and Sultan Ismā`īl, delineating the boundary of their estate east and west between the *kurus* and the *qurayr*. [Shaykh `Abd Allāh] established that the land concerning which they were disputing was [named] in the body of the documents. Shaykh `Abd Allāh said to the Muḥammadāb and the Dāniyāb: "Do you have a claim?" They themselves admitted and acknowledged, testifying against themselves without compulsion or coercion: "We have no claim to the estate of Shaykh Khōjalī. We are cut off from it. Their boundary is according to that which is in their documents, between the *kurus* and the *qurayr*." The divinely preserved and pious Shaykh `Abd Allāh ruled in favor of the Awlād al-Shaykh Khōjalī concerning the land according to what was in their documents. He cut off the dispute of the Muḥammadāb and the Dāniyāb from them, and charged them: "Whoever trespasses after this my document is subject to the reckoning, and he is subject to [a fine of] one thousand [*qirsh*]." The estate has become the property of the Awlād al-Shaykh Khōjalī. Let no troublemaker trouble them in it. Let no challenger challenge them in it.

Thereupon, after the ruling of Walad `Ajīb and his delineation of the boundaries, after [. . .] Shaykh `Abd Allāh, Ḥasan his[7] brother became angry with them, and Mubdā, Shaykh of the Dāniyāb, concerning land and crops they were cultivating on it. They came to me, Shaykh `Abd Allāh, with their men and their women, and their shaykhs, Jabāra walad `Abūd, his brother Yammām, the sons of his paternal uncle Ibrāhīm walad Muḥammad Aḥīmīr, and the sons of his paternal uncle Walad `Abd al-`Azīz, Aḥmad b. `Alī walad Ḍiyāb and `Alī walad Muḥammad, his brother. They said: "We have a right to the land; summon for us the Awlād al-Shaykh Khōjalī." So he summoned for them the great ones of the countryside and town, the great ones of Qarrī and the soldiers. He summoned his *qāḍī*, Faqīh Muḥammad walad Ḍayf Allāh, and the *fuqarā'* of al-Ḥalfāya. He made them to sit in council at his *sāqīya*, "al-Layla al-Limūna," and summoned the Muḥammadāb. He said to them: "State your claim." The Muḥammadāb said: "We have a claim to the land by *mirin* and *hadim*." The Awlād al-Shaykh Khōjalī said to them: "Take one term and we will respond to you concerning it." Thereupon they dropped the claim based upon *hadim*, and spoke of the *mirin*. The Awlād Khōjalī said to them: "Is it an old *mirin* or a new?" They replied: "Our fathers and yours made it anew." Shaykh `Abd Allāh ordered them to give evidence in support of their claim. They brought before him [some] people of the west [bank]. The Awlād al-Shaykh Khōjalī said to them: "The people of the west are your partisan advocates; we do not accept them." The shaykh ordered them to bring forward reputable individuals from the people of the east and the west, so that they might choose from among them--for by customary law a *mirin* is drawn and put into effect only with good witnesses and true, in a general assembly [of the people]--but they were unable to do that. Thereupon they spoke out and said: "Truth has come and falsehood departed; we have no evidence against the Awlād al-Shaykh Khōjalī, and we will be contented with them." Shaykh `Abd Allāh said to them: "Choose from among them." They said: "We will accept and be satisfied with the conscience of Faqīh al-Māḥī b. al-Faqīh Aḥmad." So Faqīh al-Māḥī was brought to them, and they asked him what was in his conscience. He said to them: "I do not know that you have a *mirin* or any cultivation. I have never heard of it." The Muḥammadāb and the Dāniyāb were defeated by the Awlād al-Shaykh Khōjalī. The land, the *mirin*, remains the property of the Awlād al-Shaykh Khōjalī according to their boundary which is in their documents. [It is] from the *fāṣil*, the watercourse across from the tip of Jabal Azraq, as far as the stone [marker] of Walad Ḥilyū, the *fāṣil* which is between the Nōfalāb and the Muḥammadāb. Neither the Dāniyāb nor the Muḥammadāb have a hand's breadth, [much less] a cubit, in the *qurayr* below the western *qayf*. The divinely preserved, pious, divinely assisted and victorious Shaykh `Abd Allāh ruled against the Dāniyāb and the Muḥammadāb and made the estate the property of the Awlād al-Shaykh Khōjalī. It has become their property and that of their descendants until God inherits the earth and those upon it, and He is the Best of Heirs. Let no troublemaker trouble them in it. Let no challenger challenge them in it. Beware, then beware of disobedience, and let the disobedient blame none but himself.

There were present and witnessed to that:

Ṣāliḥ, *sīd al-qūm*
Bashīr, *sīd al-qūm*
`Ajīb walad Duqays
`Uthmān walad Muḥammad Fāṭir, *shaykh al-musā`īd*
Mubdā, Shaykh of the Dāniyāb
al-Mubārak, Shaykh of al-Ḥalfāya
Aḥmad walad al-Raḍī, Shaykh of Dabarkī
Nūr, *muqaddam al-sawākira*
Walad Bishāra, *sīd al-khayl*
`Isaylī, *muqaddam al-salaṭīya*
Daf` Allāh, the *jundī* of Qarrī
Shammām walad `Abd Allāh, Shaykh of Ḥillat Ḥammad
the *wakīl*, Ḍiyāb b. al-Arbāb Bādī
the *wakīl*, `Abd Allāh b. al-Shaykh `Umar
Mālik, Ḥasan, and Mismār, sons of Shaykh `Ajīb
`Ajīb b. al-Arbāb Bādī and `Abd Allāh his brother
Muḥammad walad al-`Ajayl walad al-Shaykh `Abd Allāh
the sons of Arbāb `Alī walad Bādī, `Abd Allāh and `Ajīb
Mismār b. al-Shaykh `Umar
al-Laṭīf walad `Uthmān and his sons `Uthmān, Ḥammād, and Unsa
`Alī walad Abbakr
the sons of Abbakr, Aḥmad and Abū Ḥinna
`Umar walad al-Asīd
Muḥammad walad `Ajīb walad Makkāwī

\`Alī walad al-Asīd
Sanad walad Muḥammad walad Jammā\`, and Jammā\` his brother
Arbāb Muḥammad b. al-Faqīh \`Abd al-Ḥalīm Anwār
Muḥammad b. al-Ḥājj al-Badawī
\`Abd al-Karīm walad Muḥammad walad Balla
Madanī walad al-\`Abbās
Ḥājj Zurūq walad Muḥammad Naṣr
\`Abd al-Wāḥid walad al-Sayyid

From among the *fuqarā'*:

Faqīh Muḥammad walad Ḍayf Allāh
Faqīh Daf\` Allāh, his brother
Faqīh Muḥammad b. al-Ḥājj \`Amāra
Ḥājj Ḍaḥawī b. Makwār and \`Awaḍ Allāh his son
Muḥammad Nūr b. al-Ḥājj \`Abd al-Raḥmān
Ḥājj Idrīs b. al-Ḥājj Muḥammad Abu'l-Ma\`ālī

The writer of the original and composer of its parts is Muḥammad b. al-Ḥājj \`Amāra. He is a witness to that, and God is the Best of Witnesses. That was written on the afternoon of Friday, when eighteen days had passed of Ramaḍān the blessed, the ninth month of the year one thousand two hundred fourteen from the *hijra* of our lord and master Muḥammad, may God bless him and grant him peace.

[1]For a previously published version see Abū Salīm, *al-Fūnj wa'l-arḍ*, pp. 124-127.

[2]Muḥammad al-Nūr b. Ḍayf Allāh is better known as the author of the *Ṭabaqāt*.

[3]Spaulding, *Heroic Age*, pp. 184-187.

[4]Abū Salīm, *al-Khatm*, p. 71.

[5]Lacuna.

[6]Conjectural reading.

[7]Because of the lacuna it is not clear to whom this refers.

DOCUMENT 55

Document 55 is a charter issued by the *qāḍī* of Qarrī Muḥammad al-Nūr b. Ḍayf Allāh to the Awlād al-Shaykh Khōjalī on 18 Ramaḍān 1214/13 February 1800. The text has been taken by the editors from the original, which is frayed around all the edges.[1] It forms one of a pair of documents, discussion of which may be found above in the introduction to Doc. 54.

بسم الله الرحمن الرحيم (. . .)[2] حجة شرعية قاطعة مالكية على يدى متوليها حاكم
قاصيها و دانيها الفقيه محمد النور بن الفقه ضيف (الله)[3] / و بعد فان الشيخ
عبد الله بن المرحوم الشيخ عجيب احضره فى وجهه فى حجة المحمداب و اولاد الشيخ
خوجلى متنازعين فى فاصل الجزيره قطعيه الغربى ثم بعد ما نصب لهما ميزان الشرع
(المنيف)[3] / السالم من الزيغ و التحريف فادعوا اولاد الشيخ خوجلى ان حد
الجزيرة قطعية المذكورة (شرقا)[3] / و غربا الكرس من القرير و انكر ذلك جماعة
المحمداب و هم جباره ولد عبود و ابراهيم ولد (محمد)[4] / ولد احيمر و اخوانهم
و اولاد اعمهم و ولد عبد العزيز و احمد ولد على ولد ضياب و على (ولد)[3] /
اخوه في حجتهما لانفسهما و وكالة مفوضة مقبولة شرعا من غيرهما و قالوا الجزيرة لها
(مرن)[3] / معلوم ما بيلحق الكرس و لنا نحن فيها هدم و قالوا لهم اولاد الشيخ
خوجلى (قلتوا)[3] لنا (مرن)[3] و هدم امسكوا واحدة اما المرن او الهدم ثم ان
الحاكم الفقه محمد نور بن الفقه ضيف الله / لما سمع جوابهم امرهم ان يمسكوا الهدم
او المرن فابطلوا دعوى الهدم و مسكوا المرن و (قالوا)[3] لهم اولاد الشيخ خوجلى
مرنا قديم حرسها او جديد حدث بعد و قالوا المحمداب جديد / فعلوه ءاباءنا و
ءاباءكم و توكلوا به ثم ان الحاكم لما سمع جوابهم امرهم ان يثبتوا صحة ما (ادعوا)[3]
/ بوثيقة او جماعة مسلمين و قالوا بيعرفوه ناسا من النوفلاب و هم غير عدول و قال

لهم / شق المرن من الامور التى يطلب فى حضورها العدول و غيرهم مثل التزويج و العتق و (. . .)[2] / ثم بعد ما تعذر عليهم العدول قالوا المحداب كذبا راح و صدقا جاء المرن الفعلوه ابواتنا / و ابواتكم بيعرفه الماحى بن الفقه احمد رضينا بشهادته لنا او علينا فانه مامون ما بيغير / ثم ان الحاكم احضر الفقه الماح بن الفقه احمد و سالوه بما فى ذمته و قال ما بعلم مرنا (انفعل)[3] بين ابواتى و المحداب ثم ان الحاكم امر اولاد الشيخ خوجلى باثبات صحة دعواهما فاتوا بوثيقة / الملك بادى و صدقته للشيخ خوجلى و تحديد الدار المذكور شرقا و غربا بالكرس و ايضا (. . .)[2] / على صحة دعواهما شيوخ المحداب حموده ولد محمود و منصور بن سلفا و شهدا بما فى علمهما / ان دار الشيخ خوجلى خافسه للكرس الغربى و زكوهما بجميعة مستفيضة بانهما عدلان / مرضيان فايقان على اقرانهما فى جماعتهما و قبل الشرع شهادتهما اقرارا على انفسهما لانهم / شركاء فى الدار و شهدا على غيرهما و ايضا تحديد الملك بادى بالكرس صحيح لان السلطان / له ان يقطع البور و المعمور و على تقدير لو زاد على ذلك فرسخا فانه ماضى فى الشرع لانه / السلطان الاعلى و شيوخ الدار عماله كما قال الشيخ خليل و مضى فى جبر عامله ثم / بعد ثبوت صحة الوثيقة و شهادة البينة و قبولها شرعى و عدم الاعذار فيها / حكم بصحة التحديد المذكور شرقا و غربا بالكرس و قطع نزاع المحداب / و عجزهم من كل حجة يقومون بها و صارت الدار المذكوره بحدودها / المعلومه ملكا لاولاد الشيخ خوجلى و ذريتهم و ذرية ذريتهم (. . .)[2] حتى يرث الله الارض و من عليها و هو خير الوارثين

(حضر)[3] و شهد بذلك جمع غفير منهم

الفقه دفع الله بن الفقه ضيف الله //
و الحاج ضحوى / بن مكوار
و عوض الله / ابنه
و محمد نور بن الحاج / عبد الرحمن ولد اسيد /
و الحاج ادريس بن الحاج محمد ابو المعالى
و عثمان بن (بان)[3] / النقا الجميعاب
و الطريف (بن)[3] / الفقه عبد الهادى الضو (. . .)[2] /
و اولاد حسب النبى
محمد /
و حمدن الله
ناس ولد دليل /

و انا محمد بن الحاج عمار / كاتب و شاهد و الله خير / الشاهدين حرر ذلك عصر / الجمعه ثمانيه عشر يوم خلون / من رمضان المبارك تاسع (شهور)[3] / سنة اربعة عشر بعد الالف / و المايتين من هجرته صلى الله عليه و سلم[5]

و انا فقير / الله محمد بن احمد المعروف / بالجبيل موافق على هذا / الحكم و هذا خطى بيدى /[5]

الامر كما ذكر و الشان كما / سطر و انا محمد بن ضيف الله / حكمت بما فى الوثيقه /[5]

نعم انا الشيخ ادريس بن دفع الله / نظرت فى هذا الحكم فوجدته صحيح و هذا / خطى بيدى /[5]

نعم انا محمد عبد / الرحمن نظرت فى هذا / الحكم فوجد / ته صحيح لا خلل فيه / و هذا خطى / بيدى[5]

و انا محمد / بن اسماعيل / نظرت الحكم / فوجدته صحيحا / فوافقت و هذا خطى / بيدى

In the name of God, the Merciful, the Compassionate [. . .]. A definitive Mālikī legal charter from the hand of her warden, the governor of her far places and near, Faqīh Muḥammad al-Nūr b. al-Faqīh Ḍayf Allāh.

Thereafter: Shaykh `Abd Allāh, son of the late Shaykh `Ajīb, summoned him [the judge] into his presence because the Muḥammadāb and the Awlād al-Shaykh Khōjalī were disputing concerning the *fāṣil* of the island of Qaṭ`īya West. Thereupon, after he had set up for the two of them the scales of justice, orthodox and free from error and corruption, the Awlād al-Shaykh Khōjalī claimed that the boundary of the said island of al-Qaṭ`īya, east and west, lay between the *kurus* and the *qurayr*. The party of the Muḥammadāb denied that. They were Jabāra walad `Abūd, Ibrāhīm walad Muḥammad walad Aḥīmir, and their brothers and paternal cousins, and Aḥmad walad `Alī walad Ḍiyāb, and `Alī the son of his brother, acting on their own behalf and as authorized, legally acceptable representatives for others. They said: "The island has a known *mirin* that does not touch the *kurus*, and we have a *hadim* in it." The Awlād al-Shaykh Khōjalī said to them: "You have said to us '*mirin*' and '*hadim*.' Take one; either the *mirin* or the *hadim*." Thereupon the judge, Faqīh Muḥammad al-Nūr b. al-Faqīh Ḍayf Allāh, when he had heard their reply, ordered them to choose either the *mirin* or the *hadim*. They voided the claim to the *hadim* and chose the *mirin*. The Awlād al-Shaykh Khōjalī said to them: "Is it a *mirin* preserved from olden times, or a new that [came] later?" The Muḥammadāb said: "It is new; our fathers and yours were responsible for making it." When the judge heard their reply, he ordered them to give evidence in support of the validity of what they claimed, by document or by [the word of] the community of Muslims. They said: "Some people of the Nōfalāb know this, but they have no authorized witnesses." He said to them: "Separate the matter of the *mirin* from those that require the presence of authorized witnesses, as in the case of marriage or manumission." Thereafter, after both had failed to produce authorized witnesses, the Muḥammadāb said: "Falsehood has departed and truth has come. Al-Māḥī b. al-Faqīh Aḥmad knows the *mirin* which our fathers and yours made; we will be satisfied with his testimony for us or against us, for he is trustworthy and will not distort [his testimony]." Thereupon the judge summoned Faqīh al-Māḥī b. al-Faqīh Aḥmad, and they asked him what was in his conscience. He said: "I know of no *mirin* made between my fathers and the Muḥammadāb." Then the judge ordered the Awlād al-Shaykh Khōjalī to establish the validity of their claim. They brought a document of King Bādī and his gift of alms to Shaykh Khōjalī, which set the boundaries of the said estate, east and west, at the *kurus*. Moreover, [he summoned to comment on] the validity of their claim Ḥamūda walad Maḥmūd and Manṣūr b. Silfān, the Shaykhs of the Muḥammadāb. They testified that to the best of their knowledge the estate of Shaykh Khōjalī extended to the western *kurus*. Both were suitable to be considered sufficient [representatives of the] community [of Muslims], for they were honest, satisfactory, and superior in giving testimony on behalf of their community. The court accepted their testimony, for they are partners in the district but had witnessed against [their own partisan interests]. Further, King Bādī's delineation of the boundary at the *kurus* is valid because he is a king, who has the right to apportion the lands, whether barren or cultivated. Even if he had added a league to that, he would have prevailed at the judgment, for he is the supreme sultan and the shaykhs of the district are his agents. As Shaykh Khalīl said: "He may act effictively through orders to an agent." Thereupon, after having established the validity of the document, the attestation of the evidence and its acceptance by the court in the absence of mitigating circumstances, [the judge] ruled that the said delineation, east and west at the *kurus*, was valid. He cut off the dispute of the Muḥammadāb and voided all arguments for their remaining in it. The said estate, its boundaries known, has become the property of the Awlād al-Shaykh Khōjalī, their descendants and their descendants' descendants [. . .] until God inherits the earth and those upon it, and He is the Best of Heirs.

There were present and witnessed to that:

Faqīh Daf` Allāh b. al-Faqīh Ḍayf Allāh
Ḥājj Ḍaḥawī b. Makwār
`Awaḍ Allāh, his son
Muḥammad al-Nūr b. al-Ḥājj `Abd al-Raḥmān walad Asīd
Ḥājj Idrīs b. al-Ḥājj Muḥammad Abu'l-Ma`ālī
`Uthmān b. Bān al-Naqā al-Jimī`ābī
al-Ṭarīf b. al-Faqīh `Abd al-Hādī al-Ḍaw [. . .]
the sons of Ḥasab al-Nabī, Muḥammad and Ḥammadnā Allāh,
people of Walad Dalīl

I, Muḥammad b. al-Ḥājj `Ammār, am scribe and witness, and God is the Best of Witnesses. That was written on the afternoon of Friday, when eighteen days had passed of Ramaḍān the blessed, the ninth month of the year one thousand two hundred fourteen from his *hijra*. May God bless him and grant him peace.

I, the *faqīr* of God Muḥammad b. Aḥmad, known as al-Jubayl, agree with this ruling, and this is written in my hand.

The matter is as mentioned and the affair as written. I, Muḥammad b. Ḍayf Allāh, have ruled according to that which is in the document.

Yes. I, Shaykh Idrīs b. Daf` Allāh, have examined this ruling and found it sound, and this is written in my hand.

Yes. I, Muḥammad `Abd al-Raḥmān, have examined this ruling and found it sound. It has no flaws in it. This is written in my hand.

I, Muḥammad b. Ismā`īl, have examined the ruling and found it sound. I am in agreement, and this is written in my hand.

[1]For a previously published version see Abū Salīm, *al-Fūnj wa'l-arḍ*, pp. 121-123.

[2]Lacuna.

[3]Conjectural reading.

[4]Lacuna; a conjectural reading of the missing text has been taken from Doc. 54.

[5]Handwriting changes.

DOCUMENT 56

Document 56 is a confirming charter issued by Arbāb Ibrāhīm b. Nāyil, Malik of the Jamū`īya, to the Awlād al-Shaykh Khōjalī on 16 Jumāda II 1215/4 November 1800. The text has been taken by the editors from the original.[1] The present document may be seen as a sequel to and support for the rulings contained in Docs. 54 and 55.

الحمد لله و الصلاة و السلام على رسول الله / فهذه حجة فرعية و وثيقة ملوكيه محررة مرضية بالديار الفنجية / على يدى ملك الجموعية اجلها الله تعالى لدا متوليها و بن متوليها الارباب / الملك ابراهيم بن المرحوم الملك نايل حفظه الله و رعاه و نصره و تولاه بجاه محمد خير / انبياه اما بعد فان المحفوظ المبرور الارباب الملك ابراهيم عرضوا عليه اولاد الشيخ / خوجلى حكم الشيخ عبد الله ولد عجيب و حكم الشريعة فى دار الشيخ خوجلى من جهة / الطين المرق فى جهة الغرب المحمداب نازعوا اولاد الشيخ خوجلى فيه و شكوا على ولد / عجيب و حضروا الفريقين و انقطعوا المحمداب من دار الشيخ خوجلى ما لهم تحت / القيف في القرير و لو شبرا و انقطعوا المحمداب بالعاده و الشريعة ثم ان الملك / ابراهيم لما عرضوا عليه حكم ولد عجيب و حكم الشريعة تم و امضا لاولاد الشيخ / خوجلى حكم الشريعة و حكم العادة و قطع نزاع المحمداب من دار الشيخ خوجلى / ما لهم تحت القيف و لو شبر و ملك الدار لاولاد الشيخ خوجلى لا يعارضهم فيها / معارض و لا ينازعهم فيها منازع و من تعرض لهم بعد ذلك عليه الحسب / و ان نازع فيها واحد او اثنين او اكثر ادبته جمل الحذر ثم الحذر من الخلاف / و المخالف لا يلوم الا نفسه

حضر و شهد بذلك من جماعة الملك

(. . .)[2] بن الا / حيمر
و (. . .)[3]
و نايل بن رحمه
و خيار بن الامين ولد رحمه
و حامد بن منصور
و عبد / الجبار بن عبد القادر
و قرجاج ولد حمد
و عبد الله ولد المعيق
و سعيد بن فرح /
و نصار بن محمد
و الارباب فضل الله بن تبيدى السايق

و من جهة الفقرا

الفقه يس بن / حامد بن الملك الاحيمر
واحمد بن الفقه محمد بن الشيخ بن الفقه عبد الدافع /
و الحبيب بن حمد بن الفقه النور بن ام مريوم
و الفقه على بن ابى قصه /
و عبد الله ولد سليمان بن محمد نعيم[3]

و انا فقير الله البشير بن الفقه حسب الله بن بحر كاتب و شاهد و الله خير / الشاهدين حرر ذلك بيوم الثلاثاء نصف النهار نهار ستة عشر خلون / من جماد الثانى من شهور سنة خمسة عشر بعد الالف و المايتين من / هجرة سيد المرسلين عليه افضل الصلاة و ازكى التسليم[4]

نعم انا / فقير الله يس بن حامد بن الملك الاحيمر شاهد بما فى الوثيقه و هذا / خطى بيدى[4]

نعم انا فقير الله احمد بن الفقه محمد بن الفقه الشيخ بن الفقه / عبد الدافع شاهد بما فى الوثيقه و هذا خطى بيدى[4]

نعم انا فقير الله احمد / الحبيب ابن الفقه حمد شاهد بما فى الوثيقه و هذا خطى بيدى[4]

نعم انا فقير الله عبد الله بن سليمان شاهد بما فى الوثيقه و هذا خطى بيدى

Praise be to God, and prayers and peace upon the messenger of God. This is a subsidiary charter and royal document written and approved in the Funj territories, in the presence of the Malik of the Jamū`īya, may God Most High exalt them, in the presence of their warden, Arbāb al-Malik Ibrāhīm, son of the late Malik Nāyil. May God preserve and guard him, grant him victory, and care for him through the influence of Muḥammad, the best of His prophets.

Thereafter: The Awlād al-Shaykh Khōjalī showed the divinely preserved and pious Arbāb al-Malik Ibrāhīm a ruling of Shaykh `Abd Allāh walad `Ajīb and a ruling at Islamic law concerning cultivable land in the estate of Shaykh Khōjalī along the western side. The Muḥammadāb challenged the Awlād al-Shaykh Khōjalī concerning it and complained to Walad `Ajīb. The two parties were summoned and the Muḥammadāb were cut off from the estate of Shaykh Khōjalī; they have nothing in the *qurayr* below the *qayf*, not even a hand's breadth. The Muḥammadāb were cut off both by customary law and by Islamic law. Thereupon Malik Ibrāhīm, when he had been shown the ruling of Walad `Ajīb and the ruling at Islamic law,[5] confirmed and ratified the ruling at Islamic law and the ruling at customary law for the Awlād al-Shaykh Khōjalī. He cut off the claim of the Muḥammadāb to the estate of Shaykh Khōjalī; they have nothing below the *qayf*, not even a hand's breadth. He made the estate the property of the Awlād al-Shaykh Khōjalī. Let no troublemaker trouble them concerning it. Let no challenger challenge them concerning it. He who troubles them after that is subject to the reckoning; whoever challenges concerning it, be they one, two, or more, I will fine him a camel. Beware, then beware of disobedience, and let the disobedient blame none but himself.

There were present and witnessed to that from the entourage of Malik [Ibrāhīm]:

[. . .] b. al-Aḥīmīr

[. . .]

Nāyil b. Raḥma

Khayyār b. al-Amīn walad Raḥma

Ḥāmid b. Manṣūr

`Abd al-Jabbār b. `Abd al-Qādir

Qarjāj walad Ḥammad

`Abd Allāh walad al-Mu`īq

Sa`īd b. Faraḥ

Naṣṣār b. Muḥammad

Arbāb Faḍl Allāh b. Tabīdī al-Sāyiq

From the *fuqara'*:

Faqīh Yāsīn b. Ḥāmid b. al-Malik al-Aḥīmīr

Aḥmad b. al-Faqīh Muḥammad b. al-Shaykh b. al-Faqīh `Abd al-Dāfi`

al-Ḥabīb b. Ḥammad b. al-Faqīh al-Nūr b. Umm Maryūm

Faqīh `Alī b. Abū Quṣṣa

`Abd Allāh walad Sulaymān b. Muḥammad Na`īm

I, the *faqīr* of God al-Bashīr b. al-Faqīh Ḥasab Allāh b. Baḥr, am scribe and witness, and God is the Best of Witnesses. That was written at midday on Tuesday, when sixteen days had passed of Jumāda II from the months of the year one thousand two hundred fifteen from the *hijra* of the lord of the messengers, upon whom the best of prayers and purest peace.

Yes. I, the *faqīr* of God Yasin b. Ḥāmid, son of Malik al-Aḥīmīr, am a witness to what is in the document, and this is written in my hand.

Yes. I, the *faqīr* of God Aḥmad b. al-Faqīh Muḥammad b. al-Faqīh al-Shaykh b. al-Faqīh `Abd al-Dāfi`, am a witness to what is in the document, and this is written in my hand.

Yes. I, the *faqīr* of God Aḥmad al-Ḥabīb b. al-Faqīh Ḥammad, am a witness to what is in the document, and this is written in my hand.

Yes. I, the *faqīr* of God `Abd Allāh b. Sulaymān, am a witness to what is in the document, and this is written in my hand.

[1]Photocopies are preserved in the private collections of the editors.

[2]Lacuna.

[3]Inserted in the margin.

[4]Handwriting changes.

[5]Probably Docs. 54 and 55.

DOCUMENT 57

Document 57 is a letter from the northern provincial governor Nāṣir b. Muḥammad al-Amīn to the populace of the district of Berber, announcing the deposition of their district governor `Alī walad Muṣṭafā and the appointment of his successor Naṣr al-Dīn. The text has been taken by the editors from the original.[1] The letter was probably written during the northern campaign of the Regent Idrīs b. Muḥammad Abū Likaylik between 1800 and 1802.[2]

الحمد لله وحده / محمد عظم الله مجده /

الواثق برب العالمين
الشيخ ناصر بن الشيخ
محمد الامين
١٢١٤[3]

من حضرت صاحب المقامات العليه و الاقوال الصادقه / الوفيه المامون على دينه و الرعيه المتمسك بالشريعه المحمديه / الواثق برب العالمين الشيخ ناصر بن المرحوم الشيخ محمد الا / مين كان الله له حيث كان الى حضرت (الميرفاب)[4] و (الخواويل)[4] / و النعيماب و الشليتياب و السويكتاب / و المحمداب و الانقرياب و عامت الجماعه / يسلم عليكم الشيخ و الذى نعلمكم به من جيهت الملك / على ولد مصطفى سابق طلبنه فى اسم ابوه فوق الحرسنه / و حرس تحت اتطاعه و النفاع و الانقياد و تورته زوله / جاه مع الحاج على ولد تمساح للوفا و ما حصل منه وفا / و الحمد لله انا وفيت الربطتها معاه زوله جانه واجه / يعلن قفاه فى دار بربر كلها ما لقى من يجيبه لى اول / جيبه لى جاب لى جملا اجرب ذا الحين انا ترانه / ريحته من داره و ملكته نصر الملك نصر الدين و / دفعت اليه جميع الحرس و المستنيه (ذا)[4] الحين انتم / تموه و اتبعوه اليطيعه طاعنه // و اليخالفه خالفنه / و من تعرض له بعد / كلامى هذا فقد

عرض / نفسه للهلاك الحذر / ثم الحذر من الخلاف و / المخالف لا يلوم الا نفسه /
و القادم اليكم الياس / و السلام الف

Praise be to God Alone. May God magnify the glory of Muḥammad.

He who trusts in the Lord of the Universe
Shaykh Nāṣir, son of Shaykh
Muḥammad al-Amīn
1214/1799-1800

From the presence of the lord of high station, truthful and veracious in word, faithful to his religion and to the subjects, who holds fast to the Muḥammadan law, who trusts in the Lord of the Universe, Shaykh Nāṣir, son of the late Shaykh Muḥammad al-Amīn. May God be with him wherever he is.

To the presence of the [Mīrfāb], the Khawāwīl, the Na`īmāb, the Shilītiyāb, the Suwaykitāb, the Muḥammadāb, the Inqiriyāb, and the whole populace.

The shaykh greets you. What we are informing you is about Makk `Alī walad Muṣṭafā. Formerly we asked him, in the place of his father, to exercise stewardship over that which was assigned to his oversight, and he administered it under the conditions of obedience, usefulness, and compliance. I sent to him a messenger with Ḥājj `Alī walad Timsāḥ for satisfaction, but he did not obtain satisfaction from him. Praise be to God, I have fulfilled what I promised him. The messenger came [back] to us with empty pockets. In all the land of Berber he found nothing to present me, the first time, but a mangy camel. So now I have decided to release him from [authority over] his land; I have installed Makk Naṣr al-Dīn and delivered to him all the stewardship and what awaits him. Now you [must] endorse him and follow him. Whoever obeys him has obeyed us;

whoever opposes him we have opposed, and whoever troubles him after these my words has exposed himself to destruction. Beware, then beware of disobedience, and let the disobedient blame none but himself.

Ilyās is coming to you.

One thousand farewells.

[1]NRO Miscellaneous 1/30/530. For a previously published version see al-Ḥājj Ḥāmid Muḥammad Khayr and Jay Spaulding, "The Deposition of a *Makk* of Berber," *Sudan Texts Bulletin*, Vol. 2 (1980): 47-58.

[2]Spaulding, *Heroic Age*, pp. 371-379.

[3]The reading of the seal text given here is confirmed by Dr. `Izz al-Dīn al-Amīn, *Qarīyat Kutrānj wa-atharuhā al-`ilmī fi'l-Sūdān* (Khartoum: 1975), p. 119. Dr. Abū Salīm has elsewhere (*al-Fūnj wa'l-arḍ*, p. 128 and *al-Khatm*, p. 68) read the seal date as 1204/1789-1790; this is unlikely, however, as Nāṣir first came to power with the northern campaign of Idrīs b. Muḥammad Abū Likaylik in 1800 (Spaulding, *Heroic Age*, pp. 371-374).

[4]Conjectural reading.

DOCUMENT 58

Document 58 is a confirming charter issued by the northern provincial governor Nāṣir b. Muḥammad al-Amīn to the Awlād Dōlīb on 27 Ṣafar 1215/20 July 1800. The text has been taken by the editors from the original.[1] The present charter confirms the grant recorded in Doc. 50.

الحمد لوليه و الصلاة و السلام على نبيه /

الواثق برب العالمين
الشيخ ناصر بن الشيخ
محمد الامين
١٢١٤[2]

فهذه حجة قطعيه و وثيقه ملوكية ببندر قرى المحروسة / المحميه اجلها الله تعالى لدا متوليها و ابن متوليها و الحاكم يوميذ عليها / و ما فيها صاحب المقامات العليه و الاقوال الصادقه الوفيه المامون / على دينه و الرعيه المتمسك بالشريعه المحمديه الواثق برب العالمين الشيخ / ناصر بن المرحوم الشيخ محمد الامين نصره الله ءامين زيدت ايام عدله و / (جددت)[3] ليالى سعده بجاه محمد و ءاله و بعد فان المحفوظ المبرور / المويد المنصور الشيخ ناصر عرضت (عليه)[3] وثيقة من ابيه الشيخ محمد الامين / فان فيها صدقة جاريه لى الفقه محمد بن الفقه السيد دوليب / و تلك الصدقة ثلاثين عود فى مرن الضناقلة فى الجزيره / فى الدار التى بيد الشوشى و هى معلومة البقعة و الحدود فحدها / من جيهت السافل دارجماع و من جيهت الصعيد بقيت امها و من / جيهت الصبح البحر و من جيهت الغرب المرن المعلوم الليل (الكرس)[4] / و ذراعها ابوا ثمانية اذراع و صارت الدار المذكوره بحدودها المعلومه / صدقة ناجزة لوجه الله و لرسوله و طلبا للثواب فى دار الماب و ليوم لا / ينفع (فيه)[3] مال و لا بنون الا من اتى الله بقلب سليم و انها سالمة مسلمه من جميع الشرور و السبل العاديه و لا عليها

علوق و لا كليقه و لا قله و لا / جله و (المحفوظ)[5] المبرور المويد المنصور الشيخ ناصر تمم و امضا ما فعله / ابيه الشيخ محمد الامين لى الفقه محمد

حضر و شهد بذلك

صالح سيد القوم
و بشير سيد القوم
و عجيب ولد دقيس
و البشير (ولد النعيم شيخ)[6] المساعيد
و طه ولد احمد شيخ الدانياب
و على شيخ الخيل //
و المبارك (مقدم خيل)[3] / الحلفاية
و (. . .)[7] دفع الله / جندى قرى
و الارباب ابراهيم / مك الجموعية
و الارباب جماع
والا / رباب شمام
و الارباب بادى
و / حسن
و عمر
اولاد الشيخ الامين
و الارباب الاسيد
و الارباب اونسه
و الارباب / شاور
اولاد الشيخ مسمار
و اولاد الا / رباب على
مسمار
و محمد الامين
و اولاد / الشيخ عبد الله
الامين
و العجيل
و ناصر /

و اولاد الارباب العجيل
محمد
و احمد /
و عيسى
و كباشى المنكروكن /
و محمد سيد العدة

و الكاتب لاصلها و المحرر لفصلها عوض / الله بن الحاج ضحوى حرر ذلك / ضحوة الثلاثا نهار سبعه و عشرين / يوما خلون من شهر الله صفر / سنة خمسة عشرسنة بعد / المايتين و الالف من هجرته عليه / الصلاة و السلام

Praise be to His friend, and prayers and peace upon His prophet.

He who trusts in the Lord of the Universe
Shaykh Nāṣir, son of Shaykh
Muḥammad al-Amīn
1214/1799-1800

This is a definitive charter and royal document [issued] in the *bandar* of Qarrī, the divinely guarded and protected, may God Most High exalt her, in the presence of her warden, the son of her warden, the governor at the present time over her and what is in her, the lord of high station, truthful and veracious in word, faithful to his religion and to the subjects, who holds fast to the Muḥammadan law, who trusts in the Lord of the Universe, Shaykh Nāṣir, son of the late Shaykh Muḥammad al-Amīn. May God grant him victory. Amen. May the days of his justice be increased and the nights of his good fortune renewed through the influence of Muḥammad and his family.

Thereafter: The divinely preserved, pious, divinely assisted and victorious Shaykh Nāṣir was shown a document from his father Shaykh Muḥammad al-Amīn, in which is a presently obtaining gift of alms to Faqīh Muḥammad al-Faqīh al-Sayyid Dōlīb. This gift of alms is thirty rods in the *mirin* of the Danāqla on the island in the district in the hands of al-Shūshī. Its location and boundaries are known. Its boundary on the north is Dār Jimā`, on the south the remainder of the estate, on the east the river, and on the west the known *mirin* as far as the *kurus*. Its cubits are eight [per rod]. The said estate, its boundaries known, has become a free gift of alms for the sake of God and His messenger, asking for reward in the life to come, for a day in which neither wealth nor sons suffice, unless one comes to God with a secure heart. It is completely free from all the customary *shurūr* and *subul*. It is not subject to *`ulūq*, *kalīqa*, *qilla*, or *jilla*. The divinely preserved, pious, divinely protected and victorious Shaykh Nāṣir has confirmed and ratified what his father Shaykh Muḥammad al-Amīn did for Faqīh Muḥammad.

There were present and witnessed to that:

Ṣāliḥ, *sīd al-qūm*
Bashīr, *sīd al-qūm*
`Ajīb walad Duqays
al-Bashīr walad al-Na`īm, *shaykh al-musā`id*
Ṭaha walad Aḥmad, Shaykh of the Dāniyāb
`Alī, *shaykh al-khayl*
al-Mubārak, *muqaddam al-khayl* of al-Ḥalfāya
[. . .]
Daf` Allāh, the *jundī* of Qarrī
Arbāb Ibrāhīm, Makk of the Jamū`īya
Arbāb Jammā`
Arbāb Shammām
Arbāb Bādī
Ḥasan and `Umar, sons of Shaykh al-Amīn
Arbāb al-Asīd
Arbāb Unsa and Arbāb Shāwir, sons of Shaykh Mismār

the sons of Arbāb `Alī, Mismār and Muḥammad al-Amīn
the sons of Shaykh `Abd Allāh, al-Amīn, al-`Ajayl, and Nāṣir
the sons of Arbāb al-`Ajayl, Muḥammad, Aḥmad, and `Īsā
Kabbāshī the *Mankarūkan*
Muḥammad, *sīd al-`udda*

The writer of the original and composer of its parts is `Awaḍ Allāh b. al-Ḥājj Ḍaḥawī. That was written on the morning of Tuesday, when twenty-seven days had passed of God's month of Ṣafar in the year one thousand two hundred fifteen from his *hijra*, upon him be prayers and peace.

[1]For a previously published version see Abū Salīm, *al-Fūnj wa'l-arḍ*, pp. 75-76.

[2]See Doc. 57, note 3.

[3]Conjectural reading.

[4]Spelled *al-kursī.*

[5]Spelled as shown.

[6]Lacuna. A conjectural reading has been restored from Doc. 50.

[7]Lacuna.

DOCUMENT 59

Document 59 is an originating charter issued by the northern provincial governor Nāṣir b. Muḥammad al-Amīn at the request of Faqīh Aḥmad b. `Īsā on 17 Muḥarram 1224/4 March 1809. The text has been taken by the editors from the photocopy published by Dr. `Izz al-Dīn al-Amīn.[1] The document contains two grants. By the first, the governor excused the obligations of six men. The obligation (*`aẓm*) of each of the men named consisted of *fardatayn subā`iyāt*, probably meaning two pieces of homespun cotton cloth seven cubits (about fifteen feet) in length.[2] The assessment of a tax in the form of finished cloths was a means of obliging subjects to grow cotton and to work it into fabric to be delivered to the government. By the second grant, the governor forbade servants of the state to trespass upon the men's lands, which lay on the east bank of the Blue Nile in or near the village of Kutrang.

(الحمد لله وحده محمد عظم الله مجده)[3] /

الواثق برب العالمين
الشيخ ناصر بن الشيخ
محمد الامين
١٢١٤[4]

من حضرت صاحب المقامات العليه و الاقوال الصادقه / الوفيه المامون على دينه و الرعيه المتمسل بالشريعه المحمديه الواثق برب / العالمين الشيخ ناصر ابن المرحوم الشيخ محمد الامين نصره الله الرحمن الرحيم / امين الى حضرت كل من تقف عليه هذه الوثيقة و الناظر / لما فيها من الحقيقه من المحكمين و ولات امور الدين و بعد فان المحفوظ /

المبرور المويد المنصور بعناية الله والرسول الشيخ ناصر بن المرحوم الشيخ محمد الا /
مين قد طلب منه الفقيه احمد ولد عيسى ان يعفى له عن عظم اولاد مصطفى / محمد
و الامين اخيه و عن عظم اولاد محمد ولد رقيه احمد و النور اخيه / و عن عظم بنى
عمهم محمد و محمود و عظم كل من الستة المذكورين فردتين / سباعيات فالمحفوظ
المبرور الشيخ ناصر عفا عن عظم الرجالة المذكورين / للفقيه احمد ولد عيسى هم و
ذريتهم ما يناسلوا و طلبا للثواب فى دار / الماب و ليوم لا ينفع فيه مال و لا بنون الا
من اتى الله بقلب سليم و صاروا / هولاء الرجالة المذكورين سالمين مسلمين من جميع
السبل العادية / و المضار الصحيه لا عليهم قل و لا جل

حضر ذلك و شهد به

صالح سيد القوم
و الامين ولد على ولد بشاره مقدم الخيل
و ناصر ولد عجيب ولد دقيس /
و محمد ولد فاطر شيخ المساعيد
و طه ولد احمد شيخ الدانياب /
و احمد ولد المبارك ولد مرناتى
و الارباب ابراهيم ولد نايل ملك الجموعيه /
و الارباب مسمار وكيل قرى
و الارباب بادى بن الشيخ محمد الامين /
و الارباب عجيب ولد اونسه
و اولاد الارباب العجيل
محمد
و احمد
و عيسى /
و الارباب الفحل بن الشيخ عبد الله
و اولاد الارباب على
محمد
و حماد
و الامين
و الامين ولد الشيخ ناصر

و محمد ولد الحاج النور
و احمد ولد دفع الله / كاشى
و الفقيه محمد النور بن الحاج عبد الرحمن
و الفقيه محمد عبد الجليل عامر /

و هولا الرجالة من تعرض لهم فقد عرض نفسه للهلاك و نوكد عليكم يا جميع / الخدام و الجراى و خصوصا الدقيساب الحذر ثم الحذر من الخلاف و المخالف / لا يلوم الا نفسه

و كاتب المسطور زروق بن محمد النور عبيد / و كفى بالله شهيدا و حرر ذلك ضحوة الاحد نهار سبعة عشر خلون من / عاشور المحرم و ذلك عام اربعه و عشرون بعد الالف و المايتين من الهجره //

كذا ان صاحب المقامات العليه و الاقوال / الصادقه الوفيه الشيخ ناصر (بنى)[5]
المرحوم / محمد الامين نصره الله الرحمن الرحيم بعد عفوه عن عظم طلب
الرجال المذكورين طلب / منه ايضا الفقيه احمد عيسى ان يمنع المداخلين / فى حدود اطيان الرجال المذكورين البحريه و الخلوية / الرفاعيه المعلومه بالحدود الذى حدها من / قدام الخور ابوا عجيجه قدام التمدات و من ورى / حد رفاعه العسيلات قبل بنون الحجر و فوق / الشكريه و البطاحين و تحت البحر فاجابه بذالك الشيخ ناصر ايها المقاديم و المشايخ و رءوس / القبايل او الجراى السالف ذكرهم لا يكون لكم تداخل / فى حدود الاطيان المعلومه بحريه و خلويه / (خصوصا)[6] وضعتين الرجالة المذكورين اولاد محمد / احمد رقيه و النور اخيه و قبوش و ولد ابوا / فريسه و بنى عمهم محمد و محمود / (و)[6] اولاد مصطفى محمد و الامين الذى حدها من قدام الخور ابوا عجيجه / المذكور و من ورى ابراهيم عيسى وضعة البحر و فوق حدودها / المعلومة و تحت البحر و وضعتهم الثانية الذى / حدها من قدام الحله كترانج و من ورى الفقيه ابراهيم عيسى / و مشرع الدويمات و تحت السدر و فوق الخلا هى خاصه بهم / دون عشيرتهم لا يتداخل فيها احد و خصوصا الدقيساب و من تعرض عرض نفسه للهلاك و حرر ذلك عصر الاحد نهار سبعة عشر خلت من عاشورا و ذلك عام اربعه و عشرون بعد الالف و المايتان كما تقدم

Praise be to God alone. May God magnify the glory of Muḥammad.

He who trusts in the Lord of the Universe
Shaykh Nāṣir, son of Shaykh
Muḥammad al-Amīn
1214/1799-1800

From the presence of the lord of high station, truthful and veracious in word, faithful to his religion and to the subjects, who holds fast to the Muḥammadan law, who trusts in the Lord of the Universe, Shaykh Nāṣir, son of the late Shaykh Muḥammad al-Amīn. May God, the Merciful, the Compassionate, grant him victory. Amen.

To the presence of all who read this document and see the truth therein from among the arbiters and executors of the affairs of religion.

Faqīh Aḥmad b. ʿĪsā asked the divinely preserved, pious, divinely protected one, victorious through the providential care of God and the messenger, Shaykh Nāṣir, son of the late Shaykh Muḥammad al-Amīn, to excuse for his sake the obligation of the Awlād Muṣṭafā (Muḥammad and al-Amīn his brother), the obligation of the Awlād Muḥammad walad Raqīya (Aḥmad and al-Nūr his brother), and the obligation of the sons of their paternal uncle, Muḥammad and Maḥmūd. The obligation of each of the six mentioned is two *subāʿī farda*s. The divinely preserved and pious Shaykh Nāṣir excused the obligation of the men mentioned and of their descendant offspring for Faqīh Aḥmad walad ʿĪsā, asking for reward in the life to come, for a day in which neither wealth nor sons suffice unless one comes to God with a secure heart. These men mentioned have become completely free from all the customary *subul* and valid *maḍārr;* they are not subject to *qill* or *jill.*

There were present and witnessed to that:

Ṣāliḥ, *sīd al-qūm*
al-Amīn walad `Alī walad Bishāra, *muqaddam al-khayl*
Nāṣir walad `Ajīb walad Duqays
Muḥammad walad Fāṭir, *shaykh al-musā`īd*
Ṭaha walad Aḥmad, Shaykh of the Dāniyāb
Aḥmad walad al-Mubārak walad Marnātī
Arbāb Ibrāhīm walad Nāyil, Malik of the Jamū`īya
Arbāb Mismār, the *wakīl* of Qarrī
Arbāb Bādī b. al-Shaykh Muḥammad al-Amīn
Arbāb `Ajīb walad Unsa
the sons of Arbāb al-`Ajayl, Muḥammad, Aḥmad, and `Īsā
Arbāb al-Faḥl b. al-Shaykh `Abd Allāh
the sons of Arbāb `Alī, Muḥammad, Ḥammād, and al-Amīn
al-Amīn walad al-Shaykh Nāṣir
Muḥammad walad al-Ḥājj al-Nūr
Aḥmad walad Daf` Allāh Kāshī
Faqīh Muḥammad al-Nūr b. al-Ḥājj `Abd al-Raḥmān
Faqīh Muḥammad `Abd al-Jalīl `Āmir

Whoever troubles these men has exposed himself to destruction. We peremptorily command you, all servants of the government[7] and *jarāī*, especially the Duqaysāb. Beware, then beware of disobedience, and let the disobedient blame none but himself.

The writer of the text is Zurūq b. Muḥammad al-Nūr `Ubayd. With God, two witnesses suffice. That was written on the morning of Sunday, when seventeen days had passed of `Āshūrā, al-Muḥarram, and that is [in] the year one thousand two hundred twenty-four from the *hijra*.

Likewise the lord of high station, truthful and veracious in word, Shaykh Nāṣir, son of the late Muḥammad al-Amīn, may God the Merciful, the

Compassionate, grant him victory, after he had excused the obligation of the men mentioned was further asked by Faqīh Aḥmad `Īsā to forbid the servants of the government[7] [to cross] the boundaries of the riverain, barren and uncultivated lands of the aforementioned men. [These lands] are known by [lateral] boundaries which [run] from in front of Khōr Abū `Ujayja in front of al-Tamadāt, [and] behind the border of the uncultivated land of the `Isaylāt in front of Banūn al-Ḥajar; above [inland] are the Shukrīya and the Baṭāḥīn, and below is the river. Shaykh Nāṣir accepted that [and said]: "O you previously mentioned *muqaddams*, shaykhs, heads of tribes, and *jarāī*! You have no right to enter the boundaries of the known lands, riverain or uncultivated." Of the men mentioned--the Awlād Muḥammad, Aḥmad Raqīya[8] and al-Nūr his brother, Qabūsh,[9] Walad Abū Farīsa,[9] the sons of their paternal uncle, Muḥammad and Maḥmūd, and the Awlād Muṣṭafā, Muḥammad and al-Amīn--the details of the two positions [of their lands] are [as follows]. [First], that whose boundary is from in front of the said Khōr Abū `Ujayja and behind [the land of] Ibrāhīm `Īsā to the site of the stone; above its boundaries are known and below is the river. The position of their second [landholding] is that whose boundary is from in front of the village of Kutrang and behind Faqīh Ibrāhīm `Īsā and the watering place of the Duwaymāt; below is the *sidr* tree, and above is the wasteland. It is their very own to the exclusion of their associates; let no one, especially the Duqaysāb, enter it. Whoever makes trouble exposes himself to destruction.

That was written, as was the preceding, on the afternoon of Sunday, when seventeen days had passed of `Āshūrā in the year one thousand two hundred twenty-four.

[1]`Izz al-Dīn al-Amīn, *Qarīyat Kutrānj*, p. 118.

[2]For the *farda*, see Brocchi, *Giornale*, Vol. 5, pp. 194-195; A.E. Brehm, *Reiseskizzen aus Nord-Ost-Afrika* (Jena: 1861), Vol. 1, p. 157, and Burckhardt, *Travels in Nubia*, p. 216.

[3]Given by Dr. `Izz al-Dīn in his printed version (*Qarīyat Kutrānj*, p. 119) but not visible in the photocopy.

[4]See Doc. 57, note 3. Two seal impressions are present.

[5]Spelled as shown.

[6]Conjectural reading.

[7]The apparent meaning here of *al-khuddām* and *al-mudākhilīn*.

[8]Possibly meaning "the sons of Muḥammad walad Raqīya, Muḥammad and al-Amīn;" see above.

[9]Not previously mentioned by name.

DOCUMENT 60

Document 60 is a confirming charter issued by the northern provincial governor Nāṣir b. Muḥammad al-Amīn to the Awlād al-Shaykh Khōjalī on 4 Dhu'l-Qa`da 1226/20 November 1811. The text has been taken by the editors from the original.[1] The charter records one episode in the longstanding dispute between the Khōjalāb and their neighbors introduced in Doc. 14. Documents 60 and 61 form a pair of rulings, comparable to Docs. 54 and 55, issued respectively by the Shaykh of Qarrī and his *qāḍī* after hearing the same case at the same time in the same place. Consideration of both will be given here.

The action recorded in Docs. 60 and 61 was initiated by the Awlād Khōjalī through an appeal to the secular lord; the latter summoned the *qāḍī*, several *`ulamā'* of Qarrī and its environs, the defendants, and the latter party's secular overlord the Makk of the Jamū`īya. The *qāḍī* then instructed each group of litigants to choose a single spokesman, and Doc. 60 preserves some of the formulas by which the rights and duties of these individuals were established before the court. One may note a similarity in this regard to the practices of the court of the Shaykh of Qarrī in July 1701 as recorded by the court physician Theodoro Krump:

> Every morning and afternoon the shaykh held public court, in which both the plaintiff and the defendant chose advocates from among those present. The spokesman for the plaintiff would tell what was charged against the defendant, and then the representative of the defendant would refute the charges and justify him. When the two advocates had

> stated their cases, those present joined in, pro and con, after which the shaykh would pronounce sentence, which is without appeal.[2]

At the order of the *qāḍī*, the spokesman for the Khōjalāb as plaintiffs reviewed his party's claim to the disputed land, a claim which rested upon grants from the sultans. One is told explicitly that the defendants had previously sought to overturn these rights through an appeal to Islamic justice (Doc. 55), but that this appeal had been rejected. The defendants then submitted a case based on a document; in contrast to the action recorded in Docs. 54 and 55, the present suit would be decided through the weighing of competing documentary evidence. When examined by the court, however, the document presented by the defendants was found to be irrelevant to the case as it concerned a different site entirely, while the secular charters presented by the plaintiffs were found to be sound.

A controversy arose, however, when the plaintiffs presented Doc. 55 for consideration by the court; some objected to having it read on the grounds that this would have the effect of calling into question the presumably sound ruling of a reputable Islamic judge, while others cited legal authorities who would allow the reevaluation of a *qāḍī*'s judgment. It may be that the judge in the present case was among those who objected to seeing his brother's ruling reexamined, for Doc. 61 rather pointedly notes that it was the governor and not the *qāḍī* who ordered Doc. 55 to be read. In the event, the *qāḍī*'s ruling was found to be sound; the Khōjalāb were victorious, and their opponents again went through the customary ritual of submission to the court. Prince and judge then ruled in favor of the plaintiffs; the charter of the former was witnessed by the courtiers of Qarrī, while that of the latter is truncated, and in its present form bears only the endorsement of the *qāḍī* himself.

باسمك يا كريم بسم الله الرحمن الرحيم الحمد لله الذى بلغ الرسول و نحن ءامنا بما يقول /

الواثق برب العالمين
الشيخ ناصر بن الشيخ
محمد الامين
١٢١٤[3]

و بعد فهذه حجة فرعية و وثيقة مرضيه بالديار الفنجيه بنواحي قرى المحروسة المحمية اجلها الله / تعالى لدا متوليها و ابن متوليها و الحاكم يوميذ عليها و ما فيها صاحب المقامات العليه و الاقوال الصادقه الوفيه / المامون على دينه و الرعيه المتمسك بالشريعه المحمديه الواثق برب العالمين الشيخ ناصر بن المرحوم الشيخ محمد الامين / طابت فعاليه و دامت ايامه و لياليه بحق طه و تابعيه ءامين اءمين ءامين الى كل من تقف عليه هذه الوثيقة / و الناظر لما فيها من الحقيقه من المحكمين و اولات امور الدين و بعد فان المحفوظ المبرور المايد المنصور الشيخ / ناصر بن المرحوم الشيخ محمد الامين قد قدموا اليه اولاد الشيخ خوجلى و شكوا اليه المحمداب و الدانياب و زعموا / انهم ماخذين دارهم ظلما و عدوان و المحفوظ المبرور المايد المنصور الشيخ ناصر ارسل للمحمداب و الدانياب احضرهم / و احضر مكهم الارباب ابراهيم فى وجهه و قعد لهم ديوان و ارسل لقضيه الحاج دفع الله و احضر من العلما الفقيه / محمد المعروف بالجبيل و الفقه احمد ولد سرحان و الفقه محمد ولد على و الفقه محمد هادى و الفقه شيخ ادريس / دفع الله و اولاد الفقه محمد الفقه عبد اللطيف و الفقه نور الدين و من الفقرا جمعا كثير لا نطيل بذكرهم / فلما انحضروا هوءلاء المذكورين فى وجه الشيخ ناصر بحضرت العلما امرهم الحاكم الحاج دفع الله بالكلام فقال / لهم الحجه ما بتبق برحه يا اولاد الشيخ خوجل اوكلوا لكم زول لحجتكم و انتم يالمحمداب و الدانياب اوكلوا / فيكم زول على حجتكم ايضا اولاد الشيخ خوجل اوكلوا الفقه نور الدين ولد الامين و المحمداب و الدانياب اوكلوا عواضه ولد حريحر فقال عواضه لنور الدين حمل اولاد خوجل كله عندك فقال له نعم حمل الحاضر و الغايب / عندى التزمته و انت يا عواضه حمل المحمداب و الدانياب عندك فقال له نعم عندى و التزمته بحمل الحاضر / و الغايب فمن المحمداب الحضر المجلس شيخهم على ولد محمد ولد ضياب المعروف بجانجير و ابراهيم ولد محمد / احيمر و يمام ولد عبود و ولد حامد ولد احيمر التتميم و ولد عبد العزيز و من الدانياب الدكر ولد بشير / و فضل الله ولد على و نصر الدين و التوم ودان ولد حماد كلهم فوضوا لعواضه الامر الحاضر و الغايب / و

اوكلوه على النظر و غيره فلما سمع الحاكم اجوابهم امر المدعى فيهم بالجواب و هو الفقه نور الدين / فتكلم و زعم إن الملك بادى ولد نول تصدق على الشيخ خوجلى بدار معلومة البقعة و الحدود و اسمها / قطعيه و محدده يمينا و شمال و من الشرق و الغرب حد الكرس من القرير و بعده الملك ناصر تمم صدقة / ابيه على تحديدها ثم بعد برهة من الزمان انتم يالمحمداب و الدانياب نازعونا فى طين مرق داخل الحدود / و شكيتونا للشيخ عبد الله و طلبت منه الشريعه و (تورنا)[4] للفقه محمد ولد ضيف الله و اتحكمن معاكم / و انقطعت مننا و حكم العاده عندنا و حكم الشريعه عندنا و انتم جايرين دارنا ظلما و عدوان / فتكلم عواضه فقال للفقه نور الدين نحن داركم مان ناكرنها لاكن لنا فيها مرن فقال له الفقه / نور الدين اثبت مرنك ان كان ببينه او بوثيقة فقال له عندى وثيقة قال له نور الدين عرض / وثيقتك فعرض عواضه وثيقته للعلما فوجدوها باطله و لم تطابق الدعوه الحجه فى قطعيه / و الوثيقه فى ابوا حميده و كنك و اتى ايضا الفقه نور الدين بوثيقة الملك بادى و ابنه الملك ناصر / و اتى بوثيقة فيها حكم الفقه محمد ولد ضيف الله فلما نظر الحاكم الحاج دفع و من معه فى العلما / فى الوثايق و وجدوهن صحاح حكموا على عواضه و عامة المحمداب و الدانياب بالانقطاعه / و عجزوهم من كل حجه يقومون بها ما لهم تحت القيف فى القرير و لو شبر سوا الكرس و حده / و حكموا لاولاد الشيخ خوجلى بصحة المكاتيب و صحة الدار على ما فى مكتوب السلطان بادى / و مكتوب الشريعه و المحفوظ المبرور المايد المنصور لما سمع جواب العلما و نظر ما فى المكاتيب / و وجدهن صحاح حكم على المحمداب و الدانياب بالانقطاعه ما لهم فى القرير و لو شبر تحت / قيف الغرب سوى الكرس و حكم لاولاد الشيخ خوجلى بصحة مكاتيبهم و صحة دارهم // و ملكهم اياها الى قيام الساعة و من ينازعهم فيها بعد / حكمى هذا عليه حسبى و فوقه الف بعد / انقطاعيتهم فى وجهى و رضا عواضه بذمت الفقه محمد / ولد الجبيل كونه سواه شجره و تظلل بظله

حضر ذلك / و شهد به

صالح سيد القوم
و ناصر ولد دقيس
و فضل الله / ولد بشاره مقدم الخيل
و الشيخ محمد ولد فاطر شيخ المساعيد /
و الشيخ طه ولد احمد شيخ الدانياب
و احمد ولد المبارك وكيل / الحلفايه

و الجندى جابر جندى قرى
و الارباب ابراهيم مك / الجموعيه
و الارباب مسمار وكيل قرى
و اخوانه
حماد
و محمد
و / الامين
اولاد الارباب على
و الارباب بادى بن المرحوم الشيخ / محمد الامين
و الارباب الامين بن الشيخ ناصر
و الارباب الامين /
و الارباب ناصر
و الارباب العجيل
و الارباب ضياب
و الارباب (. . .)[5] /
و الارباب عثمان
اولاد الشيخ عبد الله
و الارباب محمد
و الارباب / احمد
و الارباب عيسى
اولاد الارباب العجيل
و الارباب اونسه / بن الشيخ مسمار
و اولاد الارباب عجيب
اونسه
و شاور /
و ابا بكر
و العجيل
و الارباب عجيب ولد قدوره
و عجيب / ولد قدوره ولد زمزم
و الارباب الاسيد ولد عبد الله / الاديغم

و من جهة عيلة الشيخ

المنكروكن نايل
و عيسى ولد دفع / فايت
و عبد الاسد
و كباشي
و عبد الامين قليمه
و مر الجواب /
و حسن ولد رابحه
و نايل ولد العينه
و فضل الله ولد نصير / و اولاده
الامين
و البخيت
و اولاد العقيد مر الجواب /
قنديل
و حسن
و اونسه
و فضل الله ولد بخيت
و محمد ولد / الحاج النور سيد العده
و احمد ولد دفع الله
و الفقه محمد / عبد الجليل

و انا محمد نور بن الحاج عبد الرحمن اسيد / كاتب و شاهد و الله خير الشاهدين
حرر ذلك / ضحوة الجمعه فى شهر الله ذى القعدة (. . .)[5] / نهار اربعة ايام خلون
منه سنة الف و مايتين و ستة و عشرون سنة من هجرته صلى الله عليه و سلم

In Thy name, O Generous One. In the name of God, the Merciful, the Compassionate. Praise be to God, Who sent the messenger. We believe in what he says.

He who trusts in the Lord of the Universe
Shaykh Nāṣir, son of Shaykh
Muḥammad al-Amīn
1214/1799-1800

This is a subsidiary charter and document approved in the Funj territories, in the regions of Qarrī, the divinely guarded and protected, may God Most High exalt her, in the presence of her warden, the son of her warden, the governor at the present time over her and what is in her, the lord of high station, truthful and veracious in word, faithful to his religion and to the subjects, who holds fast to the Muḥammadan law, who trusts in the Lord of the Universe, Shaykh Nāṣir, son of the late Shaykh Muḥammad al-Amīn. May his deeds be made pleasant, and his days and nights be prolonged, by virtue of Ṭā' Hā' and what follows.[6] Amen, amen, amen.

To the presence of all who read this document and see the truth therein from among the arbiters and executors of the affairs of religion.

The Awlād al-Shaykh Khōjalī came before the divinely preserved, pious, divinely assisted and victorious Shaykh Nāṣir, son of the late Shaykh Muḥammad al-Amīn, and complained to him against the Muḥammadāb and the Dāniyāb, charging that they were unjustly and aggressively taking their estate. The divinely preserved, pious, divinely assisted and victorious Shaykh Nāṣir sent to the Muḥammadāb and the Dāniyāb to summon them, and he summoned into his presence their *makk*, Arbāb Ibrāhīm. He set up a court for them, and he sent to his judge, Ḥājj Daf` Allāh, to summon from among the *`ulamā'* Faqīh Muḥammad, known as "al-Jubayl," Faqīh Aḥmad walad Sirḥān, Faqīh Muḥammad walad `Alī, Faqīh Muḥammad Hādī, Faqīh Shaykh Idrīs Daf` Allāh, the sons of Faqīh Muḥammad, Faqīh `Abd al-Laṭīf and Faqīh Nūr al-Dīn, and from among the *fuqarā'*, a large gathering mention of whom would be tedious. When these the aforementioned had assembled before Shaykh Nāṣir in the presence of the *`ulamā'*, the judge, Ḥājj Daf` Allāh, ordered them to speak, saying: "Argumentation does not allow for chatter. O Awlād al-Shaykh Khōjalī, delegate one from among you to present your arguments, and you too, O Muḥammadāb and Dāniyāb, delegate one from among you to present your arguments." The Awlād al-Shaykh Khōjalī chose Faqīh Nūr al-Dīn walad al-Amīn as their representative, and the Muḥammadāb and the Dāniyāb chose as their representative `Awāḍa walad Ḥarīḥīr. `Awāḍa said to Nūr al-Dīn: "Do you assume responsibility for all the Awlād Khōjalī?" He said to him: "Yes. I take responsibility for those present and absent. And you, `Awāḍa, do you assume responsibility for the Muḥammadāb and Dāniyāb?" He said to him: "Yes. I take responsibility for those present and absent." Among the Muḥammadāb present at court were their shaykh, `Alī walad Muḥammad walad Ḍiyāb, known as "Jānjīr," Ibrāhīm walad Muḥammad Aḥīmīr, Yammām walad `Abūd, Walad Ḥāmid walad Aḥīmīr al-Tatmīm, and Walad `Abd al-`Azīz. From among the Dāniyāb [there were] al-Dakr walad Bashīr, Faḍl Allāh walad `Alī, Naṣr al-Dīn, and al-Tōm Widān walad Ḥammād. All of them, present and absent, entrusted the matter to `Awāḍa to handle. When the judge heard their reply he ordered the plaintiff among them to respond, and that was Faqīh Nūr al-Dīn. He spoke, and claimed that King Bādī walad Nōl had bestowed as alms upon Shaykh Khōjalī an estate whose location and boundaries are known, named Qaṭ`īya. It is bounded on the left and right, the east and west, by the boundary of the *kurus* from the *qurayr*. After him, King Nāṣir confirmed the gift of alms of his father according to its boundaries. "Thereupon, after a short time you, O Muḥammadāb and Dāniyāb, disputed with us concerning land that runs inside the boundaries. You complained against us to Shaykh `Abd Allāh. You demanded of him a judgment according to Islamic law, so he referred us to Faqīh Muḥammad walad Ḍayf Allāh. We litigated against you there, and you were cut off from us. The ruling according to Islamic law was in our favor. You are encroaching upon our estate unjustly and aggressively." Then `Awāḍa spoke, and said to Nūr al-Dīn: "We do not deny that it is your estate, but we have a *mirin* in it." Faqīh Nūr al-Dīn said to him: "Prove that you have a *mirin*, either by evidence or by document." He said to him: "I have a document." Nūr al-Dīn said to him: "Show your document." So `Awāḍa showed his document to the *`ulamā'*, but they found it to be worthless and irrelevant to the claim; the argumentation concerned Qaṭ`īya, while the document was about Abū Ḥumayda and Kanak. Then Faqīh Nūr al-Dīn brought a document of King Bādī, and [one] of his son, King Nāṣir. He also brought a document in which was the ruling of Faqīh Muḥammad walad Ḍayf Allāh. When the judge Ḥājj Daf` [Allāh] and those of the *`ulamā'* who were with him had examined the documents and found them sound, they ruled that the claim of `Awāḍa and all the Muḥammadāb and the Dāniyāb be cut off, and they nullified any further argument remaining to them. They have nothing below the *qayf* in the *qurayr*, not even a hand's breadth--just to the *kurus* and its boundary. They ruled in favor of the Awlād al-Shaykh Khōjalī; their documents are valid and their estate is valid according to what is in the document of Sultan Bādī and the Islamic legal document. The divinely preserved, pious, divinely assisted and victorious [Shaykh Nāṣir], having heard the response of the *`ulamā'* and examined what was in the documents, having found them sound, ruled that the claim of the Muḥammadāb and the Dāniyāb be cut off. They have nothing in the *qurayr*, not even a hand's breadth, below the western *qayf*--only as far as the *kurus*. He ruled in favor of the Awlād al-Shaykh Khōjalī; their documents are valid and their estate is valid. He made the latter their property until the hour of resurrection, [saying]: "He who challenges them concerning it after this my ruling is liable to my reckoning, and subject to [a fine of] one thousand [*qirsh*], now that I have cut them off in my presence." `Awāḍa accepted the guarantee of Faqīh Muḥammad walad al-Jubayl, he being just, and a tree under whom he sought shelter.

There were present and witnessed to it:

Ṣāliḥ, *sīd al-qūm*
Nāṣir walad Duqays

Faḍl Allāh walad Bishāra, *muqaddam al-khayl*
Shaykh Muḥammad walad Fāṭir, *shaykh al-musā'īd*
Shaykh Ṭaha walad Aḥmad, Shaykh of the Dāniyāb
Aḥmad walad al-Mubārak, the *wakīl* of al-Ḥalfāya
the *jundī*, Jābir, *jundī* of Qarrī
Arbāb Ibrāhīm, Makk of the Jamū'īya
Arbāb Mismār, the *wakīl* of Qarrī
his brothers Ḥammād, Muḥammad and al-Amīn, sons of Arbāb 'Alī
Arbāb Bādī, son of the late Shaykh Muḥammad al-Amīn
Arbāb al-Amīn b. al-Shaykh Nāṣir
Arbāb al-Amīn
Arbāb Nāṣir
Arbāb al-'Ajayl
Arbāb Ḍiyāb
Arbāb [. . .] and Arbāb 'Uthmān, sons of Shaykh 'Abd Allāh
Arbāb Muḥammad, Arbāb Aḥmad and Arbāb 'Īsā, sons of Arbāb al-'Ajayl
Arbāb Unsa, son of Shaykh Mismār
the sons of Arbāb 'Ajīb, Unsa, Shāwir, Abū Bakr, and al-'Ajayl
Arbāb 'Ajīb walad Qadūra
'Ajīb walad Qadūra walad Zamzam
Arbāb al-Asīd walad 'Abd Allāh al-Idīghim

From among the household of the shaykh:

Mankarūkan Nāyil
'Īsā walad Daf' Fāyit
'Abd al-Asad
Kabbāshī
'Abd al-Amīn Qalīma
Murr al-Jawāb
Ḥasan walad Rābiḥa

Nāyil walad al-`Ayna
Faḍl Allāh walad Nuṣayyir and his sons al-Amīn and al-Bakhīt
the sons of `Aqīd Murr al-Jawāb, Qandīl, Ḥasan, and Ūnsa
Faḍl Allāh walad Bakhīt
Muḥammad walad al-Ḥājj al-Nūr, *sīd al-`udda*
Aḥmad walad Daf` Allāh
Faqīh Muḥammad `Abd al-Jalīl

I, Muḥammad Nūr b. al-Ḥājj `Abd al-Raḥmān Asīd, am scribe and witness, and God is the Best of Witnesses. That was written on the morning of Friday, in God's month of Dhu'l-Qa`da [. . .], when four days of it had passed, in the year one thousand two hundred twenty-six from his *hijra*, may God bless him and grant him peace.

[1]For a previously published version see Abū Salīm, *al-Fūnj wa'l-arḍ*, pp. 128-131.

[2]Krump, *Palm-Baum*, p. 300.

[3]See Doc. 57, note 3.

[4]Spelled as shown.

[5]Lacuna.

[6]Qur'ān 20.

DOCUMENT 61

Document 61 is a charter issued by the *qāḍī* of Qarrī Daf` Allāh b. Ḍayf Allāh; it contains a ruling favorable to the Awlād al-Shaykh Khōjalī in the longstanding dispute with their neighbors introduced in Doc. 14. The text has been taken by the editors from the original, which is truncated at both top and bottom, and frayed along either side with significant loss of text.[1] The date of the charter is missing, but internal evidence clearly indicates that it forms a pair with Doc. 60, and may therefore be assigned to 4 Dhu'l-Qa`da 1226/20 November 1811. Further discussion may be found in the introduction to Doc. 60.

(. . .)[2]   و بعد فهذه حجة شرعيه و وثيقة مرضيه قاطعه مالكية محررة مرضية بالديار الفنجيه ببندر الحلفاية المحروسة المحميه / اجلها الله تعالى لدا متوليها و حاكم قاصيها و دانيها عالم علما الملة المحمدية و امين الدولة الفنجية ذو النصر السليم الذى / سيضع حكمه على الابرام و التتميم الحاج دفع الله بن الفقيه ضيف الله و بعد فان اولاد الشيخ خوجلى قدموا الى حضرت الامير الشيخ ناصر و شكوا له المحمداب و الدانياب و زعموا انهم ماخذين دارهم فارسل الشيخ ناصر للمحمداب و الدانياب و احضرهم / بوجهه و احضر ملكهم الملك ابراهيم و ارسل لحاكمه الحاج دفع الله و احضر من العلما الفقيه محمد ولد الجبيل و الفقيه احمد ولد سرحان / و الفقيه محمد ولد على فلما انحضروا هوءلاء امر الحاكم الحاج دفع الله ان يتكلموا و هما الرجلان البالغان الرشيدان و هما الفقيه / نور الدين ولد الفقيه الامين فى خصومته لنفسه و بوكالة مفوضة مقبولة شرعا من اولاد اعمه اولاد الفقيه طه و اولاد ابراهيم و اولاد الفقيه محمد الخليفه و اولاد سراج النور و اولاد الامين و اولاد محمد و عامة الخوجلاب و كافتهم و عوضة ولد ابراهيم / ولد حريحير فى خصومته لنفسه و بوكالة مفوضة مقبولة

شرعا من المحمداب و الدانياب و من المحمداب شيخهم على ولد محمد ولد ضياب / المعروف بجانجير و ابراهيم ولد محمد ولد احيمر و يمام ولد عبود و ولد حامد ولد احيمر التتميم و ولد عبد العزيز و رجالة الدانياب / الدكر ولد بشير و فضل الله ولد على و نصر الدين و التوم ودان ولد حماد و جملة المحمداب و الدانياب فوضوا له الامر و اوكلوه على (النظر)[3] / و غيره ثم قام عوضة و قال يا نور الدين كلما ثبت على الخوجلاب عندك فقال نور الدين شلت حمل الكبير و الصغير و الحاضر و الغايب / و التزمته و انت يا عوضة حمل المحمداب و الدانياب عندك فقال عندى و شلت حمل الكبير و الصغير و الغايب و الحاضر و التزمته (فلما)[4] / حضروا من يديه امر المدعى فيهم بالجواب و هو الفقيه نور الدين المذكور و زعم ان الملك بادى ولد نول تصدق على (الشيخ خوجلى)[4] / (بدار معلومة)[4] البقعة و الحدود فقطعها له و حددها صعيد و سافل على ما فى وثيقته و شرقا و غربا حد الكرس (من القرير)[4] / و بعده الملك ناصر تمم صدقة ابيه على تحديدها ثم بعد برهة من الزمان نازعوا المحمداب و الدانياب فى طين (مرق)[4] / فى تحديدنا فى وجه الفقيه محمد ولد ضيف الله فحكم علينا و ملكنا الدار بانهم ما لهم بعد قيف الغرب شبر من (القرير)[5] / نازعونا و شكينا لولد عجيب هذا جوابه ثم ان الحاكم امر المدعى عليه بالجواب و هو عوضة المذكور اما بالانكار او بالاقرار فتكلم و قال / ان دارنا من دار الشيخ خوجلى لها مرن معلوم و حدا واقف و عندى وثايق على ذلك هذا جوابه فلما سمع الحاكم جوابهم امر كلا / منهم ان يثبت صحة دعواه فاتى الفقيه نور الدين بوثيقة فيها ان الملك بادى ولد نول تصدق على الشيخ خوجلى بالجنديه / و رفيده و القطعية و هى دار عامله ولد سرير و قطعها له لان الانقطاع جايز و ماضى كما قال (المصنف)[6] و مضى فى جبر عامل و لان / الامام يقطع البور و المعمور كذا ذكره الشيخ محمد التتاى و الشيخ شرف الدين و اتى ايضا بوثيقة فيها حكم الفقيه محمد ولد ضيف / الله و توقفوا عن نظره بدليل قول المصنف و لا يتعقب حكم العدل العالم اى لا ينظر فيه من ولى بعده بل قال الشيخ محمد الخراشى / ينظر فيه ان رءوه صوابا مضى و ان رءوا خطاء نقص ثم ان الشيخ ناصر امرهم بالنظر فيه فنظروا فاذا مغلق بالادلة / و النصوص موافق الكتاب و السنة و الاجماع فاذا فيه ان اولاد الشيخ خوجلى و المحمداب و الدانياب تخاصموا اليه (. . .)[7] / ثم انهم اعترفوا و قروا على انفسهم انه صدق جا و كذب راح ما لنا فى دار الشيخ خوجلى دعوه حدنا الكرس فى القرير ثم / بعد ثبوت اقرارهم و شهادة العدول عليهم حكم عليهم بانهم ما لهم فى الطين بعد قيف الغرب و لو شبر من القرير / فحكموا العلما بصحة حكم الفقيه محمد ولد

ضيف الله لانه عدل عالم و اتى عوضة بوثيقة فيها دار فى كنك و لم (. . .)[7] /
دعوه فقال له الحاكم الدعوى فى رفيده و قطعية و اين كنك منهما هذا باطل لا يتصور
بعيد بعضه من بعض ثم ان عوضة قال ما ارضى الا بذمة الفقيه محمد ولد الجبيل
سويته شجرة و تظللت بظله فقال الشيخ ناصر / (. . .)[7] (محمد ولد)[4] الجبيل
فقال انا موافق و حاكم بصحة هذا الحكم و ان الحاكم بعد حضور العلما و شورتهم
(. . .)[7] خوجلى و حكم لهم بالطين المتنازعين فيه و ملكهم اياه و حكم عوضة
(. . .)[7] / قطعه من ذلك الطين المتنازعين فيه و هو حد الكرس من القرير (. . .)[7]
/ (. . .)[7] و من معه و عجزهم من كل (. . .)[7] يقوم بها

حضر ذلك و شهد به (. . .)[8]

نعم الامر كما ذكرو الشان كما سطر دفع الله بن الفقه ضيف الله

[. . .] Thereafter: This is a lawful charter and approved document, definitive and Mālikī, written and approved in the Funj territories, in the *bandar* of al-Ḥalfāya, the divinely guarded and protected, may God Most High exalt her, in the presence of her warden, the governor of her far places and near, the foremost *ʿālim* of the Muḥammadan community, *amīn* of the Funj dynasty, who has secure support that will enforce his judgment conclusively and definitively, Ḥājj Dafʿ Allāh b. al-Faqīh Ḍayf Allāh.

Thereafter: The Awlād al-Shaykh Khōjalī came before the *amīr* Shaykh Nāṣir and complained to him against the Muḥammadāb and the Dāniyāb, charging that they were taking their estate. Shaykh Nāṣir sent to the Muḥammadāb and the Dāniyāb to summon them into his presence, and he summoned also their *malik*, Malik Ibrāhīm. He sent to his judge, Ḥājj Dafʿ Allāh, to summon from among the *ʿulamāʾ* Faqīh Muḥammad wad al-Jubayl, Faqīh Aḥmad walad Sirḥān, and Faqīh Muḥammad walad ʿAlī. When these had been assembled, the judge Ḥājj Dafʿ Allāh ordered the two mature and rightly-guided men to speak. They were Faqīh Nūr al-Dīn walad al-Faqīh al-Amīn, litigating on his own behalf and as an authorized and legally acceptable representative for the sons of his paternal uncles, the Awlād al-Faqīh Ṭaha, the Awlād Ibrāhīm, the Awlād al-Faqīh Muḥammad the *khalīfa*, the Awlād Sirāj al-Nūr, the Awlād al-Amīn, and all the rest of the Khōjalāb, and `Awūḍa walad Ibrāhīm walad Ḥarīḥīr, litigating on his own behalf and as an authorized and legally acceptable representative for the Muḥammadāb and the Dāniyāb; among the Muḥammadāb their shaykh, `Alī walad Muḥammad walad Ḍiyāb, known as "Jānjīr," Ibrāhīm walad Muḥammad walad Aḥīmir al-Tatmīm, Walad `Abd al-`Azīz; and men of the Dāniyāb, al-Dakr walad Bashīr, Faḍl Allāh walad `Alī, Naṣr al-Dīn, and al-Tōm Widān walad Ḥammād. All the Muḥammadāb and the Dāniyāb authorized him to represent them in regard to [the matter] and so forth. Thereupon `Awūḍa rose and said: "O Nūr al-Dīn! Do you speak authoritatively on behalf of the Khōjalāb?" Nūr al-Dīn said: "I will take it upon myself to bear the burden of the Khōjalāb, great and small, present or absent. And you, `Awūḍa, will you bear [the cause of] the Muḥammadāb and the Dāniyāb?" He said: "I will. I take it upon myself to bear the burden [for them], great and small, present or absent." [When] they came into his presence, he ordered the plaintiff among them to respond, and that was the said Faqīh Nūr al-Dīn. He claimed that King Bādī walad Nōl had bestowed as alms upon [Shaykh Khōjalī an estate], its location and boundaries [known], and apportioned it to him, and set its boundaries south and north according to what is in his document and east and west between the *kurus* [and the *qurayr*]. King Nāṣir confirmed the gift of alms of his father according to its boundaries. "Thereupon, after a short time, the Muḥammadāb and the Dāniyāb laid claim to our land [running] within our boundaries before Faqīh Muḥammad walad Ḍayf Allāh. But he ruled against them and made us the owners of the estate, for they do not have [even] a hand's breadth beyond the western *qayf* from the west [in the *qurayr*]. They disputed with us, and so we complained to the Walad `Ajīb; this is his document." Thereupon the judge ordered the defendant, and that was the said `Awūḍa, to reply either in denial or in affirmation. He spoke, saying: "Our estate has a well-known *mirin* with a fixed boundary from the estate of Shaykh Khōjalī. I have documents to that effect." That was his reply. When the judge had heard their statements he ordered each of them to establish the validity of his claim. Faqīh Nūr al-Dīn brought a document in which was, that King Bādī walad Nōl had bestowed as alms upon Shaykh Khōjalī al-Jundīya. It was his gift, apportioned by him, for it was the territory of his agent [Bādī] walad Sarīr. It was his right to apportion it, for apportionment is permissible and binding. As The Author [Khalīl b. Isḥāq] says: "He may act effectively through orders to an agent," for the *imām* may apportion barren and cultivated land. Shaykh Muḥammad al-Tatā'ī and Shaykh Sharaf al-Dīn stated this also. He also brought a document in which was a ruling of Faqīh Muḥammad walad Ḍayf Allāh, but they hesitated to examine it because of the word of The Author: "The just ruling of an *`ālim* may not be ammended," that is, the one who succeeds him may not examine it. On the other hand, Shaykh Muḥammad al-Khurāshī said: "One may examine it. If they find it to be correct, it is binding, but if they see an error, it is defective." Thereupon Shaykh Nāṣir ordered them to examine it, so they investigated whether the proofs were ambiguous, whether the terms conformed to the Book, the *sunna*, and the consensus, and whether the Awlād al-Shaykh Khōjalī and the Muḥammadāb and the Dāniyāb were litigating concerning it [. . .]. Thereupon they [the Muḥammadāb and the Dāniyāb] admitted and accepted that "truth has come and falsehood departed. We have no claim on the estate of Shaykh Khōjalī. Our boundary is the *kurus* in the *qurayr*." Thereupon, after the establishment of their admission and the authorized witnesses against them, he ruled against them, to the effect that they had no land beyond the western *qayf*, not even a hand's breadth beyond the *qurayr*. The *`ulamā'* ruled in favor of the validity of the ruling of Faqīh Muḥammad walad Ḍayf Allāh, for he was a just *`ālim*. `Awūḍa brought a document concerning an estate in Kanak and not [. . .] his claim. The judge said to him: "The claim is about Rafīda and Qaṭ`īya; which of these is Kanak? This is invalid. It seems that one is far from the other." Then `Awūḍa said: "I will only accept the conscience of Faqīh Muḥammad al-Jubayl. His fairness is a tree under which I seek shelter." Shaykh Nāṣir said: [. . .]. He [Faqīh

Muḥammad al-Jubayl] said: "I agree, and rule [in confirmation of] the validity of this ruling." After the *`ulamā'* were present and [after] their consultation, the judge [. . .] Khōjalī, he [the judge] ruled in their favor in regard to the contested land and their ownership of it. He ruled that `Awūḍa [. . .] is cut off from this disputed land, whose boundary is the *kurus* from the *qurayr* [. . .] and those with him, and nullified their every [. . .] settle on it.

There were present and witnessed to it:

[. . .]

Yes. The matter is as mentioned and the affair as written. Daf` Allāh b. al-Faqīh Ḍayf Allāh.

[1]For a previously published version see Abū Salīm, *al-Fūnj wa'l-arḍ*, pp. 108-110.

[2]The top of the document, containing the introductory protocols, is truncated.

[3]Spelled as shown.

[4]Lacuna; the missing text has been restored from Doc. 60.

[5]Conjectural reading; the last two letters of the word are missing.

[6]Conjectural reading.

[7]Lacuna.

[8]The remainder of the document is truncated; what follows is in the top margin in a different hand.

DOCUMENT 62

Document 62 is a charter issued by Qāsim walad Muḥammad, Shaykh of the Ḥalawiyīn, at al-Tumayd, in 1204/1789-1790. The text has been taken by the editors from a photocopy of the original.[1] The document is intact, but the closing protocols are crowded into a very small space at the bottom, and are written in a miniscule hand, so that some readings of the final portion are uncertain. Document 62 is the second of a pair, with Doc. 26, concerning the rival claims of two litigants to land that probably lay on the west bank of the Blue Nile slightly below modern Hassaheisa. One may infer that the judgment missing from the truncated Doc. 26 resolved the issue of right to the land itself (*dār*) in favor of Ḥājj Ḥāmid. The present dispute concerns *aṣl*, original right, but also mentions specific privileges of access that seem residual to the basic issue of ownership, which had apparently been resolved previously. The judge, Qāsim walad Muḥammad, is remembered in Ḥalawī tradition as the penultimate precolonial tribal shaykh, but also as a rather controversial figure.[2] He employed an *inscriptio* more appropriate to a private legal document of the period than a government charter, and in this he resembled his predecessor, Ibrāhīm Abū Likaylik.

بسم الله الرحمن الرحيم / فهذه حجة متقبلة خوف المكر و الملابطه / اما بعد ان الحاج
حامد و عبيد ولد ادريس / تنازعوا فى وجه قاسم ولد محمد شيخ الحلاويين / فى
(الاصل)[3] فى البحر و القاب و ادعا عبيد انه شريك / فى (الاصل)[3] و الدعا
انه ما ينهى من قطع العود / فى القاب و ما ينهى من البحر مركبه ترمى / فى البحر و
الدعا الحاج انه (اصلا)[3] ابوه وحده / ما لك فيها دعوه و لا لك فيها اصل و
الحق / معى له الحاج الاصل و الملك و ان قطع عبيد / بقى للحاج فى وجه قاسم

و حضروا و شهدوا / على ذلك جماعة كثيرة منهم

الارباب زين / العابدين ولد الفقه السيد دوليب
و الارباب محمد ولد احمد ولد ابو مزة
و الارباب محمد ولد/ سعيد ولد ابو فروع
و الارباب محمد ولد لكيل /
و محمد
و الفقه المرضى
و الضو ولد الفقه محمد / ولد الفقه قرشى
و عبد الصمد ولد الفقه / مدين
و محمد المقل
و المانكروكن ادريس ولد / عيسى
و المانكروكن محمد ولد عقاب / العجاج

و انا فقير الله على بن الفقه قرشى كاتبه و شهد به تحرير ذلك الف و مايتين
و اربعه بعد الهجره النبويه على (. . . .)[4]

In the name of God, the Merciful, the Compassionate. This is a charter made for fear of deceit and disorder.

Thereafter: Ḥājj Ḥāmid and `Ubayd walad Idrīs disputed before Qāsim walad Muḥammad, Shaykh of the Ḥalawiyīn, concerning land on the river and in al-Qāb. `Ubayd claimed that he was a partner in the land, and that he should not be prevented from cutting wood or placing his boat in the river. The claim of al-Ḥājj was that his father had owned the land alone. [He said:] "You have no claim and no right to it. I, al-Ḥājj, have a right to it, and the ownership." `Ubayd was cut off, and it remained the property of al-Ḥājj. [This took place] in the presence of Qāsim.

There were present and witnessed to that a large multitude, among them:

Arbāb Zayn al-`Abdīn walad al-Faqīh al-Sayyid Dōlīb
Arbāb Muḥammad walad Aḥmad walad Abū Mazza
Arbāb Muḥammad walad Sa`īd walad Abū Furū`
Arbāb Muḥammad walad Likayl
Muḥammad
Faqīh al-Marḍī
al-Ḍaw walad al-Faqīh Muḥammad walad al-Faqīh Qurashī
`Abd al-Ṣamad walad al-Faqīh Madīn
Muḥammad al-Maqal
Mānkarūkan Idrīs walad `Īsā
Mānkarūkan Muḥammad walad `Aqāb al-`Ajjāj

I, *faqīr* of God `Alī b. al-Faqīh Qurashī, wrote it and witnessed to it. That was written one thousand two hundred four [years] after the *hijra* of the prophet, upon [. . .].

[1]For previously published versions see Sadik Nur, "Land Tenure," p. 52 and Plate VIb, and Abū Salīm, *al-Fūnj wa'l-arḍ*, p. 141.

[2]National Records Office Dakhlia 112/5/51; G.B. Tame, "Legends of the Halawin of Blue Nile Province, *Sudan Notes and Records*, Vol. 17, No. 2 (1934): 201-216.

[3]The word *aṣl* is difficult to read.

[4]Lacuna.

DOCUMENT 63

Document 63 is an originating charter issued by Arbāb Idrīs b. Muḥammad al-Faḥl, governor of Shandī, to Faqīh Ḥammad b. Muḥammad al-Majdhūb. The text has been taken by the editors from the original, which is frayed around the edges and damaged along a fold below the middle of the document, with considerable loss of text.[1] The document was issued in 1168/1754-1755, on a Wednesday, the twenty-eighth day of a month whose name may have begun with the letters *al-*; a likely possibility would be Wednesday, 28 [Dhu']l-Qa`da 1168/5 September 1755. One impression of the seal is visible below the *invocatio*, but it is not legible. The beneficiary was the founder of the religious community of al-Dāmir,[2] and the land donated lay on an island adjoining the east bank of the Nile near an estate belonging to the demesne of the governor. The witness roster reveals that at a district court such as that of the Makk of Shandī, few titled offices were to be found; the governor's entourage consisted largely of groups of kinsmen and soldiers.[3]

الحمد لوليه و الصلاة و السلام على نبيه /

[4](. . .)

فهذه حجة سلطانيه و وثيقة (ملوكيه)[5] بديار شندى / المحروسة المحمية اجلها الله
تعالى لدا متوليها و بن متو / ليها و الحاكم يوميذ بما فيها الارباب ادريس بن المرحوم
/ الارباب محمد الفحل و بعد فان الارباب ادريس تصد/ ق على الفقيه حمدّ بن
الفقيه محمد المجذوب بماية عود / فى الجزيره ام جمل و ذراعها ابو ثلاثه و حدها /

من جهت الصعيد دار ولد دفع الله و من جهت / السافل بقيت دار الملك و مرنها من جهت الصبح / اللحلفا و من جهت المغرب البحر و صارت تلك الصد/ قه لله و لرسوله طلبا للثواب فى دار الماءب ليوم لا ينفع / فيه مال و لا بنون الا من (اتى)[6] الله بقلب سليم

حضر و شهد / (. . .)[7]

(. . . الاربا)ب[5] عبد السلام
و عبد (. . .)[7] / (. . .)[7]
سعد
و الفحل
و سليمان
و عبد السلام
ابناء / الارباب ادريس
و عبد السلام
و ميرف
و نمر
ابناء الارباب / كنبلاوى
و (اولاد)[5] / عجيب
سليمان
و ادريس
و محمد
و اولاد / رحمه
فزارى
و ميرف
و بشاره ولد سعد
و اولاد محمد // ولد دياب
عبد (. . .)[7]
و ذياب
و را (. . .)[7] / بو ادريس (. . .)[7]

و ادريس /
و بلال
و اولاد النا / قاويه
عبد الله /
و مركز
و حسين / ولد تيتانه
و عبو / ده
و عبد الحميد
و كثير من الجموع و / العسكر

و انا على / بن عوض كاتب و / شاهد و الله خير / الشاهدين تحرير / ذالك ضحوة الاربعاء / ثمانية و عشرون فى (. . .)[7] / من شهور / سنة ١١٦٨ الف و ماية و ثمانية و / ستين من الهجرة النبوية / على ساكنها الف سلام و / الف تحيه

Praise be to His friend, and prayers and peace upon His prophet.

[. . .]

This is a sultanic charter and royal document, in the territories of Shandī, the divinely guarded and protected, may God Most High exalt her, in the presence of her warden, the son of her warden, the governor at the present time of what is in her, Arbāb Idrīs, son of the late Arbāb Muḥammad al-Faḥl.

Thereafter: Arbāb Idrīs has bestowed as alms upon Faqīh Ḥammad b. al-Faqīh Muḥammad al-Majdhūb one hundred rods of three cubits [each] on the island of Umm Jamal. Its boundary on the southern side is the estate of Walad Dafʿ Allāh and on the northern side the remainder of the estate of the *makk*. Its lateral boundary on the east is al-Luḥafā', and on the west the river. This has become a gift of alms for [the sake of] God and His messenger, asking for reward in the life to come, for a day in which neither wealth nor sons suffice, unless one comes to God with a secure heart.

There were present and witnessed to it:

[. . .] al-Arbāb `Abd al-Salām
`Abd [. . .]
[. . .], Sa`d, al-Faḥl, Salmān, and `Abd al-Salām, sons of Arbāb Idrīs
`Abd al-Salām, Mīraf, and Nimr, sons of Arbāb Kanbalāwī
Sulaymān, Idrīs, and Muḥammad, sons of `Ajīb
Fazārī and Mīraf, sons of Raḥma
Bishāra walad Sa`d
`Abd [. . .] and Dhiyāb, sons of Muḥammad walad Diyāb
Rā[. . .] Abū Idrīs
[. . .]
Idrīs
Bilāl
`Abd Allāh and Markaz, sons of al-Nāqāwīya
Ḥasan walad Taytāna
`Abūda
`Abd al-Ḥamīd
and many of the entourage and the soldiers.

I, `Alī b. `Awaḍ, am scribe and witness, and God is the Best of Witnesses. That was written on the morning of Wednesday, the twenty-eighth of [. . .] from the months of the year 1168/1754-1755 from the *hijra* of the prophet, upon whom one thousand times peace and salutations.

[1][Abū Salīm] *Sādat al-Majādhīb*, II.

[2]*Ṭabaqāt*, p. 182.

[3]Spaulding, *Heroic Age*, pp. 51-56; 340-341.

[4]One illegible seal impression may be found here.

[5]Conjectural reading.

[6]This word was omitted from the formula by the scribe.

[7]Lacuna.

DOCUMENT 64

Document 64 is an originating charter issued by Arbāb Muḥammad b. Nimr, governor of Shandī, to Faqīh al-Amīn b. Ḥammad al-Majdhūb on 12 Sha`bān 1208/15 March 1794. The text has been taken by the editors from the original, which is frayed along internal folds with some loss of text.[1] The lands donated lay on both banks of the Nile in the vicinity of al-Dāmir. The present document was issued at a time when the Makk of Shandī was the last surviving major figure in the royalist movement that had sought to oust the Hamaj and restore the kings.[2]

الحمد لوليه و الصلاة و السلام على نبيه /

الواثق بالملك
المقتدر الارباب محمد
ابن الارباب
نمر ١٢٠٠

حجة (سلطانية)[3] و وثيقة ملوكية بديار شندى المحروسة المحمية اجلها الله / تعالى لدا متوليها و بن (متوليها)[3] و الحاكم حينيذ بما فيها المحترم المكرم المهاب المعظم / الامير الذى هو (وارث)[3] العقد من قريش الامير الذى ولى النهى و الامر عظيم / الجاه و القدر المويد (بالقهر)[3] و النصر المتعلق باذياله العز و الفخر القريشى من / الطرفين الامير (. . .)[4] الواثق بالملك المقتدر الارباب محمد بن المرحوم الارباب / نمر جعله الله (. . .)[4] حيث ما يتوجه على عدوه ينتصر امين يا رب العالمين / الى حضرة كل (من)[5] تقف عليه هذه الوثيقة و الناظر لما فيها من الحقيقه / ان يعمل (بمضمونها)[6] من غير المخالفة و لا انكار و بعد فان المحفوظ المبرور / المويد المنصور (الارباب)[3] محمد المذكور تصدق على الفقيه الامين / بن الفقيه حمد (بن محمد)[3]

المجذوب بالجزيره العربابيه فحدها من جهة / الصعيد يمام و (. . .)[4] منه و من
جهة السافل قناطير الملح و من جهة / الغرب البحر و من القبله القيف الليل اقانين
السواق و ايضا الارباب / محمد بن الارباب نمر تصدق على الفقيه الامين المذكور
بمايتين عود / فى الجزيره النامو (. . .)[4] فحدها من جهة الصعيد عبد القادر ابو
سج و من / جهة السافل (. . .)[4] عبد الله اخيه و من جهة الغرب البحر و من القبله
/ المسنداب و ايضا الارباب محمد بن الارباب نمر تصدق على (الفيه)[7] / الامين المذكور
بمية عود فى الجزيره الجبر ابيه فحدها من جهة / الصعيد (. . . .)[4] سعد و من
جهة السافل شمام و من القبله البحر / و من الغرب (. . .)[4] الجماعه و صارت تلك
الصدقة ناجزة / لله و لرسوله طلبا للثواب فى دار الماب و ليوم لا ينفع فيه مال / و لا
بنون (الا من اتى الله)[5] بقلب سليم

حضر و شهد بذلك /

عبد السلام (. . .)[4]
و ميرف
اولاد الارباب بشاره
و عبد السلام /
و ادريس
و سعد
و ضياب
و على
اولاد الارباب نمر
و نمر
و احمد /
اولاد الارباب محمد
و سلمان
و سليمان
اولاد الارباب ضياب
و الاسيد
و نمر
اولاد الارباب كنبلاوى

و فضل الله
و ميرف //
اولاد حجازى
و حجازى ولد ادريس /
و عبد السلام ولد محمد
و ارتنتى ادريس /
و المهدى
و العوض
و على
اولاد / الحاج عثمان
و محمد ولد الحاج يو (. . .)[4] /
و ضياب الفقير
و عبد (. . .)[4] ولد ابراهيم
و حسن ولد محمد (. . .)[4] / ابعريف
و جمع كثير من العساكر / لا نطيل بذكرهم

حرر (ذلك)[5] ضحى السبت اثنا عشر يوم خلون / من شهر الله شعبان من شهور / سنة ثمانية اعوام (بعد)[7] / المايتين و الالف من الهجرة النبوية / على صاحبها الف صلاة و الف / تحيه و مسطرها عمر بن (. . .)[4] عبد الرحمن (. . .)[4]

Praise be to His friend, and prayers and peace upon His prophet.

He who trusts in the Powerful King
Arbāb Muḥammad, son of Arbāb
Nimr 1200/1785-1786

A sultanic charter and royal document, [issued] in the territories of Shandī, the divinely guarded and protected, may God Most High exalt her, in the presence of her warden, the son of her warden, the governor at that time of what is in her, the honored, revered, respected, and exalted, the commander who inherited ties to the Quraysh, who disposes of the power to prohibit or command, exalted of rank and station, divinely assisted to conquest and victory, attached to the train of might and glory, descended from the Quraysh on both sides, the commander [. . .], he who trusts in the Powerful King, Arbāb Muḥammad, son of the late Arbāb Nimr. May God make him victorious over his enemy wherever he goes. Amen, O Lord of the Universe.

To the presence of all who read this document and see the truth therein; let [each one] act [accordingly] without disobedience or refusal.

Thereafter: The divinely preserved, pious, divinely assisted and victorious Arbāb Muḥammad has bestowed as alms upon Faqīh al-Amīn b. al-Faqīh Ḥammad b. Muḥammad al-Majdhūb the island of al-`Urbābīya. Its boundary on the southern side is Yammām and [. . .], on the northern side Qanāṭīr al-Milḥ, on the western side the river, and on the side of the *qibla* [the east] the *qayf*, as far as Aqānīn al-Sawwāq. Furthermore: Arbāb Muḥammad b. al-Arbāb Nimr has bestowed as alms upon the said Faqīh al-Amīn two hundred rods on the island of al-Nāmū[. . .]. Its boundary on the southern side is `Abd al-Qādir Abū Sajja, on the northern side [. . .] `Abd Allāh his brother, on the west the river, and on the *qibla,* al-Musanadāb. Furthermore: Arbāb Muḥammad b. al-Arbāb Nimr has bestowed as alms upon the said Faqīh al-Amīn one hundred rods on the island of al-Jabr Abīhī. Its boundary on the southern side is [. . .] Sa`d, on the north Shammām, on the *qibla* the river, and on the west [. . .] al-Jamā`a. This has become a free gift of alms for God and His messenger, asking for reward in the life to come, for a day in which neither wealth nor sons suffice, unless one comes to God with a secure heart.

There were present and witnessed to that:

`Abd al-Salām [. . .] and Mīraf, sons of Arbāb Bishāra
`Abd al-Salām, Idrīs, Sa`d, Ḍiyāb, and `Alī, sons of Arbāb Nimr

Nimr and Aḥmad, sons of Arbāb Muḥammad
Salmān and Sulaymān, sons of Arbāb Ḍiyāb
al-Asīd and Nimr, sons of Arbāb Kanbalāwī
Faḍl Allāh and Mīraf, sons of Ḥijāzī
Ḥijāzī walad Idrīs
`Abd al-Salām walad Muḥammad
Irtantī Idrīs
al-Mahdī, al-`Awaḍ, and `Alī, sons of al-Ḥājj `Uthmān
Muḥammad walad al-Ḥājj Yā[. . .]
Ḍiyāb al-Faqīr
`Abd al-Raḥmān walad Ibrāhīm [Warrāq][6]
Ḥasan walad Muḥammad [. . .] Ab`arif
and a large gathering of the soldiers, mention of whom would be tedious.

That was written on the morning of Saturday, twelve days having passed from God's month of Sha`bān from the months of the year one thousand two hundred eight from the *hijra* of the prophet, upon whose master one thousand prayers and one thousand salutations. Its writer is `Umar b. [. . .] `Abd al-Raḥmān [. . .]

1[Abū Salīm] *Sādat al-Majādhīb*, II.

2Spaulding, *Heroic Age*, pp. 340-380.

3Conjectural reading.

4Lacuna.

5Omitted from the formula by the scribe.

6Lacuna; the missing word has been restored from Doc. 67.

7Only part of this word is visible.

DOCUMENT 65

Document 65 is an originating charter issued by Arbāb Naṣr al-Dīn b. al-Ṣādiq for Faqīh al-Amīn b. Ḥammad al-Majdhūb and his brother Faqīh al-Ṭayyib in 1216/1801-1802. The text has been taken by the editors from the original.[1] The land bestowed lay in the vicinity of al-Dāmir. The charter was issued during a period of confusion and civil war in the Middle Nile area, after the conquest of Shandī by `Adlān b. Muḥammad Abū Likaylik and before the division of the district of Shandī into separate east bank and west bank governates later in 1216/1801-1802.[2]

الحمد لوليه و الصلاة و السلام[3] / على نبيه و بعد ان الارباب نصر الدين بن المرحوم الارباب الصادق / فى حال ولايته و انبرام امره تصدق على الفقيه الا / مين بن الفقيه حمد بن محمد المجذوب بماية و عشرين / عود بابوا ثلاثة ذراع فى ولد ام قصير و حدودها / و من جهة الصعيد دار سليمان الحداد و من جهة / السافل دار الفقيه حمد بن محمد المجذوب و ايضا ان / الارباب نصر الدين تصدق على الفقيه الطيب بن / الفقيه حمد بن محمد المجذوب ثلاثين عود / فى ولد ام قصير و حدها من جهة (الصعيد)[4] الفقيه حمد / و من جهة السافل دار (الازيداب)[5] و هذ[6] الصا / دقات المذكورات صدرت من الارباب نصر الدين / طلبا لثواب الاخره فى يوم لا ينفع مال و لا / بنون الا من اتى الله بقلب سليم و تاريخه / سنة بعد الف و ميتين[6] و ستة عشر سنة / من الهجرة و هى قابل سنة قدوم عدلان / فى الشندى و قبض محمد ولد نمر

و الشهدا على / ذالك

الفقيه المدنى بن الفقيه محمد ولد / عبد الوهاب
و مصطفى ولد ريشابى /
و الفقيه محمد ولد اللقا

و الشاهد كاتب / فقير الله قريش بن حسن نسل محمد / ابن عيسى و السلام //[7]

نعم انا محمد / اللقا شاهد بما / فى الوثيقه و هذا / خطى بيدى /[7]

انا فقير الله / المدن / بن الفقيه / محمد بن / عبد الوهاب / شاهد بما / فى الوثيقه
/ و هذا خطى / بيدى /

Praise be to His friend, and prayers and peace upon His prophet.

Thereafter: Arbāb Naṣr al-Dīn, son of the late Arbāb al-Ṣādiq, in a state of legal competence and established authority, has bestowed as alms upon Faqīh al-Amīn b. al-Faqīh Ḥammad b. Muḥammad al-Majdhūb one hundred twenty rods of three cubits [each] in Walad Umm Quṣayyir. Its boundaries are on the southern side the estate of Sulaymān the blacksmith and on the northern side the estate of Faqīh Ḥammad b. Muḥammad al-Majdhūb. Furthermore: Arbāb Naṣr al-Dīn has bestowed as alms upon Faqīh al-Ṭayyib b. al-Faqīh Ḥammad b. Muḥammad al-Majdhūb thirty rods in Walad Umm Quṣayyir. Its boundary on the southern side is Faqīh Ḥammad and on the northern side the estate of the Azīdāb. These said gifts of alms originated from Arbāb Naṣr al-Dīn, asking for reward in the life to come, for a day [in which] neither wealth nor sons suffice, unless one comes to God with a secure heart. Its date is the year one thousand two hundred sixteen from the *hijra*, the year after that of `Adlān's descent upon Shandī and seizure of Muḥammad walad Nimr.

The witnesses to that are:

Faqīh al-Madanī b. al-Faqīh Muḥammad walad `Abd al-Wahhāb
Muṣṭafā walad Rīshābī
Faqīh Muḥammad al-Laqā

The witness and scribe is the *faqīr* of God Qurayshī b. Ḥasan from the offspring of Muḥammad b. `Īsā. Farewell.

Yes. I, Muḥammad al-Laqā, am a witness to what is in the document, and this is written in my hand.

I, *faqīr* of God al-Madanī b. al-Faqīh Muḥammad b. `Abd al-Wahhāb, am a witness to what is in the document, and this is written in my hand.

[1][Abū Salīm] *Sādat al-Majādhīb*, II.

[2]Spaulding, *Heroic Age*, pp. 379-380.

[3]Two impressions of the seal appear in the right margin here; they are not legible.

[4]Inserted in the left margin.

[5]Conjectural reading.

[6]Spelled as shown.

[7]Handwriting changes.

DOCUMENT 66

Document 66 is a confirming charter issued by Arbāb Muḥammad Musā`ad b. Sa`d for Faqīh Ibrāhīm al-Ḥawwāḍ b. `Abd al-Salām on 10 Ṣafar 1220/10 May 1805. The text has been taken by the editors from the original.[1]

الحمد لوليه و الصلاة و السلام / على نبيه /

الواثق بالله القدير
الارباب محمد (مساعد)
بن الارباب
محمد سنه (. . .)[2]

فهذه حجة سلطانية و وثيقه ملوكية ببندر شندى / المحروسة المحمية اجلها الله تعالى لدا متوليها و بن متوليها / و الحاكم حينيذ بما فيها المحفوظ المبرور المويد المنصور الارباب / محمد مساعد بن المرحوم الارباب سعد تمم و امضا مكا / تيب جده الارباب ادريس و والده الارباب سعد للفقيه / ابراهيم الحواض بن الفقيه عبد السلام و من جهة الجاه / من دار (الفي يده)[3] شرق و غرب و الحيران و المتروس (فحد هذه من جهة الصعيد بطن الواد ابو هجليج و من جهة السافل واد الحيران و مرنها الما المدلى حول الفقيه و الما السدر[4] حول الملك)[3] و عفا منهن / لله و الرسول طلبا للثواب فى الدار الاخرة و ليوم لا ينفع فيه / مال و لا بنون الا من اتى الله بقلب سليم و من تعرض لهولاء / الجاه المذكور فقد عرض نفسه للهلاك الحذر ثم الحذر من / الخلاف و المخالف لا يلوم الا نفسه

حضر و شهد بذلك

بان / النقا بن الارباب ادريس و اخوانه
ميرف
و العجيل
و صالح /
و سلمان
و سليمان
و الفحل ولد عبد السلام و اخوانه
بلام /
و العجيل
و محمد
و سليمان
و ضياب
و الزبير
و ادريس ولد / سالم و اخوانه
سعد
و بشارة
و دفع الله
و على
و عبد الرازق /
و محمد ابو لكيلك و اخوانه
ادريس
و الفحل
و عبد السلام /
و ضياب
و البشير
و حموده
و عبد الرحيم
و عبد الله اخيه /
و عبد الرحمان بن ابراهيم وراق
و كباشي

و مسطر الحروف / احمد الناسخ شهد بذلك و كفى بالله شهيدا / تاريخ ذلك ضحوة الجمعة نهار عشرة ايام خلت من // صفر من شهور سنة / الف و مايتين و عشرين / من الهجرة النبويه / صلى الله و سلم على صا / حبها بكرة و عشية

Praise be to His friend, and prayers and peace upon His prophet.

He who trusts in God the Almighty
Arbāb Muḥammad [Musā`ad]
b. al-Arbāb
Sa`d Year [. . .]

This is a sultanic charter and royal document, [issued] in the *bandar* of Shandī, the divinely guarded and protected, may God Most High exalt her, in the presence of her warden, the son of her warden, the governor at that time of what is in her.

The divinely protected, pious, divinely assisted and victorious Arbāb Muḥammad Musā`ad, son of the late Arbāb Sa`d, has confirmed and ratified the documents of his grandfather Arbāb Idrīs and his father Arbāb Sa`d concerning the grant to Faqīh Ibrāhīm al-Ḥawwāḍ b. al-Faqīh `Abd al-Salām of the estate which is in his possession--east and west, al-Ḥīrān and al-Matrūs. The boundary of this on the southern side is the middle of Wādī Abū Hijlīj, and on the northern side Wādī al-Ḥīrān. Its *mirin* is the water that comes down near the *faqīh* and the water that originates near the *makk*. He has relinquished this for God and the messenger, asking for reward in the life to come, for a day in which neither wealth nor sons suffice, unless one comes to God with a secure heart. Whoever troubles them [concerning] the said grant has exposed himself to destruction. Beware, then beware of disobedience, and let the disobedient blame none but himself.

There were present and witnessed to that:

Bān al-Naqā b. al-Arbāb Idrīs and his brothers
Mīraf, al-`Ajayl, Ṣāliḥ, Salmān, and Sulaymān
al-Faḥl walad `Abd al-Salām and his brothers
Ballām, al-`Ajayl, Muḥammad, Sulaymān, Ḍiyāb, and al-Zubayr
Idrīs walad Sālim and his brothers
Sa`d, Bishāra, Daf` Allāh, `Alī, and `Abd al-Rāziq
Muḥammad Abū Likaylik and his brothers
Idrīs, al-Faḥl, `Abd al-Salām, Ḍiyāb, al-Bashīr, and Ḥamūda
`Abd al-Raḥīm and `Abd Allāh his brother
`Abd al-Raḥmān b. Ibrāhīm Warrāq
Kabbāshī

The writer of the letters, Aḥmad the Copyist, is a witness to that, and with God two witnesses suffice. The date of that is the morning of Friday, ten days having passed in Ṣafar from the months of the year one thousand two hundred twenty from the *hijra* of the prophet. May God bless its master morning and evening and grant him peace.

[1][Abū Salīm] *Sādat al-Majādhīb*, II. For the rule of Musā`ad see Spaulding, *Heroic Age*, pp. 377-380.

[2]Lacuna.

[3]Written in the margin.

[4]Spelled as shown.

DOCUMENT 67

Document 67 is a charter issued by Arbāb Nimr b. Muḥammad, governor of Shandī, for the Awlād al-Faqīh Ḥammad al-Majdhūb on 14 Ṣafar 1228/16 February 1813. The text has been taken by the editors from the original.[1]

الحمد لوليه و الصلاة و السلام على نبيه /[2] (فهذه حجة)[3] سلطانيه و وثيقة
ملوكية ببندر شندى المحروسة المحمية / لدا متوليها و بن متوليها و الحاكم حينيذ بما
فيها المحترم المكرم / المهاب المعظم الامير الذى هو (وارث)[3] العقد من قريش الامير
الذى ولى / النهى و الامر عظيم الجاه و القدر المويد بالقهر و النصر المتعلق باذياله
العز / و الفخر القريشى من الطرفين الصادق فيما وعد الواثق بالله الصمد الارباب
نمر / ابن المرحوم الارباب محمد كان الله له حيث كان امين يا (رب العالمين)[3] الى
حضرة / كل من تقف عليه هذه الوثيقة و الناظر لما فيها من الحقيقه ان يعمل /
بمضمونها من غير مخالفة و لا انكار اما بعد ان اولاد الارباب ضياب / ولد عبد الله
(. . .)[4] الفحل و اخوانه و سليمان و عمر اولاد سلمان و الفقيه البشير / ولد
مدينه فى زمن الارباب نمر ادعوا دار الفقيه حمد بن الفقيه محمد المجذوب / اليلت
شموك فى طينها التحتانى من جهة البحر بانه اصلا لهم من ابيهم الارباب / ضياب و
اولاد الفقيه حمد منهم الفقيه الطيب بنفسه و الطيب بن الفقيه (الامين)[3] / اتوا
بوثايق من السلطنه من السعداب و الفونج القطع حد (. . .)[4] / (. . .)[4] بحضرة
المحفوظ المبرور المويد المنصور / (الارباب)[3] نمر المذكور تركوا و انقطعوا و عفوا من
دار الفقيه عفواء / لله و لرسوله و صارت دار الفقيه على ما لها كما فى الدفاتر تابعة
(. . .)[4] / (حيث)[3] غرب لا احد يتعرض لها فى شى و لا احد ينازع سالمه
(مسلمه)[3] / من (. . .)[4] و الدعوى و النزاع و الارباب نمر حكم عليهم
(بالانقطاع)[3] / و الراحه من النزاع ثانيا فى دار الفقيه و رضيوا[5] بذلك صاروا
(. . .)[4] / نزاع لا دعوى و لا طلب و لا فضه و لا ذهب و لا يمينا بالله

اذا وجب / بشهاده

سعد
و ضياب
و البشير
و سليمان
و بشاره
وسلمان
ابناء / الارباب نمر
و احمد
و ادريس
و عمر
ابنا الارباب محمد
وسعد و (. . .)[4] /
و سعد
و ادريس
اولاد عبد السلام ابنا الارباب بشاره و (. . .)[4] /
و سعد ولد حجازى (. . .)[4] اولاد الارباب (عبد)[3] السلام (. . .)[4] /
و (. . .)[4] الفحل
و ارتنتى محمد
و العوض
و ادريس (. . .)[4] // (. . .)[4] /
(طاهر ولد)[3] / (ايوب)[3]
و حمد (. . .)[4] /
عبد الرحمن ولد وراق
و عبد (. . .)[4] / العنقر
و حسن بن محمد (. . .)[4] /
و جمع كثير من العساكر (لا نطيل بذكرهم)[3] /

حرر ذلك ضحا الاربعا اربعة عشر (خلون)[3] / من شهر الله صفر من شهور عام ثمانيه / و عشرين بعد المايتين و الالف / من الهجرة النبويه (. . .)[4]

Praise be to His friend, and prayers and peace upon His prophet.

[This is a] sultanic [charter] and royal document, [issued] in the *bandar* of Shandī, the divinely guarded and protected, in the presence of her warden, the son of her warden, the governor at that time of what is in her, the honored, revered, respected, and exalted, the commander who inherited ties to the Quraysh, who disposes of the power to prohibit or command, exalted of rank and station, divinely assisted to conquest and victory, attached to the train of might and glory, Qurayshī on both sides, truthful in what he promises, he who trusts in God the Eternal, Arbāb Nimr, son of the late Arbāb Muḥammad. May God be with him wherever he is. Amen, O Lord of the Universe.

To the presence of all who read this document and see the truth therein; let [each one] act accordingly without disobedience or refusal.

Thereafter: In the time of Arbāb Nimr the Awlād Ḍiyāb walad `Abd Allāh [. . .] al-Faḥl and his brothers, and Sulaymān and `Umar, sons of Salmān, and Faqīh al-Bashīr walad Madīna claimed the estate of Faqīh Ḥammad b. al-Faqīh Muḥammad al-Majdhūb as far as Shumūk, its lower land on the side of the river, [saying] that it belonged to them from their father Arbāb Ḍiyāb. The Awlād al-Faqīh Ḥammad, among them Faqīh al-Ṭayyib himself and al-Ṭayyib b. al-Faqīh [. . .] came with documents from the rulers of the Sa`dāb and the Funj that delineated the boundary [. . .]. In the presence of the said divinely preserved, pious, divinely protected and victorious Arbāb Nimr they relinquished, were cut off, and abandoned the estate of the *faqīh*, a relinquishment for the sake of God and His messenger. The estate of the *faqīh* is according to what it has in the documents, following [. . .] on the west. Let no one trouble it concerning anything; let no one trouble. It is completely free from [. . .], claim, or dispute. Arbāb Nimr ruled against them. [They are] cut off, and freed from further dispute concerning the estate of the *faqīh,* and they consented to that. [. . .] challenge, nor claim, nor demand, neither silver nor gold, nor oath by God.

If witnessing is required:

Sa`d, Ḍiyāb, al-Bashīr, Sulaymān, Bishāra, and Salmān, sons of Arbāb Nimr
Aḥmad, Idrīs, and `Umar, sons of Arbāb Muḥammad
Sa`d, [. . .], Sa`d, and Idrīs, sons of `Abd al-Salām
sons of Arbāb Bishāra [. . .]
Sa`d walad Ḥijāzī [. . .] sons of Arbāb [`Abd] al-Salām
[. . .] al-Faḥl
Irtantī, Muḥammad, al-`Awaḍ, Idrīs [. . .]
Ṭāhir walad Ayyūb, Ḥammad [. . .]
`Abd al-Raḥmān walad Warrāq
`Abd [. . .] al-`Anqar
Ḥasan b. Muḥammad [. . .]
and a large gathering of the soldiers, mention of whom would be tedious.

That was written on the morning of Wednesday, when fourteen days had passed of God's month of Ṣafar, from the months of the year one thousand two hundred twenty-eight from the *hijra* of the prophet [. . .].

1[Abū Salīm] *Sādat al-Majādhīb*, II. See also Spaulding, *Heroic Age*, pp. 377-380.

2One impression of the seal is visible here; it is not legible.

3Conjectural reading.

4Lacuna.

5Spelled as shown.

REGISTER OF FIXED DATES

1702 (1 May)	Doc. 1 issued		
1724-1725	Seal of Bādī b. Nōl		1137
1729 (31 January-1 March)	Doc. 2 issued	Rajab	1141
1732-1733	Doc. 3 issued		1145
1733 (17 January-14 February)	Doc. 4 issued	Sha`bān	1145
1733 (17 January-14 February)	Doc. 5 issued	Sha`bān	1145
1734 (27 May)	Doc. 6 issued	23 Dhu'l-Ḥijja	1146
1734 (3 June)	Doc. 7 issued	1 Muḥarram	1147
1743-1744	Doc. 9 issued		1156
1744 (10 August-8 September)	Doc. 10 issued	Rajab	1157
1746 (27 August)	Doc. 11 issued	9 Sha`bān	1159
1747-1748	Seal of Muḥammad "Abū Likaylik" b. Bādī		1160
1753 (4-31 May)	Doc. 12 issued	Rajab	1166
1754-1755	Doc. 63 issued		1168
1761-1762	Seal of Nāṣir b. Bādī		1175
1762 (7 June)	Doc. 14 issued	15 Dhu'l-Qa`da	1175
1762-1763	Seal of `Adlān b. Ṣubāḥī		1176
1763 (11 August-8 September)	Doc. 15 issued	Ṣafar	1177
1765 (22 October)	Doc. 16 issued	7 Jumāda I	1179
1766-1767	Sinnār first fears invasion from Egypt		1180
1766-1767	Seal of `Ajīb b. `Abd Allāh		1180
1767 (30 August)	Doc. 46 issued	4 Rabī` II	1181
1768 (10 January)	Doc. 47 issued	19 Sha`bān	1181
1769-1770	Seal of `Abd al-`Azīz b. Muḥammad al-Mahdī		1183
1769-1770	Seal of Ismā`īl b. Bādī		1183
1770-1771	Seal of Muḥammad al-Amīn b. Mismār		1184
1770 (5 July)	Doc. 18 issued	11 Rabī` I	1184
1772	Doc. 19 issued		
1772	Doc. 20 issued		
1772	Doc. 21 issued		
1774 (9 May)	Doc. 22 issued	27 Ṣafar	1188
1776-1777	Seal of `Adlān b. Ismā`īl		1190

1778 (17 September)	Doc. 23 issued	24 Sha`bān	1192
1780 (28 November)	Doc. 24 issued	1 Dhu'l-Ḥijja	1194
1781 (4 December)	Doc. 25 issued	17 Dhu'l-Ḥijja	1195
1785-1786	Seal of Muḥammad b. Nimr		1200
1788-1789	Seal of `Umar b. Ibrāhīm		1203
1789 (4 March)	Doc. 27 issued	6 Jumāda II	1203
1789-1790	Seal of Nāṣir b. Muḥammad Abū Likaylik		1204
1789-1790	Doc. 62 issued		1204
1790-1791	Seal of `Abd Allāh b. `Ajīb		1205
1791-1792	Seal of Bādī b. Mismār		1206
1791 (9 November)	Doc. 28 issued	12 Rabī` I	1206
1794 (15 March)	Doc. 64 issued	12 Sha`bān	1208
1794 (25 December)	Doc. 51 issued	2 Jumāda II	1209
1795 (12 August)	Doc. 30 issued	26 Muḥarram	1210
1798-1799	Doc. 32 issued		1213
1798-1799	Seal of Ranfā b. Bādī		1213
1798 (21 June)	Doc. 53 issued	7 Muḥarram	1213
1799-1800	Seal of Nāṣir b. Muḥammad al-Amīn		1214
1799 (20 June)	Doc. 33 issued	16 Muḥarram	1214
1800 (13 February)	Doc. 54 issued	18 Ramaḍān	1214
1800 (13 February)	Doc. 55 issued	18 Ramaḍān	1214
1800-1801	`Adlān b. Muḥammad Abū Likaylik captures Shandī		1215
1800 (20 July)	Doc. 58 issued	27 Ṣafar	1215
1800 (4 November)	Doc. 56 issued	16 Jumāda II	1215
1801-1802	Doc. 65 issued		1216
1803-1804	Seal of Wāwrit b. Hārūn		1218
1805-1806	Seal of Bādī b. Ṭabl		1220
1805 (10 May)	Doc. 66 issued	10 Ṣafar	1220
1809 (4 March)	Doc. 59 issued	17 Muḥarram	1224
1810 (22 May)	Doc. 35 issued	17 Rabī` II	1225
1811 (20 November)	Doc. 60 issued	4 Dhu'l-Qa`da	1226
1813 (13 January)	Doc. 38 issued	10 Muḥarram	1228
1813 (15 January)	Doc. 39 issued	12 Muḥarram	1228
1813 (16 February)	Doc. 67 issued	14 Ṣafar	1228
1815 (17 October)	Doc. 40 issued	13 Dhu'l-Qa`da	1230
1815-1816	Seal of Muḥammad b. `Adlān b. Muḥammad Abū Likaylik		1231
1820 (12 February)	Doc. 42 issued	27 Rabī` II	1235

THE COURT OF SINNĀR

Dates:	Sultans:	Regents:
1103/1692	Bādī III	
1128/1716	Unsa III	
1132/1720	Nōl	
1136/1724	Bādī IV	
1175/1762	Nāṣir	Muḥammad Abū Likaylik
1182/1768-1769	Ismā`īl	
1190/1775-1776	`Adlān	Bādī wad Rajab
1194/1780		Rajab wad Muḥammad
1200/1786		death of Rajab
		Interregnum
1202/1787-1788	Idrīs, Awkāl	Nāṣir wad Muḥammad
1203/1788-1789	Ṭabl, Rubāṭ	
1204/1789-1790	Bādī V	
1205/1790-1791	Ḥasab Rabbihī	
1206/1791-1792	Nuwwār	
1207/1792-1793	Bādī VI (First Reign)	
1213/1798-1799	Ranfā	Idrīs wad Muḥammad
1218/1803		`Adlān wad Muḥammad
		Muḥammad wad Rajab
1220/1805-1806	Interregnum	Ḥusayn wad Muḥammad
	Bādī VI (Second Reign)	
1221/1806-1807	`Ajbān, Bādī VI	
1236/1820-1821	Fall of Sinnār	Fall of Sinnār

Source:	the *amīn*:	the *jundī*:	Date:
(Doc. 2)		Muḥammad (father of Yūnus)	?
Doc. 2	Yūnus b. Muḥammad	Irdāb	1729
Doc. 4	Raḥma b. Yūnus	Yūnus (b. Muḥammad)	1733
Doc. 5	Raḥma b. Yūnus	Yūnus (b. Muḥammad)	1733
Doc. 6	Raḥma b. Yūnus		1734
Doc. 7	Raḥma b. Yūnus	Yūnus (b. Muḥammad)	1734
Doc. 8	Bashar (b. Yūnus)	Muḥammad (b. Darīsh?)	1743-4
Doc. 9	Bashar (b. Yūnus)	Muḥammad (b. Darīsh?)	1743-4
Doc. 10	Bashar (b. Yūnus)	Muḥammad (b. Darīsh?)	1744
Doc. 12	Anqala b. Yūnus	Muḥammad b. Darīsh	1753
Doc. 15	Ḥasab Allāh b. Yūnus	Hārūn b. Yūnus	1763
Doc. 16	Ḥasab Allāh b. Yūnus	Hārūn b. Yūnus	1765
Doc. 18	Hārūn b. Yūnus	Shawwāl b. Yūnus	1770
Doc. 22	Hārūn b. Yūnus	Shawwāl b. Yūnus	1774
Doc. 23	Hārūn b. Yūnus		1778
Doc. 24	Hārūn b. Yūnus	Shawwāl b. Yūnus	1780
Doc. 25	Hārūn b. Yūnus	Shawwāl b. Yūnus	1781
Doc. 27	Hārūn b. Yūnus	\`Alī b. Shawwāl	1789
Doc. 28	Hārūn b. Yūnus	\`Alī b. Shawwāl	1791
Doc. 37	Wāwrit b. Hārūn		1803-4
Doc. 39	Wāwrit b. Hārūn	Kitfāwī (b. Muḥammad Taktak)	1813
Doc. 40	Wāwrit b. Hārūn	Kitfāwī b. Muḥammad Taktak	1815
Doc. 42	Wāwrit b. Hārūn	Wāwrit b. Hārūn	1820

Source:	the *sīd al-qūm* or his representative at court:		Date:
	Ismā\`īl	executed the *wazīr* Dōka and seized power	1729
Doc. 2	Ismā\`īl	(maternal uncle of the king)	1729
Doc. 4	Ismā\`īl	maternal uncle of the king	1733
Doc. 5	Ismā\`īl	maternal uncle of the king	1733
Doc. 7	Ismā\`īl	maternal uncle of the king	1734
	Ismā\`īl	overthrown and executed	1743-4

Doc. 8	`Azūza	representative	1743-4?
Doc. 9	`Azūza	representative	1743-4
Doc. 10	`Azūza	representative	1744
Doc. 12	`Azūza	representative	1753
Doc. 14	`Azūza	representative	1762
Doc. 15	`Azūza	representative	1763
Doc. 16	`Azūza	representative	1765
Doc. 18	Jum`a b. `Azūza	representative	1770
Doc. 22	al-Ḍaw (b. Murīsa)	representative	1774
Doc. 23	al-Ḍaw b. Murīsa	representative	1778
Doc. 24	al-Ḍaw b. Murīsa	representative	1780
Doc. 25	al-Ḍaw b. Murīsa	representative	1781
Doc. 27	Sabbāb b. `Abd al-Rāziq	representative	1789
Doc. 28	Ṣabbāb b. `Abd al-Rāziq	representative	1791
Doc. 32	Maḥmūd b. Muḥammad	representative	1798-9
Doc. 40	Bādī b. Diyāb	representative	1815

Source:	Shaykh of Qarrī:	Date:
Doc. 1	Muḥammad (al-`Ajayl?)	1702
Doc. 44	Ḥammad b. `Alī, "al-Simayḥ"	before 1706?
	`Ajīb b. Muḥammad al-`Ajayl	
	Bādī b. `Ajīb b. Muḥammad al-`Ajayl	
Doc. 45	Ḥammād b. Muḥammad al-`Ajayl	before 1729
Doc. 2	Diyāb	1729
Doc. 4	`Abd Allāh b. `Ajīb	1733
Doc. 5	`Abd Allāh b. `Ajīb	1733
Doc. 8	`Abd Allāh b. `Ajīb	1743-4?
Doc. 9	`Abd Allāh b. `Ajīb	1743-4
Doc. 10	`Abd Allāh b. `Ajīb	1744
	`Abd Allāh b. `Ajīb	died 1747
	Mismār b. `Ajīb (or, b. `Abd Allāh?)	after 1747
Doc. 12	Muḥammad al-Amīn b. Mismār	1753
Doc. 14	Muḥammad al-Amīn b. Mismār	1762

Doc. 15	Muḥammad al-Amīn b. Mismār	1763
Doc. 16	Muḥammad al-Amīn b. Mismār	1765
Seal	`Ajīb b. `Abd Allāh	1180/1766-7
Doc. 46	`Ajīb b. `Abd Allāh	1767
Doc. 47	`Ajīb b. `Abd Allāh	1768
Doc. 18	`Ajīb b. `Abd Allāh	1770
Seal	Muḥammad al-Amīn b. Mismār	1184/1770-1
Doc. 50	Muḥammad al-Amīn b. Mismār	c. 1772?
	Nāṣir b. Shammām (invested and deposed)	c. 1774
	`Ajīb b. `Abd Allāh (second investiture)	c. 1774
	`Ajīb b. `Abd Allāh (died)	1193/1779-80
	`Umar (invested and deposed)	1193/1779-80
Doc. 24	Muḥammad al-Amīn b. Mismār	1780
Doc. 25	Muḥammad al-Amīn b. Mismār	1781
	Bādī b. Mismār (first investiture)	1198/1783-4
Doc. 27	`Abd Allāh b. Muḥammad al-Amīn (or, b. `Ajīb?)	1789
	Muḥammad al-Amīn b. Mismār (died)	1205/1790-1
Seal	`Abd Allāh b. `Ajīb (invested and deposed)	1205/1790-1
Seal	Bādī b. Mismār (second investiture)	1206/1791-2
Doc. 28	Bādī b. Mismār	1791
Doc. 29	Bādī b. Mismār	1794?
Doc. 51	Bādī b. Mismār	1794
Doc. 53	`Abd Allāh b. `Ajīb	1798
Doc. 54	`Abd Allāh b. `Ajīb	1800
Doc. 55	`Abd Allāh b. `Ajīb	1800
	`Abd Allāh b. `Ajīb (died)	1800
Seal	Nāṣir b. Muḥammad al-Amīn	1214/1799-1800
Doc. 57	Nāṣir b. Muḥammad al-Amīn	c. 1800
Doc. 58	Nāṣir b. Muḥammad al-Amīn	1800
Doc. 59	Nāṣir b. Muḥammad al-Amīn	1809
Doc. 60	Nāṣir b. Muḥammad al-Amīn	1811
Doc. 61	Nāṣir b. Muḥammad al-Amīn	1811
Doc. 39	Nāṣir b. Muḥammad al-Amīn	1813
Doc. 40	Shammām b. Muḥammad al-Amīn	1815
Doc. 42	Nāṣir b. Muḥammad al-Amīn	1820

Source:	Shaykh of al-Tāka:	Date:
Doc. 2	`Awaḍ	1729
Doc. 8	`Alī b. Shāwir	1743-4?
Doc. 9	`Alī b. Shāwir	1743-4
Doc. 10	(`Alī b. Shāwir ?)	1744
Doc. 12	`Abd Allāh b. `Awaḍ	1753
Doc. 14	`Abd Allāh b. `Awaḍ	1762
Doc. 15	`Abd Allāh b. `Awaḍ	1763
Doc. 16	`Abd Allāh b. `Awaḍ	1765
Doc. 18	`Abd Allāh b. `Awaḍ	1770
Doc. 22	Mismār (b. Ḥammad "al-Zīr" Darīsh ?)	1774
Doc. 24	Mismār b. Ḥammad "al-Zīr" (Darīsh)	1780
Doc. 25	Mismār b. Ḥammad "al-Zīr" (Darīsh)	1781
Doc. 27	`Umar "Jūr" b. Ḥammad ("al-Zīr") Darīsh	1789
Doc. 28	`Umar "Jūr" b. Ḥammad "al-Zīr" (Darīsh)	1791

Source:	Shaykh of Atbara:	Date:
Doc. 8	`Alī b. Ḥasan	1743-4?
Doc. 9	(`Alī) b. Ḥasan	1743-4
Doc. 10	`Alī (b. Ḥasan)	1744
Doc. 12	Sabat b. Ḥaydar	1753
Doc. 14	Bādī b. Ḥaydar	1762
Doc. 15	`Alī b. Ḥasan	1763
Doc. 16	`Alī b. Ḥasan	1765
Doc. 18	al-Faḍīl b. Mismār b. Ḥasan	1770
Doc. 22	al-Faḍl (sic) b. Mismār	1774
Doc. 24	al-Faḍīl b. Mismār	1780
Doc. 25	al-Faḍīl b. Mismār	1781
Doc. 27	`Ajīb b. Hākīt	1789
Doc. 28	`Ajīb b. Hākīt	1791
Doc. 32	(Kannān) b. al-Faḍīl	1798-9
Doc. 39	Kannān b. al-Faḍīl	1813
Doc. 40	Kannān b. al-Faḍīl	1815
Doc. 42	Kannān (b. al-Faḍīl)	1820

Source:	Shaykh of Bayla:	Date:
Doc. 2	Muḥammad Qaylī	1729
Doc. 8	Muḥammad Qaylī	1743-4?
Doc. 9	Muḥammad Qaylī	1743-4
Doc. 10	Muḥammad Qaylī	1744
Doc. 12	`Abd al-`Aṭā b. Muḥammad Qaylī	1753
Doc. 14	`Abd al-`Aṭā b. Muḥammad Qaylī	1762
Doc. 15	`Abd al-`Aṭā b. Muḥammad Qaylī	1763
Doc. 16	`Abd al-`Aṭā b. Muḥammad Qaylī	1765
Doc. 18	`Abd al-`Aṭā b. Muḥammad Qaylī	1770
Doc. 22	(`Abd al-`Aṭā b. Muḥammad Qaylī)	1774
Doc. 24	`Abd al-`Aṭā b. Muḥammad Qaylī	1780
Doc. 25	`Abd al-`Aṭā b. Muḥammad Qaylī	1781
Doc. 28	Ibrāhīm b. `Abd al-`Aṭā	1791
Doc. 32	(Ibrāhīm b. `Abd al-`Aṭā ?)	1798-9
Doc. 39	Aḥmad al-`Arakī	1813
Doc. 40	Muḥammad al-`Arakī b. `Abd al-`Alī	1815
Doc. 42	Muḥammad al-`Arakī (b. `Abd al-`Alī)	1820

Source:	Shaykh of al-Qarbīn:	Date:
Doc. 2	`Uthmān	1729
Doc. 4	Ḥammad	1733
Doc. 5	Ḥammad	1733
Doc. 7	Ḥammad	1734
Doc. 8	Qāsim	1743-4?
Doc. 9	Qāsim	1743-4
Doc. 12	Qāsim	1753
Doc. 14	Qāsim	1762
Doc. 15	Balūl b. Bādī b. Kābir	1763
Doc. 16	`Umar b. Qāsim	1765
Doc. 18	`Umar b. Qāsim	1770

Doc. 22	`Umar b. Qāsim	1774
Doc. 24	`Umar b. Qāsim	1780
Doc. 25	`Umar b. Qāsim	1781
Doc. 27	`Umar b. Qāsim	1789
Doc. 32	`Umar b. Qāsim	1798-9
Doc. 39	al-Nūr b. Muḥammad	1813
Doc. 40	Muḥammad b. al-Nūr	1815
Doc. 42	Muḥammad b. al-Nūr	1820

Source:	Shaykh of al-Baḥr:	Date:
Doc. 2	Bādī	1729
Doc. 4	Shā` al-Dīn (Darwīsh)	1733
Doc. 5	Shā` al-Dīn (Darwīsh)	1733
Doc. 7	Shā` al-Dīn Darwīsh	1734
Doc. 8	Fāṭir	1743-4?
Doc. 9	(Fāṭir?)	1743-4
Doc. 10	(Fāṭir?)	1744
Doc. 12	al-Ḍaw b. Arbāb	1753
Doc. 14	`Adlān b. Ṣubāḥī b. Ṣaqar	1762
Doc. 15	`Adlān b. Ṣubāḥī (b. Ṣaqar)	1763
Doc. 16	`Adlān b. Ṣubāḥī (b. Ṣaqar)	1765
Doc. 18	`Adlān b. Ṣubāḥī b. Ṣaqar	1770
Doc. 20	`Adlān b. Ṣubāḥī (b. Ṣaqar)	1772
Doc. 21	`Adlān b. Ṣubāḥī (b. Ṣaqar)	1772
Doc. 22	Aḥmad (b. `Alī)	1774
Doc. 24	Aḥmad b. `Alī	1780
Doc. 25	Aḥmad b. `Alī	1781
Doc. 27	Muḥammad Kamtūr (b. Aḥmad)	1789
Doc. 28	Ṣubāḥī b. `Adlān	1791
Doc. 32	(Muḥammad) Kamtūr b. Aḥmad	1798-9
Doc. 39	(Muḥammad) Kamtūr b. Aḥmad	1813
Doc. 40	Muḥammad Kamtūr b. Aḥmad	1815
Doc. 42	(Muḥammad) Kamtūr (b. Aḥmad)	1820

Source:	Shaykh of Arbajī:	Date:
Doc. 12	Shanbūl b. (Walad Nūh)	1753
Doc. 14	Shanbūl b. Walad Nūh	1762
Doc. 15	Shanbūl b. (Walad) Nūh	1763
Doc. 16	Shanbūl b. (Walad) Nūh	1765
Doc. 18	Shanbūl b. Walad Nūh	1770
Doc. 22	Shanbūl (b. Walad Nūh)	1774
Doc. 28	Madanī b. Shanbūl	1791
Doc. 32	`Adlān b. Shanbūl	1798-9
Doc. 38	`Adlān b. Shanbūl	1813
Doc. 39	`Adlān b. Shanbūl	1813
Doc. 40	`Adlān b. Shanbūl	1815
Doc. 42	`Adlān b. Shanbūl	1820

Source:	Shaykh of Alays:	Date:
Doc. 2	Shāṭir	1729
Doc. 8	Sulaymān (b. Bādī)	1743-4?
Doc. 9	Sulaymān (b. Bādī)	1743-4
Doc. 10	(Sulaymān b. Bādī)	1744
Doc. 12	Sulaymān b. Bādī	1753
Doc. 15	(Irdāb) b. Badr	1763
Doc. 16	Irdāb b. Badr	1765
Doc. 18	Sabat b. Badr	1770
Doc. 22	Sabat b. Badr	1774
Doc. 24	Sabat b. Badr	1780
Doc. 25	Dakīn	1781
Doc. 39	Muḥammad b. Badr	1813
Doc. 40	Muḥammad b. Badr	1815
Doc. 42	Sulaymān b. Badr	1820

Source:	Shaykh of Kordofāl:	Date:
Doc. 12	`Alī Karrār b. `Umar (al-Ghadawī)	1753
Doc. 14	`Alī Karrār b. `Umar	1762
Doc. 15	`Alī Karrār b. `Umar	1763
Doc. 16	al-Nūr b. `Umar	1765
Doc. 18	Idrīs b. `Alī Karrār b. `Umar	1770
Doc. 28	`Alī b. al-Nūr	1791
Doc. 32	Sa`īd b. `Alī	1798-9

Source:	Sultan of the Sinnār Musabba`āt:	Date:
Doc. 2	Khamīs (b. Janqal)	1729
Doc. 8	Khamīs	1743-4?
Doc. 9	Khamīs	1743-4
Doc. 10	Khamīs	1744
Doc. 12	(Badr) b. Khamīs	1753
Doc. 14	Badr b. Khamīs	1762
Doc. 15	Badr b. Khamīs	1763
Doc. 16	Badr b. Khamīs	1765
Doc. 18	Baḥr b. Khamīs	1770
Doc. 22	Ghurdām b. Khamīs	1774
Doc. 25	Adam b. Khamīs	1781
Doc. 28	`Abd Allāh b. Bādī	1791
Doc. 40	Abkīr	1815

Source:	Keeper of the King's Son:	Date:
Doc. 18	Muḥammad b. Khiḍr b. Nāyil	1770
Doc. 22	Muḥammad (b.) Khiḍr (b. Nāyil)	1774
Doc. 24	Muḥammad b. Khiḍr b. Nāyil	1780
Doc. 25	Muḥammad b. Khiḍr (b. Nāyil)	1781
Doc. 39	Muḥammad b. Idrīs	1813
Doc. 40	Muḥammad b. Idrīs	1815
Doc. 42	Muḥammad b. Idrīs	1820

Source:	*muqaddam al-sawākira*:	Date:
Doc. 2	`Abd Allāh	1729
Doc. 4	Abū Shōwa	1733
Doc. 5	Abū Shōwa	1733
Doc. 8	Idrīs (b. Nāyil)	1743-4?
Doc. 9	Idrīs (b. Nāyil)	1743-4
Doc. 12	Idrīs b. Nāyil	1753
Doc. 14	Idrīs b. Nāyil	1762
Doc. 15	Idrīs b. Nāyil	1763
Doc. 16	Nāyil b. Idrīs b. Nāyil	1765
Doc. 24	Qāsim b. Idrīs b. Nāyil	1780
Doc. 25	Qāsim b. Idrīs b. Nāyil	1781
Doc. 27	Qāsim b. Idrīs (b. Nāyil)	1789
Doc. 28	Qāsim b. Idrīs b. Nāyil	1791
Doc. 32	Mūsā b. Idrīs	1798-9
Doc. 40	Qāsim b. Rubāṭ	1815

Source:	*muqaddam al-quwwārīya*:	Date:
Doc. 2	Maḥmūd	1729
Doc. 8	Maḥmūd	1743-4?
Doc. 9	Maḥmūd	1743-4
Doc. 10	Maḥmūd	1744
Doc. 12	Muḥammad b. Maḥmūd	1753
Doc. 14	Muḥammad b. Maḥmūd	1762
Doc. 15	Muḥammad b. (Maḥmūd)	1763
Doc. 16	Muḥammad b. Maḥmūd	1770
Doc. 18	Aḥmad b. Maḥmūd	1770
Doc. 24	Muḥammad Taktak b. al-Nūr Qandilāwī	1780
Doc. 25	Muḥammad Taktak b. al-Nūr Qandilāwī	1781
Doc. 32	Bādī n. al-Nūr	1798-9
Doc. 38	Aḥmad b. al-Nūr	1813
Doc. 40	Aḥmad b. al-Nūr	1815

Source:	*malik bursāj*:	Date:
Doc. 2	Maḥmūd	1729
Doc. 8	Nuwwār	1743-4?
Doc. 14	`Adlān	1762
Doc. 15	(`Adlān)	1763
Doc. 16	`Adlān	1765
Doc. 18	`Adlān	1770
Doc. 24	al-Ḍaw b. Ḥawā (his mother)	1780
Doc. 25	al-Ḍaw b. Jamīl (his father)	1781
Doc. 27	Aḥmad b. `Adlān	1789
Doc. 28	Aḥmad b. `Adlān	1791
Doc. 32	Aḥmad b. `Adlān	1798-9
Doc. 40	Muḥammad b. `Adlān	1815

Source:	*muqaddam al-sajjāda*:	Date:
Doc. 2	Shalnakī	1729
Doc. 4	Muḥammad	1733
Doc. 5	Muḥammad	1733
Doc. 7	Muḥammad	1734
Doc. 8	(Muḥammad?)	1743-4?
Doc. 14	Bādī	1762
Doc. 15	(Bādī)	1763
Doc. 16	Bādī	1765
Doc. 18	Bādī	1770
Doc. 22	Balūla b. Bādī	1774
Doc. 24	Balūla b. Bādī	1780
Doc. 25	Balūla b. Bādī	1781
Doc. 32	Jammā`a b. Bādī	1798-9

Source:	*muqaddam (bayt) al-`udda*:	Date:
Doc. 2	Nāyil	1729
Doc. 8	Nāyil	1743-4?
Doc. 14	Faḍl Allāh b. Shabradal	1762
Doc. 15	Faḍl Allāh b. Shamradal	1763
Doc. 16	Ḥammād b. Dōka	1765

Source:	*muqaddam al-khayl*:	Date:
Doc. 2	Rajab	1729
Doc. 8	(`Alī b. Tūma)	1743-4?
Doc. 9	`Alī b. Tūma	1743-4
Doc. 10	(`Alī b. Tūma)	1744
	`Alī b. Tūma killed in Kordofan	1747

Source:	*muqaddam al-qawāwīd*:	Date:
Doc. 6	Maḍuwī	1734
Doc. 8	Jābir	1743-4?
Doc. 9	Jābir	1743-4
Doc. 10	Jābir	1744
Doc. 18	Yaḥyā	1770
Doc. 32	`Abd Allāh b. Jābir	1798-9
Doc. 40	Aḥmad b. Bān al-Naqā	1815

Source:	*khaṭīb*:	Date:
Doc. 2	`Abd al-Ḥafīẓ b. Nūnū	1729
Doc. 7	`Abd al-Laṭīf	1734
Doc. 8	`Abd al-Laṭīf	1743-4?
Doc. 9	`Abd al-Ḥafīẓ (b. Nūnū)	1743-4
Doc. 16	Su`ūdī b. Khayyārī	1765
Doc. 18	`Abd al-`Azīz al-Maghribī	1770
Doc. 24	Aḥmad b. `Abd al-Ḥafīẓ b. Nūnū	1780
Doc. 25	Aḥmad b. `Abd al-Ḥafīẓ b. Nūnū	1781
Doc. 28	Nuwwār b. `Ammār	1791
Doc. 32	Nuwwār (b. `Ammār)	1798-9
Doc. 40	Nuwwār (b. `Ammār)	1815

Source:	*qāḍī*:	Date:
Doc. 2	`Abd al-Ḥamīd	1729
Doc. 4	`Abd al-`Azīz	1733
Doc. 4	Ibrāhīm	1733
Doc. 5	Ibrāhīm	1733
Doc. 7	Ibrāhīm	1734
Doc. 8	`Abd al-Ḥamīd	1743-4?
Doc. 14	Muḥammad b. `Abd al-Ḥamīd	1762
Doc. 15	Muḥammad b. `Abd al-Ḥamīd	1763
Doc. 46	`Abd al-`Azīz b. Muḥammad al-Mahdī	1769-70
Doc. 18	`Abd al-`Azīz al-Maghribī	1770
Doc. 22	Aḥmad b. al-Ḍaw	1774
Doc. 24	`Abd al-`Azīz al-Maghribī al-Marākashī	1780
Doc. 25	`Abd al-`Azīz	1781
Doc. 28	`Umar	1791
Doc. 32	`Umar	1798-9
Doc. 33	`Umar	1799
Doc. 40	`Abd al-Raḥmān	1815

GLOSSARY

The following are brief working definitions of terms left untranslated; more complete discussion may be found in the Introduction to this volume and the sources cited therein.

``āda: (1) customary law, as opposed to Islamic law, *sharī`a*; (2) an obligation to the state, possibly involving the payment of first fruits to the lord.

`ādil, pl. `udūl: authorized witnesses according to Islamic law.

afṭār: an obligation to the state.

`ālim, pl. `ulamā': an individual trained in Islamic jurisprudence.

amān: truce, safeconduct.

`āmil, pl. `ummāl: generic term for government officials.

amīn (al-sulṭān): a court official, usually the highest in rank before the rise of the Hamaj.

amīr: commander; in the present collection, a secular nobleman.

`āna/`anāda: an obligation to the state; possibly a penalty for fornication or adultery similar to *zinā'* in Dār Fūr.

arbāb: title of personal status; originally, a son of a Funj woman, but with the adoption of patrilineal succession, any individual so ennobled by his superior.

aṣamm: literally, "deaf;" an epithet usually applied to the month of Rajab, but in Doc. 11, to Sha`bān.

a`shār, sing. `ushr: an obligation to the state; literally, "tithes."

awlād: see **walad**.

`aẓm: an obligation to the state, exemplified here by a payment of homespun cloths.

bandar: authorized center for trade, especially the import-export trade.

bursāj, malik al-: a court official.

Caliph: see **khalīfa** (2).

dabba: mound, especially one formed by the ruins of previous habitations.

damm: an obligation to the state; possibly a communal fine levied on a community where homicide took place, prerequisite to the arrangement of a wergild payment.

danga: audience hall of a Funj nobleman.

dār: land, estate, administrative district, kingdom.

dīnā: an obligation to the state; possibly intended to be *zinā*; see *`āna*.

ḍiyāfa: an obligation to the state; literally "hospitality," probably while billeting.

fard, al-: literally "the unique;" epithet for the month of Rajab.

farda: unit of homespun cotton cloth; two *farda*s comprised one *tōb*, or standard garment. A *subā'ī farda* was probably about fifteen feet in length.

faqīh, pl. **fuqarā'**: an Islamic holy man in the Sudan; a title of personal status.

faqīr: literally "poor man," usually in the religious sense of "poor man of God."

fāṣil: survey line drawn at right angles to the midriver (or midchannel) *mirin* as far inland as the limits of irrigated cultivation, but excluding basin (*kurrū*) lands where such were present.

fuqarā': see **faqīh**.

Gezira: the region between the Blue and White Niles.

ḥabl: a linear measure of eight cubits.

hadim: literally "wrecking" or "destruction;" a basis for a legal claim to riverine land.

Ḥājj: (1) title of personal status, indicating completion of the pilgrimage, (2) a proper name.

ḥajr al-qashsh: an obligation to the state, possibly the reservation of a farmer's stubble as forage for his lord's horses and livestock.

ḥall: an obligation to the state.

ḥarāz: *acacia albida.*

ḥasab: an obligation to the state, possibly of homespun cloths.

hijra: the journey of Muḥammad from Makka to Madīna in AD 622, marking the beginning of the Islamic calendar.

imām: the legitimate leader of the community of Muslims in any generation.

jabal: hill, mountain.

jabāya: an obligation to the state, possibly the basic levy in grain or livestock.

jada'a: a unit of land measure, a square of 60 (in some districts, 64) rods on each side.

jarāī: subordinate government officials, especially perambulatory tax assessors and collectors.

jarf: (1) sloping riverbank, usually covered by the Nile flood and suitable for *salūka* cultivation with no additional irrigation as the water recedes; (2) a landholding located in the *jarf.*

jill/jilla: an obligation to the state.

jundī: a court official, usually second in rank before the Hamaj period.

jusāra: an obligation to the state; possibly labor dues to build or repair irrigation works.

kalīqa: an obligation to the state; possibly a levy of fodder for the lord's horses.

kersha: an obligation to the state; possibly a herding duty.

khalīfa: (1) "successor;" in the Sinnār literature, usually to the leadership of a community of *fuqarā'*; (2) successor to the political role of Muḥammad as the leader of the community of Muslims, here translated as "Caliph."

khaṭīb: preacher; a member of the mosque staff.

khayl, muqaddam/sīd al-: a court official and military commander.

khidam/khidma: an obligation to the state; probably in the form of labor.

khōr: channel of a seasonal watercourse; gulch.

khusāra: an obligation to the state.

kisra: an obligation to the state; literally, "bread."

kiyāb: an obligation to the state.

kurus: flat, fertile land adjoining the **qurayr**, but too high to be irrigated by a **sāqīya** situated at the top of the **jarf**.

laqab: nickname.

maḍārr: obligations to the state.

makk: see **malik**.

malik: literally, "king;" a part of several titles.

Mālikī: appertaining to the *madhhab* of Mālik.

mānjil: a Funj title of personal status; usually a provincial governor.

mankarūkan/mankrōknā: a Funj title of military rank.

maṣḥaf: a manuscript of the Qur'ān.

matūra/matūrāt: an obligation to the state; possibly the provision of draft animals.

mirin: (1) a survey line dividing riverbank agricultural plots, drawn parallel to the course of the river; (2) a landholding demarcated by a **mirin**; (3) a basis for a legal claim to land.

mithqāl: a measure of gold equivalent to two **qism**.

mu`allim: title of respect bestowed upon Christian missionaries in Sinnār; literally, "teacher."

muezzin: member of the mosque staff; responsible for giving the call to prayer.

muḥallaqāt: small coins of Sinnār.

mukhlā/mukhlāya: an obligation to the state; literally, "nose-bag."

munawwara: an obligation to the state.

muqaddam: supervisor, foreman; part of several court titles.

muqran: tip of the land enclosed by the junction of two rivers, for example, the Blue and White Niles.

mursāl: messenger, courier.

musā`id, shaykh al-: a court office, especially in Qarrī.

naḥās: copper kettledrum, a symbol of royal authority.

nār: an obligation to the state; possibly a penalty for starting destructive fires--a perennial hazard to both homes and fields.

nāyib: assistant; member of the mosque staff.

nuzūl: an obligation to the state; possibly the housing component of billeting.

qāḍī: Islamic judge.

qawāwīd, muqaddam al-: a court officer; responsible for the corps of hostage pages.

qawwād al-shaykh: a court title.

qayf: edge; the natural divide between the **jarf** and the **qurayr**, or between the **qurayr** and the **kurus**.

qibla: the direction of prostration for prayer; in Sinnār, due east.

qill/qilla: an obligation to the state.

qirsh: a small coin.

qism: a measure of gold; see **mithqāl**.

qōz: a fossil dune of sandy soil, usually slightly elevated above the surrounding clay soil, and easier to cultivate successfully with eighteenth-century technology.

qubba: domed structure erected at the tomb of an eminent individual, usually an Islamic holy man; occasionally, a similar structure placed elsewhere to honor such an individual.

qurayr: flat, fertile land adjoining the **jarf**, and suitable for irrigation by means of a **sāqīya** situated near the riverbank at the crest of the **jarf**.

quwwār: an obligation to the state; possibly market fees.

quwwārīya, muqaddam/shaykh al-: a court officer with fiscal duties.

raghm: an obligation to the state.

rāw, al-: an elevated, fortified tower.

rubāṭ/rabṭ: an obligation to the state.

sajjāda, shaykh/muqaddam al-: a court office.

salaṭīya: a government-sponsored slave raid.

salūka: (1) a digging stick used in planting crops on land irrigated by innundation during the Nile flood; (2) land suitable for cultivation by means of a **salūka**, notably the **jarf**.

sāqīya: (1) an ox-driven waterwheel; (2) a landholding irrigated by such a waterwheel, including its appertaining **jarf**.

sawākira: hostage princes of the royal family.

sawākira, shaykh/muqaddam al-: a court office; supervisor of the royal princes.

sharī`a**: Islamic law, often in contrast to **`āda, customary law.

sharīf: title of personal status; a biological descendant of the prophet Muḥammad.

shurūr: obligations to the state.

sīd al-qūm: a court office; originally, the maternal uncle of the king.

sidr: *Zizyphus spina Christi.*

sinsina: an obligation to the state; possibly the supply of travel rations when billeting.

subul, sing. **sibla**: obligations to the state; sumptuary laws.

sunna: the legally binding precedents set by the words and deeds of the prophet Muḥammad.

tūrāt: see **matūrāt**.

turus, pl. **turūs**: (1) a low ridge around a rainland field to retain runoff moisture; (2) a landholding enclosed by a **turus**.

ʽudda, muqaddam/sīd [bayt] al-: a court office; supervisor of the arsenal.

ʽudūl: see **ʽādil**.

ʽulamā': see **ʽālim**.

ʽulūq: an obligation to the state; possibly the provision of fodder.

wakīl: agent.

walad, pl. **awlād**: "the son[s] of."

Walad ʽAjīb: the head of the **ʽAbdallāb**, the eighteenth-century ruling house of the northern province of Sinnār.

waqf: religious endowment according to the **sharīʽa**.

waqīya: measure of gold; equivalent to four **mithqāl**, or one ounce.

wazīr: minister in the political sense; when applied to the Hamaj, translated as "Regent."

zarība: (1) an enclosure of thorn branches; (2) a homestead enclosed by a **zarība**; (3) an obligation to the state.

zayyāt al-shaykh: a court office.

REFERENCES

Abdulla, Abdelgadir Mahmoud, ed. *Studies in Ancient Languages of the Sudan*. Khartoum: 1974.

Abū Salīm, Muḥammad Ibrāhīm. *al-Fūnj wa'l-arḍ: wathā'iq tamlīk*. Khartoum: 1967.

________. *al-Fūr wa'l-arḍ: wathā'iq tamlīk*. Khartoum: 1975.

________. *al-Khatm al-Dīwānī fi'l-Sūdān*. Khartoum: 1983.

[________, ed.] *Sādat al-Majādhīb*. 3 Vols. No place or date; no pagination.

Adams, William Y. *Nubia: Corridor to Africa*. Princeton: 1977.

[Aḥmad b. Ismā`īl al-Azharī]. *Khulāṣat al-iqtibās fī ittisāl nasabinā bi'l-Sayyid al-`Abbās*. Unpublished: Sudan Archive, University of Durham, G//S 555(4), uncatalogued, from the papers of Douglas Newbold.

[________.] "Nisba of Ahmed al-Azhari." Unpublished: National Records Office, Khartoum, Intelligence 5/1/3.

Aḥmad al-Mu`taṣim al-`Abbās, `Alī `Osmān Muḥammad Ṣāliḥ and Jay Spaulding, "A Colophon from Eighteenth-Century Sinnār," *Fontes Historiae Africanae Arabicae: Bulletin d'Information*, Vol. 6 (1981): 13-18.

`Alī `Osmān Muḥammad Ṣāliḥ. "The Economy and Trade of Medieval Nubia." Ph.D. Diss., Christ's College, Cambridge University, 1978.

Anonymous [Hiob Ludolf?]. *Sonderbarer Lebens-Lauf Herrn Peter Heylings aus Lübec*. Halle: 1714.

Beccari, C. *Rerum Aethiopicarum Scriptores Occidentales Inediti a Saeculo XVI ad XIX*. Rome: 1905-1917.

Biberfeld, Eduard. *Der Reisebericht des David Reubeni*. Berlin: 1898.

Björkelo, Anders. "From King to Kāshif: Shendī in the Nineteenth Century." Ph.D. Diss., University of Bergen, 1983.

Björkman, W. *et al*. "Diplomatic." *The Encyclopaedia of Islam*. 2nd ed., Vol. 2 (Leiden: 1965): 301-316.

Brehm, A.E. *Reiseskizzen aus Nord-Ost-Afrika*. Jena: 1861.

Brocchi, Giovanni Battista. *Giornale delle osservazioni fatte ne'viaggi in Egitto, nella Siria e nella Nubia*. Bassano: 1843.

Brockelmann, Carl. *Geschichte der Arabischen Litteratur*. Weimar: 1898-1902.

Bruce, James. *Travels to Discover the Source of the Nile*. 2nd ed. Edinburgh: 1805.

Burckhardt, John Lewis. *Travels in Nubia*. 2nd ed. London: 1822.

Cahen, Claude. "Notes de Diplomatique Arabo-Musulmane." *Journal Asiatiques*, Vol. 251 (1963): 311-325.

Cahen, Claude. "A Propos des *Shuhūd*." *Studia Islamica*, Vol. 31 (1970): 71-79.

Donzel, E. van. *Foreign Relations of Ethiopia, 1642-1700*. Istanbul: 1979.

Ernst, Hans. *Die mamlukischen Sultansurkunde des Sinai-Klosters*. Wiesbaden: 1960.

Ewald, Janet. "Leadership and Social Change on an Islamic Frontier: The Kingdom of Taqalī, 1780-1900." Ph.D. Diss., University of Wisconsin-Madison, 1982.

El Fatih El Houssein El Hasan. "The Fung and Mehadyia At Abu Haraze Site." B.A. Honours Diss., Pt. II, Department of Archaeology, University of Khartoum, 1977-1978.

Giamberardini, C. *I Viaggiatori francescani attraverso la Nubia dal 1698 al 1710*. Cairo: 1963.

Grohmann, Adolf. *Allgemeine Einführung in die Arabischen Papyri nebst Grundzügen der Arabischen Diplomatik*. Wien: 1924.

Holt, P.M. "Four Funj Land-Charters." In *Studies in the History of the Near East*, edited by P.M. Holt, 104-120. London: 1973.

________. "The genealogy of a Sudanese holy family." *Bulletin of the School of Oriental and African Studies*, Vol. 44 (1981): 262-272.

________. "A New History of [sic] Funj." *Journal of African History*, Vol. 27, No. 3 (1986): 562-564.

Huntingford, G.W.B. *The Land Charters of Northern Ethiopia*. Addis Ababa: 1965.

`Izz al-Dīn al-Amīn. *Qarīyat Kutrānj wa-atharuhā al-`ilmī fi'l-Sūdān*. Khartoum: 1975.

Jackson, H.C. *Notes on the Yacubabi Tribes of Sennar*. Khartoum: 1912.

Kapteijns, Lidwien. "The Organization of Exchange in Precolonial Western Sudan." In *Trade and Traders in the Sudan*, edited by Leif O. Manger, 49-80. Bergen: 1984.

________. *Mahdist Faith and Sudanic Tradition*. London: 1985.

________ and Jay Spaulding. "Precolonial Trade Between States in the Eastern Sudan, c. 1700 - c. 1900." *African Economic History*, Vol. 11 (1982): 29-62.

________ and Jay Spaulding. *After the Millennium*. East Lansing: 1988.

________ and Jay Spaulding. "History, Ethnicity and Agriculture in the Sudan." In *The Agriculture of the Sudan*, edited by Jill Craig. Oxford: forthcoming.

Krump, Theodoro. *Hoher und Fruchtbarer Palm-Baum des Heiligen Evangelij*. Augsburg: 1710.

McHugh, Neil. "Land, Lords and Holy Men in Eighteenth-Century Sinnār: Two Documents." *Fontes Historiae Africanae Arabicae: Bulletin d'Information*, Vol. 7/8 (1982-1983): 12-32.

________. "Holymen of the Blue Nile: Religious Leadership and the Genesis of an Arab Islamic Society in the Nilotic Sudan, 1500-1850." Ph.D. Diss., Northwestern University, 1986.

Montano, G.M. *L'Etiopia Francescana nei Documenti dei secoli XVII e XVIII*. Quaracchi: 1948.

Murray, Alexander. *Account of the Life and Writings of James Bruce of Kinnaird*. Edinburgh: 1808.

O'Fahey, R.S. *State and Society in Dār Fūr*. London: 1980.

________ and M.I. Abū Salīm. *Land in Dār Fūr*. Cambridge: 1983.

________and J. L. Spaulding. "Hāshim and the Musabba`āt." *Bulletin of the School of Oriental and African Studies*, Vol. 35, No. 2 (1972): 316-333.

________ and J.L. Spaulding. *Kingdoms of the Sudan*. London: 1974.

________and Jay Spaulding. "A Sudanese Battle in About 1800." *Sudan Texts Bulletin*, Vol. 2 (1980): 42-46.

Orhonlu, Cengiz. *Habeş Eyaleti*. Istanbul: 1974.

Poncet, Charles-Jacques. In *The Red Sea at the Close of the Seventeenth Century*, edited by William Foster, 93-165. London: 1949.

Prudhoe, Lord. "Extracts from private Memoranda kept by Lord Prudhoe on a journey from Cairo to Sennar, in 1829, describing the Peninsula of Sennar." *Journal of the Royal Geographical Society*, Vol. 5 (1835): 135-149.

[Robinson,] A.E. "The Fung Drum or Nehas." *Sudan Notes and Records*, Vol. 4 (1921): 211-212.

Sadik Nur. "Land Tenure during the Time of the Fung." *Kush*, Vol. 4 (1956): 48-53.

Sainte Marie, Jean de. *Les estranges evenemens du voyage de son altesse, le serenissime prince Zaga-Christ d'Ethiopie*. Paris: 1635.

Santillana, David. *Istituzioni di Diritto Musulmano*. Rome: 1925.

Schneider, Madeleine. "Deux actes de Donation en Arabe." *Annales d'Ethiopie*, Vol. 8 (1970): 79-88.

al-Shāṭir Buṣaylī `Abd al-Jalīl, ed. *Makhṭūṭat Kātib al-Shūna fī ta'rīkh al-sulṭāna al-Sinnārīya wa'l-idāra al-Miṣrīya*. Cairo: 1961.

Shinnie, Peter L. "The Ancient Languages of the Northern Sudan." In *Aspects of Language in the Sudan*, edited by Robin Thelwall, 82-96. Londonderry: 1978.

Spaulding, Jay. "A Mortgage Foreclosure from Sinnār." *Sudan Texts Bulletin*, Vol. 1 (1979): 26-31.

________. "A Confirming Charter of Sultan Bādī b. Ṭabl of Sinnār." *Sudan Texts Bulletin*, Vol. 1 (1979): 18-25.

________. "Two Credit Documents from Sinnār." *Sudan Texts Bulletin*, Vol. 2 (1980): 59-61.

________. "*Kora*: A Theme in Nubian Cultural History." *Africa Today*, Vol. 28, No. 2 (1981): 61-68.

________. "A Confirming Charter of Sultan `Adlān b. Ismā`īl of Sinnār." *Sudan Texts Bulletin*, Vol. 3 (1981): 20-37.

________. "A Grant by the 'Great *Mānjil*' to the 'Great *Faqīh*' of Sinnār." *Sudan Texts Bulletin*, Vol. 4 (1982): 20-28.

Spaulding, Jay. "The Misfortunes of Some--The Advantages of Others: Land-Sales by Women in Sinnār." In *African Women and the Law: Historical Perspectives*, edited by Margaret Jean Hay and Marcia Wright, 3-18. Boston: 1982.

________. "Two documents from the days of Nāṣir b. Muḥammad Abū Likaylik, Hamaj Regent of Sinnār." *Fontes Historiae Africanae Arabicae: Bulletin d'Information*, Vol. 7/8 (1982-1983):: 33-37.

________. "A Charter of Bādī b. Rajab, Hamaj Regent of Sinnār." *Sudan Texts Bulletin*, Vol. 5 (1983): 68-72.

________. "Taxation in Sinnār." *Northeast African Studies*, Vol. 6, No. 1/2 (1984): 127-146.

________. "The Management of Exchange in Sinnār, c. 1700." In *Trade and Traders in the Sudan*, edited by Leif O. Manger, 25-48. Bergen: 1984.

________. "The Chronicle of Aḥmad b. `Īsā." *Sudan Texts Bulletin*, Vol. 6 (1984): 37-43.

________. "A Charter of Sultan Bādī b. Nōl of Sinnār, 1145/1732-3." *Fontes Historiae Africanae Arabicae: Bulletin d'Information*, Vol. 9/10 (1984-1985): 8-11.

________. "The End of Nubian Kingship in the Sudan." In *Modernization in the Sudan*, edited by M.W. Daly, 17-27. New York: 1985.

________. "Numerical Notation and Token Counters in Nubia." *Findings* (1985): 9-12.

________. *The Heroic Age in Sinnār*. East Lansing: 1985.

________ and Abdel Ghaffar Muhammad Ahmed. "A Seal from Nineteenth-Century Sinnār." *Sudan Notes and Records*, Vol. 55 (1974): 175-176.

________ and `Abd al-Ghaffār M. Aḥmad. "The Sinnār King-List of the *sīd al-qūm* Aḥmad." *Fontes Historiae Africanae Arabicae: Bulletin d'Information*, Vol. 7/8 (1982-1983): 38-42.

________ and Ḥājj Ḥāmid Muḥammad Khayr. "The Deposition of a *Makk* of Berber." *Sudan Texts Bulletin*, Vol. 2 (1980): 47-58.

________ and J.L. Spaulding. "The Democratic Philosophers of the Medieval Sudan: Pigs." *Sprache und Geschichte in Afrika*, forthcoming.

Stern, S.M. "Two Ayyūbid Decrees from Sinai." In *Documents from Islamic Chanceries*, edited by S.M. Stern, 9-38. Oxford: 1965.

Tame, G.B. "Legends of the Halawin of Blue Nile Province." *Sudan Notes and Records*, Vol. 17, No. 2 (1934): 201-216.

al-Ṭayyib Muḥammad al-Ṭayyib. *al-Turāth al-sha`bī li-qabīlat al-Ḥamrān*. Khartoum: 1970.

Walz, Terence. "The Paper Trade of Egypt and the Sudan in the Eighteenth and Nineteenth Centuries." In *Modernization in the Sudan*, edited by M.W. Daly, 29-48. New York: 1985.

INDEX OF NAMES